INTERNATIONAL EXTRADITION AND WORLD PUBLIC ORDER

by

M. Cherif Bassiouni

LL.B.; J.D.; LL.M.; J.S.D.
Professor of Law, De Paul University

1974

A. W. SIJTHOFF -LEYDEN

OCEANA PUBLICATIONS INC. – DOBBS FERRY, N. Y.

ISBN 90 286 0044 2 (Sijthoff)
ISBN 0-379-00203-5 (Oceana)

Printed in The Netherlands.

INTERNATIONAL EXTRADITION AND WORLD PUBLIC ORDER

This book is the product of six years of research and study which grew out of a doctoral dissertation completed at George Washington University and several publications by this author on the same subject. The research and documentation is comprehensive if not exhaustive in many respects. Some of the ideas and proposals presented herein have been tendered by this writer at several international conferences and have benefited from that test. Among these conferences deserving particular mention are: The International Colloquim on Extradition held under the auspices of the Max-Planck Institute for International and Comparative Criminal Law, Freiburg, Germany (1968); The International Pre-Congress on International Criminal Law, Italy (1969) and the $\overline{X}$ th. International Penal Law Congress, Rome, Italy (1969). Each of these international gatherings received favorably some of the ideas advanced herein in particular those on the role and rights of the individual in the extradition system and specific Human Rights guarantees.

The traditional view of extradition by practicing states is that it is an instrument of inter-state cooperation designed primarily to serve the very interests of these states. Thus its processes, norms and practices derive from this premise, and the whole constitutes a system which comprises multiple participants who are employing common strategies to achieve identical outcomes. This system, with its underlying assumptions, its processes, norms, and practices is critically appraised and often challenged.

The United States is the legal system selected as the main focus of inquiry into the framework of the practice, its legal bases, processes, norms and practices. But, the analysis of that country's law and practice is undertaken in a historical and comparative context whereby landmark extradition cases decided in thirty-two countries are contrasted to the some one hundred and twenty United States cases discussed. The eighty-eight United States treaties in force are referred to as well as selected bilateral treaties and, all multilateral treaties and draft conventions.

The appraisal of that system is conducted at two different but interrelated levels: the first is the international law level, framed in a world public order model which encompasses internationally protected human rights; while the second level is that of the municipal criminal laws of the United States and its constitutional framework. The interraction of these two levels as well as their international legal implications are presented as an integrated whole through a methodology which combines contemporary theories of international law, criminal law, criminal procedure and constitutional law with some related aspects of social and behavioral sciences. Hopefully that approach will reflect the distinctive character of the discipline of international criminal law.

The two most recurring themes throughout this book are the world public order model, as applied to extradition, and human rights through the emergence of the individual as a participant in extradition processes. The outcome of this approach is the development of a new framework of analysis which identifies the need for developing new international legal norms.

The continuity and homogeneity of the subject matter as traditionally perceived is preserved by the pervasive method through which developing trends and proposed ideas are intertwined in the study and treatment of the extradition system.

Each chapter of the book deals with a specific aspect of that system in a historical and comparative context, appraising policy considerations. This critical appraisal is undertaken in the context of a policy-oriented inquiry into the values, strategies, goals and outcomes of the multiple processes of the extradition system and the interaction of its participants. This approach lead the author to propose a new framework for extradition and to explore some alternative approaches to present normative applications, stressing two basic values: the preservation of minimum world order and the protection of fundamental human rights.

To that extent, the proposals made herein constitute a conceptual departure from traditional extradition law and practice; nevertheless, careful concern is given not to confuse the *lex lata* and the *lex ferenda*.

Over the last six years in which this book has been in progress, I have also worked on other aspects of international criminal law particularly two volumes entitled <u>International Criminal Law: Crimes and Punishment</u>, and <u>International Criminal Law: Jurisdiction and Cooperation</u> (Charles C. ThomasPublisher, Springfield, Ill. 1973). During this time I came to the conclusion that Internanational Criminal Law will develop in the next decade as an important area which will require the combined efforts of penalists, publicists and other social and behavioral scientists. It is with this multi-disciplinary ideal that I approached the study of extradition. To what extent I have been able to integrate nonlegal disciplines in this book is admittedly little because the thrust of my efforts was to integrate international law and criminal law. To that extent I hope to have been successful enough so that others can continue to build up the discipline of international criminal law as a new integrated, multi-disciplinary and cross-cultural branch of the law.

In the course of the preparation of this book I have benefited from the views of several world-renowned experts who have contributed through personal contact and exchange of views and through their writings to the refinement of my ideas, and particular mention goes to Professors H. H. Jescheck, Director of the Max-Planch Institute; G. Levasseur of the University of Paris; H. Schultz of the University of Berne; A. Evans of the University of Puget Sound; G.O.W. Mueller of New York University; P. O'Higgins of Cambridge's Christ College; I. Shearer of the University of Western Australia; E. Wise of Wayne State University; H. Grutzner, retired Legal Adviser, Ministry of Justice, Germany; and W. T. Mallison, Jr., R. Allen, H. Liebesny of George Washington University.

The influence of Professors Myres McDougal and Harold Lasswell of Yale University will also no doubt be obvious with respect to the World Public Order model relied upon even though it was adapted to fit the author's own conceptual framework and method. Maybe I should add that although I credit all those persons (and others who have made their contributions to the field) with their beneficial influence, I nonetheless confess to all heresies in this book as being only mine.

M. Cherif Bassiouni

Chicago, April 1, 1974

TABLE OF ABBREVIATIONS*

Hackworth, <u>Digest</u>

- Green, H. Hackworth, A Digest Of International Law (8 Volumes, 1940-1944).

Hyde, <u>International Law</u>

- Charles C. Hyde, International Law Chiefly as Interpreted and Applied by the United States (2 Volumes, 1922).

Malloy, <u>Treaties</u>

- William M. Malloy, Treaties, Conventions, International Acts, Protocols and Agreements between the United States of America and Other Powers (4 Volumes, 1910-1938).

Moore, <u>Digest</u>

- John B. Moore, A Digest of International Law as Embodied In Diplomatic Discussions, Treaties and other International Agreements, International Awards, The Decisions of Municipal Courts, and the Writings of Jurists (8 Volumes, 1906).

Moore, <u>Extradition</u>

- John B. Moore, A Treatise on Extradition and Interstate Rendition (2 Volumes, 1891).

Whiteman, <u>Digest</u>

- Marjorie Whiteman, Digest of International Law (14 Volumes, 1963-1970).

*All abbreviations in the text and notes are in accordance with The Harvard Law Review Association, <u>A Uniform System of Citations</u>.

TABLE OF CONTENTS

PREFACE   vii-xi

TABLE OF ABBREVIATIONS   xii

CHAPTER I - THE LEGAL FRAMEWORK OF EXTRADITION IN
            INTERNATIONAL LAW AND ITS APPLICATION
            IN THE LAW AND PRACTICE OF THE UNITED
            STATES   1

1. Historical Introduction   1

2. Characteristics of the Process of Extradition
    in International Law and Practices   6

    2.1 - The duty to extradite   6

    2.2 - Extradition in the absence of a treaty   9

    2.3 - Extradition by bilateral treaty; the
          prevailing practice   13

    2.4 - Extradition by multilateral regional
          arrangements   19

3. Characteristics of the Process of Extradition
    in the Law and Practice of the United States   24

    3.1 - The basis for extradition; treaty
          relations   24

    3.2 - The Constitution, treaty-making and
          treaty-interpretation   29

    3.3 - The extent of treaty application:
          state succession   33

    3.4 - The effects of war on continued appli-
          cation of extradition treaties . . .   39

TABLE OF CONTENTS

3.5 - Appraisal of state succession and

war on the extradition treaties of

the United States 42

4. An Appraisal of the Contemporary Framework

of Extradition and a Proposed Policy-Oriented

Framework 45

Footnotes 53

Appendix A 78

CHAPTER II - ASYLUM AND EXTRADITION 86

1. Historical Introduction 86

2. Rationale Asylum 90

2.1 - Rationae materiae 94

2.2 - Rationae personae 95

2.3 - Difference between rationae materiae

and rationae personae 96

3. Legal Bases for Asylum 97

4. The Position of the United States on Asylum . 104

5. An Appraisal of the Relationship Between

Asylum and Extradition 107

Footnotes 114

CHAPTER III - UNLAWFUL SEIZURES AND IRREGULAR

RENDITION DEVICES AS ALTERNATIVES

TO EXTRADITION 121

1. Typology and Rationale 121

1.1 - Abduction and kidnapping 124

1.2 - Informal Rendition 128

    1.3 - Disguised extradition

2. Unlawful Seizures, State Responsibility
and International Protection of Human
Rights 143

    2.1 - The validity of *mala captus bene*
         detentus 143

    2.2 - State responsibility 145

    2.3 - Human rights and state responsibility . 151

    2.4 - Remedies 173

3. An Appraisal of Rendition Devices as Alternatives to Extradition and World Public Order . 176

Footnotes 186

CHAPTER IV - THEORIES OF JURISDICTION AND THEIR
              APPLICATION IN EXTRADITION LAW AND
              PRACTICE 202

Introduction 202

1. Territorial Jurisdiction and Its Extensions . 205

    1.1 - Special status territory 211

    1.2 - Subjective-objective territorial theory 217

    1.3 - Floating territoriality, the law of
         the flag 224

    1.4 - Special environments 244

2. The Active Personality (Nationality) Theory . 251

3. The Passive Personality Theory 255

4. The Protected Interest (Protective) Theory . 259

5. The Universality Principle 261

6. A Policy-Oriented Inquiry into the Problems
   of Jursidiction in Extradition and World
   Public Order 270

Footnotes 277

CHAPTER V - SUBSTANTIVE REQUIREMENTS: EXTRADITABLE
            OFFENSES, DOUBLE CRIMINALITY, AND THE
            DOCTRINE OF SPECIALITY 311

Introduction 311

1. Extraditable Offenses and Double Criminality 314
   1.1 - The relationship of extraditable
         offenses, double criminality and
         reciprocity 314
   1.2 - Methods of determining extraditable
         offenses 315
   1.3 - Rationale for defining extraditable
         offenses 319
   1.4 - Double Criminality 322
   1.5 - Definitional theories of extraditable
         offenses and their relationship to
         double criminality 326

2. A Case Study Analysis of Judicial Application
   of Extraditable Offenses and Double Criminality with Emphasis on the Practice of the
   United States, England and Canada 329

3. The Doctrine of Specialty 352
   3.1 - The doctrine of specialty and variance

TABLE OF CONTENTS

in prosecution 357

3.2 - Extension of the doctrine: limitations

on reextradition and death penalty . . 359

Footnotes 361

CHAPTER VI - DENIAL OF EXTRADITION: DEFENSES, EXCEP-

TIONS, EXEMPTIONS AND EXCLUSIONS . . . 368

Introduction 368

1. Grounds Relating to the Offense Charged . . . 370

1.1 - The political offense 370

1.1(1) - Historical meaning 370

1.1(2) - Ideologically motivated

offenders and political

offenses 375

1.1(3) - The purely political offense . 379

1.1(4) - The relative political offense 383

1.1(5) - A proposed juridical standard

of inquiry for municipal

tribunals 411

1.1(6) - International crimes: The

exception to the political

offense exception 416

1.1(7) - The political offense excep-

tion and world public order:

A proposed international

solution 425

1.2 - Offenses of a military character . . . 429

1.3 - Offenses of a fiscal character 433

2. Grounds Relating to the Person of the Relator 435

2.1 - Exclusion of nationals 435

2.2 - Persons performing official acts and

persons protected by special immunity

under international law 442

3. Grounds Relating to the Prosecution of the

Offense Charged 443

3.1 - Introduction to the defenses of:

legality of the offense charged, trial

in absentia, statute of limitation and

immunity 443

3.2 - Trial *in absentia* 445

3.3 - Statute of limitation and immunity in

municipal law 447

4. Grounds Relating to the Penalty and

Punishability of the Relator 450

4.1 - Amnesty and pardon 450

4.2 - Double jeopardy - *ne bis in idem* . . . 452

4.3 - Death penalty 459

4.4 - Cruel and unusual punishment 463

Footnotes 467

CHAPTER VII - EXTRADITION PROCEDURE IN THE UNITED

STATES 502

1. Sources of Procedural Rules: Some Comparative

Aspects 502

TABLE OF CONTENTS

2. Procedure in the United States 511

    2.1 - Initiation of the process 511

    2.2 - The initial executive process 512

    2.3 - The judicial process 513

        (1) - The complaint 514

        (2) - The hearing 515

        (3) - The evidence 518

        (4) - Review and *habeas corpus* 524

        (5) - *Habeas corpus* and the rule of
        non-inquiry 527

        (6) - Executive discretion 531

        (7) - Procedure for requests by the
        United States 534

Footnotes 538

CHAPTER VIII - A POLICY-ORIENTED FRAMEWORK FOR
        INQUIRY INTO THE PROCESSES AND VALUES
        OF EXTRADITION 558

1. The Individual in International Law in the
   Scheme of Extradition 558

2. A Policy Inquiry into Factors Bearing on the
   Framework and Processes of Extradition . . . 566

3. Appraisal of the Conceptual Framework of
   Extradition as an International Process . . . 570

Footnotes 576

INDEXES 581
      Subject Index, Table of Cases, Index of Names,
      Index to International Conventions and Treaties Cited

Chapter I

The Legal Framework of Extradition in International Law and Its Application in the Law and Practice of the United States

1. Historical Introduction

Extradition, throughout the history of the practice, has remained a system consisting of several processes whereby one sovereign surrenders to another sovereign a person sought after as an accused criminal or a fugutive offender. The practice originated in earlier non-Western civilizations such as the Egyptian, Chinese, Chaldean, and Assyro-Babylonian civilizations. [1] In these early days of the practice the delivery of a requested person to the requesting sovereign was undertaken in solemn formulas and performed with solemn pomp. This delivery of individuals to a requesting sovereign was usually based on facts or treaties but they also occurred by reciprocity and comity as a matter of courtesy and good will between sovereigns. The delivered person was usually a subject of the requesting sovereign or that of another sovereign but seldom if ever was the person delivered a subject of the requested sovereign. Undertakings involving the rendition of fugitives were deemed an essential feature of friendly relations between sovereigns, and consequently the performance of such acts was often unsolicited. Thus, rendition did not always derive from the process of extradition but was more likely a gesture of friendship and cooperation between sovereigns. Indeed, the formal processes of extradition are only one of the modes of rendition. In fact extradition to this time is in comparison to other means of rendition the one least resorted to. In fact, in contemporary practice there are more persons who are surrendered, delivered or returned by one state to another in a variety of ways (both legal and extra-legal), than there are renditions through formal extradition; Chapter III discusses some of these alternative rendition devices.

In contemporary practice extradition means a formal process through which a person is surrendered by one state to another by virtue of a treaty, reciprocity or comity as between the respective states. The participants in such a process are, therefore, the two states and, depending upon value-perspectives, the individual who is the object-subject of the proceedings. To a large extent, the processes and its participants have not changed much in the course of time but the rationale and purposes of the practice have changed, and as a consequence so have the formal aspects of the proceedings.

The emergence of humanitarian international law gave rise to a new legal status to one of the participants, i.e., the individual, thus, placing some limitations on the power of the respective sovereigns.

The rendition of a person to another sovereign presupposes that the person in question is in the requested state either because he or she believes refuge can be found there or because of fortuitous circumstances. In any event the surrender of a person who has been granted the privilege of presence or refuge in the requested state

2

has always been deemed an exceptional measure running against the traditions of asylum and hospitality. This gave rise to a speculation about the name of this rendition process, i.e., "extra-tradition", which ultimately evolved into "extradition". A more commonly accepted explanation for the term "extradition" is its Latin origin *extradere* which means forceful return of a person to his sovereign.

Because the requested and requesting participants are states it is clear that there is a nexus between the interests of these respective states and the granting or denial of extradition. In fact, the whole history of extradition has been little more than a reflection of the political relations between the states in question. This explains why whenever a state maintained in its relations with another state a certain degree of formality, extradition was bound in solemn formulas and treaties, but whenever relations between the interested states were informal other informal modes of rendition were resorted to as a sign of cordial cooperation. This cleavage between interstate relations and the processes of extradition is true today as it was in the earliest recorded times.

The first recorded extradition treaty in the world dates *circa* 1280 B.C. In that second oldest document in diplomatic history, Ramses II, Pharaoh of Egypt, signed a peace treaty with the Hittites after he defeated their attempt to invade Egypt.[2] King Hattusili III signed it for the Hittites and the document written in hieroglyphics is carved on the Temple of Ammon at Karnak and is also preserved on clay tablets in Akkodrain in the Hittite archives of Boghazkoi. The peace treaty provided expressly for the return of persons sought by each sovereign who had taken refuge on the other's territory. Since then however only the practice of Greece and Rome's extradition arrangements found their way into European texts of international law.

Surrendering persons sought by another state did not necessarily mean that the person sought after was a fugitive from justice charged with a common crime. In fact, from antiquity until the late eighteenth century, such persons were sought because of political reasons.[4] Sovereigns obliged one another by surrendering those persons who most likely affected the stability of their political order of the requesting state. Thus, the stronger the relationship between the sovereigns, the more interest and concern they had for each other's welfare and the more intent they would be on surrendering those political offenders who had created the greatest dangers to their respective welfare. Common criminals were the least sought after species of offenders because their harmful conduct affected only other individuals and not the sovereign or the public order.

The history of extradition can be divided into four periods: (1) ancient times to seventeenth century--a period revealing almost exclusive concern for political and religious offenders; (2) the eighteenth century and half of the nineteenth century--a period of treaty-making chiefly concerned with military offenders characterizing the condition of Europe during that period; (3) from 1833 to present--a period of collective concern in suppressing common criminality;[5] and (4) post 1948 developments which ushered a

4

greater concern for protecting the human rights of persons and reveals and awareness for the need to have international due process of law regulate international relations.

The historical development of the practice of extradition leads to the conclusion that the surrender of fugitives which originated with the need to preserve the internal order of the respective states, was not deemed a tool of international cooperation for the preservation of world societal interests. This later concern was articulated in 1624 by Hugo Grotius and then gained momentum between the sixteenth and eighteenth century as part of the efforts of the world community to combat piracy. This was not due to altruistic motives but for essential economic reasons because the channels of European commerce had to be preserved. To a large extent extradition remains the most important instrument of cooperation between states. At one time it had manifested itself in the preservation of the political and religious interests of states, gradually shifting to serve xenophobic and militaristic tendencies and finally it is becoming an international means of cooperation in the suppresssion of common criminality.[6] This was due in part to philosophers of the Age of Enlightenment such as Rousseau and Voltaire who paved the way for penal reformers such as Beccaria and Bentham.[7] Since their writings, extradition which had focused on common criminals gradually became concerned with the human rights of accused criminal and fugitive offenders. This development accounts for the contemporary intricacies of the practice and its many formalities.

The history of international extradition in Europe has not paral-

leled that of the southern Mediterranean basin or even elsewhere.
In fact up until the eighteenth century, the relatively new and
independent sovereign states of Europe found no need for cooperative undertakings, particularly in view of an almost constant state
of suspicion and threat of war. Consequently, asylum was generally
granted to fugitives from justice of other states and a sovereign
could enforce the return of fugitives only by force of arms. Since
the threat of war was almost always impending, the threatened resort to such means was no great deterrent to asylum. Extradition
as an inducement to peaceful relations and friendly cooperation
between states remained of little practical significance until
after World War I.

2. *Characteristics of the Process of Extradition in International
   Law and Practice*

2.1 *The duty to extradite*

The classics of international law did not dispute the efficacy of
the practice of rendition carried through the means of extradition.
They differed however as to its rationale, its modalities and particularly as to whether a legal or moral obligation existed which
required the surrender of accused criminals or fugitives of another
system's justice. Hugo Grotius took the former view and held that
the state of refuge should either punish the criminal or surrender
him back to the state seeking his return. Accordingly, the legal
basis was not so much a duty to deliver up the fugitive criminal
as it was a disjunctive duty to either prosecute him in the state
of refuge or to surrender him to be tried in the requesting state. [9]

This notion was embodied in the maxim *aut dedere aut punire,* which should however more appropriately be phrased as *aut dedere aut iudiare.* The scholar Vattel regarded extradition as a clear legal duty imposed upon states by international law in the case of serious crimes. [10] The views of Grotius and Vattel were supported by such diverse scholars as Heineccius, Burlemaqui, Rutherford, Schmelzing and Kent. [11]

Proponents of the opposing viewpoints like Pufendorf regarded extradition only as an imperfect obligation requiring a special compact to secure the full force and effect of international law. [12] He was supported by Voet, Martens, Klüber, Leyser, Luit, Saalfeld, Schmaltz, Mittermaier and Heffter. [13]

The contemporary practice reflects to some extent the latter point of view, but the trend has favored the former position advocated by Grotius and Vattel. After some divergent judicial opinions, the Supreme Court of the United States definitely laid down in 1840 the principle that no obligation to extradite existed apart from that imposed by treaty. [14] This position has since been steadfastly maintained. [15] The British courts have maintained the same attitude since 1815 even though before that date, the view was held by the Law Officers of the Crown that the Royal Prerogative extended to the power of surrendering aliens to foreign states and that there existed judicial authority to the same effect. [16] In 1815, however, the Law Officers advised that without statutory authority no person might be surrendered to a foreign state. [17] Since this time, British practice has consistently maintained that no power to extradite existed apart from statute and treaty. [18]

The English Extradition Act of 1870 [19] however left no doubt as
to its intended purpose to apply to all aspects of extradition
making the existence of an extradition treaty a condition precedent
for granting requests to foreign states. That surrender may not
be granted in the absence of a treaty obligation and statutory
warrant have since been amply confirmed by judicial decisions of
British and Commonwealth courts. [20]

Contrasting with what had become known as the common law approach,
the civil law countries demonstrated a greater willingness to grant
extradition in the absence of a treaty. The view espoused was that
extradition in such circumstances was based on comity or reciprocity.
As an example, the French Minister of Justice issued on July 30,
1872, a *circulaire* which stated that on the basis of reciprocity
extradition might take place in the absence of a treaty, in which
case the applicable body of rules were those emanating from international law. [21] No legal duty to extradite was thereby recognized
and only in the absence of treaty or statute could the government
regulate such matters by relying on international law.

Some South American states recognized at times a legal duty to
extradite in the absence of a treaty. The Supreme Court of Venezuela, for example, in 1953 surrendered an American national to
Panama in the absence of an extradition treaty with that country.
In granting the request the court expressly acted on the notion
that surrender was "in conformity with the public law of nations
(whereby) friendly states recognize a reciprocal obligation to
surrender offenders who have taken refuge in their respective countries." [22] This judgment reflected an opinion long held by the

Venezuelan courts.[22] Earlier a Brazilian court in 1924 surrendered

a Brazilian national to Great Britain without a treaty, but only

after it felt assured that the law of Great Britain allowed recip-

rocity (an assurance which, in point of fact, was quite false).[23]

Argentina, in Article 646 of the Argentine Code of Criminal Pro-

cedure provides for extradition in the absence of treaties in

cases where "extradition is proper according to the principle of

reciprocity or the uniform practice of States."[24] This statement,

however, does not clarify what is to be regarded as "the uniform

practice of States."

The practice of most states, however, confirms the observation

of Wheaton that extradition has not been looked upon as an absolute

international duty, and that if a state wishes to ensure that it

secures the return of its own criminals it must enter into treaties

with other states,[25] which is mainly accomplished by bilateral

treaties.

2.2 Extradition in the absence of a treaty

Few countries in the world possess no extradition treaties at all,

but a number of them are parties to surprisingly few extradition

treaties. Some examples are: Brazil - ten treaties; Thailand -

three treaties; Great Britain has treaties with forty-four states;

and the United States with eighty-eight states (see Appendix A).

Some states prefer as a matter of principle or convenience to enter

into treaties only with selected states, such as with states which

will not extradite in the absence of a treaty or with which, by rea-

son of territorial contiguity or because of close commercial ties it

is deemed especially desirable to have formal and binding extradition commitments. With respect to those states, where the occasions for extradition seem to be infrequent, there are few formal arrangements. The question often arises as to the possibility of securing the surrender of a criminal from one country to another in the absence of an extradition treaty. As has been noted above that the common law countries, as a general rule, do not extradite in the absence of a treaty while Western European states and other civil law states are inclined to do so. The United States requires the existence of a "treaty or convention for extradition,"[26] and the extradition legislation of Great Britain applies only "where an arrangement has been made with any foreign state."[27] The word "arrangement" has arguably a broad significance and might even apply to an exchange of diplomatic correspondence concerning a particular individual, even though this extreme view has never been tested. The Act requires in any event that an Order-in-Council must follow the "arrangement" in order to bring the Act into force with respect to the given State (for the duration of the "arrangement"). Most of the Commonwealth States are similarly limited by their laws from extraditing in the absence of a treaty. The United States has however on occasion sought extradition without a treaty on the basis of comity but considered the practice as exceptional.[28]

Extradition in the absence of treaties had early and consistent support starting from 1880[29] in the form of a resolution by the Institute of International Law up to the Xth International Penal Law Congress of 1969.[30] That position has been sanctioned by the practice of most Civil Law countries and French judicial

10

decisions as early as 1827 have recognized it. The French writer
Billot stated that it is an "established principle that extradition may be authorized in the absence of a treaty,"[31] and in this
view he is joined by other writers including Donnedieu de Vabres.[32]
The French Extradition Law of 1927 expressly applies in the absence of a treaty; in fact, the Law was designed principally to
regulate such extradition since in France treaties, duly approved
and promulgated, operate without the need of legislative implementation. This is due to the fact that France adheres to the monis-
tic view of international law. There are, however, a few exceptions in the practice of civil law countries. The Constitution of
the Netherlands requires the existence of a treaty before extradition may be conceded. The laws of Zaire, Ethiopia, Israel and
Turkey for example also require the existence of treaty arrangements. Although there is no specific prohibition in Norwegian
law, in practice a treaty is regarded as indispensable for the
surrender of fugitive criminals from Norway to countries outside
the multilateral Nordic Treaty area.[33]

Unlike France and several other countries,[34] the extradition
legislation of a number of states requires the giving of a guarantee of reciprocity as a condition precedent to its operation in
the absence of a formal treaty. The German Extradition Law of
1929,[35] for example, provided that extradition is not permissible
unless reciprocity is guaranteed.[36] Similar provisions are contained in the laws of Argentina, Austria, Belgium, Iraq, Japan,
Luxembourg, Mexico, Peru, Spain, Switzerland, and Thailand.[37]

The position of the United States was stated in an 1886 decision

of the Supreme Court which was unequivocal in its interpretation
of international law in <u>United States v. Rausher</u>[38] and reaffirmed
it in 1933 as follows:

> ". . . [T]he principles of international law
> recognize no right to extradition apart from treaty.
> While a government may, if agreeable to its own con-
> stitution and laws, voluntarily exercise the power
> to surrender a fugitive from justice to the country
> from which he has fled, and it has been said that it
> is under a moral duty to do so, . . . the legal right
> to demand his extradition and the correlative duty to
> surrender him to the demanding country exist only
> when created by treaty."[39]

In sharp contrast, the Supreme Court of Ireland, in 1950, stated:

> "A study of the history of extradition shows that
> a change has come about in the attitude of States in
> regard to it. Grotius and other well-known writers
> took the view that according to the law and usage of
> civilised nations every sovereign state was obliged
> to grant extradition freely and without qualification
> or restriction. In the view of other jurists of
> high authority extradition was at most a duty of im-
> perfect obligation.
>
> The negative doctrine that independent of special
> compact no state is bound to grant extradition seems
> now to be generally accepted."[40]

The common law states rely on the treaty approach while the European and European-influenced states differ in that they rely on reciprocity and comity as well.[41] These two conflicting approaches resulted in the proliferation of bilateral treaties by those adhering to one view which in turn caused those who did not to follow suit or opt for the multilateral extradition convention formula. Although it would seem that multilateral conventions on extradition (or multilateral conventions on subjects other than extradition but containing provisions on the subject) would have been the ideal compromise between the different approaches to the practice, so far this has not materialized.

2.3 Extradition by bilateral treaty: the prevailing practice

All developed, and most developing, countries are parties to at least some bilateral treaties. For those states whose laws or established practice prevent them from extraditing in the absence of a formal international agreement, extradition treaties are the sole means by which they cooperate with other states in surrendering fugitive criminals to jurisdictions competent to try them. The number and effectiveness of such treaties is,therefore, of vital importance. Even for those states whose laws permit extradition in the absence of a treaty, bilateral treaties are still shown to be of importance for the reasons given above.

An attempt has been made in multilateral conventions on international criminal law subjects to encompass extradition within their scope.[42] Thus, in the International Convention for the Suppression of Counterfeiting Currency of 1929, it is provided that the offense created by the Convention shall be regarded as an extraditable offense in any extradition treaty already in force, or which might later be concluded, between any of the Contracting Parties.[43] Similar provisions, widening the application of pre-existing and subsequent treaties, appear in some of the narcotics agreements, such as the 1936 Convention for the Suppression of Illicit Traffic in Dangerous Drugs.[45] Similarly, in an area protective of human rights, the 1910 Slavery Convention has an extradition clause[46] but paradoxically the 1948 Genocide Convention, only requires states not to qualify genocide and other offenses described in the Convention as political offenses.[47] By contrast, 1923 Conventions on Obscene Publications did not attempt to create new extradition offenses.[48] The 1963 Tokyo Convention on Offences on Board Aircraft[49] expressly disclaimed an obligation to grant extradition for the offenses dealt with therein, while the 1970 Hague Convention established a duty to prosecute or extradite.[50]

A universal extradition Convention is regarded as the ideal if yet unrealizable form of international arrangement for extradition. Meanwhile, bilateral treaties continue in the meantime to form the main basis of international practice. Whenever they are kept up to date and exist in sufficient numbers to provide a comprehensive and effective system they may be a sufficiently satisfactory basis, but these conditions are seldom fulfilled. The present system of bilateral treaties is therefore far from being effective. The gaps in almost every country's treaty network is both loose and full of loopholes.

At least four factors have contributed to this state of affairs:

(1) There tends to exist a certain resistance or reluctance on the part of states to enter into new bilateral treaties or make supplementary treaties to existing ones. States tend to give a lower priority to the negotiation of extradition treaties which is readily understandable since extradition is not usually a pressing issue in international relations. All too often, states unduly defer consideration of their extradition relations until a particular crisis or urgency shocks them out of their inertia. This may be due in no small measure to the often complicated and arduous process of negotiating and ratifying a treaty and where needed, to pass implementing legislation.

(2) It is the practice of a few states to denounce all their extradition treaties in anticipation of a fundamental revision of their municipal extradition laws. This was done by Brazil in 1913 and by Sweden in 1950, which led to serious breaks in the continuity of their relations with other states, especially those constitutionally unable to extradite in the absence of a treaty. This created a gap in relations between Brazil and the United States of some fifty years making Brazil a haven for futives from the United States until a treaty was signed in 1964.[51] The situation with Sweden did not give rise to such disruptive consequences,[52] even though twelve years passed before Sweden and Great Britain concluded a new treaty to replace that denounced in 1951 and the one with the United States was signed in 1964.[53]

(3) The effect of war on treaties generally has had a severe impact on extradition treaties. It seems that the only generalization which may safely be made under the present state of

international law is that the effect of war on treaties must be assessed in the light of the nature of the particular treaty obligation in question.[54] Extradition treaties do not lie at any extreme position of compatibility with a state of war such as treaties of alliance at one end of the spectrum and treaties respecting treatment of prisoners of war at the other. The effect of war on an extradition treaty was directly put in question in the United States in _Argento v. Horn_.[55] In that case the relator argued that, despite the purported "revival" by the United States of the extradition treaty with Italy after World War II, the treaty had been abrogated by the outbreak of war and could only be replaced by an altogether new treaty (see State succession, section 3.1). The Court avoided the theoretical question by basing its decision on a consideration of the "background of the actual conduct of the two nations involved, acting through the political branches of their governments."[56] The provisions of the Peace Treaties following World War II did not advert to the question whether any classes of treaty irrevocably disappeared as a result of war. The provisions of these treaties merely invited the signatories to notify the former belligerents which treaties it desires to keep in force or "revive" and declared that treaties not so notified shall be regarded as abrogated. Extradition treaties have figured prominently among the treaties which were revived under the provisions of the Peace Treaties with Bulgaria, Finland, Hungary, Italy, Japan and Romania. The disruptive effect of war on extradition treaties has been felt most keenly in respect of Germany, with whom no Peace Treaty has yet been concluded

16

by the Allied Powers. However, extradition relations between the Federal Republic of Germany and other states have since been restored.[57] The German Democratic Republic has entered into extradition treaties with countries of the Socialist Bloc only.

To a much lesser extent, the cessation of diplomatic relations has been interpreted by some states as suspending the process. This had been the position of the United States vis-a-vis Cuba from 1962 to 1973 even though this view is arguable so long as a treaty was in force and another state represents the interests of the requesting state in the requested state and can act in an official capacity.[58]

(4) Legal doubts surround the effect of state succession on extradition treaties, especially in the most common present-day form of succession namely the accession to independence of former colonies, protectorates and trust territories. Some successor states have clarified their attitudes towards pre-existing treaties by entering into inheritance agreements with the predecessor states or by making unilateral declarations of continuity.[59] Other successor states have taken no formal steps with regard to treaties in general, and the fate of extradition treaties has thus been left in doubt. While most successor states have acted in accordance with their expressed intentions, others which signed inheritance agreements have in fact since adopted negative attitudes towards succession to extradition treaties. There is no evidence, for example, that Indonesia has ever granted extradition on the basis of the Netherlands' treaties.[60] Some other states, although parties to an inheritance agreement or the makers of unilateral

declarations of continuity, have seen fit to make a specific novation of particular treaties, as did Kenya and the United States with regard to the extradition treaty with England of 1931.[61] Furthermore, some states which have taken no such general steps in relation to treaties concluded by the former sovereign have, in practice, acknowledged continuity of specific preindependence treaties.[62] If the attitudes of the successor states themselves have not always been consistent, neither have been the attitudes of other states. The United States for example has consistently relied on the doctrine of state succession in its relations with newly independent states seeking specific inheritance agreements and even implied acceptances of the applicability to pre-independence agreements. Most states however adopt a wait-and-see policy, preferring to deal with each problem of state succession as it arises.[63] Although there is evidence of increasing judicial recognition of succession by new states to extradition treaties,[64] the overall picture is uneven and uncertain. Flight by criminals to newly independent states could be encouraged by the belief that the status of a formerly applicable treaty is obscure and might not be clarified in time for action to be taken against them. In any event, the delay in settling the question would be enough of an inducement to many a fugitive as it would give him time to prepare for yet another flight elsewhere if matters ultimately turned to his detriment.

2.4 Extradition by multilateral regional arrangements

In addition to bilateral treaties, some states are parties to schemes of extradition between a group of nations having geographical or political affinity. These multilateral convention schemes take two forms: (1) A multilateral convention on extradition, replacing, supplementing, or complementing bilateral treaties, such as the Arab League Extradition Agreement and the European Extradition Convention, or (2) conventions whereby states undertake to adopt reciprocal national legislation modelled on an agreed pattern, such as among the member states of the Commonwealth and the Nordic Treaty States.

The obvious advantages of such schemes over the bilateral and multilateral extradition treaties are that they greatly reduce, if not entirely eliminate, the divergence in national legislation that so perplexes national authorities when dealing with extradition matters on a bilateral or multilateral basis. They are, therefore, less susceptible to a process of attrition likely to cause a breakdown in the relationship as is the case with a large number of individual bilateral arrangements. A less immediate but important long-term advantage of such arrangements is that they contribute to the trend of creating a "common law of extradition" and could conceivably one day result in a universal extradition convention.

No single collective treaty has as yet wiped the slate clean of pre-existing bilateral treaty commitments so as to give procedural as well as substantive cohesion to the extradition law and practice of a given region.

A brief description of the eight existing regional arrangements follows:

1 - Arab League Extradition Agreement

This agreement was approved by the Council of the League of Arab States on September 14, 1952, and was signed by Egypt, Iraq, Jordan, Lebanon, Saudi Arabia and Syria.[65] Only Egypt, Jordan and Saudi Arabia proceeded to ratification and the agreement has been operative only between these states since August 23, 1954.

2 - The Benelux Extradition Convention

On June 27, 1962, Belgium, Luxembourg and the Netherlands signed a Convention on Extradition and Judicial Assistance in Penal Matters.[66] The close economic ties between these three states, which have been part of but not entirely subsumed within the wider European Economic Communtiy, serve to explain why in some respects the convention is more permissive than other multi-lateral arrangements.

The substantive provisions of the Convention follow those of the European Convention,[67] but in a number of respects reflect the closer relationship between the parties.

3 - The Commonwealth Scheme

Although the "Scheme relating to the Rendition of Fugitive Offenders within the Commonwealth"[68] was drawn up at a meeting of Commonwealth Law Ministers held in London in 1966, it did not represent a sudden and belated recognition of the possibilities of Commonwealth cooperation in this field. The genesis of the present scheme lies as far back as 1843 when the first statute providing for the surrender of fugitive criminals between British possessions was passed by the Imperial Parliament.[69] This measure was replaced by the Fugitive Offenders Act in 1881.[70] Although some important changes were made in the 1966 Scheme, reflecting the evolution of the British Empire into the Commonwealth of Nations, the Scheme retains many of the features of the Act of 1881.

The proposal of a multilateral treaty was rejected in 1966 in favor of the agreed Scheme which would form the basis of reciprocal legislation enacted in each Member State of the Commonwealth. Australia was the first Member to pass implementing legislation.[71]

The Scheme does not preclude the making of bilateral arrangements between Member States establishing additional or alternative provisions to those of the Scheme. In particular, it is probable that neighboring Commonwealth countries may wish to preserve the simplified form of surrender contained in Part II of the Act of 1881, by making similar new provisions.[72]

4 - The European Extradition Convention

The preamble of this Convention, signed on December 13, 1957, recites that its object is the acceptance of uniform rules with regard to extradition as part of the more general aim of achieving greater unity between Member States of the Council of Europe.[73] The Convention secured the signatures of eleven States but not all proceeded to ratification. The Convention entered into force on April 18, 1960, after the deposit of ratifications by Norway, Sweden, and Turkey. Since coming into force, the Convention has also been ratified by Denmark, Greece, Ireland, Italy and Switzerland.

The Convention is at present limited to the Continent of Europe, but already its effects have been felt as a model for bilateral treaties concluded elsewhere. The Convention may be opened to accession by non-Members of the Council of Europe, if the unanimous consent of those States which have already ratified the Convention is obtained. Although reservations are permissible under the Convention and a number have in fact been made, the essential aim of uniformity has been largely achieved.

5 - The Inter-American Conventions

The first treaty was the Montevideo Convention of 1889 which attracted the support of five states. A second Convention was signed in Mexico in 1902 by seventeen states, including the signatories of the 1889 Convention. Five states signed the Bolivarian Convention at Caracas in 1911 which in turn was followed by the Bustamante Code, adopted at Havana by the Sixth International Conference of American States in 1928, whose provisions were only supplementary to pre-existing treaties. In 1933, the Second Montevideo Convention was concluded; this Convention did not abrogate existing bilateral or collective treaties in force between the parties but was to enter into force automatically in the event of the lapse of prior treaties. Further revisions took place in 1940 and in 1957. On February 7, 1973 the O.A.S. proposed a DRAFT INTER-AMERICAN CONVENTION ON EXTRADITION.

6 - The Nordic States Scheme

The Nordic Treaty of 1962, in which Denmark, Finland, Iceland, Norway and Sweden agreed on broad principles of cooperation, including the attainment of "the highest possible degree of juridicial equality" of all Scandinavian citizens in their territories,[74]

22

was in fact preceded by an agreement on extradition. Effect was given to the scheme of extradition by the enactment of similar legislation by each Member State.[75]

7 - *The O.C.A.M. Convention*

Twelve of the fourteen former French territories in Equatorial and West Africa formed the Union Africaine et Malgache in 1961 and signed a convention on judicial cooperation at Tananarive on September 12, 1961.[76] The Union was subsequently renamed the Organisation Communale Africaine et Malgache (O.C.A.M.) and was enlarged by the accession of Togo.

8 - *The Bilateral Treaties of the Socialist States of Eastern Europe*

The system of extradition among the Socialist States of Eastern Europe and the Soviet Union conforms to a uniform pattern. Uniformity has been achieved, in contrast to the method of uniform legislation adopted by the Commonwealth, by a network of virtually identical bilateral treaties which have been concluded by the individual members of the European Socialist States.[77] The treaties in which the extradition provisions are contained deal with other matters as well and extradition forms but one chapter of a treaty which makes comprehensive provision for legal assistance in civil, family and criminal matters.

A typical extradition treaty declares the general obligation undertaken by the parties in terms similar to the following: "The Contracting Parties agree to extradite to each other, in the circumstances stated in the present Agreement, those persons who, being accused or convicted of criminal offenses or such acts of

23

social deviance based on the specific traits which characterize
the new kind of relationship between the Socialist States." [78]
The choice of means or channels in the transmission of requests
for extradition is avoided to permit direct communication between
national Ministries of Justice as an alternative to diplomatic
channels.

The content of the treaties of the Socialist Bloc follows generally the pattern of modern bilateral and multilateral treaties in
the Western World. It is perhaps surprising that a practice so
bourgeois in origin as the non-extradition of nationals finds its
place in that scheme but it is coupled, however, with an obligation to prosecute nationals for crimes committed elsewhere whenever there is sufficient evidence available to the prosecuting
state, and to notify the authorities of the *locus delicti* of
the sentence passed.

3. *Characteristics of the Process of Extradition in the Law and*
   Practice of the United States

3.1 *The basis for extradition: treaty relations*
In the case of United States v. Rauscher, the Supreme Court of
the United States stated the American view of extradition in these
terms:

> It is only in modern times that the nations
> of the earth have imposed upon themselves the obli-
> gation of delivering up these fugitives from justice
> to the states where their crimes were committed, for
> trial and punishment. This has been done generally

by treaties . . . Prior to these treaties, and

apart from them there was no well-defined obli-

gation on one country to deliver was often

made, it was upon the principle of comity; . . .

and it has never been recognized as among those

obligations of one government towards another which

rest upon established principles of international

law.[79]

In the United States as in England, it is the general rule and

practice neither to ask nor to permit extradition in the absence

of a treaty obligation. Exceptions, however, did occur.[80]

Furthermore, it must be noted that the United States also reverts

to other modes of rendition.[81] Nonetheless, the United States

profess exclusive adherence to treaties as the sole basis for

extradition.[82] In its application of international law, the

United States does not recognize asylum and extradition as part

of customary international law and deems itself only bound by

such treaties or undertakings as it may elect to bind itself

thereby.[83] Furthermore, it considers the processes of extradi-

tion, its proceedings and practice a question of domestic law

and will not recognize any part of customary international law as

applicable to any part or phase of extradition and asylum pro-

ceedings. This could be a consequence of its election to rely

exclusively on treaties because recognition of substantive or

procedural norms of international law as applicable to the sub-

stance or procedure of extradition and asylum would disrupt the

exclusivity of norms emanating from treaties and domestic laws of

international law and would supersede or supplement them. There
can be, therefore, no reliance in the United States on international law to aid in interpreting substantive treaty obligation or
to supplement a treaty in case of absence of specific provisions.
Consequently, the United States developed a significant practice
of treaty-making and the resulting necessity to keep them *a giorno*
is a major undertaking leading to an almost constant process of
negotiating new treaties or renegotiating supplementary ones.
Furthermore, this approach has all of the problems pertaining to
treaties, such as: state succession, the effects of war, break
of diplomatic relations, and the perenial question of maintaining
a network of treaties, covering all parts of the world and providing in detail for all matters ranging from extraditable offenses to modes of delivery of the relator. As a result this practice suffers many weaknesses which will be discussed throughout
this study.

The first international extradition treaty entered into by the
United States was with Great Britain in 1794, Jay's Treaty.[84]
Article 27 of that treaty states:

> "It is further agreed that His Majesty and the
> United States on mutual requisition, by them respec-
> tively, or by their respective ministers or officers
> authorized to make the same, will deliver up to jus-
> tice all persons who, being charged with murder or
> forgery, committed within the jurisdiction of either,
> shall seek an asylum within any of the countries of
> the other, provided that this shall only be done on

such evidence of criminality as, according to
the laws of the place where the fugitive or person
so charged shall be found, would justify his apprehension and commitment for trial if the offence
had there been committed. The expense of such
apprehension and delivery shall be borne and de-
frayed by those who make the requisition and receive the fugitive."[85]

International extradition in American law and practice remains
a subject of legal debates and does not only extend to the causes
celebres of extradition, but goes to the doctrinal basis of the
process as well.[86] The contemporary state of American extradition
law and practice gives rise to the following definition of that
process:

"A process by which, in accordance to treaty
provisions and subject to its limitations one
state requests another to surrender a person
charged with a criminal violation of the laws of
the requesting state who is within the jurisdiction of the requested state, for the purposes
of answering criminal charges, stand trial or
execute a sentence arising out of the stated
criminal violation."[87]

In comparison to other modes of penal cooperation between states,
the definition offered above though correctly interpreting the
United States position is nonetheless a narrow one. As one author
stated:

"This act of rendition of an alleged criminal
was known in international law as extra-tradition,
from which the modern word extradition is derived.
It includes not only all modes by which a state
effects the return of a fugitive offender to the
demanding state against whose laws he may have
committed some offense, but also the acts or processes by which one sovereign state, in compliance
with a formal demand, prepares to surrender to
another state for trial the person of criminal
character who has sought refuge in its boundaries."[88]

The United States, as stated earlier, relies on treaties and
statutes insofar as the processes of extradition are concerned.[89]
This gives treaty interpretation a very important aspect of that
system. With respect to the definition of a treaty in international
law, one author proposes the following:

"A treaty is a written agreement by which two
or more states create or intend to create a relation between themselves operating within the sphere
of international law. Though international law prescribes no special form or procedure for the making
of an international agreement, yet a treaty which
is an international agreement creates certain legal
rights and obligations between the parties and binds
them to observe the rules of conduct laid down therein as law."[90]

If this definition would be taken *in extenso*, then the narrow

28

approach followed in United States interpretation of extradition
treaties is not required by the law of treaties. Such, however,
is not the case. The practice of the United States since Jay's
Treaty in 1794 is to have extradition treaties drawn separately
and not made part of any other agreement and to link the existence
of that treaty to the relations existing between the respective
states. This explains the number of extradition treaties which
the United States has with other states (see Appendix A).
Extradition treaties may be deemed declarative of an existing
reciprocal relationship or creative of the substantive basis of
the very process. The choice of theory relied upon will determine
its applicability.[91] As stated by Whiteman:

> "Extradition treaties do not, of course, make
> crimes. They merely provide a means whereby
> a State may obtain the return to it for trial
> or punishment of persons charged with or con-
> victed of having committed acts which are
> crimes at the time of their commission and
> who have fled beyond the jurisdiction of the
> State whose laws it is charged, have been
> violated."[92]

3.2 *The Constitution, treaty-making and treaty-interpretation*

In the United States, international extradition is regarded as an
exclusive national power pertaining solely to the Federal Government and denied to the several states. The rationale rests on
two grounds: the first being that as a treaty-founded process,

it is a matter of conduct of foreign affairs which is within the enumerated powers of the Federal Government and specifically vested in the President, and the second being that treaties are ratified by means of the "Advice and Consent" of the Senate.

Shortly after Jay's Treaty (1794), the United States had to settle an issue which had not been contemplated until then. That issue was the scope of the "due process" clause of the Fourteenth Amendment to the United States Constitution in extradition pro-ceedings. United States v. Robins[93] was a case of first impres-sion on that subject. Under Jay's Treaty, the relator stood ac-cused of an extraditable offense but the treaty made no provisions for a judicial hearing or the manner in which the proceedings were to be undertaken. The President ordered the case heard in United States District Court and the court held that the judicial power indeed extended to treaties under Article III of the Constitution. Having thereby established its jurisdiction over the subject mat-ter, the court ruled that the relator should be surrendered to the requesting state. The difficulty with this instance was that there was no statutory provision authorizing the court to act pursuant to the treaty or the presidential mandate.

The question which arose was whether extradition treaties are self-executing, in reliance on international legal doctrine, or require national legislation for their implementation, in reliance on constitutional law doctrine. The debate lasted from 1794 until 1848. During that period, the proponents of the view that extradition treaties are self-executing prevailed and extradition proceedings were adjudicated by Federal District Courts on request of the President or Secretary of State. It was not until 1848 that Congress passed the first extradition statute setting forth that extradition is to be undertaken by virtue of a treaty and subject to judicial proceedings in Federal District Court in accordance with the provisions of the statute.[94]

Since then, the statute has been revised several times,[95] and the present statute in force passed in 1964 states: "The provisions of this chapter relating to the surrender of persons who have committed crimes in foreign countries shall continue in force only during the existence of any treaty of extradition with such governments."[96]

The prevailing judicial doctrine rests on the grounds that no executive prerogative can dispose of a person's individual liberty, but that the right to restrict personal freedom in a manner not inconsistent with the Constitution is the existence of a treaty duly ratified by the Senate, thus becoming part of the law of the land and implemented through federal legislation.

The United States Supreme Court declared in 1936:

". . .[A]pplying as we must, our law in determining the authority of the President, we are constrained to hold that this power, in the absence of statute conferring an independent power, must be found in the terms of the treaty and that, as the treaty with France fails to grant the necessary authority, the President is without power to surrender the respondent."[97]

Clarifying the principle of exclusive national power in extradition affairs, the Supreme Court, as early as 1886, stated:

". . . There is no necessity for the states to
enter upon the relations with foreign nations which
are necessarily implied in the extradition of fugitives from justice found within the limits of the
state, as there is none why they should in their own
name make demand upon foreign nations for the surrender of such fugitives.

At this time of day, and after the repeated
examinations which have been made by this Court
into the powers of the Federal Government to
deal with all international questions exclusively,
it can hardly be admitted that, even in the absence of treaties or acts of Congress on the
subject, the extradition of a fugitive from
justice can become the subject of negotiation
between a state of this Union and a foreign
government."[98]

Thus, it is firmly established that the various states have no
power to negotiate extradition treaties, that international extradition is regarded as an exclusive national power, and that
there can be no extradition under present practice without a
treaty.[99] This doctrine is also at the basis of "executive discretion" which permits the chief executive or whomever he may
delegate to refuse the surrender of a person who was ordered
delivered to a requesting state by the judiciary.

A duly ratified treaty becomes the "Supreme law of the land,"[100]

32

but often the question arises as to the continued existence and application of a treaty in municipal law and who makes such a determination. In _Ivancevic v. Artukovic_,[101] the court, in determining whether an extradition obligation existed under treaties gave much weight to the views of the executive branches of the parties to the treaties.[102] In _Ivancevic_,[103] the government of the People's Federal Republic of Yugoslavia requested the extradition from the United States of Andrija Artukovic for the crime of murder, under the Treaty of Extradition of 1902 between the United States and The Kingdom of Serbia. The Federal District Court held that no extradition treaty existed between the United States and Yugoslavia. The ninth circuit reversed on the ground that the Treaty of 1902 was in force, holding that the People's Federal Republic of Yugoslavia had evolved as a nation through internal political changes from the Kingdom of Serbia and was, therefore, not a new country, but merely formed as a result of the desire of the Slav people for self-determination as one nation. The court decided that these internal changes did not affect the validity of the treaty with The Kingdom of Serbia which provided the core of the Yugoslav nation now a party to the pending extradition proceedings. Furthermore, the court noted that both the United States and Yugoslavia had continued to act under the premise that "the entity as it existed after the union was the political successor of the original Serbia with international political compacts continuing."[104] Thus the judiciary, relying on the President's "Power, by and with the Advice and Consent of the Senate, to make Treaties,"[105] looks at executive practice to determine the existence and applicability of treaty obligation. Adherence to this view was also illustrated in <u>Charlton v. Kelly</u>.[106] In this case which dealt with the surrender of nationals, the question presented before the Supreme Court was whether Italy's refusal to permit the extradition of its own citizens abrogated the extradition treaty between the Kingdom of Italy and the United States. The treaty provided for the surrender of "persons" convicted of or charged with specific crimes. Italy maintained that this term did not include its own citizens and that it would try its own citizens in its own courts; the United States contended that "persons" did include citizens.[107] The Court, following the interpretation of the Department of State, held that the treaty was not abrogated, concluding:

> "The executive department, having thus elected
> to waive any right to free itself from the obliga-
> tion to deliver up its own citizens, it is the
> plain duty of this court to recognize the obligation
> to surrender the appellant as one imposed by the
> treaty as the supreme law of the land and as af-
> fording authority for the warrant of extradition."[108]

Thus, the judicial position of the United States is to defer judgment on that issue to the Executive as a matter falling within the perogatives of that branch of government in its exercise of the powers to conduct foreign affairs.[109]

3.3 The extent of treaty application and state succession

The two leading cases discussed in 3.2, Ivancevic v. Artukovic and Charlton v. Kelly, reveal much about the constitutional authoritative framework of the United States doctrine of separation of powers. In these cases the judiciary revealed how and to what extent it will defer to the executive in matters of treaty interpretation and state succession and in fact abstain from interfering in the powers of another co-equal branch of government.

The major concern with respect to the state succession doctrine focuses on the question of "how extradition relations are affected when a state or territory covered by such a treaty changes its form of government, or becomes a part of a nation other than that which the United States has the formerly applicable treaty?"[110] The significance of this question lies in the fact that if the treaty is deemed abrogated by such changes, the United States, for example, will not grant an extradition request because its extradition practice is based exclusively on the existence of a treaty in force.[111]

Generally, the question of state succession arises whenever there is a change in the country's status, rather than in its government. This question arose recurringly whenever former colonies of a given state became independent.[112]

Upon gaining independence, several states have voluntarily assumed the treaty obligations applicable to their respective territories and which were formerly binding on the parent state. As an illustration, the Provisional Government of Burma assumed all applicable obligations of the United Kingdom, agreeing with the

United Kingdom that:

> All obligations and responsibilities here-
> tofore developing on the Government of the
> United Kingdom which arise from any valid in-
> ternational agreement shall henceforth, inso-
> far as such instrument may be held to have
> application to Burma, devolve upon the Pro-
> visional Government of Burma. The rights and
> benefits heretofore enjoyed by the Government
> of the United Kingdom in virtue of the ap-
> plication of any such international instrument
> to Burma shall henceforth be enjoyed by the
> Provisional Government of Burma. [113]

Such approach obviously avoids state succession problems but it
may not correspond with the emerging national policy of the new
state. One illustrative case is Shehadeh v. Commission of Prisons,
Jerusalem. [114]   In Shehadeh, the relators (applicants in the
case) had been detained by the respondent at the request of the
Lebanese Government pursuant to the Provisional Agreement for the
Extradition of Offenders between Syria and Lebanon and Palestine
made in 1921. The applicants applied for a writ of *habeas corpus*
in order to challenge the extradition proceedings, and obtained
a *nisi* order. The applicants contended *inter alia* that the
change of government in Lebanon from a Mandate to an independent
Republic invalidated the Provisional Agreement of 1921, (and
further that the offense for which their extradition was being
requested had not been committed within Lebanese territory). [115]

In discharging the rule and remanding the applicants to custody, the Supreme Court of Palestine held:

> . . . The change of status from a mandated
> territory to independent Republic in Lebanon
> had no effect on the continuing validity of
> the Extradition Agreement of 1921 between
> Palestine and Syria and Lebanon. The fact
> that the Lebanese Government had requested
> and the Government of Palestine had assented
> to the extradition of the applicants inferred
> that both Governments were satisfied that the
> place where the alleged crime was committed
> was within Lebanese territory.[116]

Thus, the Supreme Court of Palestine, in denying the *habeas corpus* petition, stated that it is an established principle of international law that the continued effectiveness of a state's international obligations are not affected by governmental or constitutional changes in that state.[117] The Supreme Court of Palestine in another landmark case, Perlin v. Superintendent of Prisons,[118] further clarified the effect of change of government in the requested state on the continued obligations created by treaty. In Perlin, the Superintendent of Prisons was called upon to show cause why the petitioner, Abraham Perlin, should not be released from custody and the extradition proceeding against him set aside. The petitioner was arrested in Palestine on September 19, 1942, and was eventually ordered by the Chief Magistrate of Tel-Aviv, on October 17, 1942, to be handed over to agents competent to receive him on

37

behalf of the High Commissioner for Syria and the Lebanon on the grounds that: "Extradition between Palestine and the Lebanon is governed by the terms of the Provisional Agreement between Syria and Palestine dated the 5th and 11th of July, 1921."[119] The accused had nonetheless contended, *inter alia*, that there was no extradition agreement in existence at the time of the request between Palestine and the Lebanon and that there was no longer such official authority as the French High Commissioner for Syria and Lebanon.[120] The court rejected the argument and held that the obligation to extradite must be discharged and stated:

> It seems to be settled practice in International
> Law that treaties and international agreements are
> not affected by a change in government, or in the
> form of government of one of the contracting par-
> ties, and remain in force until denounced by the
> new government or they expire by effluxation of
> time. Thus if a State changes its form of govern-
> ment from a monarchial to a republican one, treaties
> to which it was a party still remain in force.[121]

While some newly independent states specifically assume the treaty obligations of the predecessor state,[122] many do not.[123] In 1948 Israel proclaimed its statehood, and in 1949 it held that the Extradition Treaty of 1931 between the United States and the United Kingdom was not in force with respect to Israel. As a result of this position taken by Israel, it was necessary for the United States and Israel to negotiate a new extradition treaty and it was not until 1964 that it was signed.[124] Thus, the Israeli Government's

38

rejection of the treaties applicable to Palestine serves to illustrate the controlling principle operative in such state succession situations: the government of the successor state determines whether or not a given treaty remains effective with that state.[125] The prevailing position of the United States is that a treaty is in force *sua sponte* and binding on the successor state until that state repudiates it.

3.4 *The effects of war on the continued application of extradition treaties*

There are widely divergent views in international law on the subject, ranging from total abrogation of the treaty to continued enforcement of the treaty. The doctrine sometimes asserted, especially by earlier writers, is that war *ipso facto*, abrogates treaties of every kind between the warring parties.[126] The contemporary view is that whether the stipulations of a treaty are annulled by war depends upon their extrinsic character.[127] It is obvious that war must extinguish certain treaties, such as those of friendship and alliance, because of their very nature, whereas treaties contemplating a permanent arrangement of rights are not to be abrogated by the occurrence of war, but merely suspended during the conflict.[128] The effect of war on an extradition treaty was at issue in Argento v. Horn.[129] In this case, upon application of the Republic of Italy, certified by the United States Secretary of State, and upon complaint of the Italian consul for Ohio and Kentucky, extradition proceedings were initiated against the appellant in the United States District Court for the Northern District of Ohio. After a hearing pursuant to 18 U.S.C.A. § 3184, the United States Commissioner concluded that the evidence was sufficient to sustain the charge that the appellant was the same Tommaso Argento who had been convicted *in absentia* and sentenced to life imprisonment in Italy in 1931 for a murder committed there in 1922. The Commissioner accordingly committed the appellant to custody pending the surrender to the Republic of Italy. Argento argued that despite the purported "revival" by the United States of the extradition treaty with Italy pursuant to Article 44 of the peace treaty of 1947, the treaty had been abrogated by the outbreak of war and could be replaced only by an altogether new treaty. Argento claimed that no valid extradition treaty existed between the United States and the Republic of Italy, and that in the absence of such a treaty, there is no legal authority for the extradition proceedings. The court avoided the theoretical question by basing its decision on a consideration of the "background of the actual conduct of the two nations involved, acting through the political branches of their government."[130] The court found that in light of the peace treaty which contained a provision inviting notification of revival of treaties and the notification by the Department of State of its intention to revive the treaty, and the subsequent conduct of the parties evidencing an understanding that the treaty was in force, the conclusion was that the treaty had been merely suspended during the war not abrogated by it. [131]

A subsequent landmark decision containing an interesting opinion on the effect of war on extradition treaties can be found in In Re Extradition of D'Amico.[132] On the application of the Republic of Italy, extradition proceedings were begun against the relator

40

before the United States Commissioner for the Southern District of New York. The Commissioner found that the relator was the same Vito D'Amico who had been convicted *in absentia* in Italy in 1952 for robbery and kidnapping committed in Italy on or about April 15, 1946, and that there was probable cause to believe that D'Amico had committed the crimes charged. The Commissioner therefore committed D'Amico to custody pending surrender to the Republic of Italy. D'Amico petitioned for a writ of *habeas corpus*, contending: (1) that the Convention between the United States and Italy of 1868 for the surrender of Criminals was abrogated by the outbreak of war between the Parties in 1942, and was not validly revived by the notification of the United States to Italy on February 6, 1948; (2) that the revival of the Treaty of 1868 did not make it applicable retroactively to crimes committed during the existence of a state of war between the Parties; and (3) that the offence was not committed in territory subject to the jurisdiction of the demanding state because it was committed while the Italian Government was subject to Allied Control.[133] In discharging the writ of *habeas corpus* and remanding D'Amico to the custody of the United States Marshal, the court concluded that the extradition treaty was merely suspended by the outbreak of war between the Parties and was revived by the formal cessation of hostilities. In effect the court held that an extradition treaty could operate retroactively and apply to offenses committed while the treaty was suspended prior to its revival.[134] It would seem that such a doctrine violates the principle *nulla poene sine legge - nullum crimen sine legge.*

3.5 *Appraisal of state succession and war on the extradition treaties of the United States*

The effects of state succession and war on extradition treaties as a legal basis for extradition, depend upon this question: "if the United States may extradite a fugitive in the absence of treaty relations with the requesting state and whether it is barred from requesting extradition in the absence of a treaty with the asylum state."[135] The answer for both instances is negative in the practice of the United States because it chooses to reject the applicability of customary international law to extradition and asylum matters. This self-imposed restriction condemns the practice to depend exclusively on one source of international law, namely, treaties, and lose the benefit of an alternative source.[136] As has been noted very few countries in the world possess no extradition treaties at all, nevertheless, a majority of the countries in the world are parties to relatively few extradition treaties. One reason seems to be that some states prefer as a matter of principle or convenience not to enter into treaties and be formally bound and will usually enter its treaties only with those states that will not extradite in the absence of a treaty. The many reasons advanced by states who are reluctant to enter such treaties are basically reasons of convenience and self-interest.[137] It must be noted, however, that the existence of a treaty is not indispensable for extradition, but of great significance is the existence of a domestic legal framework to regulate the process. Without such a framework there is no likelihood that a sustained practice will exist. Treaties, however, tend to insure that the state in question will examine its own structure and internal procedures to insure the continuity and regularity of the practice. To that extent the extinction of treaty relations have no effect on the continuity of the process internally. The domestic laws of a given state may, however, give the executive branch of government discretionary power to surrender fugitives to foreign governments in certain situations. In such cases the domestic legal framework relies on the doctrine of comity to pursue the practice.[138] The position of the United States as to the doctrine of comity has been stated as follows:

> Generally, this Government does not request surrender as an act of comity, since in the few cases where it has done so, it has been necessary to point out to the government of the asylum country that this Government would be unable to comply with such a request if it should receive one. Such a statement usually has the effect of causing the requested government to decline surrender.[139]

It must be noted however that the extinction of a treaty obligation by reason of war or its abrogation by a successor state would not have a definitive effect on extradition if the United States were to accept the existing alternative under international law, i.e., reciprocity or comity. A better policy in state succession would be to rely on an alternative basis for extradition pending treaty negotiations which is the case whenever a former colony usually of a Western nation acquires its independence.

It is at that crucial time of a nation's existence that a previous treaty obligation sought to be continued has been contracted with what has become a foreign state (and maybe not on good terms with the newly independent state).[140] Politically and psychologically, the approach and timing are often bad and the result is the rejection of the previously contracted obligation. The alternative policy is to urge the negotiation of a new treaty and in the interim to rely on comity. The problem is different in respect to the effect of war, even though it would seem that with the outlawry of war in the United Nations Charter, Article 2-4,[141] only a party guilty of aggression would see all treaty obligations suspended if not abrogated. Any other process of coercion short of aggression, would at best suspend extradition treaties. This conclusion depends on whether extradition between states is considered an aspect of foreign policy furthering the national interest or is deemed a form of international cooperation against common criminality. If the former approach is adopted then extradition treaties are dependent upon the friendly relations of the signatories and would thus be suspended during unfriendly periods. If the latter approach is adopted then world societal interest would prevail over the prevailing conditions of bilateral relations and no common criminal would benefit from the political conditions existing between the respective states at the time he is sought by justice. The United States so far adheres to the narrower position of self-interest and this explains the preponderant role played by the executive in extradition matters as expressed in Terlinden v. Ames by the Supreme Court: "The

44

decisions of th executive department in matters of extradition
are within its own sphere and in accordance with the Constitution
are not open to judicial revision." [142]

4. *An Appraisal of the Contemporary Framework of Extradition and A Proposed Policy-Oriented Framework*

The proposed framework outlined in this section will be referred
to throughout this book. Certain terms will be used recurringly
and because they are given a peculiar meaning which relates to
the proposed framework their definition is set forth herein.

IDEOLOGY: Body of doctrine or thought based on
values supporting a social or political movement,
institution or class.

VALUES: The ideals to which a measure of regard,
significance and importance is subjectively a-
scribed by one who estimates the worth and quality
of the said ideals.

VALUE-JUDGMENT: A preference, choice of a form
of action or thought over another without a fixed
evaluation but in reliance upon ideology and values.

IDEOLOGICALLY MOTIVATED OFFENDER: One who knowingly commits a violation of positive law, with the
belief that it is warranted or justified by a
higher order or superior values than those a-
scribed to the law which he violates.

A person moved by ideology who has made a value-judgment that for him justifies such conduct.

AUTHORITATIVE PROCESS: A system by virtue of which there is power and ability to direct the actions of others in a desired manner without reasoned persuasion or choice.

DECISION-MAKING PROCESS: A system through which persons at varying levels, holding authority (ability to direct others) coordinate and produce a final result.

ORDER: The product of a system of action and interaction, having a value-oriented goal for the purpose of a value realization.

WORLD PUBLIC ORDER: Is "order" oriented to that which affects mankind and is brought into being by the collective action and interaction of all constitutive forces of the various world authoritative decision-making processes.

International law in the twentieth century is entering a pronounced phase of changing structures which entails the broadening of its scope and application. The individual who has been historically alien to the scope of this discipline is gradually acquiring a limited place therein. This is manifested by the recognition and enunciation of certain fundamental human rights and by the subjection of the individual to personal responsibility

46

under international criminal law.[143] Relations between nation-states are ceasing to be a matter of limited interest and exclusive concern of the parties immediately involved, but are broadening to encompass some aspect of the world community's interests in the maintenance and preservation of world public order.[144] The impact of these factors on classical norms of extradition law and practice are causing a re-evaluation of this institution's purposes and functions.[145]

The classical definition of extradition is that it is a process by which one state (the state of refuge or asylum) surrenders to another (the requesting state) an individual (the relator) accused or convicted in the requesting state of an offense for which the requesting state is seeking to subject the relator to trial or punishment.[146] This definition reflects a conceptual approach which does not account for all inter-active interests.

The proposed conceptual framework for extradition is therefore based on five interlocking factors, namely: (1) the recognition of the 'national interest" of the states who are parties to the extradition proceedings; (2) the existence of an international duty to preserve and maintain world public order; (3) the effective application of minimum standards of fairness and justice to the relator in the extradition process; (4) a collective duty on the part of all states to combat criminality; and (5) the balancing of these factors within the juridical framework of the Rule of Law.[147]

The interrelationship of these five factors is based on the following rationale : (1) The existence of a duty to preserve and maintain world public order does not destroy national sovereignty. The interests of the world community can be considered within the scope of the "national interest" because this latter concept is founded on the notion that "national independence (is better served) within international interdependence."[148] The enforcement of individual rights in extradition proceedings is not only a matter of humanitarian concern, but also a recognition that the individual is a party in interest vis-a-vis the respective states and the world community. Such recognition does not detract from a nation's sovereignty if for no other reason than that the individual is ultimately the bearer of the consequences of institutionalized conflicts and personally accountable before the world community for acts in violation of international law. (2) Mutual cooperation and assistance in penal matters reinforces the effectiveness of the municipal public order of all states and does not have to depend for its effectiveness on political compromises or denial of individual rights. (3) Adherence to the Rule of Law is the ultimate safeguard and guarantee for the survival of mankind. Such a framework lends credence to the merits of the process through which decisions are reached. Credibility in the process makes acceptance of its results more likely and thus greatly diminishes opportunities for conflict over the decisional outcome.

In our contemporary, politically factionalized world, it would be naive to believe that in balancing these five factors in this proposed concept of extradition all said factors are equal; some are more equal than others. The first of these factors, the nationally perceived interest of the state, will remain the foremost consideration. The second factor, concern for world public order, will be largely shaped by considerations ancillary to the first and, therefore, of lesser impact in the course of the authoritative decision-making process leading to the granting or denial of extradition. The third, concern for the individual, will remain the least considered factor in the over-all balancing of the equities and interests involved, as weighted by today's politically value-oriented decisions of institutional authoritative processes.[149] The fourth, if it is ever considered, will be regarded as part of national interest and not as an international obligation arising under general principles of international law. With respect to the "Rule of Law" concept, it will most likely be received perfunctorily and given lip service adherence by the following of certain forms and formalities with little or no regard for its substance. Somehow, even this bleak picture may become encouraging if a break-through is accomplished through greater adherence to the Rule of Law when we consider that in the history of law, forms, formalities and essentially adjective law determined outcomes which shaped some of the most fundamental and substantive human rights. The rights of the individual in extradition reflect the position of the individual in international law.[150] Extradition is regarded throughout the world, with some variations in application but not in substance, as in institutional practice. Governments are the subjects of its regulation, while individuals are the objects of its outcome. The individual who is contemplated by extradition proceedings is not the primary party contemplated by extradition law and practice. Restrictions,

49

limitations, or defenses which exist under extradition law are not, with a few exceptions, primarily designed for the benefit of the individual, but rather for the benefit of the states involved. While it is sustainable to argue that the individual is the beneficiary of the political exception to extradition, the fact that his right thereto is limited to the raising of the issue is indicative of the real center of interest.[151] The state of refuge has the sole discretion of recognizing or rejecting the relator's contention that his alleged conduct falls within the scope of the political offense exception to extradition, but it does so in accordance with its own self-serving standards.[152]

To further emphasize the inter-governmental nature of the practice, nowhere in extradition law and practice can the individual -- the object of the proceedings -- compel the demanding state or the state of refuge to adhere to internationally recognized principles of extradition law if the states wish not to recognize them or to circumvent or waive their application.[153] As recently as 1972 a United States Court of Appeals held that the doctrine of specialty was one of convenience between the respective states and not a right which the relator could claim.[154] This decision illustrates the classical approach in its narrowest sense. Many states deny that asylum or extradition are part of customary international law and reject any international obligations arising therefrom. It must be noted, however, that customs evidenced by consistent practice are one of the sources of international law and are, therefore, as binding upon those nations as are their treaty obligations. The history of extradition treaties

and customary practice of extradition developed certain principles
which by their consistency and wide acceptance could be said to
have become "general principles of international law,"[155] and
therefore creative of binding obligations upon the nation-states
to adhere to such principles. These are primarily principles
regulating relations between states and so far there are no rights
conferred upon the individual which he can claim, let alone enforce, against either of the respective states involved. The
individual who is the subject of extradition proceedings is still
dependent upon the good faith and benevolence of the interested
states.[156] The protection of individual rights are still considered a matter of municipal law even though they may be covered
by international treaties and covenants on human rights. This
situation exists because the individual is still not considered
a full fledged subject of. international law and, also, because
there are no practical means for the implementation of human
rights which would allow individual redress against a given state
which can still find protection in the Doctrine of Sovereignty.
The exception to this situation arises under the terms of the
European Convention on Human Rights.[157] The failure by states to
follow their own treaty obligations designed to protect individuals
rights will not even create a right under international law which
the individual can raise against such states, except whenever
municipal law allows a specific remedy in which case the issue
will be of domestic rather than international law. A mutual or
consensual failure by states engaged in extradition proceedings
to abide by a treaty obligation designed to inure to the relator's

benefit may not even constitute a breach of the treaty since the individual who bears its consequences is not a party to the treaty. However, lack of fairness or good faith by the parties in the application of rights which they have stipulated in favor of third parties, or conceded to individuals as parties beneficiary under the treaty, may be said to violate principles of fairness engaging state responsibility for injury to aliens. Even then, however, the claim must be made by the state of which the alien is a national. When, as is usually the case, that state is the requesting state the individual remains without protection.

A different approach to this problem could be that treaties rights containing a stipulation for the benefit of the individual are, to that extent, enforceable rights made in favor of a third party regardless of that party's status under international law.[158] In furtherance thereof a claim could be asserted that a state's failure to grant the relator those rights created for his benefit by treaty create implications of illegibility of the proceedings. Because such a claim could be asserted and in order to avoid political embarrassment states seldom conferred upon or granted the individual any specific rights. All provisions likely to be interpreted as such are couched in vague terms to preclude the assertion of any such rights or claims thereto. These observations are particularly significant in respect to defenses available to an individual in the course of extradition proceedings, which are discussed in Chapter VII.

Chapter 1

Footnotes

1. Kutner, "World Habeas Corpus and International Extradition,"
   41 U. Det. L. J. 25 (1964), and *infra* notes 2-3 and 4.

2. Langdon and Gardner, 6 Journal of Egyptian Archeology 179
   (1930); also referred to in Franz Von Haltzendorf, Völkrreclits,
   169 (1885).

3. See Phillipson, I., The International Law and Custom of
   Ancient Greece and Rome, 358-374 (1911).

4. De Visscher, Theory and Reality in Public International Law
   243 (1957); Nussbaum, A Concise History of the Law of Nations
   214 (1954). Consider the British Extradition Law which listed
   five treaties between 1174 and 1794 and referring almost
   exclusively to the surrender of political offenders; see,
   Clark, Extradition, 18-22 (4th ed. 1903) and O'Higgins, "The
   History of Extradition in British Practice," 13 Indian Y. B.
   Int'l Aff. 78 (1964); and 6 Brit. Dig. Int'l. L. (1965) which
   considers "treason" and "rebellion" the two main extraditable
   offenses as nonpolitical even though they are both deemed
   examples of political offenses par excellence.

5. See, G.F. Martens, Recueil des Traités, 7 Vols. and Supplements
   au receuil des principaux traites, 20 Vols. (1802-42).

6. These observations are confirmed by an examination of
   eighteenth century treaties between 1718 and 1830 compiled
   by G.F. Martens. Of the ninety treaties concluded during
   this period, twenty-eight deal exclusively with military deserters.

7. For Beccaria, see _Dei delitti e delle pene_ (1704) translated
   by J.A. Farrer, _Crimes and Punishments_ 193-194 (1880). For
   Bentham, see _An Introduction to the Principles of Morals and
   Legislations_ (Harriman, 1948); also, Phillipson, _Three Criminal
   Reformers: Beccaria, Bentham and Romilly_ (1923).

8. _Supra_, notes 1, 2, 3, 4.

9. _De Jure Belli ac Pacis_, bk. 2, c. 21, § § 3, 4. Consider its
   modern application in the 1970 Hague Convention on Unlawful
   Seizure of Aircrafts, etc., _infra_, note 50, which provides for
   the alternative of punishment or extradition.

10. _Le Droit des Gens_, bk. 2, c. 6 § § 76, 77.

11. See Wheaton, _Elements of International Law_ at 188 (5th ed.,
    1916).

12. Puffendorf, _Elements of International Law_, bk. 8, ch. 3,
    § § 23, 24.

13. Wheaton, _supra_, note 11, at 188.

14. _Holmes v. Jennison_, 14 Pet. 540 (1840).

15. _Rausher v. United States_, 119 U.S. 407 (1886); _Factor v.
    Laubenheimer_, 290 U.S. 276 (1933); _Valentine v. United States
    ex rel. Neidecker_, 299 U.S. 5 (1936); 4 _Hackworth Digest_, 11
    et seq. (1942); 6 Whiteman _Digest_ 732 (1968).

16. Blackstone, 1 _Commentaries_ 355; II McNair, _International Law
    Opinions_, 43 (1963).

17. _Ibid._, McNair, p. 44.

18. 6 _British Digest of International Law_ 454-461 (1965). The law
    officers pronounced the following opinion in 1842 concerning
    The Creole, where slaves arose against the vessel, owned by the

United States, killed the master and a passenger and sought refuge in the Bahamas: "[I]n the practice of some States to deliver up persons charged with crimes who have taken refuge, or been found within their dominions, on demand of the government of which the alleged criminals are subjects but such practice does not universally, or even generally prevail, nor is there any rule of the Law of Nations rendering it imperative on an independent state to give up persons residing or taking refuge within its territory. The brutal surrender of criminals is indeed sometimes stipulated by treaty, but as there is not at present any subsisting treaty to that effect with the United States of America, we think that Her Majesty's Government is not bound on the demand of the Government of the United States to deliver up the persons in question, or any of therein, to that Government to be tried within the United States." pp. 455-456.

19. 33 and 34 Vict. c. 52 (1870).

20. Brown v. Lizars, 2 Comm. L. R. 837 (1905) (High Court of Australia); Babu Ram Saksena v. the State (1950) Sup. Ct. Rep. 573 (Sup. Ct. of Indian); Reg. v. Governor of Brixton Prison ex parte Soblen, 2 Q. B. 283, 299-300 (1963) (Court of Appeal, England). Canadian legislation provides for extradition in the absence of a treaty: Revised Statutes of Canada, 1952, c. 322, Part II, but this Part has not been brought into effect: LaForest, Extradition to and from Canada, 13 (1961).

21. Billot, Traite de l'extradition, 422-423 (1874).

22. <u>In re Tribble</u>, 20 <u>I. L. R.</u> 366 (1953), Venezuela Federal
    Court (May 26, 1953).

23. <u>In re Milton Gomes</u> [1929-1930] <u>Ann. Dig.</u> 280 (No. 177).

24. Harvard Research in International Law, Draft Convention on
    Extradition, 29 <u>A. J. I. L., Spec. Supp.</u> 360 (1935).

25. *Supra*, note 11, p. 193.

26. 18 U.S.C. § 3184; Neidecker, 299 U.S. 5, 9 (1936).

27. <u>Regina v. Wilson</u>, 3 Q. B. D. 42, 46 (1877).

28. Among these cases see that of <u>Arguelles</u> who was returned to
    Spain in 1864 without a treaty, discussed in I, Moore, <u>A</u>
    <u>Treatise on Extradition and Interstate Rendition</u> (1891),
    pp. 33-35; the case of <u>John H. Suratt</u> charged with the
    assassination of Lincoln, who was surrendered by Egypt to the
    United States at the request of the latter without the exis-
    tence of a treaty, discussed in 2, Moore (1906), cites three
    other cases at p. 35, 42, 45; the case of <u>William H. Adsetts</u>,
    who was surrendered by the United States without a treaty
    and was tried and executed in Hong-Kong discussed in 4
    Hackworth, <u>Digest</u> (1942), pp. 14-15. It is noteworthy that
    Whiteman's <u>Digest</u> does not mention any of these cases nor
    does it discuss "comity" and "reciprocity" as a legal basis
    for extradition; see 6 Whiteman, <u>Digest</u> (1968), pp. 732-737.
    See also <u>United States v. Paroutian</u>, extradition from Leba-
    non, 299 F. 2d 486 (2d cir. 1962), <u>aff'd</u> 319 F. 2d 661 (2d
    cir. 1963), <u>cert. denied</u>, 375 U.S. 981 (1964); also <u>United</u>
    <u>States v. Accarch</u>, extradition from Italy on a nonextraditable
    offense, 241 F. Supp. 119 (S.D.N.Y. 1964), <u>aff'd</u> 342 F. 2d

697 (2d cir. 1964), <u>cert. denied</u>, 382 U.S. 954 (1954);
another exception appears in 18 U.S.C. § 3185 permitting
extradition without treaty to and from countries occupied
by the United States; see <u>in re Kraussman</u>, 130 F. Supp. 926
(D. Conn. 1955); also, <u>Neely v. Henkel</u>, 180 U.S. 109 (1901);
see opinion of Hackworth on the subject in 4 Hackworth,
<u>Digest</u>, 20-21; another exception is for offenses committed
on United States military bases abroad, 6 Whiteman, <u>Digest</u>
744-745. Ruling on the constitutionality of such surrenders
the Supreme Court upheld the validity of status of forces
agreements in <u>Wilson v. Girard</u>, 354 U.S. 524 (1957).

29. 5 <u>Annuaire de l'Institut de Droit International</u> 127 (1880).

30. See 39 and 40 <u>Revue Internationale de Droit Penal</u> (1969)
(1970).

31. Billot, *supra*, note 21, p. 259.

32. <u>Les Principes Modernes du Droit Penal International</u> 249
(1927).

33. See Kutner, *supra*, note 1.

34. No express condition of reciprocity appears in the legislation of Algeria (the other former French States of Africa),
Denmark, Finland, Italy, Lebanon, Libya, Sweden and Yugoslavia.

35. Law of December 23, 1929, art. 4(1), Harvard Research,
Extradition, *supra*, note 24, 385.

36. Continuing declarations of reciprocity are listed and kept
up to date in <u>Richtlinien fur den Berkehr mit dem Ausland
in Strafrechtlichen Angelegenheiten</u> (1959 to date). For the

German practice see Grützner as well as Vögler in 39 <u>Revue Internationale de Droit Penal</u>, pp. 379-448 (1968).

37. Shearer, <u>Extradition in International Law</u> (1971).

38. 119 U.S. 407 (1886).

39. <u>Factor v. Laubenheimer</u>, *supra*, note 15 at 387 (1933); see, however, note 28, *supra*.

40. <u>The State (Duggan) v. Tapley</u>, 28 I. L. R. 336, 337 (No. 109) (1957).

41. Compare 1 Moore, <u>A Treatise on Extradition and Interstate Rendition</u> (1891) (hereinafter referred to as "Moore, Extradition"); and 6 Whiteman, <u>Digest</u>, pp. 732-738 (1968) to the various European national reports in 39 <u>Revue Internationale de Droit Penal</u> (1968).

42. See Bassiouni and Nanda, <u>A Treatise on International Criminal Law</u>, Vol. (1973).

43. 112 L. N. T. S. 371, art. 10.

44. 198 L. N. T. S. 299, art. 9.

45. 520 U. N. T. S., 204 T. I. A. S. 62; see also the Amending Protocol of 24 March 1972, U.N. Doc. E Conf. 63/8, which is patterned after the similar provision of 1970 Hague Convention, *infra*, note 50; for a detailed analysis of all Narcotics Conventions, see Bassiouni, "The International Narcotics Control Scheme--A Proposal," 46 <u>St. John's L. Rev.</u> 713 (1972), and Bassiouni, <u>Work Paper on International Drug Control</u>, 1973 Abidjan World Peace Through Law Conference; see also Bassiouni, "Transnational Control of Narcotics," 1972, <u>Proceedings of the American Society of International</u>

Law 227.

46. 103 B. F. S. P. 244, art. 5, and the Supplementary White
     Slave Traffic Convention, 1921, 9 L. N. T. S. 415, art 4,
     and the Convention for the Suppression of the Traffic in
     Persons and of the Exploitation of the Prostitution of
     Others, 1950, 96 U. N. T. S. 271, art. 8. See, e.g., Nanda
     and Bassiouni, "Slavery and White Slavery--Steps toward
     Eradication," 12 Santa Clara Lawyer 424 (1972).

47. 78 U. N. T. S. 277, art. 7; see also art. 8 of the 1935
     Convention for the Prevention and Punishment of Terrorism
     even though it never entered into force; 7 Hudson, Interna-
     tional Legislation (1937); see also Bassiouni, International
     Terrorism (1974).

48. 46 U. N. T. S. 201, and 47 U. N. T. S. 159.

49. I. C. A. O. Doc. No. 8364 (1963), art. 16(2)--for text see
     58 A. J. I. L. 566 (1964); for a general analysis see Evans,
     "Aircraft Hijacking: Its Causes and Cure," 63 A. J. I. L.
     695 (1969). For a detailed comment see 20 DePaul L. Rev.
     485 (1972).

50. For a text of the 1970 Hague Convention for the Suppression
     of Unlawful Seizure of Aircraft, see Appendix I to Sundberg,
     "Piracy: Air and Sea," 20 DePaul L. Rev. 337 et seq. (1970)
     reprinted in Bassiouni and Nanda, A Treatise on International
     Criminal Law, Vol. I, p. 455 (1973).

51. See Evans, "The New Extradition Treaties of the United States,"
     59 A. J. I. L. 351 (1965). The author discusses the treaties
     with Brazil, Sweden, and Israel concluded in 1964.

52. *Ibid.*

53. *Ibid.*

54. O'Connell, International Law 286 (1965).

55. 241 F. 2d 258 (6th cir. 1957), cert. denied, 355 U.S. 818.

56. *Id.*, 262, cf. the approach of the Supreme Court in Terlinden v. Ames, 184 U.S. 270 (1902) with regard to State succession and extradition treaties; and in Charlton v. Kelly, 229 U.S. 447, 468 (1913) in respect of the nonextradition of nationals.

57. The treaty with Belgium of 1874 was reapplied by an exchange of notes in 1952; a new treaty was concluded in 1958. Although a new treaty was concluded with France in 1951, it did not enter into force until 1959. The new treaty with Great Britain of 1960 did not reactivate the old treaty with respect to Commonwealth Member States. Unpublished correspondence with the United States reactivated the treaty of 1930: McIntyre, Legal Effect of World War II on Treaties of the United States, 148 (1958).

58. See Extradition Treaty with Cuba, 33 Stat. 2265 (1905), upholding the view of the Department of State, holding that the break of diplomatic relations precluded making extradition requests. On February 15, 1973, a memorandum of understanding was signed between the United States and Cuba on the extradition of hijackers of aircrafts and vessels, see Vol. 10-5, The Globe, March 1973, Bassiouni ed. See Evans, *supra*, note 49, pp. 695-696, contra, Bassiouni, "Ideologically Motivated Offenses and the Political Offense Exception in Extradition--A Proposed Juridical Standard for an Unruly

Problem," 19 DePaul L. Rev. 217 at 219 (1969).

59. Barbados, Botswana, Burma, Ceylon, Congo (Brazzaville),
Congo (Kinshasa), Cyprus, Gambia, Chana, Guyana, India,
Indonesia, Jamaica, Jordan, Kenya, Laos, Lesotho, Malagasy,
Republic, Malaqi, Malaysia, Malta, Mauritius, Morocco, Nigeria,
Pakistan, Rwanda, Sierra Leone, Singapore, Somalia, Tanzania
Trinidad and Tobago, Uganda, Vietnam, Western Samoz, Zambia.
For the history of techniques of achieving continuity of
treaties and for a critique of their effectiveness, see
O'Connell, State Succession in Municipal Law and International
Law, II, 113-140 (1967). See Appendix A.

60. But Indonesia has requested extradition on the basis of a
preindependence treaty; Re Westerling, 17 I.L.R. 82 (No.
21) (1950).

61. Exchange of Notes, May 14 - August 19, 1965, T. I. A. S.
5916.

62. E.g., Mali: 2 Whiteman, Digest 983-984 (1963).

63. Cf., the Survey by O'Higgins, "Irish Extradition Law and
Practice," 34 Brit. Y. B. Int'l L. 274, 296, 306-311 (1958).

64. Shehadeh v. Commissioner of Prisons, 14 I. L. R. 42 (No. 16)
(1947), Palestine Supreme Court; Re Westerling, 17 I. L. R.
No. 21, 82 (1950), Singapore High Court; Ex parte O'Dell
and Griffen (1953), 3 D. L. R. 207; State v. Bull (1967),
2 South African Law Reports 636 (distinguishing the earlier
South African decisions of State v. Eliasov (1965), 2 South
African Law Reports 770; In re Jere, District Court, District of Columbia, 1966 (unreported); Ministere Public v.

Sabbe, Cour d'appel de Leopoldville, No. 7995 (1966).

65.   159 British and Foreign State Papers 606.

66.   De Schutter, "International Criminal Law in Evolution:
      Mutual Assistance in Criminal Matters between the Benelux
      Countries," 14 Netherlands J. of Int'l. L. 382-410 (1967),
      and Bassiouni and Nanda, A Treatise on International Criminal
      Law, Vol. II, p. 249, (1973).

67.   See below, p.

68.   H. M. S. O. London, Cmnd. 3008.

69.   Cited in Shearer, *supra*, note 37, p. 55, 56 and 57 Vict.
      c. 34.

70.   Cited in Shearer, *supra*, note 37, p. 55, 44 & 45 Vict. c.
      69.

71.   Extradition (Commonwealth Countries) Act, 1966, Act. No.
      75 of 1966. See also Great Britain, Fugitive Offenders Act,
      1967, c. 68, and Malaysia, Commonwealth Fugitive Criminals
      Act, 1967, No. 54 of 1967.

72.   See, e.g., the Australian Extradition (Commonwealth Coun-
      tries) Act, 1966, Part III, which applies between Asutralia,
      the British Solomon Islands Protectorate, Fiji, the Gil-
      bert and Ellice Islands Colony and New Zealand.

73.   Council of Europe, European Treaty Series, No. 24, see
      generally O'Higgins, "The European Convention on Extradi-
      tion," 9 Int'l. & Comp. L. O. 491 (1960).

74.   434 U.N.T.S. 145.

75.   See, e.g., the Swedish Law of June 5, 1959, No. 254.

76.   The parties were: Cameroun, Central African Republic,

Chad, Congo (Brazzaville), Dahomey, Gabon, Ivory Coast, Malagasy Republic, Mauritania, Niger, Senegal and Upper Volta. Concerning other treaties of these countries, see O'Connell, State Succession in Municipal Law and International Law, 58-88 (1967).

77. See, e.g., Romania - Hungary, 1958, 416 U.N.T.S. 199.

78. Conesco, "l'extradition dans les Traites d'Assistance Juridiques Conclus par l'Etat Socialiste Roumaine avec les Autres Etats Socialistes d'Europe," 9 Revue roumaine des sciences sociales (serie de sciences juridiques) 279, 282 (1965). For a survey of the criminal procedure of the USSR, see Bassiouni, "The Criminal Justice System of the Union of Soviet Socialist Republics and the People's Republic of China," 11 Revista de derecho Puertorriqueno 164 (1972).

79. 119 U.S. 407, 411 (1886), see also Factor v. Laubenheimer, supra, note 15.

80. See supra, note 28.

81. See Chapter II, Section 2.

82. See 6 Whiteman, Digest (1968), pp. 732-737.

83. Ibid.

84. I. Malloy, Treaties, Conventions, International Acts, Protocols and Agreements between the United States of America and other Powers, 490 (1910) and S.F. Bemis, Jay's Treaty: A Study in Commerce and Diplomacy (2nd Edition, 1965).

85. For a discussion of that treaty and its effect in American extradition, see I. Moore, Extradition, p. 90 (1891).

86. See Symposium on Extradition in 16 N.Y.L.R. 1970 and compare e.g., Evans at p. 525 with Brown at p. 578 and Rogge at 378. Brown relying on Bassiouni in support, pp. 578-580, 583-584, 590-591 - contrasts with Evans; see Bassiouni, "International Extradition: A Summary of the Contemporary American Practice and a Proposal, 39 Revue Internationale de Droit Penal 494 (1968) reprinted in 15 Wayne L. Rev. 739 (1969), and Bassiouni, "International Extradition in American Practice and World Public Order," 36 Tenn. L. Rev. 1 (1968). See also Wise in Symposium N.Y.L.F., p. 5621, who also differs from the position of Evans and Rogge, but remains consistent in his views expressed in "Some Problems of Extradition," 39 Revue Internationale de Droit Penal 518 (1968), reprinted in 15 Wayne L. Rev. 709 (1968). The view of Wise and Bassiouni coincide in many respects, see Wise in N.Y.L.F. Symposium citing Bassiouni, note 48, p. 575.

87. For a similar definitional approach see 6 Whiteman, Digest, 727-728 (1968); also Terlinden v. Ames, supra, note 56 (1902).

88. Bedi, Extradition in International Law and Practice, p. 16 (1968).

89. See appendix for treaties.

90. Bedi, supra, note 88 at 33.

91. See supra, note 58 and corresponding text.

92. 6 Whiteman, Digest, pp. 753-754.

64

5. An Appraisal of the Relationship Between Asylum and Extradition

Political asylum, even if commendable and to be encouraged in
municipal laws and practice, is not one of the recognized principles embodied in the Universal Declaration of Human Rights.
Asylum for crimes predicated on race, color, religion or national
origin or persecution on account thereof, however, do fall within
the category of recognized principles enunciated by the Universal
Declaration of Human Rights, the 1951 Refugee Convention, the
1967 Protocol, the International Covenant on Economic, Social
and Cultural Rights, the Refugee Convention of the Organization
of African Unity of 1969, the Inter-American Human Rights Convention of 1969 and the 1967 General Assembly Resolution on Territorial Asylum. [25] Thus, politically motivated crimes wherein the
actor engages in some material conduct deemed violative of the
laws of a given state do not fall within the purview of the international protective scheme unless they relate to race,
religion or origin. It becomes necessary, therefore, to distinguish between political and humanitarian asylum, if such a distinction can be made, to ascertain whether or not a right of
asylum exists under international law or whether the conduct of
the relator falls within the treaty definition of a "political
offense" exception to extradition, in both cases the relator
would have to raise the question under the municipal laws of
state wherein he is located at the time of the extradition proceedings and the only significance of this distinction is that
humanitarian asylum, as described in the 1948 Universal Declara-

tion, the 1951 Refugee Convention, the 1967 Protocol, the 1967
General Assembly Resolution on Territorial Asylum, the 1969
Organization of African Unity Convention of Refugees and the
1969 Inter-American Human Rights Convention, offers more specificity and certainty than the vaguely drafted provisions on political offense exception contained in extradition treaties.

A further distinction must be made between asylum in the sense
of permission by one state to an individual to enter its territory or remain therein when such individual is not sought by
another state, and asylum in the sense of allowing a person
sought by another state to be shielded from its processes by a
denial of extradition. The first does not necessarily contain a
political consideration element which the second instance usually
involves. It must be noted that this situation, involving large
numbers of refugees seeking asylum, is often laden with political
factors. Unlike instances of individual asylum, refugee asylum
in large numbers have the official support of the United Nations
High Commissioner for Refugees which counterbalances other
political considerations. As is invariably the case, the individual asylum seeker attracts less interest, unless he is a
celebrity, and consequently has the most to gain or lose from
his lack of notoriety. The granting of asylum must be distinguished from the decision to refuse extradition even though both
may at times be intimately intertwined. This is due to the fact
that the state of refuge may decide the issue of extradition
irrespective of, and separate from, the issue of allowing the
relator to remain on its territory or to grant him asylum. The

extradition question may be decided on narrow, technical grounds, particularly where treaty interpretation may be involved and that decision is usually left to the judiciary while the asylum issue is dealt with by the executive and is more often than not resolved on political or pragmatic grounds. Unlike the issue of humanitarian asylum, that of political asylum is a question of municipal law, except to the extent that it is within the scope of extradition and in some cases be subject to international law. It is apparent that any arguments to sever asylum from extradition whenever both questions are presented in the same case are strained. Whenever political or humanitarian asylum are granted and extradition proceedings are pending, the request shall be denied on grounds of the "political offense exception." However, so intricately linked that a state can deny extradition on the basis of the "political offense exception," but also refuse to grant the fugitive asylum in such a case the request of state will allow him the opportunity to choose his destination and to leave freely thereto. When the "political offense exception" is relied upon to deny extradition and the alien fugitive is permitted to remain, he is, in effect granted asylum. Thus, asylum, when granted concomitant with an extradition request, subtracts the individual from extradition, but denial of an extradition request does not confer asylum status on the relator.

It is likely that a person seeking to avoid extradition will, therefore, first seek asylum as a means of blocking the extradition request. Such a person is, therefore, likely to seek refuge in a state which has the least pendency to preserve the political interests of the requesting state from which the individual is seeking asylum. Whatever the offender's prior conduct was, he is most likely to seek refuge in a state which has either the least interest in what he did or the most interest in what he did in the requesting state. In fact, the offender is not likely to seek refuge in a state which, by reason of identical or similar political ideology or form of government, is likely to feel even vicariously affected by his conduct, be it purely criminal or political.

The arguments offered in favor of granting asylum, political or humanitarian, are affected by four considerations: (1) a balancing of the extent to which granting asylum will affect political relations with the state whose extradition request was denied; (2) the political value of the refugee to the state of refuge; (3) the degree of national commitment to the values embodied in the refugee's prior conduct for which he is sought, and (4) the extent to which the refugee will present a domestic problem to the municipal public order. While the first three considerations are purely ideological, the fourth can be evaluated in the following manner: Assuming that the criminality of the refugee is predicated and dependent upon certain conditions which brought about his violative conduct, then the removal of these conditions, or his removal from their environment, eliminates the basis of his criminality. In the absence of any other factors indicating a propensity to criminality, and if the accused offender abstains from such activities against the state from whose processes he was shielded, he will not represent a greater threat to the municipal public order of the asylum state than any other individual. This argument is advanced to rationalize the denial of extradition for such an offender as not being in derogation to the theory of mutual assistance and cooperation in combatting criminality. Furthermore, that refugee does not fall within the contemplated category of common criminals for whom there is an international reciprocal interest in bringing him to prosecution and punishment.

The decision to seek extradition of a fugitive is arrived at by the executive, authoritative decision makers of the requesting state. The decision to recognize or reject the requesting state's petition, either for political reasons or humanitarian ones, lies with the executive, authoritative decision maker's process of the state of refuge even though a judicial intervention may occur in the interim. It is thus apparent that conflicts of interest are likely since the opposing parties are two distinct, authoritative decision making processes which are pitted against each other without alternative recourses.

The manner in which extradition is denied or asylum granted can, therefore, create a threat to world public order.

Since World War II, the immigration laws of many states have been revised to provide asylum for political refugees, however differently it is defined. [26] This has been done in the avowed interest of protecting individuals from persecution in the country from which they fled. The decision to request extradition by the demanding state, or that of its granting or denial by the asylum state may, however, involve the whole spectrum of their political relations. The standard by which the relator's conduct will be evaluated and whether he will be extradited or granted asylum will, therefore, depend on the overall political relations between the states involved. The fugitive is, therefore, in a position to pit one state against the other. Furthermore, since the issue of his extraditability is left to the decision making process of the asylum state (which decides in accordance to its own laws), there is no shelter for that asylum state which is forced to elect between its political interest and its humane concern for the refugee, which could be conflicting.

In denying extradition, a state claims that the offense for which the relator is sought is not within the offenses specified in the treaty, or that it falls within an exception thereto and, therefore, no obligation exists to exercise its jurisdictional power over the person of the relator and deliver him to the requesting state. Whether the state of refuge is concerned with the fate of the offender, desirous of upholding a national commitment to certain values, or simply to further its own self-serving political interests, the consequence is that the relator will be shielded from the processes of the requesting state, and will evade the consequences of his conduct altogether, assuming that conduct constituted a common crime. Thus, to be exclusively concerned with the relator is tantamount to granting him impunity, which is detrimental in two ways: (1) as it affects world public order, by disruption of the political relations between the respective states, and (2) as it affects the duty to combat criminality, by lack of concern for the prosecution or punishability of a potential common criminal. Whether or not the state of refuge, in addition to denying extradition, will also grant asylum will be another internal decision based on potential considerations. In view of the precarious nature of this situation, the asylum state has to exercise the greatest discretion and caution when granting asylum and refusing extradition. Thus, states often employ certain subterfuges to reach their desired result extra-legally.

Footnotes

1. Caillemer, "Asylia," in <u>Dictionnaire des Antiquites Grecques et Romaines d'apres les Textes et les Documents</u>, p. 505 (1877).

2. *E.g.*, Sinha, <u>Asylum and International Law</u>, pp. 5-49 (1971).

3. See 6 Whiteman, <u>Digest</u>, pp. 279-427 (1968).

4. Garcia-Mora, <u>International Law and Asylum as a Human Right</u>, p. 5 (1956).

5. As stated in 6 Whiteman, <u>Digest</u>, p. 428 (1968), "Asylum in foreign embassies and legations within a country is known as "diplomatic asylum." Where granted, and recognized by the local sovereign, it thus constitutes in effect an exemption from the territorial jurisdiction of that State. It may, of course, be argued that a foreign embassy or legation is in some respects exterritorial, but this is true only to the limited extent and in the sense that the receiving State may not exercise acts of jurisdiction within the premises of the foreign State. The concept of "diplomatic asylum" is to be distinguished from that of "political asylum" or "territorial asylum" which is granted by a receiving State to such refugees or fugitives from justice as that State may receive or permit. Thus, "political" or "territorial" asylum does not constitute an exemption from the jurisdiction of the local sovereign State. While "diplomatic asylum," where granted and recognized, is accorded to "political offenders," as distinguished from common criminals, it does not thereby become "political

114

asylum" as herein used.

6. For the relationship between the law of asylum, the political
offense exception, and the penal policy of some foreign coun-
tries, see Ronning, Diplomatic Asylum, Legal Norms and Polit-
ical Reality in Latin American Relations (1965); Rousseau,
"Preface" to Koziebrodzki, Le Droit D'asile (1962); Vieira,
Derecho de Asilo Diplomatico (Asilo Politico). Montevideo,
Biblioteca de Publicaciones Oficiales de la Facultad de
Derecho Ciencias Sociales de la Universidad de la Republica
(1961); La Forest, Extradition to and from Canada (1961);
Kircheimer, Gegenwartsprobleme der Asylegewährung (1959);
Grutzner, Staatspolitik und Kriminal-Politik in Auslieferngs-
recht Zietshrift für die Gesaute Strafrechtswissenshaft, Tome
68 (1956); Greenburgh, "Recent Developments in the Law of
Diplomatic Asylum," 41 Trans. Grotius Soc. 103 (1955); Papa-
thanassiou, L'Extradition en Matiere Politique (1954); Planas-
Suarez, El Asilo Diplomatico. Estudio Juridico Y Politico
Sobre Este Execrable Uso Latinoamericano Destructor de la
Soberania Nacional Y de la Cordialidad Internacional (1953);
Quintana, Derecho de Asilo (1952); Morgenstern "Diplomatic
Asylum," 67 Law Q. Rev. 362 (1951); Africa, Political Offen-
ses in Extradition (1927); Morgenstern, "The Right of Asylum,"
(1949) 26 Brt. Y.B. Int'l L. 327; Morgenstern, "Extraterr-
itorial Asylum," (1958) 25 Y.B. Int'l L. Comm'n 236; Piccott,
Extradition, A Treatise on the Law Relating to Fugitive
Offenders (1910); Green, "Recent Practice in the Law of
Extradition," 6 Current Legal Problems 287 (1953);

Hambro, "New Trends in the Law of Extradition and Asylum," 5 West. Pol. Q. 11 (1952); McNair, "Extradition and Extra-territorial Asylum," (1951) 28 Y.B. Int'l L. Comm'n 172.

7. Evans, "Reflections upon the Political Offense in International Practice," 57 A.J.I.L. 16 at 18 (1963); see also, note 19, *infra*.

8. "The purpose of immunity is to enable representatives to fulfill their function fully. In other matters they should yield entire respect to the jurisdiction of the territorial government." 2 Hackworth, Digest 623 (1941).

9. That view was put forward by many nineteenth century authors who used the "fiction" of exterritoriality as a useful descriptive term, but denied that it is "so absolute" as to justify a right of asylum, Twiss, Law of Nations, Vol. I, p. 218 (1884). Amongst twentieth century writers, Fauchilee claims that modern theory has "completely rejected" the idea of exterritoriality, see Traité de Droit International Public, Vol. I, pp. 64 and 78 (1926). His view is supported by the report of the League of Nations Codification Sub-Committee on Diplomatic Privileges and Immunities, League Doc. C. 196. M. 70. 1927. V., p. 79, stating that: "It is perfectly clear that exterritoriality is a fiction which has no foundation either in law or in fact . . . The mere employment of this unfortunate expression is liable to lead to legal consequences which are absolutely inadmissible."

10. See examples in Constitution of Nations (3d Rev. ed. 1970).

11. Sinha, "An Anthroprocentric View of Asylum in International

Law," Col. J. Trans. L. 78, 86 (1971).

12. (1927). P.C.I.J., Sec. An., No. 10, at 28; Hudson, The Permanent Court of International Justice, 1920-1942 (1943).

13. Id. at 610; see also, 1 Oppenheim, International Law, p. 25 (8th ed. 1955).

14. Asylum Case (Colombia v. Peru) 20 Nov. 1950, I.C.J. Reports 1950, 266 at 277; see also, Garcia-Mora, "The Colombian-Peruvian Asylum Case and the Doctrine of Human Rights," 37 Va. L. Rev. 925 (1951). Judge Alvarez, in his dissenting opinion in the Asylum Case, stated that: "A principle, custom, doctrine, etc., need not be accepted by all of the state of the New World in order to be considered as a part of American international law. The same situation obtains in this case as is the case of universal international law," I.C.J. Reports 294 (1950).

15. The human rights approach to asylum was prevalent in the Havana Convention on Asylum, 4 Hudson, International Legislation 2412 (1931) and 22 A.J.I.L. Supp. 158 (1928); The American Declaration of the Rights and Duties of Man Adopted at the Ninth International Conference of American States held in Bogata in 1948, 43 A.J.I.L. Supp. 133 (1949); The Institute of International Law Resolution of September, 1950 in 45 A.J.I.L. Supp. 15 (1951); The International Law Commission of the United Nations in its Draft Declaration on Rights and Duties of States in 44 A.J.I.L. Supp. 8 (1950); The 1933 Montevideo Convention on Political Asylum, 6 Hudson, International Legislation 607 (1937); and other international

instruments which are stated below in notes 16, 17, 18 and
corresponding text. As to the doctrine on the subject, see
Garcia-Mora, *supra*, note 4, pp. 120-39, referring to decisions
upholding the right of asylum; Krenz, "The Refugee as a Subject of International Law," 15 Int'l & Comp. L.Q. 90, 104
(1966); Weis, "The International Protection of Refugees,"
48 A.J.I.L. 193, 198 (1954).

16. The Universal Declaration of Human Rights, G. A. Res. 217,
U. N. Doc. A/810 (1948); Article 14 of the Declaration in 43
Am. J. Int'l L. 127 (Supp. 1949); Lauterpacht, "The Universal
Declaration of Human Rights," (1948) 25 Brt. Y.B. Int'l L. 354;
Kunz, "The United Nations Declaration of Human Rights," 43
Am. J. Int'l L. 316 (1949). The Draft of the International
Declaration on Asylum, prepared by the Commission on Human
Rights of the United Nations and transmitted to the U. N.
General Assembly in July, 1960, declares in Article 3 that,
"(n)o one seeking or enjoying asylum in accordance with the
Universal Declaration of Human Rights should, except for over-
riding reasons of national security or safeguarding of the
population, be subjected to measures such as rejection at the
frontier, return or expulsion which would result in compelling him to return to or remain in a territory, if there is
a well-founded fear of persecution endangering his life,
physical integrity or liberty in that territory." See U. N.
Doc. E/3335/CN.4/804, 21 March 1960.

17. See Convention Relating to the International Status of Refugees, 28 October 1933; 159 L.N.T.S. No. 3663 and the Refugee

Convention of 25 July 1951, 189 U.N.T.S. 137 No. 2545, The

1967 Protocol Relating to the Status of Refugees, U.N.T.S.

18. G. A. Res. 2200, 21 U. N. GAOR Supp. 16, at #7g U. N. Doc.
A/6316 (1966).

19. 1 Whiteman, Digest, 717-718 (1960) and 3 Hackworth, Digest,
690-705 (1945). While the United States takes a very restrictive view of diplomatic asylum, there are numerous
occasions at which it was practiced, viz, The Case of Cardinal
Midzenty, 6 Whiteman, Digest, p. 463, *et seq.* (1968); see
also, United States Foreign Relation Report which, according
to Whiteman at p. 430, by 1968 contained fifty reported
cases of diplomatic asylum. See also, Evans, "Observations
of the Practice of Territorial Asylum in the United States,"
56 A.J.I.L. 148 (1962); Garcia-Mora, "The Present Status of
Political Offenses in the Law of Extradition and Asylum,"
14 U. Pitt. L. Rev. 371 (1953); and Deere, "Political Offenses in the Law and Practice of Extradition," 27 A.J.I.L. 247
(1933). As to territorial asylum, in 1965, Congress amended
Section 243 (h) of the Immigration and Nationality Act of
1952, 66 Stat. 163, 214 (1952), 8 U.S.C. §1253(h), as amended
by §11(f), 79 Stat. 911 (1965) to allow for political asylum
only in such cases involving "persecution on account of race,
religion or political opinion." In 1967, the United States
became a party to the 1967 Protocol Relating to the Status
of Refugees, 19 U.S.T. 6223, T.I.A.S., No. 6577; 63 A.J.I.L.
385 (1969). After the incident of the Lithuanian sailor,
Kudirka, the Department of State made its position clear in

a document entitled, "General Policy for Dealing with Requests
for Asylum by Foreign Nationals," 4 January 1972, 66 Dept. of
State Bull. 124 (1972). The policy of the Department of State
and the Immigration and Naturalization Service is to encompass in categories eligible for political asylum cases involving "physical persecution" as had been specifically stated
in Section 243(h) prior to its amendment in 1965. Interpretation by Immigration Board decisions, and judicial decisions
remain consistent with this position, see Evans, "The Political Refugee in United States Immigration Law and Practice,"
3 Int. Lawyer 204 (1969); Evans, "Political Refugees and the
United States Immigration Laws: A Case Note," 62 A.J.I.L.
921 (1968); Evans, "Political Refugees and the United States
Immigration Laws: Further Developments," 66 A.J.I.L. 571
(1972).

20. 65 Department of State Bulletin 404 (1971).

21. 19 U. S. Treaties 6223, T.I.A.S. No. 6577.

22. 66 Department of State Bulletin 124 (1972).

23. *Ibid.*, 124-125.

24. Page 132.

25. *Supra,* notes 16 to 18.

26. See, *e.g., supra,* note 19.

*Unlawful Seizures and Irregular Rendition Devices as
Alternatives to Extradition*

1. Typology and Rationale

The title of this chapter does not suggest that alternatives to
extradition means extradition other than by treaty. This clarification is made because those states who adhere to extradition
only by treaty regard any other basis for extradition (reciprocity
and comity) as an alternative to extradition. What is meant by
alternatives to extradition are legal and extralegal devices
which do not fall within the framework of extradition. This
assertion is true even though the end result of all such processes is the rendition of a person against his or her will by one
state to another because what is at issue is not the end result
but the processes employed. These rendition techniques, which
are outside the framework of extradition, fall into three categories:

(1) abduction and kidnapping of a person by the
agents of another state;

(2) informal surrender of a person by the agents
of one state to another without formal or
legal process;

(3) the use of immigration laws as a device to
directly or indirectly surrender a person or

place a person in a position where he or she
can be taken into custody by the agents of
another state.

Professor O'Higgins classifies these situations as follows: [1]

(1) Recovery of fugitive criminals in violation
    of international law--(i) seizure in violation
    of customary international law; (ii) seizure
    in violation of conventional international law.

(2) Apprehension of a fugitive criminal in the
    territory of State B by private individuals,
    Nationals of State A, with the connivance of
    the officials of State A.

(3) Apprehension of a fugitive criminal in the
    territory of State B by private individuals,
    Nationals of State A, without the connivance
    of the officials of State A.

(4) Irregular apprehension of a fugitive criminal
    in State B by an official of State B prior
    to his extradition to State A.

(5) Mistaken surrender of a fugitive criminal by
    one state to another.

This typology is important to determine the existence and extent
of state responsibility (which is discussed below). These various
techniques exist, in fact, because of the inappropriate application of the maxim *mala captus bene detentus* whereby municipal
courts will assert *in personam* jurisdiction without inquiring into
the means by which the presence of the accused was secured. [2]

122

Most of the devices and strategies listed above are extralegal, either in form, substance or both; but there is no deterrent to them because their consequences are allowed to produce legally valid results. Aside from the flagrant violation of the individual's human rights, such practices affect the stability of international relations and subvert the international process.

The techniques stated above are extraordinary in the legal sense, since an ordinary legal process does exist, i.e., extradition. However, the recourse to these practices may well be due to the frustration of the legitimate efforts of a requesting state following formal channels, thus leading one writer to ask: "When extradition fails, is abduction the solution?" [3] Indeed, there are numerous examples which illustrate this unfortunate dilemma. The difficulties encountered in some instances by states desirous of securing a fugitive or convicted offender and which result in failure for unwarranted reasons have in part caused the resort to these alternatives. The length and costs involved in formal extradition proceedings is often advanced as another reason. The alternative, however, is to make extradition more workable and not to subvert it by resorting to unlawful means.

To place states in a position where they can benefit from these practices encourages further violations of the sort and erodes voluntary observance of international law whether by other states or by individuals. Consider, for example, the attempts to control individual terrorism and the inevitable argument which arises in the context of kidnapping: why is it terrorism if the act is committed by a private person acting alone or on behalf of a political group and not terrorism when the same act is committed by agents of a state?

At this stage of development of international law it is no longer possible to rationalize violations of international law on grounds of *raison d'etat* or to allow such violations to be perpetuated without an adequate deterrent - remedy.

1.1 Abduction and Kidnapping

This device is characterized by the fact that agents of one state acting under color of law unlawfully seize the body of a person within the jurisdiction of another state without its consent and in violation of its sovereignty and territorial integrity. This involves three distinct violations; they are: (a) disruption of world public order; (b) infringement on the sovereignty and territorial integrity of another state, and (c) violation of the human rights of the individual unlawfully seized.

This technique must be distinguished from any other formal or quasi-formal means of rendition or even the erroneous exercise of a formal process such as when an unauthorized public official acting under color of law surrenders or causes to be surrendered a fugitive who sought refuge in his state to the agents of another state. [4] The most dramatic *causes célèbres* remain the Soblen, Eichmann, Argoud, Ahlers and Tshombe cases. [5] In these spectacular cases, the method by which the fugitive was sought and brought to trial can be characterized as exceptional and violative of international due process of law. [6] The most recent such cases occurred in February, 1973, when eleven persons were forcefully seized by Israeli armed forces in Lebanon and tried

in Israel by a military tribunal on the grounds that they be-
longed to an organization which caused harm or intended to cause
harm to Israel, regardless of where such acts actually occurred.
In rejecting the arguments of the first defendant, a Turkish
citizen named Faik Bulut, the military tribunal relied in part on
the Eichmann case as valid precedent. [7]

There are, of course, other cases maybe less notorious, but
nonetheless equally violative of international law. [8]

As stated above, the inducement for the continuation of these
practices is the proposition that whenever a fugitive is presented to a domestic court, the tribunal will consider the physical
presence of the fugitive sufficient to cause jurisdiction to
attach to the person notwithstanding the manner in which it was
secured. The case of Kerr v. Illinois [9] is the example cited by
almost every court before which such a case has been presented;
but, all too often, the facts are not similar and a careful
reading of Kerr would reveal that it is not always applicable.

One such inappropriate applicate of Kerr was in the Trial of
Faik Bulut, a Turkish citizen seized by Israeli armed forces in
February, 1973, in a Palestinian refugee camp located one hundred miles inside Lebanese territory. Bulut, who was seized
with ten other persons, citizens of various Arab states were
charged with an Israeli law purporting to apply to anyone, anywhere who participates in an organization intending to cause
harm to the state or its citizens. Counsel for defendant Bulut
raises a jurisdictional question on the grounds that Bulut and
the others were seized in violation of international law and

that the Israeli law could apply to him if he had committed a crime in Israel or against Israeli citizens, which was not the case. The military tribunal on July 23, 1973, rejected both arguments and cited Eichmann and Kerr as authority. [10] Prescinding from the issue of unlawful seizure the two cases cited were inappropriately relied upon because in Kerr, Illinois had territorial jurisdiction since a crime had been committed there, while in Eichmann, there was universal jurisdiction since he had committed international crimes. This indicates the confusion made between subject matter jurisdiction and jurisdiction over the person.

The United States has been on both sides of abduction cases, but remains fixed to the Kerr position, [11] provided there is valid subject matter jurisdiction. This is also the position of England as enunciated since 1829 in *ex parte* Suzannah Scott. [12] The position of the United States was reaffirmed by a unanimous decision of the Supreme Court as late as 1952. [13] Many other countries have found themselves enbroiled in the same application of the maxim *mala captus bene detentus*. It is advanced that to be unlawful under international law, the abductors must be public agents or other persons acting under color of state law and that they cannot be bona fide volunteers. [14] This argument relies on the notion that international law is designed to restrict state conduct and not to secure the integrity of a process when violated by individuals acting in their private capacity. Presumably, that would be left to national legislation.

This argument was presented in the Eichmann case, but it was established that those "private volunteers" were operating "with the connivance of the Israeli government." Eichmann was duly tried and convicted. In contrast, in the Vincenti case, United States Department of Justice agents unlawfully seized a United States citizen in England, but on complaint of England. He was released and the United States apologized to Great Britain for the improper seizure stating that the agents "acted on their own initiative and without the knowledge or approval of this government." [15] If the rationalization that the practice is valid because committed by private volunteers is to stand, it would mean that states would only have to allow their agents to act as "private volunteers," *sic*, and thus avoid the whole problem. This, however, would not square with efforts to curb terrorism by private individuals who resort to the same technique. The paradox is quite interesting in that states on the one hand seek to curb terrorism which includes kidnapping, yet condone it when committed by their agents or by "private volunteers" when it is to their benefit. This dual standard is all too evident and only leads to further disregard of international law which after all relies on voluntary compliance.

The question of connivance between officials may be classified as a form of abduction, but a distinction ought to be drawn between these two techniques. Abduction occurs only whenever the state of refuge or asylum is not a party to the plot, otherwise, when two interested states through their agents, whether public or private, acting under color of law or by official connivance, the instance should be placed in another category separate from abduction. This distinction is predicated on the fact that an abduction differs from an informal surrendering of a person by means approved by the respective states because in this case there is no violation of the territorial integrity or sovereignty of the state of refuge and, consequently, there is little likelihood that the practice would lead to disruptive relations between the respective states. There remains, however, a violation of the human rights of the individual. This category is referred to as informal rendition and is discussed below. The existence of such cooperative undertaking by state agents, even though violative of international due process, evidences the cooperation and friendly relations of the respective states, except when the agents of the respective states are acting on their own, without their superiors' knowledge and approval and undertake such ventures on a purely personal basis. There are no such cases in legal or diplomatic records which are available to this writer to illustrate this type of practice. There are, however, numerous cases occurring between agents of neighboring states who may seek to cut through the red tape of formal processes and who act on their own, but in most such cases, their conduct is either known or condoned by their superiors and their actions cannot be deemed private or personal ventures.

The Legal Doctrine expressed in the writings of scholars remains, however, opposed to these practices and the application of the maxim *mala captus bene detentus*. [16]

1.2 Informal Renditon

These are cases wherein the officials of the state of refuge will act outside the framework of a formal process or without authority in order to facilitate the abduction or cause the surrender of the fugitive by other means producing the same result. These cases, however, are difficult to document since they presuppose the connivance of the two agencies which could bring the matter to the attention of the judiciary. [17] The present position of the individual in international law and in most states is such that very likely he is not going to be capable to raise the issue in a domestic court.

The plea of kidnapping by connivance between officers of the Federal Bureau of Investigation and Mexican Security Police was advanced unsuccessfully in United States v. Sobell, a case in which the Second Circuit Court of Appeals, sustaining the jurisdiction of the District Court to try Sobell on espionage charges said:

"But it can hardly be maintained, still assuming the truth of appellant's charges that the unlawful and unauthorized acts of the Mexican police acting in behalf of subordinate agents of the executive branch of the United States Government were any more acts of the United States than the unlawful and unauthorized acts of the emissary of the Chief Executive (in Kerr). We think the question presented is indistinguishable from that before the Supreme Court in Kerr and that our decision here is controlled by that case." [18]

Most such cases occur as between neighboring states and, in particular, when the individual who is the object of those devices is a national of the state to whose agents he is delivered. The commonplace examples occur as between the United States and Canada and the United States and Mexico. [19]

In Kerr [20] and Sobell, [21] United States public agents participated in the abduction of a United States citizen in a foreign country, respectively, Peru and Mexico, with the assistance and cooperation of public agents of the two states. These facts distinguish these two cases from the pure abduction ones as exemplified by Eichmann.

In the Kerr case, a private detective from the United States, while in Peru, received duly executed extradition papers from the U. S. Government, conforming to the requirements of the extradition treaty between the United States and Peru. He did not use them, however, because he had no access to the proper Government of Peru, which was disorganized as a result of military occupation of the capital city by Chilean forces. The latter assisted the American officers in forcing Kerr to board a U. S. vessel. At no time did Peru object to the proceedings.

If Peru had protested, the question would have arisen whether the occupation by a foreign force had so deprived the Peruvian Government of sovereignty over the place where Kerr was found that it had no standing to object to police action by foreign authorities.

130

It was just such a situation that enabled the U. S. Government in 1946 to have Douglas Chandler seized in Germany by U. S. military forces and forcibly returned to the United States for trial on charges of treason. [22] There was no sovereign whose sovereignty was offended by the action of foreign officers on its soil.

In the Sobell case the abducting party in Mexico was allegedly made up originally of Mexican officers. Sobell was carried, against his will, to the U. S. border and there turned over to U. S. authorities even before crossing into the United States. The latter took him to New York, where he was tried for conspiracy to commit espionage and convicted. He lost in his efforts to obtain release on various grounds, including a charge that the treaty of extradition had been violated. It seems clear that the collaboration of the Mexican police, like the French in the Savarkar case, [23] deprived Mexico of any basis for complaint, even if it had wanted to raise an objection. Many years before, however, the Mexicans had protested vigorously against retention by the United States of one Martinez, who was forcibly taken from Mexico to the United States by another Mexican. The latter was extradited by the United States to stand trial in Mexico for kidnapping, but the United States refused to release Martinez. [24]

The compelling argument in such cases is that the length and
formalism surrounding extradition processes as well as its exclusive dependence on the decision making process of the state of
refuge without other alternative recourse, if denied, leaves the
requesting state with no choice but to seek other means to secure
the return of the fugitive. The classic example where such an
instance could have arisen, but did not, is the <u>Artukovic</u> case. [25]
Indeed, suppose as Professor Cardozo wrote that headlines in
United States press would state:

"War Criminal Abducted from California Home:
Spirited to Yugoslavia by Serbian Patriots"--(and
commenting) Would we be outraged at the evident
offense to our sovereignty? Or would we be glad
to be rid of a fugitive who had been accused of
responsibility for wartime atrocities on a massive
scale under Nazi auspices? The questions are not
just academic, for there lives in California one
Andrija Artukovic, against whom the Yugoslavs
level charges of enough murders of bishops, priests,
rabbis, Serbs, Croats, Gypsies, Jews, women and
children to brand him a major war criminal. Their
efforts to have him formally extradited under
treaty and statutory procedures have finally been
frustrated by decisions of the United States
courts. It would hardly be incredible if a group
of Serbs, inspired by hatred, revenge, and

patriotism, should try to emulate the "volunteers"

who successfully contrived to move Adolph Eichmann

for his refuge in Argentina to a prison in Israel.[26]

Artukovic was charged with war crimes and mass murder on a geno-

cidal scale, but his extradition was denied after almost nine

years of attempts by Yugoslavia to extradite him. He was not

extradited because the U. S. courts found such crimes to fall

within the "political offense exception" in the treaty between

the United States and the (former) Kingdom of Yugoslavia to which

the new government of Yugoslavia was deemed to have succeeded.

In cases involving "ideologically motivated offenders," the more

wanted species, extradition is denied without recourse, thus

making likely the resorting to one of the alternatives discussed

in this chapter.

1.3 *Disguised Extradition*

This is the process by virtue of which a person is placed in such

a condition that he or she falls or is likely to fall under the

control of authorities of a state which has an interest in sub-

jecting such a person to its jurisdictional control. The manner

in which it is done is not illegal under international law since

the fugitive is not abducted. It is not an informal process of

rendition in that agents of the interested state do not connive

or plan the seizure of the person, nor do they undertake it as a

joint venture. It is a method by which a state uses or relies

upon its immigration laws to deny an alien the privilege of re-

maining in that state and then, in carrying out the exclusion,

133

expulsion or deportation provisions of such laws against the individual, it places him directly or indirectly in the control of
the agents of another state who seek him. This device presupposes
(1) the use of immigration laws and regulations, because (2) the
individual is within the jurisdiction of a state wherein he seeks
refuge or asylum, (3) he is then denied refuge or asylum, and (4)
he is either removed (deported) or required to leave (voluntary
departure) or caused to leave (denied legal entry), and (5) his
"departure" (if not deported to a given country) is executed in
such a manner as to cause him to fall within the hands of agents
of an interested state.

The right of a state to admit and extend residence privileges
to an alien is part of immigration laws and thus subject to municipal law. Some states consider that right as exclusive and
deny the application thereto of international law. This is the
position of the United States. [27] It must be noted, however,
that this position is highly questionable in light of several
treaties and other sources of international law which govern the
rights of refugees and supersede municipal law. [28] A compelling
case can be made under existing international law showing that
rights conferred upon a refugee entitle him to equal treatment
granted non-refugees and that injuries to aliens subject a state
to international responsibility. [29] Professor Evans writing
about the problem states:

> The potentiality of expulsion as a method for the
> rendition of fugitive offenders has been recognized
> by government officials for many years. The long

borders with Canada and Mexico, the relative ease
of crossing them, and the generally friendly relations prevailing between the United States and
these two states have been conducive to the use of
this method of rendition. For example, where a
fugitive from justice in the United States has been
known to be in prison in Canada, an indication to
Canadian authorities of American interest in the
prisoner's whereabouts upon the completion of his
sentence might lead to his deportation with prior
notice to interested federal or state officials
of the time and place of his departure from Canada.
Again, Mexican authorities, having been alerted by
United States authorities to the presence in that
country of a fugitive from the United States, might
order his deportation on grounds of illegal entry
into Mexico. Expulsion might be suggested where
extradition was not available as in the case of a
known "confidence man" whose offense of using the
mails to defraud was not covered by treaty with
the United Kingdom, or as a relatively inexpensive
and more convenient alternative to extradition.
It might also be held in reserve in the event
that extradition should fail.
Apart from deliberate rendition by expulsion, it is
possible that the strict execution of a deportation
order would result in placing an individual in

jeopardy of criminal process in the State of
destination; however, both judicial and administrative authorities have held that such ultimate
result constitutes no bar to expulsion. [30]
A landmark English case is <u>Regina v. Secretary of State for Home
Affairs</u>, <u>ex p. Duke of Chateau Thierry</u> (1917), [31] in which

. . .the validity of the use of the power of
deportation in order to secure the return of the
Duke to France and place him within the control of
the French military authorities was challenged.
It was argued on his behalf (i) that the Home
Secretary had no power to order the deportation of
an alien to a particular country, and (ii) that
the Duke was, in fact, a political refugee and
would be punished for a political offense in
France. The Divisional Court found that immigration
laws gave no power to the Secretary of State to
order deportation to any particular named country. [32]
Although the deportation order did not on the face
of it purport to prescribe the destination of the
alien, it was nonetheless shown that immigration
authorities admitted to the court that the decision
of expulsion had been made for the purpose of returning the Duke to France. Lord Reading C. J. said:
". . .In form the order is correct, but the court
must look behind the mere form, and when there is
no doubt that the intention is to deport the alien

to a particular country, though the form of the
order does not state that this is the object and
intention of the executive in making the order,
we must treat it as if the order did, in effect,
state that the alien was to be deported to
France." [33]

On appeal the Court of Appeal reversed this
decision. [34] Its judgment is authority for a
number of important principles:

(i) The Secretary of State has no power to order
the deportation of an alien to a foreign state
specified in the deportation order.

(ii) Since, however, the Aliens Act entitled
the Secretary of State to cause an alien to be
detained and placed on board a particular ship
selected by the Secretary of State and there
detained until the ship finally left the United
Kingdom with the result that an alien may be
obliged to disembark at the port to which the
vessel sailed, the Secretary of State could
lawfully, but indirectly by selecting the means
of departure, effect what he had no power to do
directly, i.e., secure an alien's deportation
to a particular state. In the case of the Duke
of Chateau Thierry, the order made against him
was good. It did not purport to order his deportation to France. Although it was admitted

that the executive intended under the order to
send the Duke to France this was immaterial
provided the procedure employed was to specify
the Duke's departure by a particular ship and
not to require in the order itself that he be
deported to France.

(iii) The fact that an alien is a political
refugee, or is likely to be punished for a
political offense in the country to which it
is intended that he should, albeit indirectly,
be deported, will not invalidate a deportation
order made against him. [35] However, the authorities expressly disclaimed any intention of
using deportation proceedings against political
refugees.

". . . It should, however, be stated that the
Attorney General, on behalf of the Government,
expressly stated that the Executive had no intention whatever of taking advantage of their
powers over aliens to deport political refugees." [36]
The same view is held by the British Government
today. [37] It may be added that, in fact, the
Duke of Chateau Thierry failed to satisfy the
court that he was a political refugee.

(iv) A court can invalidate a deportation order
only on very limited grounds, principally that
the intended deportee is not an alien.

(v) The Court of Appeal took the view that the use of deportation proceedings to secure, in effect, the surrender of military deserters is quite lawful. This can readily be seen from the following extracts from the judgments:

". . .In early July, last inquiry was made at the request of the French Government as to the failure of the respondent (who is a Frenchman, within military age, whether reckoned according to the French or the British standard) to discharge his military duties . . . These (French) authorities dispute that he is a political refugee; they state that his return to France is sought in connection with his 'irregular military situation' and for no other cause, and that he is not known to the French police for any other offense. An assurance has been given by the French Government that the respondent, if returned to France, would be treated as a military absentee, and not as liable to prosecution for any other offense.

"We were informed that there exists an agreement between this country and France by which this country undertakes to return to France subjects of that country who are of military age and liable to military service, and that it was by reason of this agreement that the Secretary of State made this (deportation) order."[39]

Subsequently, in _Regina v. Superintendent of Chiswick Police Station, ex p. Sacksteder,_ [40] the Court of Appeal again upheld the validity of the use of deportation orders to secure the return of military deserters to France.

It is highly significant that in the case of the surrender of the Duke of Chateau Thierry it was admitted on behalf of the states concerned that the principles of specialty and non-surrender of political offenders should apply. The states themselves treated the surrender as a special form of extradition to which the general rules governing extradition should be applied.

Notwithstanding the apparent ease and convenience of the "expulsion" device as a substitute for a formal process of extradition, the fugitive is still entitled to the benefits of the domestic legal process. For example, the alien must first be deportable and that determination is subject to its limitations as was evidenced in the _Horne_ case. [41]

Horne was a prisoner in a federal penitentiary, wanted by Canadian authorities during the First World War on charges of sabotage. The Department of Justice was at first inclined to deport him to Canada, upon completion of his sentence, as an enemy alien whose presence in the country constituted a threat to the safety of the United States. The Department, however, decided against this procedure, apparently on grounds of

140

its doubtful legality as an alternative to extradition. Expulsion would not be an available remedy where the fugitive could show that he had entered the country legally and had not otherwise transgressed the immigration laws, that he was a national of the state from which deportation was proposed or sought, or where the immigration authorities were satisfied that he was not actually implicated in an offense in the requesting state as alleged by the latter's authorities.

Thus, the alien was not surrendered to Canada because he was not deportable and was not extraditable under the treaty. There is always, however, the possibility of deporting the alien to the country of his own choice, and thereby avoiding his compulsory return to a country in which he might be liable to criminal prosecution. The discretionary power of the executive in such cases are likely to be used to make a bargain with the foreign authorities. Such was the case in 1941 in the deportation of Mikhail Gorin, and the exchange of Colonel Abel and U-2 Pilot Francis Gary Powers. [42] The device of expulsion finds a counterpart in the device of exclusion, which is a measure designed to prevent the alien from staying in the country whether he had been temporarily admitted on a visa or on parole. A means of carrying out the exclusion order is to leave the alien with limited options to depart and thus causing him to fall within the control of the agents of the foreign state. A state desirous of securing a person without resorting to extradition or after the process failed to produce the expected results is to request another state (the state of refuge) and surrounding states to exclude the

fugitive, thus, leaving no alternative (*sic*) to the state of
refuge who excludes the alien but to remand him to his country
of origin. [43] The landmark case remains the <u>Soblen</u> case. [44]

Dr. Soblen was accused of espionage in the United States. Released on bond, he fled to Israel claiming asylum and citizenship
as a Jew under the Israeli law of return. Israel, under the
United States pressure, found that he did not qualify and he was
placed on an El Al flight bound for New York. Interestingly,
there were no other passengers aboard except U. S. marshals.
Close to England, Soblen attempted suicide; the plane landed,
and he was taken to a hospital. The United States wanted Soblen,
but the crime he was accused of was clearly a "political offense"--
non-extraditable under the Anglo-American treaty of 1931. [45]
England then found that Soblen had not been "legally admitted"
and ordered his departure on the first available flight of the
day, presumably to be returned to Israel. It so happened that
there were no Israel bound flights that day--only a Pan Am
flight, to New York, upon which he was to be placed (instead, he
died in an English hospital). In so doing, the legal process of
extradition was to be evaded while the result desired by the
states involved would have been attained.

In 1896, J. B. Moore, with what turned out to be prophetic in-
sight, drew attention to the possibility of the immigration laws
of the United States being utilized for the purpose of extradition:

"It is, however, worthy of notice that the immigration
laws of the United States require the return to the
country from which they came, of all non-political

convicts. Though this measure is not in the nature
of an extradition treaty, the execution of which
another government may require, its full significance,
as affecting the subject of extradition, has, perhaps,
hardly been appreciated. With such a provision in our
statutes, it is difficult to set a limit to which the
system of extradition may logically be carried. [46]

The most vulnerable person is the one who is sought for political
reasons, [47] so long as there are no nationally enforced international law rules.

2. *Unlawful Seizures, State Responsibility and International Protection of Human Rights*

2.1 *The Validity of Mala Captus Bene Detentus*

The importance of drawing a distinction between the types of unlawful seizures and irregular methods of rendition discussed
above is to ascertain the existence and extent of state responsibility. It is noteworthy prior to discuss the subject of state
responsibility to dwell on the premise upon which these practices
rely, namely the maxim *mala captus bene detentus*. The application
of this maxim by municipal courts in the past one hundred years
has been inconsistent with other Roman Law maxims. Such improper
application is due to the existence of two higher principles which
have been consistently disregarded.

The first of these is procedural, namely: *Nunquam decurritur ad
extraordinarium sed ubi deficit ordinarium,* or never resort to the
extraordinary until the ordinary fails. Thus, *mala captus bene
detentus,* as an extraordinary process in order to be valid, must

143

be preceded by an exhaustion of all ordinary procedures available and cannot be admitted as a surrogate procedure while existing ordinary channels are ignored.

This same rule of exhaustion of ordinary remedies is well established in international law and was reaffirmed in the 1959 decision of the International Court of Justice in the <u>Interhandel case</u> (Switzerland v. United States) [48] wherein it was held that where rights claimed by one state have been disregarded by another in violation of international law, all local remedies and means of redress must first be resorted to before recourse to the International Court of Justice. In other words, the ordinary must be exhausted before resorting to the extraordinary.

The second of these is substantive, namely the principle *ex injuria ius non oritur*. This principle was the Roman Law's counterpart to the "exclusionary rule" developed in the United States,[49] that certain violations of law could not ripen into lawful results. Such a remedy was deemed under Roman Law, as well as some contemporary laws, an indispensible corollary to certain rights without which these rights would have no real significance. In Roman Law, these protected rights were those interests whose violation was considered an *injuria* (which is not to be confused with injury as understood in the common law of torts). Every *injuria* had its legal remedy apart from the general principle that no legal validity attached to consequences of an *injuria*. The author of an *injuria* had to redress in a prescribed manner the wrong committed, and in addition thereto there could not be any lawful consequences deriving from the transgression. The principle *ex injuria ius non*

144

oritur was not, therefore, designed to redress the wrong perpetrated against the legally protected interest which had its specific remedy, but was intended to sanction the transgression of the
law itself. In this sense, the law was meant *lato senso,* or the
integrity of the law and the legal process.

A threshold question now arises, namely, whether the violations
which take place by virtue of the practices discussed above constitute an *injuria* in international law? The peculiarity of international law compels us to examine this question in light of
existing law of state responsibility.

2.2 State Responsibility

Before considering the applicable principles of state responsibility, it is important to bear in mind the three categories of violations which are at issue in the practices as discussed in the
preceding sections of this chapter. These categories of violations are:

1. Violations of the sovereignty, territorial
    integrity and the legal process of the state
    wherein such acts occurred.

2. Violations of the human rights of the individual
    involved.

3. Violation of the international legal process.

The law of state responsibility has clearly applied to violations of the first category, [50] and also in some respect to violations of the second category, [51] but at best tenuously to violations of the third category. It is the opinion of this writer
that the general principles and policies of state responsibility

are broad enough to encompass without ambiguity the three categories of violations stated above [52] in support of this contention, consider the following statement made by Garcia-Amador, special rapporteur for the International Law Commission on the subject of state responsibility:

An analysis of the traditional doctrine and practice shows that the acts or omissions which give rise to international responsibility fall into the one or other of the following two categories of wrongful acts: (a) acts which affect a state as such, i.e., those which injure the interests or rights of the state as a legal entity; and (b) acts which produce damage to the person or property of its nationals. The first category comprises the most diverse acts or omissions, some being ill-defined or even undefinable. Acts in this category include failure to comply with the terms of a treaty, whatever the nature or purpose of the treaty, failure to respect diplomatic immunities and, in general, the violation of any of the rights which are intrinsic attributes of the personality of the state--political sovereignty, territorial integrity, property rights. The second category includes acts or omissions which give rise to the "responsibility of states for damage done in their territories to the person or property of foreigners." This is the principal subject of the literature, private and official codifications and

judicial decisions which treat of the responsibility
of states.

As will be seen hereunder, the above classification,
from the traditional point of view, is more concerned
with form than with substance, for it has been said
that, whichever category they fall into, the acts or
omissions in question have this in common: they
damage interests which, in the final analysis, vest
in the state exclusively. Apart from this aspect
of the question, which will be examined in its
proper context in a later chapter (Chapter V) the
classification may become meaningless in some cases
which come within the scope of both categories. An
example of such a case would be the nonperformance
of a treaty, where the interests of the nationals
of one of the contracting states are prejudiced and
the claim is based on this prejudice. In any case,
for the specific purposes of the present chapter,
we shall now consider what acts or omissions are
more generally regarded as giving rise to an international responsibility on the part of the state.

Within the second subdivision, too, the wrongful
acts capable of giving rise to responsibility on
the part of the state are not all of the same
character. Although in these cases the international responsibility does not originate in the
act itself but rather in the conduct of the state

in relation to the act (failure to exercise due diligence, connivance, manifest complicity, etc.), the nature of the act committed by a private person or of acts committed during internal disturbances is bound to influence the way in which the law regards the state's conduct as a source of international responsibility. Typical examples of wrongful acts which can be committed by private persons are: attacks or insults against a foreign state, in the person of the head of that state, its agencies or diplomatic representatives; acts offensive to its national flag; and illegal acts--whatever their degree of seriousness may be--which cause damage to the person or property of the nationals of a foreign state. When disturbances occur in a state, the acts concerned are usually of a more serious character; in some cases, they are specifically intended to cause damage to the property or person of foreigners.

Although not exhaustive, the foregoing enumeration presents a fairly accurate picture of the acts and omissions which according to traditional doctrine and practice, give rise to international responsibility on the part of the state. In any case, it makes it possible to define the character of those acts and so to determine the type of responsibility to which they can give rise. [53]

The general statement quoted above indicates that state responsibility attaches to actions by the state through its agents for
specific acts as well as failure to act by a state, presumably
wherever there is a preexisting legal obligation to do so. This,
therefore, raises two essential questions in the context of the
statement quoted above: (1) What is the degree of connection
which must be established between the state and its agents or
between the agents of the state and individuals acting in their
private capacity in order for state responsibility to attach; and,
(2) Is a state obligated merely to refrain from engaging in violative conduct, is there an obligation to prevent such conduct
from occurring, or is a state an insurer of lawful conduct?

As to the first point raised, it is clear that state responsibility attaches to acts committed by agents of a state or by private individuals acting for or on behalf of the state. [54] In this
latter instance, the type of connection which has to be established
between the individual (acting privately, *sic*) and the state (in
order to impute that individual's act to the state) is not very
clear nor does customary international law provide us with relia-
ble criteria. There is, however, no ambiguity in cases where the
state, through its agents incited, encouraged or induced private
individuals to undertake such actions with a view to benefit from
its outcome. It is obvious that the less direct the connection
is between the state and the individual acting privately, the
more difficult it will be to ascribe state responsibility for
individual conduct even when it inures to the benefit of the state.

As to the second point raised, a policy question arises in the context of the practices at issue, namely, whether responsibility is to be based only on positive conduct such as when a state causes a given act to take place or does it extend also to passive conduct such as when a state merely permits conduct to take place. In this latter instance, one may ask whether there is a duty on the part of a state to prevent unlawful conduct if it has the knowledge or capacity to prevent it from occurring or if a state is to be held responsible, even without prior knowledge of the contemplated action or without the capacity to prevent it. The statement of state responsibility quoted above raises an inference that states are in some instances insurers of outcomes, but in this context it could hardly be so argued. The general statement quoted above would seem, however, to encompass a range of doctrines of responsibility, but neither customary nor conventional international law have applied these doctrines to the law and practice of extradition except in respect of cases wherein a state through its agents or private persons acting on its behalf have committed abductions. The Eichmann case is probably the most illustrative example of this position. The search for state responsibility criteria in this area leads this writer to suggest resorting to analogies with other aspects of state responsibility. The parallel would be the regulation of armed conflicts and general principles of international criminal responsibility from which to derive applicable rules for state and individual responsibility in cases of violations of international extradition law.[55] Nothing in the writing of scholars, however, suggest this analogy and to the extent that it is a novel doctrine, it requires refinement. Consider, however, the applicability of this doctrine in respect of command responsibility and defenses such as the defense of obedience to superior orders. [56] If such rules of individual responsibility would be made applicable to individual perpetrators of abductions they would be considered responsible under international criminal law without benefit of the defense of obedience to superior orders; and, superiors of such agents would also be accountable by reason of command responsibility.

As stated above, state responsibility attaches under contemporary international law to unlawful seizures of persons when committed by agents of a state or individuals acting for or on its behalf. Such responsibility attaches because an *injuria* has been perpetrated. The only established remedies are reparations and diplomatic apologies, and the additional remedy of the return of the person seized unlawfully is not yet recognized, even though some courts have, however, seen fit to apply it. (The cases in which such return was ordered are discussed *infra* 2.4). This latter approach is in compliance with the higher principle of *ex injuria ius non oritur*. Indeed, without such a remedy the integrity of the international legal order would not be preserved.

2.3 *Human Rights and State Responsibility*

State responsibility hinges on the existence of an international right or duty the transgression thereof would cause certain consequences requiring a remedy and sanction to attach. This applies to the second category of violations involved in the practices discussed herein, namely, violations of human rights. The questions which arise in this context, therefore, are: What are these

151

rights? Where do they arise from? What is their legally binding effect? What sanction applies? Who applies them?

In judicial terms this means:

1. The legally binding nature of human rights.

2. The self-executing nature of obligations to preserve and protect human rights.

3. The penetration of international law into municipal law.

4. The enforcement of human rights provisions.

A complete treatment of all these questions is obviously beyond the scope of this analysis, but some general observations must be made.

An initial observation is with respect to the attitudes of municipal courts *vis-a-vis* internationally protected human rights. Time and again, decisions on the subject of unlawful seizures and irregular rendition practices distinguish between violations of international law and violations of municipal law. Once this dichotomy is accepted, it is relatively simple for municipal courts considering the issue not to deem themselves jurisdictionally impaired by international law violations and to proceed with the case as if the international law violation did not exist.

The rationale sustaining this dichotomy between violations of internal law and violations of international law is predicated on one interpretative approach to the doctrine of separation of powers in municipal law. Under this approach, violations of international law are deemed within the prerogatives of the executive, furthermore, municipal courts, it is asserted, have no

152

enforceable sanctioning powers with respect to such violations.
Governments, on the other hand, also argue that human rights are
non-enforceable by municipal courts for a variety of reasons
among which are:

1. There are no binding international sanctions for
    violations of human rights, except as provided by
    treaty.

2. There are no existing binding obligations arising
    out of internationally enunciated human rights,
    which are applicable to municipal courts, except
    as provided by treaty.

3. Self-executing enforcement of internationally
    enunciated human rights would violate state
    sovereignty.

The answers to these questions in the present state of international law are by no means as clear cut as the proponents of human
rights or the proponents of state sovereignty claims that they are.
In fact, no other area of international law is as riddled with
confusion between the *lex lata* and *de legge ferenda* as is the
literature on international protection of human rights. One may
even occasionally find some arguments in the nature of *lex
desiderata*, which are advanced as *lex lata*.

The observations which follow by no means purport to exhaust
the arguments debated on these issues, but are intended to present
a cursory view of the present state of the law and its likely
immediate development.

The central issue is not whether they are human rights, [57] but whether there are rules with enough specific content which are contained in one of the sources of international law to be deemed binding upon states and requiring enforcement. Thus, the need to identify the sources of such rights and then to determine whether these sources contain a specific right with a defined content which applies to unlawful seizures and irregular rendition practices. The applicable sources of law, arise out of the following:

1. The United Nations charter.

2. The Universal Declaration on Human Rights.

3. Multilateral treaties.

4. Decisions of international courts.

5. United Nations resolutions.

This classification is based on the degree of applicability and binding nature of specific obligations falling within the meaning of internationally protected human rights.

1. The United Nations Charter

The Charter refers to respect for human rights in Articles 1 (3), 13 (1) (b), 55(c), 62(2) and 76(c). The language of Article 55 is quite revealing as it states:

> "With a view to the creation of conditions of stability
> and well being, which are necessary for peaceful and
> friendly relations among nations based on respect for
> the principles of equal rights and self-determination
> of peoples, the United Nations shall promote:
>
> (c) Universal respect for, and observance of,
>   human rights and fundamental freedoms for
>   all without distinction as to race, sex,

language or religion."

The language quoted above has been considered by some as a statement of principles or a goal to aim at, while others read it as stating charter obligations. Consider, however, that Article 56 states:

"All members pledge themselves to take joint and
separate action in cooperation with the organization for the achievement of the purposes set forth
in Article 55."

Such a clear statement of obligation places in issue not whether an obligation to "achieve (of) the purposes" of human rights exist, but rather their specific content.

A comprehensive summary of these issues and the arguments of the proponents of various positions has been made by Professor Schwelb in a recent article. [58] One answer appears in the position of the International Court of Justice in its Advisory Opinion on "The Legal Consequences for States of the Continued Presence of South Africa in Namibia, notwithstanding Security Council Resolution 276 (1970)," [59] which was unequivocal in the recognition that the charter impose human rights obligations on member states and that they are self-executing obligations. The court in paragraph 129 of its opinion stated that South African apartheid laws and decrees "constitute a violation of the purposes and principles of the charter of the United Nations." [60]

In paragraph 130 the court held: "Under the charter of the United Nations, the former mandatory had pledged itself to ob- serve and respect, in a territory on international states, human

155

rights and fundamental freedoms for all without distinctions as to race. To establish, indeed to enforce distinctions, exclusions, restrictions and limitations exclusively based on grounds of race, color, descent or national or ethnic origin which constitute <u>a denial of fundamental human rights is a flagrant violation of the purposes and principles of the charter</u>." [61] (Emphasis added). Thus, the charter, by enunciating its purposes and principles on human rights, established self-executing obligations which acquire their specific content from the charter as well as other sources of internationally protected human rights.

As this writer sees the issue, it is whether the charter, having established certain general principles and purposes, can be said to incorporate by reference those specific rights which by virtue of the evolutionary nature of that subject have and will continue to develop through various sources of international law? The answer is affirmative and, therefore, these specific rights must be ascertained to determine their applicability, which as specific rights interpreting the charter become self-executing obligations by virtue of Article 56. Furthermore, specific obligations which are expressed in multilateral treaties and thus find another source of applicable law, run into those general purposes of the charter. As an advocate of human rights, this writer maintains that such specific rights should be considered as interpretative of the charter becoming self-executing under Article 56.

2. The Universal Declaration of Human Rights [62]

This document was adopted in 1948 as a General Assembly resolution and enunciates specific rights among these are some which are

156

affected by the practices of unlawful seizures and irregular renditions, namely:

Article 3 — "everyone has the right to life,
liberty and the security of person."

Article 9 — "no one shall be subjected to arbitrary arrest, detention or exile."

Article 10 — "everyone is entitled in full equality
to a fair and public hearing by an independent and military tribunal, in
the determination of his rights and
obligations and of any criminal charge
against him."

These three specific provisions apply to the following instances: (1) unlawful seizures such as abductions; (2) connivance between agents of two states to seize a person without lawful means, and (3) actions by private volunteers acting for or on behalf of a state.

The question, however, arises as to the legally binding effects of the declaration. One school of thought holds that as a General Assembly resolution, it has no binding effect on states, while another one claims that it interprets charter obligations. The most persuasive argument found by this writer is contained in the separate opinion of Vice President Ammoun of the International Court of Justice in the "Advisory Opinion on the Continued Presence of South Africa in Namibia (South West Africa)" wherein he states:

The Advisory Opinion takes judicial notice of the
Universal Declaration of Human Rights. In the case

157

of certain of the Declaration's privisions,
attracted by the conduct of South Africa, it
would have been an improvement to have dealt
in terms with their comminatory nature, which
is implied in paragraphs 130 and 131 of the
Opinion by the references to their violation.

In its written statement the French Government,
alluding to the obligations which South Africa.
accepted under the Mandate and assumed on becoming a Member of the United Nations, and to
the norms laid down in the Universal Declaration
of Human Rights, stated that there was no doubt
that the Government of South Africa had, in a
very real sense, systematically infringed those
rules and those obligations. Nevertheless,
referring to the mention by resolution 2145 (XXI)
of the Universal Declaration of Human Rights, it
objected that it was plainly impossible for noncompliance with the norms it enshrined to be
sanctioned with the revocation of the Mandate,
inasmuch as that Declaration was not in the nature
of a treaty binding upon states.

Although the affirmations of the Declaration are
not binding qua international convention within
the meaning of Article 38, paragraph 1(a), of the
Statute of the Court, they can bind states on the
basis of custom within the meaning of paragraph 1(b)

of the same Article, whether because they
constituted a codification of customary law
as was said in respect of Article 6 of the
Vienna Convention on the Law of Treaties, or
because they have acquired the force of custom
through a general practice accepted as law, in
the words of Article 38, paragraph 1(b), of the
Statute. One right which must certainly be considered a preexisting binding customary norm which
the Universal Declaration of Human Rights codified
is the right to equality, which by common consent
has ever since the remotest times been deemed
inherent in human nature.

It is not by mere chance that in Article 1 of the
Universal Declaration of the Rights of Man there
stands, so worded, this primordial principle or
axiom: "All human beings are born free and equal
in dignity and rights."

From this first principle flow most rights and
freedoms. The ground was thus prepared for the
legislative and constitutional process which
began with the first declarations or bills of
rights in America and Europe, continued with the
constitutions of the nineteenth century, and
culminated in positive international law in the
San Francisco, Bogota and Addis Ababa charters,
and in the Universal Declaration of Human Rights

159

which has been confirmed by numerous resolutions
of the United Nations, in particular the above
mentioned declarations adopted by the General
Assembly in resolutions 1514 (XV), 2625 (XXV) and
2627 (XXV). The Court in its turn has now confirmed it. [63]

A quarter of a century ago the Declaration expressed the consensus of the member states and since then it has become part of
those "General Principles of International Law recognized by
civilized nations." Thus, the provisions of the Declaration can
be construed as legally binding because they interpret the principles and purposes of the charter and are applicable to member
states as the embodiment of Article 55 whose execution is required
by Article 56. Furthermore, as part of international law's "General Principles," the transgression of its norms would constitute
a violation of international law to which state responsibility
would attach.

3. Multilateral Treaties

In this category of specific norms of human rights the provisions
applicable to unlawful seizures and irregular means of rendition
are clear and unambiguous. The application of these treaties can
be viewed, as in the case of the Universal Declaration, as those
specific norms which interpret the principles and purposes of the
charter and consequently, they could be considered as self-executing under Article 56 of the charter. In addition thereto, as
international treaties, they are part of conventional international
law and derive their binding force from that source of interna-

tional law.

A. The International Covenant on Civil and Political Rights--

It is noteworthy that it was first adopted as a resolution of the
General Assembly. [64] The Covenant is so far not in force, however,
should it enter into force the following provisions would apply
to the instances at hand.

Article 9

1. Everyone has the right to liberty and security of person.
    No one shall be subjected to arbitrary arrest or detention.
    No one shall be deprived of his liberty except on such grounds
    and in accordance with such procedure as are established by
    law.

2. Anyone who is arrested shall be informed, at the time of
    arrest, of the reasons for his arrest and shall be promptly
    informed of any charges against him.

3. Anyone arrested or detained on a criminal charge shall be
    brought promptly before a judge or other officer authorized
    by law to exercise judicial power and shall be entitled to
    trial within a reasonable time or to release. It shall not
    be the general rule that persons awaiting trial shall be de-
    tained in custody, but release may be subject to guarantees
    to appear for trial, at any other stage of the judicial pro-
    ceedings, and, should occasion arise, for execution of the
    judgment.

4. Anyone who is deprived of his liberty by arrest or detention
    shall be entitled to take proceedings before a court, in

order that that court may decide without delay on the lawfulness of his detention and order his release if the detention is not lawful.

5. Anyone who has been the victim of unlawful arrest or detention shall have an enforceable right to compensation.

Article 12

1. Everyone lawfully within the territory of a state shall, within that territory, have the right to liberty of movement and freedom to choose his residence.

2. Everyone shall be free to leave any country, including his own.

3. The above mentioned rights shall not be subject to any restrictions except those which are provided by law, are necessary to protect national security, public order (*ordre public*), public health or morals or the rights and freedoms of others, and are consistent with the other rights recognized in the present Covenant.

4. No one shall be arbitrarily deprived of the right to enter his own country.

Article 13

An alien lawfully in the territory of a State Party to the present Covenant may be expelled therefrom only in pursuance of a decision reached in accordance with law and shall, except where compelling reasons of national security otherwise require, be allowed to submit the reasons against his expulsion and to have his case reviewed by, and be represented for the purpose before, the competent authority or a person or persons especially designated by the competent authority.

B. The Convention Relating to the Status of Stateless Persons [65]

Article 31

Expulsion

1. The Contracting States shall not expel a stateless person lawfully in their territory save on grounds of national security or public order.

2. The expulsion of such a stateless person shall be only in pursuance of a decision reached in accordance with due process of law. Except where compelling reasons of national security otherwise require, the stateless person shall be allowed to submit evidence to clear himself, and to appeal to and be represented for the purpose before competent authority or a person or persons specially designated by the competent authority.

3. The Contracting States shall allow such a stateless person a reasonable period within which to seek legal admission into another country. The Contracting States reserve the right to apply during that period such internal measures as they may deem necessary.

C. The Convention Relative to the Status of Refugees [66]

Article 32

Expulsion

1. The Contracting States shall not expel a refugee lawfully in

163

their territory save on grounds of national security or public order.

2. The expulsion of such a refugee shall be only in pursuance
of a decision reached in accordance with due process of law.
Except where compelling reasons of national security otherwise require, the refugee shall be allowed to submit evidence
to clear himself, and to appeal to and be represented for the
purpose before competent authority or a person or persons
specially designated by the competent authority.

3. The Contracting States shall allow such a refugee a reasonable period within which to seek legal admission into another
country. The Contracting States reserve the right to apply
during that period such internal measures as they may deem
necessary.

Article 33

Prohibition of Expulsion or Return ("Refoulement")

1. No Contracting State shall expel or return ("refouler") a
refugee in any manner whatsoever to the frontiers of territories where his life or freedom would be threatened on
account of his race, religion, nationality, membership of a
particular social group or political opinion

2. The benefit of the present provision may now, however, be
claimed by a refugee whom there are reasonable grounds for
regarding as a danger to the security of the country in which
he is, or who, having been convicted by a final judgment of
a particularly serious crime, constitutes a danger to the

community of that country.

D. The European Convention for the Protection of Human Rights
    and Fundamental Freedoms [67]

Article 5

1. Everyone has the right to liberty and security of person. No
    one shall be deprived of his liberty save in the following
    cases and in accordance with a procedure prescribed by law:

    (a) the lawful detention of a person after
        conviction by a competent court.

    (b) the lawful arrest or detention of a person
        for non-compliance with the lawful order
        of a court or in order to secure the ful-
        filment of any obligation prescribed by law.

    (c) the lawful arrest or detention of a person
        effected for the purpose of bringing him
        before the competent legal authority on
        reasonable suspicion of having committed an
        offense or when it is reasonably considered
        necessary to prevent his committing an
        offense or fleeing after having done so.

    (d) the detention of a minor by lawful order for
        the purpose of educational supervision or his
        lawful detention for the purpose of bringing
        him before the competent legal authority.

    (e) the lawful detention of persons for the pre-
        vention of the spreading of infectious

diseases, of persons of unsound mind,
alcoholics or drug addicts or vagrants.

(f) the lawful arrest or detention of a person
to prevent his effecting an unauthorized
entry into the country or of a person
against whom action is being taken with a
view to deportation or extradition.

2. Everyone who is arrested shall be informed promptly, in a
language which he understands, of the reasons for his arrest
and of any charge against him.

3. Everyone arrested or detained in accordance with the provisions of paragraph 1(c) of this Article shall be brought promptly before a judge or other officer authorized by law to
exercise judicial power and shall be entitled to trial within
a reasonable time or to release pending trial. Release may
be conditioned by guarantees to appear for trial.

4. Everyone who is deprived of his liberty by arrest or detention
shall be entitled to take proceedings by which the lawfulness
of his detention shall be decided speedily by a court and his
release ordered if the detention is not lawful.

5. Everyone who has been the victim of arrest or detention in
contravention of the provisions of this Article shall have an
enforceable right to compensation.

E. The Inter-American Convention on Human Rights

Article 7

Right to Personal Liberty

166

1. Every person has the right to personal liberty and security.

2. No one shall be deprived of his physical liberty except for the reasons and under the conditions established beforehand by the constitution of the State Party concerned or by a law established pursuant thereto.

3. No one shall be subject to arbitrary arrest or imprisonment.

4. Anyone who is detained shall be informed of the reasons for his detention and shall be promptly notified of the charge or charges against him.

5. Any person detained shall be brought promptly before a judge or other officer authorized by law to exercise judicial power and shall be entitled to trial within a reasonable time or to be released without prejudice to the continuation of the proceedings. His release may be subject to guarantees to assure his appearance for trial.

6. Anyone who is deprived of his liberty shall be entitled to recourse to a competent court, in order that the court may decide without delay on the lawfulness of his arrest or detention and order his release if the arrest or detention is unlawful. In States Parties whose laws provide that anyone who believes himself to be threatened with deprivation of his liberty is entitled to recourse to a competent court in order that it may decide on the lawfulness of such threat, this remedy may not be restricted or abolished. The interested party or another person in his behalf is entitled to seek these remedies.

F. The International Right to the Due Process of the Law

In addition to these specific rights, there is the general right
that every accused is entitled to the due process of the law.
This general right is not stated specifically in human rights
documents, but is inferred therefrom. It emanates from the total
fabric of human rights treaties and doctrines and from specific
protections. It emerges as an overall concept of fairness which
is inherent to the international scheme of human rights protection. Even though it is specifically mentioned in Article 32 of
the Convention Relative to the Status of Refugees, its absence
from other specific provisions underscores its obviousness. Indeed, what can specific rights signify in the absence of the
basic framework of a lawful process. There are many provisions
in the international instruments referred to above which relate
to the judicial process and its fairness and it is the cumulative
effect of these provisions which gives rise to this right.

4. Decisions of International Courts

The International Court of Justice dealt with the issue of human
rights in its decisions on Namibia. In the latest Advisory Opinion rendered in 1971 it made its position on the legally binding
effects of human rights unequivocal. [69] (In Item 2 of this subsection, the court's decision was referred to and relevant excerpts were quoted). The court thus affirmed the justiciability
of human rights issues and interpreted charter references to
human rights as legally binding obligations which acquire their
specific content from other international instruments such as the

Universal Declaration on Human Rights.

The only other international court rendering judgments with respect to human rights as applied to those states subscribing to its jurisdiction is the European Court of Human Rights which was created by virtue of the European Convention on Human Rights. Since its creation, it has had the sole purpose and function of adjudicating disputes arising out of the Convention. [70]

This unique experience in the history of mankind augures well for the development of human rights, particularly because it demonstrated that the barriers of state sovereignty can be lowered without any shattering effects resulting therefrom. Insofar as the adjudication of human rights questions, the court decides only cases involving violations of human rights as established in the convention. As to the question of the legally binding effects of such provisions, they are no longer at issue. The experience of European states in this case ought to allay some of the apprehensions which arise whenever the justiciability of human rights issues is advanced.

A survey of this sort should not omit a reference to decisions of Arbitral Tribunals and national courts which add their weight to the recognition of state responsibility for violations of human rights. Such cases are plentiful in the annals of international law and to cite only one example, the _Chattin_ [71] case between the United States and Mexico wherein violations of the human rights of a United States defendant in Mexican criminal proceedings were arbitrated between the two states and resulted in an award for damages to the individual. The protection of

minorities in the post World War I period arising out of the
Minorities Treaty of 1919 and other decisions of the Permanent
Court of International Justice as well as Arbitral Tribunals
offer an equally abundant source of precedents for justiciability
of those issues under principles of state responsibility.

5. United Nations Resolutions

It is appropriate to state at first the impact on the United
Nations of the 1971 Advisory Opinion of the International Court
of Justice on Namibia (South West Africa). The Security Council
in a resolution of 20 October 1971 by a vote of 13 in favor, none
against, 2 absentions expressed its appreciation to the court
stating expressly that it "agrees with the court's opinion expressed in paragraph 133 of the Advisory Opinion" (this paragraph
is quoted in Item 2 of this subsection). Shortly thereafter,
the General Assembly in a resolution of 20 December 1971, stated
that it "welcomed" the Advisory Opinion "as expressed in paragraph 133." This statement of approval was voted by 111 in favor,
2 against and 10 absentions. [72] Clearly, insofar as the applicability of human rights under international law and their binding
effect there could be no stronger support for this position than
the overwhelming endorsement of the International Court of Justice
Advisory Opinion by the Security Council and the General Assembly.

United Nations resolutions emanate from the Security Council
and the General Assembly. The significance of such resolutions,
particularly General Assembly ones, which are recommendatory, is
to express a world community position. Such positions, however,

acquire their legal significance from the re-citation of these resolutions [73] and their relationship to further developments of the same subject through other international instruments. Such developments combined with a record of consistent support by the General Assembly exhibits and confirms the existence of "General Principles" as well as international customs which are two of the sources of international law. There is no greater and more over-whelming record of support for the human rights program than that expressed by the General Assembly and other United Nations special-ized agencies which have consistently referred to and upheld the recognition, application and implementation of the principles and purposes of the charter in respect of human rights and other inter-national instruments. Suffice it to record that the most important of such international instruments have at first emerged as General Assembly resolutions. Among these are: The Universal Declaration on Human Rights; The International Covenant for the Protection of Social and Cultural Rights; The International Covenant for the Pro-tection of Civil and Political Rights; The Genocide Convention; The Convention for the Elimination of all Forms of Racial Discrim-ination. There are many others concerning refugees, labor and other subjects which also deserve special consideration when deal-ing with the topic of human rights in general.

The conclusion is that General Assembly resolutions consistently re-cited or relied upon and which find tangible expression in other international law developments rank among those expressions of world community prescriptions which are among the sources of inter-national law having legally binding effects on the world community.

2.3.1 Treaty Interpretation and Human Rights

The Vienna Convention on the Law of Treaties of 1969 states in Article 31:

1. A treaty shall be interpreted in good faith in accordance with the ordinary meaning to be given to the terms of the treaty in their context and in the light of its object and purpose.

. . . . .

3. There shall be taken into account, together with the context:

   (a) any subsequent agreement between the parties regarding the interpretation of the treaty or the application of its provisions.

Subsequent agreements and customs as per subparagraph (b) of the same Article 31 are sources of interpretation of prior treaty provisons. It is the contention of this writer that the Universal Declaration of Human Rights is a subsequent agreement which interprets Article 55 of the charter by reason of its intended import as stated in its Preamble, namely:

> *Whereas*, the people of the United Nations <u>have in the charter reaffirmed their faults in fundamental human rights</u> in the dignity and worth of human persons and in the equal rights of men and have determined to promote social progress and better standards of life in larger freedom. (Emphasis added).

The link between Article 55 of the Charter and the Universal Declaration having so been established and Article 31 of the

172

Vienna Convention allowing the interpretation of Article 55 to be accomplished through subsequent agreements, it is valid to advance that the Declaration interprets Charter provisions. Consequently, its specific guarantees are incorporated in the general meaning of Charter provisions on "Human Rights" and are binding as well as self-executing under Article 56 of the Charter. Furthermore, other Human Rights sources should be considered as interpretative of Charter provisions. Violations of such obligations constitute a breach of international law and, therefore, states are estopped from further recurring violations of human rights in their processes of unlawful seizures and irregular rendition devices.

2.4 Remedies

From all of the above mentioned sources there can be no doubt that violations of certain specific internationally protected human rights constitute internationally enforceable rights in the nature of an *injuria* to which state responsibility attaches and which in addition to specific remedies cannot be productive of legitimate outcomes. The question is first whether arbitrary arrest and detention falls within the category of serious violations of internationally protected human rights to be considered an *injuria* warranting a legal remedy.

The answer seems obvious as there can be no greater internationally protected human right after the right to life than the right to liberty. The second question relates to the extent of a states' obligation to protect such rights. [73] Clearly, a state cannot infringe upon these rights without due process of law, but does

173

this extend to an obligation on the part of the state to insure against such results occurring when committed by other states? Such a proposition is not as of yet recognized because of the relatively recent development of the law of human rights, but if this was the case, then the state wherein such a violation occurred would be aggrieved in two ways: The first is its obligation to secure the right of freedom from arbitrary arrest and detention which would be violated by the actions of another state; and, the second arises by virtue of the first in that all states sharing a common duty to insure the safeguard of internationally protected human rights are affected by a transgression of such commonly binding obligations.

By that argument, it can be asserted that the rights of an injured state cannot be severed from those of the individual whose internationally protected rights were infringed. The remedy applicable to an international *injuria* should bar the ripening of such violations into lawful outcomes.

A paradigm example where such a remedy found its expression is the Jacob-Solomon case [74] wherein a former German citizen was taken into Germany from Switzerland by force and deceit. Because of a 1921 treaty between Germany and Switzerland concerning unresolved disputes the matter was submitted to an international court of arbitration. [75] Shortly after the case was initiated, Germany admitted error and returned Jacob to Swiss authorities.

Three other cases deserve mention. A case wherein a Belgian citizen was seized by French agents and brought to trial in France. The Tribunal Correctional d'Avesnes held in 1933 [76] that

174

the defendant should be returned to Belgium because he was illegally seized. The defendant was returned immediately to Belgium. In
a 1965 issue between Italy and Switzerland the Affaire Mantovani,[77]
an unlawfully seized person was returned to Switzerland and the
Italian authorities extended their apologies to the Swiss government. A 1962 case known as The Red Crusader[78] between Denmark and
the United Kingdom involved the seizure of a fishing boat captain
by Denmark which sought to prosecute him for illegally fishing in
its territorial waters. On England's complaint of the illegal seizure he was returned to his country. In September 1974 a U.S. de-
serter was seized by U.S. agents 50 yards inside Canada after a
hot pursuit commenced in U.S. territory. On Canada's complaint he
was returned to Canada within days.

These cases upheld and vindicated the principle ex injuria non
oritur. It must also be noted that world community standards were
enunciated to that effect in the unanimous resolution of the Security Council in the complaint of Argentina against Israel in the
Eichmann case wherein the Council stated:

> ". . . That acts such as that under consideration, which
> affect the sovereignty of another state and, therefore,
> cause international friction, may, if repeated, endanger
> peace and security. Requests the government of Israel to
> make appropriate reparation in accordance with the Charter
> of the United Nations and the rules of International Law."[79]

Surely, Charter principles and rules of international law include international protection of human rights which are the very violations
involved in such practices. The conclusions of this writer are:

1. States must abide by specific human rights, norms and in spirit fulfil the principles and purposes of the Charter and those instruments which interpret it.

2. Unlawful seizures in violation of international law and improper means conditions executed without benefit of a legal process insuring minimal standards of due process or in violation of specific human rights provisions are to be held violative of international law and sanctioned in this answer:

   a. The perpetrators, their aiders and abettors and responsible superiors are to be held internationally responsible.

   b. The person who was subjected to these practices is to be returned to the state from which he was seized and be entitled to homage.

   c. The state wherein the act occurred is entitled to reparation and apologies.

3. The Internatonal Court of Justice is to exercise compulsory jurisdiction in hearing petitions by states on behalf of individuals who were the object of such treatment and to issue Writs of World Habeas Corpus.

3. *An Appraisal of Rendition Devices as Alternatives to Extradition and World Public Order*

If the premise is accepted that extradition is the only legitimate process to secure rendition of a person sought by a state other than the one where the fugitive sought refuge, then all other means of rendition are illegitimate. The alternatives to extradition discussed above in this section are all irregular and extraordinary. They range from outright illegal, i.e., abduction to the irregular use of legal devices available under the immigration laws of the state of refuge. What, however, are the alternatives available when the only legitimate process, i.e., extradition fails? This is only one of the questions raised by these irregular methods, others are: (1) Is the individual entitled to have the requesting state and the state of asylum follow exclusively a single process, i.e., extradition, in the exercise of their mutual cooperation in penal matters? (2) Can either state insist on that single process as the exclusive means of cooperation between them? (3) Should international law prohibit the use of irregular devices to secure rendition other than through extradition? (4) Should there be a formal alternative process to extradition? (5) Should there be some recourse from the exclusiveness of that process in case it fails?

There is an obvious correlation between the resort to irregular methods of rendition and either the failure of the formal process of extradition or the stringency of its requirements. This conclusion tends to raise doubts about the endemic weakness of a process which relies on many legal formalities and is shrouded with the formalism that appears to have become inherent to the very process. As stated by Professor Evans:

Accepting the premise that the established method of

recovery of the international fugitive offender is
by extradition proceedings which are ordinarily
governed by both treaty and statute, it may be
asked whether Eichmann, Ahlers and similar cases
are the exceptions which prove the rule. If,
however, resort to methods of recovery other than
extradition is a common occurrence, it may be
asked whether the extradition process is failing
to serve its objective of providing a state with
a formal method of acquiring custody of a fugitive
offender in which the interests of the asylum
state, the requesting state and of the accused
are procedurally protected. In other words, does
the relative stringency of the extradition process
make it an anachronism in an age of rapid communication? Again, approaching the issue from the
broader context of that public concern with the
recognition of the rights of the individual and
their protection under international law which
has gained increasing momentum during the past
two decades, it may be asked whether the international fugitive offender has any right as against
the asylum state to demand surrender only through
extradition proceedings. Conversely, it may be
asked whether the asylum state is under an
obligation to disregard any request for surrender
other than one through the formal channel of

extradition and to refrain from using such legal
processes as exclusion or expulsion as convenient
substitutes for extradition and from condoning
the use of irregular methods of recovery of
fugitives by other states.

The answers to these questions are not readily
supplied, for each question tends to raise other
questions about the scope of the territorial jurisdiction of the state, the plenary power of the
state over the alien, the responsibility of the
state for enforcing law and order by bringing
criminals to justice, the right of the state to
protect itself from becoming a haven for criminals.
In the last analysis the answers must be found in
information about the nature of state practice in
the matter of acquiring custody over international
fugitive offenders by methods other than extradition.[80]

Among the practices which were discussed and which seem endemic
to the need of rendition, consider the following factors bearing
on policy and which may well have brought about the practical
necessity for these alternative devices:

1. A large number of states grant extradition only
   on the basis of an existing treaty and not on
   reciprocity or comity.

2. The requesting state's network of treaties has
   gaps usually known to the fugitive and exploited
   by him.

3. The treaty itself may be limited or loosely
   worded, or provide in its language for ways
   of evading its application, or simply not up
   to date to meet new contingencies.

4. The extraditable offenses listed in the treaty
   in question may not cover the specific offense,
   and even if it could be so construed, the jurisprudence of the state of refuge could give it a
   stricto sensu interpretation.

5. Political and practical considerations in given
   cases may require a political barter between
   two persons sought by both states. These persons
   may be beyond the respective reach of each state
   or in the respective custody of each of the
   given states.

6. Commencement of formal proceedings are likely
   to give notice to the fugitive and time to
   flee the jurisdiction of the state of refuge,
   thus, starting a merry-go-round chase from
   country to country.

7. The length of the formal process further
   delayed by appeals and collateral attack
   dilutes its certainty and swiftness.

8. The cost of extradition for both states is
   often significant.

9. The potential for use of executive discretion
   as a last resort to deny actual surrender after

extradition has been judicially permitted is
always present.

10. The weaknesses of the requesting state's case
at the time extradition is sought may be a
bar to it.

11. The necessity of the requesting state to with-
hold some of the evidence against the fugitive
for trial strategy or other reasons.

12. Exceptions and exemptions such as the political
offense exception may contribute to the dilution
of the effectiveness of the process.

All of these considerations bear heavily on decision makers and
contribute to making the process unattractive for the attainment
of a swift result accomplished in an efficient and economic
manner. The alternatives, therefore, become more appealing and
even though less legitimate in their means, they grow more acceptable to decision makers as a substitute to the legitimate process
which becomes more and more cumbersome and less effective. At
the policy level the dilemma is characteristic: it is a conflict
between two processes, one which is _means_ oriented and the other
which is _result_ oriented. The choice between such divergent
policies will depend on the value-oriented goals of the system
of justice as administered in that particular state.

From the point of view of preservation of minimum world order,
a distinction must be drawn as between irregular situations which
result from the cooperative undertakings of the respectively
interested states and situations where one state resorts to a

method which violates the territorial integrity, sovereignty or legal processes of another state. In both types of instances, the main deterrent to their use would be the recognition of a principle of legality of process which would disallow the application of *mala captus bene detentus*, and establish the primacy of a formal legal process over any irregular processes by declaring any resort thereto as unlawful under international law. Such, however, is still not the case even if the writings of publicists continue to decry violations of international due process of law. In the case where one state acts without the cooperation or consent of another, threats to minimum world order have three dimensions:

1. Violation of the state of refuge's sovereignty, territorial integrity and domestic process.

2. Violation of the individual's right to freedom from arbitrary arrest and detention and international due process and fairness.

3. Violation of the integrity of the international process.

Insofar as instances of mutual cooperation and consent between agents of both interested states are concerned, threats to minimum world order are reduced to two dimensions:

1. Violation of the individual's right to freedom from arbitrary arrest and detention and international due process and fairness.

2. Violation of the integrity of the international process.

The factors involved in each one of these instances demonstrates that the latter group is much less likely to cause disruption of world public order. In fact, in the latter type of instances, the activities of both states exhibit a high level of cooperation not exhibited by the former type of instances and, therefore, does not warrant the same level of apprehension of disruption of world public order as does that former type. Nonetheless, preservation of internationally protected human rights are impaired in both categories.

As to the fugitive who has committed a common crime and is legitimately sought to answer these charges and not for other concealed purposes, the question is whether or not any other means to secure him for prosecution or punishment supersedes all considerations of formal process to attain that same result. The following considerations should be taken into account in formulating a policy response to this inquiry:

1. The integrity of the internationally recognized process of extradition should not be subverted for practical considerations, particularly when the very nature of the process is intended to achieve the same desired result as the irregular means resorted to.

2. The recognition of the need to preserve the integrity of the judicial and legal processes of all states.

3. The practical considerations of justifying invalid means by a purportedly valid end

must be rejected.

4. The premise that the fugitive is sought for a common crime otherwise extraditable (and not for a concealed purpose for which extradition would not be granted) cannot be presumed and its determination should properly be made by judicial proceedings.

5. The protection of individual human rights should be insured by the requested state and not deferred to the requesting state.

The conclusion is that alternative devices to extradition should not be allowed, but that extradition needs to be streamlined.

The practice reveals that this subsystem of alternative devices developed mainly because of the practical considerations stated above and that this subsystem subverts the formal process, and if it is permitted to continue, it may well render the formal process obsolete and useless. One authority, however, stated the problem as applicable to the United States less emphatically:

Judging by available sources, the United States has resorted to, or acquiesced in other states' requests for, disguised extradition frequently enough during the past five decades to suggest that operating officials find in such quasi-formal methods as exclusion, expulsion or special arrangements, practical alternatives to extradition. These "alternatives" supplement, but do not supplant, nor are they intended to supplant, the formal process of extradition. Founded upon bilateral agreements "tailored" to the particular conditions of law and legal procedure obtaining within each signatory state, not to speak of the diplomatic relations obtaining between them, extradition cannot meet all contingencies arising out of a fugitive's taking asylum abroad. The choice between seeing an accused person go free from answering the charges against him or an escaped convict remaining at large and resorting to some form of disguised extradition can be readily rationalized in the circumstances. But even in the period 1910-33 when exclusion, expulsion or special arrangements were utilized on behalf of the United States or by the United States at the request of other states often enough to approach to a policy, the point was made time and again that such measures of rendition were "not usual." That such "exceptional" measures continue to be used today is partly the fault of the extradition process itself, which like any other legal pro-ceeding, tends to be cumbersome, for speed is not its *raison d'etre*; and partly the fault of operating officials whose zeal gets the better of their judgment, or who are attracted by the ease of informal methods especially in conditions prevailing in border states. [81]

Chapter III

Footnotes

1. O'Higgins, "Unlawful Seizure and Irregular Extradition," 36
    <u>B.Y. Int'l. L.</u> 279, 280 (1960).

2. <u>Id</u>. and Garcia-Mora, "Criminal Jurisdiction of a State over
    Fugitives Brought from a Foreign Country by Force or Fraud:
    A Comparative Study," 32 <u>Ind. L.J.</u> 427 (1957); Scott, "Crim-
    inal Jurisdiction of a State over a Defendant Based upon Pre-
    sence Secured by Force or Fraud," 37 <u>Minn. L. Rev</u>. 91 (1953);
    and <u>Kerr v. Illinois</u>, 119 U.S. 436 (1886), cited by numerous
    countries as a landmark for the *mala captus bene detentus*
    rule. See Hunt, "Kerr v. Illinois Revisited," 47 <u>A.J.I.L.</u>
    678 (1953); Preuss, "Settlement of the Jacobi Kidnapping
    Case," 30 <u>A.J.I.L</u>. 123 (1936); Preuss, "Kidnapping of Fugitives
    from Justice on Foreign Territory," 29 <u>A.J.I.L</u>. 502 (1935);
    Dickinson, "Jurisdiction Following Seizure or Arrest in Vio-
    lation of International Law," 28 <u>A.J.I.L</u>. 231 (1934).

3. Cardozo, 55 <u>A.J.I.L</u>. 127 (1961).

4. See the classic <u>Savarkar</u> case in Scott, <u>Hague Court Reports</u>,
    p.276 (1916). Also compare D.S. M.S. File No. 211.12 Hino-
    jos, Efren/2 (Mexico, 1936), in which it appeared that the
    Governor of Chihuahua mistakenly assumed that he was empowered
    by Article IX of the Extradition Treaty of 1899, 31 Stat. 1818,
    to extradite fugitives to the United States. Where a fugitive
    was removed to Canada without court order". . .by the precip-
    itate action of the representatives of the Canadian Govern-

ment. . ." before he could appeal against the dismissal of his petition for *habeas corpus* in extradition proceedings, Canadian authorities returned him at the request of the United States. His appeal was then heard; the grant of extradition was affirmed; Judge, Sixth Circuit Court of Appeals (Hamilton), to Secretary of State (Hull), 6 September 1938; same to same, 13 July 1939; D.S. M.S. File No. 211.42 Miller, C.E./10/27. In People v. Pratt, an attempted plea to the jurisdiction failed where a fugitive was returned from Japan at the request of the Governor of California after the Department of State refused to request extradition in the absence of a treaty. The Supreme Court of California noted that the Governor's action was probably illegal, but that this did not oust the court's jurisdiction over the fugitive; 78 Cal. 345 (1889). Illegal action by Mexican authorities in returning a fugitive to the United States did not oust the Court's jurisdiction; Wentz v. United States, 244 F.2d 172 (9th Cir. 1957), cert. denied 355 U.S. 806 (1957).

5. For an analysis of the legal issues in the Soblen case, see Paul O'Higgins, "Disguised Extradition: The Soblen Case," Modern Law Review, 27 (1964), p. 521. The case has aroused considerable interest, see comments listed, Ibid., note 1 at p. 1. Dr. Soblen was party to the following cases: R. v. Secretary of State for Home Affairs, Ex parte Soblen, (1962) 3 All E.R. 373; R. v. Governor of Brixton Prison, Ex Parte Soblen, (1962) 3 All E.R. 641; United States v. Soblen, 199 F. Supp. 11 (S.D.N.Y. 1961), affirmed 301 F. 2d 236 (2d Cir. 1962), cert. denied 370 U.S. 944 (1962). For a brief account

of the Israeli phase of the case, see "Soblen Case Summarized,"
The Israeli Digest, 5 (August 1962), p. 8. "Deportation in the
broadest sense comprehends exclusion and expulsion among other
methods for the ouster of aliens from a country. As these are
hardly terms of art, depending as they do for definition upon
particular national law and practice; United States, Ex rel.
Paktorovics, v. Murff, 260 F. 2d 610 (2d Cir. 1958). For a
discussion of Eichmann, see Attorney General of Israel v.
Adolf Eichmann, 36 I.L.R. 5 (District Court of Jerusaleum,
1961) and the Supreme Court opinion in 36 I.L.R. 277 (1962);
also, Papadatos, The Eichmann Trial (1964), and Musmanno, "The
Objections in Limine to the Eichmann Trial," 35 Temp. L.Q. 1
(1961). For a discussion of Argoud: See B. DeSchutter "competence of the national judiciary power in case the accused has
been unlawfully brought within the national frontiers." Revue
Belge de droit international 1965-1, pp. 88-124. Decision
in Argoud was rendered by the Cour de Surete de L'Etat Dec.
28, 1963. Argoud was leader of the military revolt against
President DeGaulle during the Algerian controversy, was kidnapped from Munich in February, 1963, and later sentenced to
life imprisonment. West Germany protested the kidnapping;
New York Times, 31 December 1963, p. 3, col. 4; 1 January 1964,
p. 3, col. 5 (city ed.). For Conrad Ahlers, "one of the
editors of Der Spiegel, fled to Spain after police raids on the
magazine following his criticism of the state of military
preparedness in West Germany. He was summarily deported from
Spain to Germany at the request of German authorities. Defense

Minister Strauss was subsequently dropped from the Government

for his part in the affair. In October, 1964, Ahlers and two

others were indicted for treason on the charge of publishing

State secrets in the magazine;" New York Times, 28 October 1964,

p. 3, col. 1; 9 November, p. 11, col. 1; 11 November, p. 15,

col. 1 (late city ed.): The Observer (London), 18 October 1964,

p. 6, col. 3. Charges against Ahlers and the publisher of Der

Spiegel were dismissed by the Federal Supreme Court in May,

1965; New York Times, 15 May 1965, p. 5, col. 5. On the Tshombe

case see Bulletin of the International Commission of Jurists,

No. 32 at 28-29, Dec. 1967.

6. See Argentina's protest against Israel for the kidnapping of

Eichmann and the Security Council's action, 15 U.N. SCOR,

U.N. Doc. S/4349; and Brennan, "International Due Process and

the Law," 48 Va. L. Rev. 1258 (1962).

7. Jerusalem Pact Weekly, August 14, 1973, P.U.; Time Magazine,

August 20, 1973, p. 31; New York Times, July 24, 1973.

8. See, e.g., Egyptian agents attempted to kidnap Mordechai Luk,

an alleged double agent for Egypt and Israel by shipping him

in a trunk to Egypt. Two Egyptain diplomats were expelled

from Italy in the matter. Luk returned to Israel, where he was

wanted for military desertion; New York Times, 18 November 1964,

p. 1. col. 5; 19 November, p. 1. col. 2; 25 November, p. 6,

col. 4. The disappearance of Professor Jesus de Galindez from

New York in March, 1956, has never been solved. He was alleg-

edly kidnapped by agents of Trujillo to the Dominican Republic.

and killed; <u>New York Times</u>, March–December, 1956. See also "Department of State Bulletin," 36 (1957), p. 1027. The particularly vigorous campaign for the "repatriation" of defectors, conducted in the late 1950's by the Soviet Union and other Communist-bloc States, can also be classed as a form of "irregular recovery;" see Evans, "Observations on the Practice of Territorial Asylum in the United States," 56 <u>A.J.I.L.</u> p. 148, at pp. 151-3 (1962). Following the West German Government's offer of a $25,000 reward for the recovery of Martin Bormann, a government official was reported to have pointed out that if Bormann were recovered by kidnapping, "the reward would be paid only if the country of hiding later gave its approval;" <u>New York Times</u>, 24 November 1964, p. 12, col. 4.

9. 119 U.S. 436 (1886), see also Fairman, <u>Kerr v. Illinois Revisited</u>, 47 <u>A.J.I.L.</u> 678 (1953).

10. <i>Supra,</i> note 7. Also, Israel's law of 21 March 1972.

11. <u>State v. Brewster</u>, 7 Vt. 118 (1835); <u>Myers and Tunstall</u> case (1862), 4 Moore, <u>Digest</u>, p. 332; <u>Adsetts</u> case (1907), 4 Hackworth, <u>Digest</u>, pp. 14-15 (1945); <u>Lawshe v. State</u>, 121 S.W. 865 (1909); <u>Converse and Blatt</u> case (1911), <u>Foreign Relations</u>, 1911, p. 606 (1918); <u>United States v. Unverzagt</u>, 299 F. 1015 (W.D. Washington, 1924), affirmed <i>sub nom.</i> <u>Unverzagt v. Benn</u>, 5 F. 2d 492 (9th Cir. 1925), <u>cert. denied</u> 269 U.S. 566 (1925); <u>Ex parte Campbell</u>, 1 F. Supp. 899 (S.D. Texas 1932); <u>Frisbie v. Collins</u>, 342 U.S. 519 (1952); <u>United States v. Sobell</u>, 142 F. Supp. 515 (S.D.N.Y. 1956), affirmed 244 F. 2d 520 (2d Cir.

1957), cert. denied 355 U.S. 873 (1957), rehearing denied
355 U.S. 920 (1958). For an excellent survey of the United
States practice see Evans, "Acquisition of Custody over the
International Fugitive Offender--Alternatives to Extradition:
A Survey of the United States Practice," 40 Brit. Y.B. Int'l
L. 77 (1966).

12. A, B and C 446; 109 E.R. 166 - see also O'Higgins, supra,
note 1. As for the practice between England and the United
States, see also the case of Townsend, concerning the kidnapping of an American national from the United Kingdom by an
American police officer. The Law Officers of the Crown, in
an Opinion of 1865, did not challenge the validity of the
jurisdiction so acquired; however, they did suggest that". . .
it would be proper and expedient that the attention of the
Government of the United States should be called to this
case, in order that such instructions may be given to their
police authorities as may prevent the possibility of the re-
petition of similar proceedings;" Parry, 5 British Digest of
International Law, 1860-1914, pp. 480-1 (1965). In Blair's
case involving the forcible removal of a British subject from
the United States, the Law Officers in 1876 did not challenge
the validity of jurisdiction so acquired as matter of law,
but questioned it as a matter of policy; Parry, id., pp. 482-3.

13. Frisbie v. Collins, 342 U.S. 519 (1952).

14. Cardozo, supra, note 6, p. 133, and a critique by Dickinson,
"jurisdiction following seizure or arrest in violation of
international law," 28 A.J.I.L. 231 (1934).

15. Discussed in 1 Hackworth, _Digest_, p. 624 (1940).

16. O'Higgins, _supra_, note 1, and DeSchutter, _supra_, note 5, also for a comparative view, see 39 _Revue Internationale de Droit Penal_ (1968).

17. Professor Evans cites some cases, mostly from diplomatic archives, see Evans, _supra_, note 11, at 90-92. See also _Vaccaro v. Collier_, 38 F. 2d 826 (D. Md. 1930); _Collier v. Vaccaro_, 51 F. 2d 241 (S.D. Texas 1931); _Ex parte Lopez_, 6 F. Supp. 324 (S.D. Texas 1934) and the discussion of Hackworth following the _Vincenti_ case, _supra_, note 15.

18. 244 F. ed. 520-525 (1957).

19. Evans, _supra_, note 11.

20. 119 U.S. 436 (1886).

21. 142 F. Supp. 515 (S.D.N.Y. 1956); _aff'd._, 244 F. 2d 520 (2d Cir., 1957), _cert. denied_, 355 U.S. 873; _rehearing den._, 355 U.S. 920 (1958).

22. _Chandler v. United States_, 171 F. 2d 921 (1948), _cert. denied_, 336 U.S. 918 (1949); _rehearing denied_, 336 U.S. 947 (1949).

23. 19 Scott, _Hague Court Reports_, 276 (1916).

24. 1906, _U.S. Foreign Relations_ 1121-1122; see also _Ex parte Lopez_, 6 F. Supp. 342 (S.D. Tex. 1934). See also France and Great Britain: _The Savarkar Case_, _Hague Permanent Court of Arbitration_ (1911), Scott, _The Hague Court Reports_, 276 (1916); reprinted in 5 _A.J.I.L._ 520 (1911), and Fenwick, _Cases on International Law_, 420 (2d ed., 1951).

25. _U.S. v. Artukovic_, 170 F. Supp. 383 (S.D. Col. 1959).

26. Cardozo, _supra_, note 6 at 127.

27. Ekiu v. United States, 142 U.S. 651 at 659 (1892) holding
    that as "an accepted maxim of international law," the powers
    of exclusion and expulsion are inherent in sovereignty;
    Scales v. United States, 367 U.S. 203 at 222 (1961) in which
    Harlan, J., referred to Congress' plenary power over aliens."
    "It is a universally recognized sovereign right of a State
    to admit or refuse to admit aliens of certain classes into
    its territory." See 1 Hyde, Digest, pp. 216-18, §212(e),
    66 Stat. 188; 8 U.S.C. §1182(e), §§241(a)(1), 241(e), 66
    Stat. 204, 208; 8 U.S.C. §§1251(a)(1), 1251(e), and Harisiades
    v. Shaughnessey, 342 U.S. 580 (1952), wherein the court
    stated that Congress' plenary power in those cases "bristles
    with severity" at 587.

28. See Chapter II and A. Gahl-Madsen, The Status of Refugees in
    International Law, Vol. I (1966).

29. For a state's responsibility toward aliens in international
    law, compare 4 Moore, Digest 95 (1901), with 5 Whiteman,
    Digest 221, et seq. (1963). See also, Guha-Roy, "Is the
    Law of Responsibility of States for Injuries to Aliens a
    Part of Universal International Law?" 55 A.J.I.L. 863 (1961);
    and Spiegel, "Origin and Development of Denial of Justice,"
    32 A.J.I.L. 63 (1938). On the United States position and
    aliens rights with respect to due process in exclusion cases,
    see Chin Yow v. United States, 208 U.S. 8 (1908), noted in
    66 Harv. L. Rev. 643, 661-76 (1953), 37 Minn. L. Rev. 440
    (1953), 20 U. Chi. L. Rev. 547, 551 (1953), 62 Yale L. J.
    1000 (1953).

In <u>Shaughnessy v. United States</u>, 345 U.S. 206 (1953), noted
in 34 <u>B. U. L. Rev.</u> 85 (1954), 67 <u>Harv. L. Rev.</u> 99 (1954),
51 <u>Mich. L. Rev.</u> 1231 (1953), 37 <u>Minn. L. Rev.</u> 453 (1953),
33 <u>Neb. L. Rev.</u> 94 (1953), 28 <u>N.Y.U.L. Rev.</u> 1042 (1953), 26
<u>Rocky Mt. L. Rev.</u> 192 (1954), and 27 <u>So. Cal. L. Rev.</u> 315
(1954), it was held that a twenty-five year resident who left
the United States temporarily to visit his mother could on his
return, be excluded without a hearing and confined indefin-
itely on Ellis Island since no other state could be found to
which he could be sent.

30. See Evans, *supra*, note 11 at 85, also citing: 4 Moore,
<u>Digest</u>, p. 259; and see 4 Hackworth, <u>Digest</u>, p. 30; D.S.
M.S. File No. 242.11 B 17 (Canada, 1922), wanted for obtain-
ing money under false pretenses; D.S. M.S. File No. 242.11
Cerafisi, Michael (Canada, 1935), wanted in New York for
parole violation; D.S. M.S. File No. 242.11 Finkelstein,
Sam (Canada, 1937), wanted in Illinois for parole violation;
D.S. M.S. File No. 212.11 Steele, Robert (Mexico, 1940-1);
D.S. M.S. File No. 259.11 Rosen, Samuel (Denmark, 1931-3);
e.g., D.S. M.S. File No. 211.41 (United Kingdom, 1932);
D.S. M.S. File No. 211.55 D 47 (Belgium, 1926); D.S. M.S.
File No. 248.11 Long, John M. (Union of South Africa, 1932);
<u>United States, ex rel.</u> <u>Giletti v. Commissions of Immigration</u>,
35 F. 2d 687 (2d Cir. 1929); <u>Moraitis v. Delaney</u>, 46 F. Supp.
425 (D. Md. 1942); <u>Matter of S-C-</u>(1949), <u>I. & N. Decisions</u>,
Vol. 3, p. 350; <u>Matter of Banjeglav</u> (1963), Interim Dec. No.
1298. In <u>Johnson v. Eisentrager</u>, Justice Jackson noted that

a "resident enemy alien is constitutionally subject to summary arrest, internment and deportation whenever a 'declared war' exists," 339 U.S. 763 at 775 (1950). In the Kendler case, deportation was ordered on grounds that the alien had concealed a previous criminal record in Canada; he was "turned over to the Royal Canadian Mounted Police, who wanted him on forgery charges." Immigration and Naturalization Service, Annual Report (1962), p. 9.

31. (1917) 1 K.B. 552 (Divisional Court), and 922 (Court of Appeal).

32. B.I.L.R. 146 (1946). In this case the Attorney General admitted on behalf of the Home Office that there was no power to order deportation to a particular named country. Nonetheless the police and other authorities had indicated to the intended deportee that it was proposed to deport her to Czechoslovakia. Cf. Papadimitriou v. Inspector General of Police and Prisons et al., (1943-1945) Ann. Dig. 146 (No. 68), (Supreme Court of Palestine).

33. (1917) 1 K.B. 552 at pp. 555-556. Cf. Lord Reading's judgment in R. v. Governor of Brixton Prison, ex p. Sarno (1916) 2 K.B. 742 (K.B.D.) where dealing with the validity of an order for the deportation of a Russian he said: ". . . If we were of opinion that the powers were being misused, we should be able to deal with the matter. In other words, if it was clear that an act was done by the Executive with the intention of misusing those powers, this court would have jurisdiction to deal with the matter" (at p. 749).

34. (1917) 1 K.B. 922; see also C. v. E. (1946) 62 T.L.R. 326; *supra*, note 62.

35. Cf. Regina v. Governor of Brixton Prison and the Secretary of State for Home Affairs, ex p. Sliwa (1952) 1 K.B. 169; (1951) I.L.R. 95.

36. (1917) 1 K.B. 922 at p. 929, per Swinfen Eady L. J.

37. E. Lauterpacht, "The Contemporary Practice of the United Kingdom in the Field of International Law: Survey and Comment, VI" (1958) 7 Int. & Comp. L. Q. 515-576 at pp. 553-555.

38. Cf. Regina v. Secretary of State for Home Affairs, ex p. Venicoff (1920) 3 K.B. 72, and Regina v. Superintendent of Chiswick Police Station, ex p. Sacksteder (1918) 1 K.B. 568 at p. 576.

39. (1917) I.K.B. 922, 928-932.

40. (1918) I.K.B. 578.

41. Horne v. Mitchell, 223 F. 549 (D. Mass. 1915), affirmed 232 F. 819 (1st Cir. 1916), appeal dismissed 243 U.S. (1917); see, however, Stevenson v. United States, 381 F. 2d 142 (9th Cir. 1967), wherein the court stated:

> "While the formalities of extradition may be waived by the parties to the treaty, Gluckman v. Henkel, 221 U.S. 508, 31 S. Ct. 704, 55 L. Fd 830 (1910), a demand in some form by the one country upon the other is required, in order to distinguish extradition from the unilateral act of one country, for its own purposes, deporting or otherwise unilaterally removing unwelcome aliens. See Fong Yue Ting v. United States, 149 U.S. 698, 709, 13 S. Ct. 1016, 37 L. Ed. 905 (1893).
>
> "In the instant case the evidence shows that the removal of the appellants from Mexico was not initiated by the United States. At the hearing in the district court on the appellant's motion

to dismiss, the Sonoita Chief of Police who had arrested the appellants in Mexico testified that to his knowledge no demand for extradition was ever made by the United States; that the appellants were deported by Mexican immigration authorities as undesirable aliens found in Mexico under suspicious circumstances; that it is the Mexican practice to refuse, in such circumstances, to permit aliens to remain in Mexico; that regardless of any interest of the United States in the appellants, they would have been returned to the Mexican-American border. The evidence showed that it was the Mexican authorities who first contacted American officials with regard to the appellants." (p. 144)

42. Foreign Relations, 1941 (1958), Vol. I, p. 937; the exchange of Colonel Abel, convicted in the United States on espionage charges, for U-2 Pilot Francis Gary Powers, convicted in the U.S.S.R. for espionage by "overflight," Donovan, Strangers on a Bridge: The Case of Colonel Abel (1964), pp. 371 et seq. The return to Mexico of one Lopez, who had been kidnapped from Mexico by Hernandez and Villareal, in exchange for Mexico's dropping its extradition request for Hernandez was suggested to the Mexican Government in 1935; Villareal and Hernandez v. Hammond, 74 F. 2d 503 (5th Cir. 1934).

43. The Insull case provides a good example of the use of requests for exclusion addressed to countries in the vicinity of Greece in order to force the fugitive to return to face charges in the United States. Foreign Relations, 1933 (1949) Vol. 2, pp. 552 et seq., Foreign Relations, 1934 (1951), Vol. 2, pp. 566 et seq.

44. O'Higgins, "Disguised Extradition: The Soblen Case," 27 Modern L. Rev. 521 (1964). The converse can also occur whenever expulsion is used to defeat extradition; see In re

Esposito (1933-1934) Ann. Dig. 332 (No. 138),
Supreme Court of Brazil, 1932.

45. 47 Stat. 2122 (1933).

46. The Collected Works of John Bassett Moore, Vol. 1, p. 277 (1944).

47. See *infra*, Chapter V, Section 1, on the political offense exception; and see Evans, "The Political Refugee in United States' Law and Practice," 3 Int'l Law, 205 (1969); DeVries and Novas, "Territorial Asylum in the Americas--Latin American Law and Practice of Extradition," 5 Inter-American L. Rev. 61 (1963). Section 243(h) of the Immigration and Nationality Act of 1952, 8 U.S.C. §1253 (1965), provides that the political refugee who has been admitted into the country and is then found to be a deportable alien may request a temporary withholding of deportation on the plea that he would be subjected to persecution on account of race, religion or political opinion in the country to which he is to be deported. Section 203(a)(7) added to the Act in 1965, 8 U.S.C. §1153 (1965), provides for conditional entry of political refugees. The refugee is considered to be an excludable alien whose status can be adjusted to that of a permanent resident at the discretion of the Attorney General and subject to the approval of Congress.

48. (1959) I.C.J. Rep. 6.

49. For a discussion of the rule and relevant cases, see Bassiouni, Criminal Law and its Processes, p. 370-375 (1969).

50. See e.g., Eichmann case discussed throughout this section 36

I.L.R. 5 (1968) and *infra*, note 79.

51. <u>Chattin</u> case (United States v. United Mexican States) General
    Claims Commission 1927, IV <u>U.N. Rep. Int'l Arbitral Awards</u>
    282. For state responsibility towards aliens see also
    <u>Barcelona Traction, Light and Power Company Limited</u> (Belgium
    and Spain) (1970) <u>I.C.J. Rep</u>. 3. The latest decision on
    Namibia (South West Africa) also stands for the proposition
    advanced, see (1971) <u>I.C.J. Rep</u>. 16. The case is discussed
    in the text of this section.

52. Eagleton, <u>Responsibility of States in International Law</u>
    (1928), also Bassiouni, "The Nationalization of the Suez
    Canal and the Illicit Act in International Law" 14 <u>DePaul</u>
    <u>L. Rev</u>. 258-263 (1965).

53. <u>Yearbook of the International Law Commission</u>, pp. 173, 181
    (1965 Vol. II).

54. Eagleton, *supra*, note 52 at p. 80 states: "A state owes at
    all times a duty to protect other states against injurious
    acts by individuals from within its jurisdiction."

55. See Bassiouni and Nanda, <u>A Treatise on International Criminal</u>
    <u>Law</u>, Vol. I, Part I, p. 158 (1973).

56. <u>Ibid</u>., Part II, p. 450. Also, Part V, pp. 559-635.

57. See Bassiouni, "The Human Rights Program: The Veneer of
    Civilization Thickens," 21 <u>DePaul L. Rev</u>. 271 (1971). Also,
    Sohn and Buergenthal, <u>International Protection of Human</u>
    <u>Rights</u> (1973).

58. "The International Court of Justice and the Human Rights
    Clauses of the Charter," 66 <u>A.J.I.L</u>. 337 (1972).

59.   (1971) I.C.J. Rep. 16

60.   Ibid., p. 57.

61.   Ibid.

62.   G. A. 217A(111) 10 December 1968.

63.   (1971) I.C.J. Rep. 16, 76.

64.   G. A. Res. 2200A(XXI) 16 December 1966.

65.   G. A. Res. 429(V) 14 December 1950.

66.   G. A. Res. 526A(XVII) 26 April 1954.

67.   213 U.N.T.S. 221, 4 November 1950.

68.   O.A.S. Treaty Series No. 36, 22 November 1969.

69.   *Supra,* note 59.

70.   See The Annual Reports prepared by the Council of Europe,
      Commission on Human Rights entitled "Stock-taking on the
      European Convention on Human Rights" and Linke, "The Influ-
      ence of the European Convention of Human Rights on National
      European Criminal Proceedings," 21 DePaul L. Rev. 397 (1971).

71.   *Supra,* note 51.

72.   S. C. Res. 301.

73.   G. A. Res. 2871 (XXVI).

74.   Preuss, "Settlement of the Jacob Kidnapping Case," 30 A.J.I.L.
      123 (1936).

75.   12 LNTS 281, No. 320.

76.   in re Jovis (1933–1939) Ann. Dig. 191 (No. 77).

77.   See Rousseau in 69 Revue Generale de droit International
      Public 761 (1965).

78.   An incident involving Japan and South Korea was resolved
      in November, 1973. In August, 1973, Kim Dae Jung, spokes-

man for the opposition of the South Korean Government, was

abducted from a hotel room in Tokyo. <u>Time</u> magazine, November 12, 1973, states at p. 72:

> "After a week of intensive negotiations, South
> Korea dispatched Prime Minister Kim Jong Pil to
> Japan to bow and offer an apology for the kid-
> naping to Prime Minister Kakuei Tanaka. Under
> the terms of the compromise, the government of
> President Chung Hee Park conceded that the chief
> "suspect" in the kidnaping was Kim Dong Woon, the
> former first secretary of the Korean embassy in
> Tokyo and a suspected agent of South Korea's
> Central Intelligence Agency. South Korea, though,
> insisted that whatever Kim Dong Woon might have
> done was not in any way an official act, but
> entirely private. That distinction was essential
> to the compromise. The government of Prime
> Minister Tanaka had stated earlier that Japanese
> sovereignty would have been violated only if it
> turned out that the kidnaping was an "official"
> act of the Seoul government.
>
> As for Kim Dae Jung, Korean's Foreign Minister
> said that he had been freed from protective
> custody in Seoul. South Korea would waive any
> action against Kim for past activities if he
> did not repeat his "crimes" -- presumably public
> opposition to the Park regime."

79. U. N. Doc S/1439, June 23, 1960.

80. *Supra*, note 11 at 78-79.

81. Evans, *supra*, note 11 at 103.

Chapter IV

*Theories of Jurisdiction and Their Application in Extradition
Law and Practice*

Introduction

Extradition, whether by treaty, reciprocity or comity, is premised
on the assumption that the interest of a given state has been
affected by the conduct of a given individual who is not within
that state's jurisdiction but within the jurisdiction of another
state. The issue of extradition is, therefore, of primary significance, yet few, if any, treaties refer to theories of jurisdiction except to the extent of using such terms as jurisdiction
or territory without further clarification. The assumption
stated above presupposes that: (1) the interest of the requesting
state has been affected in such a manner that it seeks to subject
the individual in question to its jurisdictional authority, and
(2) the state wherein the individual sought after is located has
no greater interest in that person. Consequently, the requested
state will not shield that person from the jurisdictional control
of the requesting state by denying its extradition request. This
balancing of interests theory bears upon the granting or denying
extradition and also on the outcome of conflicting jurisdictional
claims.

The term jurisdiction in international law refers to two
aspects of the authoritative decision making, the first is rule-

making and the second is rule-enforcing. Both of these aspects are present in extradition because the setting in motion of the process presupposes that the requesting state has a legal basis to exercise its authoritative control over the individual because: (1) it has jurisdiction over the subject matter of a given interest which had been or is being affected by the conduct of the person sought after, and (2) that once surrendered that state would have *in personam* jurisdiction over that person and consequently through this process it requests the state which has actual jurisdictional control over the individual to formally surrender that individual and relinquish jurisdiction over him or her.

The first substantive aspect of extradition is, therefore, the determination of the requesting state's jurisdiction over the subject matter for which the individual is sought. Theories of jurisdiction will therefore be discussed to determine whether under international law and the national laws of the requesting state such jurisdiction exists and whether under international law and the national laws of the requested state the individual should be surrendered.

Prior to initiating a request for the surrender of an individual sought after, a state first determines it jurisdiction over the subject matter of the alleged conduct perpetrated by the relator because the state of refuge which has jurisdiction control of the individual sought after by the requesting state will not entertain an extradition request unless it determines that the requesting state does have such jurisdiction over the subject matter and

and over the individual if and when that person is returned to face those charges alleged in the request. Because of this requirement which chronologically precedes the initiation of the formal process, the existence of jurisdiction is a condition precedent both to the request and to the granting of extradition.

The significance of the issue of jurisdiction will also be manifest with respect to the substantive conditions of extradition discussed below in Chapter V, namely, "extraditable offenses" and "double criminality". This is true in part because the determination of the legal existence of an offense also inquires into the applicable jurisdictional theory underlying the creating of the offense charged. However it must be noted that this question raises sovereignty questions.

It is universally recognized that every state has the power to regulate conduct within its territory and such other conduct which may affect those interests it would seek to protect. The power of a state to proscribe conduct within its territory and such other conduct which affects its interests is a concomitant to the principle of sovereignty. [1] Thus, the interrelationship between sovereignty and jurisdiction delineates the extent and limits of a state's power to proscribe conduct in relationship to other states. However, since conduct performed by individuals or legal entities may be committed within and without the given territory of a state and can affect any one or more interests of any or more states, the power to proscribe conduct may rest on several theories and consequently result in potential conflicts. These jurisdictional conflicts assume an international character, giving rise to the need for solutions or guidelines for the resolution of these conflicting jurisdictional claims.

There are five theories of jurisdiction recognized by international law as giving rise to rule-making and rule-enforcing power by national authoritative decision-making processes. Not all of these theories enjoy the same degree of recognition with respect to rule-making and rule-enforcing. They are:

1 - Territorial: based on the place of commission of the offense.

2 - The Active Personality or Nationality: based on the nationality of the accused.

3 - Passive Personality: based on the nationality of

4 - Protective: based on the national interest affected, (and as such is in part related to the passive personality).

5 - Universality: based on the international character of the offense.

1 - Territorial Jurisdiction and Its Extensions

The theory of territorial jurisdiction, often referred to as "territorial principle" because of its universal recognition, is the criterion by which a state prescribes and enforces rules of conduct within its physical boundaries. This principle, more than any other, is a concomitant of sovereignty; and, therefore, all states adhere to the territorial principle. It is, therefore, upon the two tenets of sovereignty and equality of sovereign that the principle of territorial jurisdiction is founded.

Every state exercises jurisdiction over all persons whether
they be nationals, resident aliens or nonresident aliens, asso-
ciations or legal entities other than natural persons and objects tangible or intangible within its physical boundaries.
The right to prescribe and enforce rules of conduct within a
state is not, however, absolute, since certain limitations exist
which restrict or compete with the exclusive jurisdiction of
states. These limitations may be self-imposed limitations under
municipal law or those imposed by international law. It may be
stated that it is universally recognized that states are competent to declare conduct as violative of their interests and embody
it into national legislation and, therefore, punish all offenses
committed in or within the said territory. As stated by Whiteman:

> "While a state which has an offender against
> its laws in custody can prosecute him for
> offenses committed within its jurisdiction,
> as it defines that jurisdiction, difficulties
> may arise when it attempts to extradite an
> offender from a country which does not share
> its concept of criminal jurisdiction. Many
> states have, under their laws, jurisdiction
> to punish their nationals for offenses committed
> anywhere, whereas common law countries, such as
> the United States and Great Britain, exercise
> jurisdiction, generally, only over crimes committed
> within their territory. Accordingly, these latter

countries usually apply their concept of
jurisdiction and limit, either specifically
or by interpretation of the extradition
agreement involved, their obligation to grant
extradition to cases where, were the circumstances reversed, they would have jurisdiction
over the offense." [2]

The interrelationship of the sovereignty and territorial jurisdiction is stated by Chief Justice Marshall in the case of the
Schooner Exchange v. McFaddon:

"The jurisdiction of the nation, within its
own territory, is necessarily exclusive and
absolute. It is susceptible of no limitation not imposed by itself. Any restriction
upon it, deriving validity from an external
source, would imply a diminution of its
sovereignty to the extent of its restriction,
and an investment of that sovereignty,
to the same extent, in that power, which could
impose such restriction." [3]

This absolutist position, adopted by Chief Justice Marshall,
has been carried rather consistently throughout United States
extradition law and practice, even though it is challengeable
in its exclusiveness.

Treaties, as well as the writing of some scholars, use the
terms "territory" and "jurisdiction" interchangeably; however it is indispensable to establish that territory and juris-

diction do not mean the same. Jurisdiction is a legal theory whereby a political entity, namely a state, claims the power to prescribe and enforce its laws, while territory is the object upon which jurisdiction is exercised.

There are, however, certain cases in which a distinction has been drawn between the two concepts in the interpretation of a particular treaty. In one such instance, the Judicial Committee of the Privy Council refused the surrender of one Kossekechatko and others to France which had exercised its jurisdiction over the relators and had found them guilty but England held that Article I of the 1873 Extradition Treaty with France applied only:

> to crimes committed within the territory of the
> Power which is seeking extradition . . . in their
> Lordships' opinion no one of the appellants was
> liable to be extradited under the treaty, unless the
> crime of which he was convicted was, in fact, committed
> within the territory of the French republic. [4]

Similar views had been expressed by the Attorney General of the United States in the case of <u>In re Stupp</u> in 1873, when he recommended:

> I am quite clear that the words "committed within the
> jurisdiction," as used in the treaty, do not refer to
> the personal liability of the criminal, but to <u>locality</u>.
> The *locus delicti,* the place where the crime is committed,
> must be within the jurisdiction of the party demanding
> the fugitive. [5]

As indicated above, "jurisdiction" refers to rule-making and rule-enforcing. In both cases the authoritative decision making body must exercise a certain dominion and control over the territory upon which it claims that such power extends to.

In the international legal system "jurisdiction" is regarded as the perogative of a state to subject certain persons, events and places to its authoritative decision-making processes. That system does not delve into the constituent units or political subdivisions of a state in the exercise of these perogatives. Thus the jurisdictional question is one of recognizing the allocation perogatives inter-states and not intra-state. Furthermore it does not prescribe the basis upon which such perogatives are to be claimed unless the claims made by a given state conflict with those of another state. Similarly the international legal system does not distinguish between power to proscribe and power to enforce except when these powers conflict, with those of another state. The role of the international legal system is to define rules by which to resolve conflicts between states as to their power to proscribe and enforce their laws. The practical aspect of such a role lies in the effect of state action which may transcend internationally recognized limits (see in this respect Chapter III concerning unlawful seizure of persons for the effects of improperly secured jurisdiction).

The very purpose of jurisdictional power is to the ability to enforce and therefore an illustrative case is In re Lo Dolce.[6] In this case, Sergeant Lo Dolce and Major Holohan were United States OSS military personnel and were parachuted behind German lines in Italy in 1944. Major Holohan was reported by Sergeant

Lo Dolce as killed in action, but the money which the Major carried to finance partisan operations in Italy was never recovered. After the war ended, it was alleged that the Sergeant had killed him. Lo Dolce, who returned to live in New York, could not be charged under the Uniform Code of Military Justice because he was no longer subject to its jurisdiction. [7] He could not be tried in the United States because the alleged crime had not been committed within the territorial jurisdiction of the United States. The United States did not rely on the application of any other doctrine or theory of jurisdiction except the territorial principle, and, therefore, Lo Dolce could only be tried where the alleged crime took place. The Italian authorities, therefore, requested the extradition of Lo Dolce in 1952 pursuant to the Treaty of 1869 then in force between Italy and the United States. The court recognized the criminality of the acts charged and that they fell under the treaty provisions but that Italy had no jurisdiction because the territory wherein the alleged crime took place was then under the control of the German forces which occupied it and, therefore, Italy at that time exercised no dominion and control over that territory and, therefore, Italy had no "jurisdiction" over that territory at that time the alleged crime was committed. Consequently, Italy could not be granted the surrender of Lo Dolce since he was not amenable to Italian jurisdiction when he allegedly committed the crime. If Germany would have attempted to extradite Lo Dolce it probably would not have succeeded either since it would likely have been argued *inter alia* that it had no present jurisdiction to enforce any laws upon which it would have

relied upon at that time. It is also doubtful that German laws
would have made the killing of an enemy office a crime, but if
they held the act not to be part of the war or as justified by
military laws and international rules of armed conflicts, they
could have prosecuted him. The question of dominion and control
as a basis for territorial jurisdiction was also in part relied
upon in the denial of the surrender of one Artukovic to Yugoslavia
for alleged crimes committed in that country during World War II. [8]
The territorial principle has several extensions and applications
which will be discussed below.

1.1 *Special Status Territories*

The term "territory" is often a dependable variable of the notion
of jurisdiction, i.e., the power to exercise dominion and control
over a determinable physical area. Consequently, this power to
exercise jurisdiction will extend to certain various territories
whose legal status may vary. Such is the case of certain territories which by reason of exceptional circumstances or special
conditions are called "Special Status Territories." A factor
common to all cases of "Special Status Territories" is that the
area over which the jurisdictional control of one state extends
is usually excepted from that of another state's control either
in whole or in part and varying in extent and duration because
of peculiar circumstances such as military occupation, treaty
or other arrangements. The term "Special Status Territories,"
therefore, does not include "Special Environments" (discussed
below in 1.4).

Section 3185 of Title 18, United States Code, makes provision for the return from the United States to "any foreign country or territory or any part thereof" occupied by or under the control of the United States of any person found in the United States who is charged with cimmitting any of certain enumerated offenses in violation of the "criminal laws in force" in such country or territory on the written requisition of "the military governor or other chief executive office in control of such foreign country or territory." Provision is made for proceedings "before a judge of the courts of the United States only, who shall hold such person on evidence establishing probable cause that he is guilty of the offense charged" and that the person so held shall be returned "on the order of the Secretary of State of the United States."

The application of this authority extended to occupied zones in Germany. In the case of In re Kraussman [9] the court stated:

> . . . The question which presents itself here is whether or not this right of the courts to continue to function in the heart of a foreign nation whose sovereignty has been restored, is occupation or control of part of that country by the United States within the intent and purpose of the extradition statute, Section 3185. I do not think so. The occupation and control mentioned in the statute refers to full governmental authority based upon a dominating police or military force which makes the authority effective, . . . The United States

High Commission is not now in the words of the
statute the "chief executive officer in control
of such foreign country."

Although the treaty excludes Berlin and Germany
as a whole, the fair implication to be drawn
from this exclusion is that the retention of
powers by the signatories is principally for
the purpose of dealing with the Soviet Republics
relative to the reunification of Germany and a
peace treaty, and that, in so far as it is
practically possible, local governmental authority
will be turned over to the Federal Republic of
Germany as soon as and to the extent that it si
feasible. The Government has offered no proof
that the situation in the American Sector of
Berlin is factually different from this. Therefore,
in the face of a retention of joint over-all power
de jure and a policy de facto to turn over to the
Federal Republic of Germany as much of the administration of local government as possible, it
cannot be said that the situation is one which
comes within Section 3185. [10]

Whenever there is jurisdiction over a military base or
territory, the state having such authority cannot only prosecute
the violator, repatriate him to the mother country for trial
but can, if he excapes to another state, seek his extradition
by treaty or comity. [11] In addition to military occupation,

territories may be leased by agreement whether for military or non-military purposes and such an agreement may have an extra-territorial clause or a special jurisdiction clause permitting the lessee-state to exercise jurisdiction over the leased terr-itory, completely, partially, concurrently or with respect to its nationals only. Such an example is the Guantanamo base. Article IV of the Lease Agreement signed on July 2, 1903, by the United States and Cuba, under which the United States was granted the right to establish and maintain a naval station at Guantanamo, provides:

> Futitives from justice charged with crimes or
> misdemeanors amenable to Cuban law, taking
> refuge within said areas, shall be delivered up
> by the United States authorities on demand by
> duly authorized Cuban authorities.
>
> On the other hand the Republic of Cuba agrees
> that fugitives from justice charges with crimes
> or misdemeanors amenable to United States law,
> committed within said areas, taking refuge in
> Cuban territory, shall on demand, be delivered
> up to duly authorized United States authorities. [12]

The same basis for jurisdiction, established by the treaty, exist between the United States and the Philippines in the Mili-tary Bases Agreement of 1947. This treaty contains provisions regarding jurisdiction over offenses and the delivery of fugitives to the authorities having jurisdiction over the particular offen-ses. Article XIII, Paragraph 7 of the Military Bases Agreement of 1947 between the United States and the Philippines provides that:

> 7. The United States agrees that it will not grant
> asylum in any of the bases to any person fleeing
> from the lawful jurisdiction of the Philippines.
> Should any such person be found in any base, he
> will be surrendered on demand to the competent
> authorities of the Philippines. [13]

Even though the state enjoying special status rights over a given territory can exercise its jurisdiction within the framework of the existing agreement between the respective states, it does not have to exercise it. In the case of <u>Wilson v. Girard</u>, [14] the Supreme Court recognized the right of the United States acting through its agents to waive jurisdiction over an American citizen and relinquish it to Japan even though the territory wherein the crime was committed was a United States military installation which by treaty was excepted from Japan's territorial surisdiction. The District Court held that since Girard's act was committed in the performance of official duty he was, under United States law, "accountable only to United States federal jurisdiction" and his delivery to the Japanese authorities would be "illegal and in violation of the Constitution and laws of the United States." [15]

However, the Supreme Court of the United States, noting that "a sovereign nation has exclusive jurisdiction to punish offenses against its laws committed within its borders, unless it expressly or impliedly consents to surrender its jurisdiction," reversed the judgment of the District Court stating:

> The issue for our decision is, therefore, narrowed
> to the question whether, upon the record before us,
> the Constitution or legislation subsequent to the
> Security Treaty prohibited the carrying out of this
> provision authorized by the Treaty for waiver of
> the qualified jurisdiction granted by Japan. We
> find no constitutional or statutory barrier to the
> provision as applied here. In the absence of such
> encroachments, the wisdom of the arrangement is
> exclusively for the determination of the Executive
> and Legislative Branches. [16]

The _Girard_ case arose under a special agreement with Japan,
namely the Security Treaty of 1952; however, the problems raised
in that case are no different from those of Status of Forces
Agreements, whether _N.A.T.O._ or _S.O.F.A._ as examples of multilateral agreements or other bilateral ones.

As to _N.A.T.O._, the North Atlantic Treaty of April 4, 1949,
states: "considering that the forces of one Party may be sent,
by arrangement, to serve in the territory of another Party,"
the parties agreed in Article VII of the Status of Forces Agreement of June 19, 1951, that:

> 5.--(a) The authorities of the receiving and sending
> States shall assist each other in the arrest of
> members of a force or civilian component or their
> dependents in the territory of the receiving State
> and in handing them over to the authority which is

to exercise jurisdiction in accordance with the
above provisions. [17]

1.2 *Subjective-Objective Territorial Theory*

Traditional Anglo-American practice has followed the general principle of territorial jurisdiction [18] with respect to both nationals
and aliens who have violated federal or state law even when all
or part of the acts were committed outside its territory [19] provided its effects were within the territory. The fact that a
crime was not entirely consummated within the state's territory
or that the preparation for or effects of the crime occurred in
another state, does not prevent the territorial state where some
of the acts or results occurred from asserting jurisdiction. [20]
These extensions of the territorial principle have been such
that it is often difficult to distinguish between cases relying
on their theory and other theories such as the protected interest
or nationality. United States courts have freely extended the
territorial principle in many cases to where it would have
appeared that another theory would be more appropriate. Among
such cases are those in which United States citizens have committed violations of the United State's law outside of United
States territory but having an effect within the United States.
Usually, these cases have involved acts detrimental to United
States national security [21] or economic interests [22] as well as
other categories of violative conduct. [23] The fact remains that
in these cases the more appropriate theory would be nationality
or protected interest and not territoriality.

217

Where aliens have been involved both United States and English courts have expanded the traditional application of the territorial principle, generally through the use of what may be referred to as the subjective-objective territorial theory. This theory is better described as an extension of the territorial theory rather than as a separate one. Under it, aliens acting outside territorial boundaries are considered as having committed crimes within the state if the offense has a certain impact within the territory of the state. Under the subjective-objective territorial theory, the important factor is that the effect of the crime occurred within the territory of the rule-enforcing state. That state would have objective territorial jurisdiction. The state from which the acts were committed would have subjective territorial jurisdiction. This principle has been recognized, although not under the nomenclature, by the *Restatement on Foreign Relations Law of the United States*, [24] and has been relied upon in some cases, such as violations of prohibition laws. [25] English and other Commonwealth courts have extended its application to cases involving national security [26] and other matters. [27]

Whenever courts are faced with the problem of acts committed outside the jurisdiction but having effects within it, the perpetrator is deemed constructively present in the state where the effects of the conduct took place and which requests that actor's delivery.

The case which seems to be relied upon most frequently in the United States is <u>Strassheim v. Daily</u>, [28] wherein the Supreme Court held that:

Acts done outside a jurisdiction, but intended to
produce and producing detrimental effects within
it justified a State in punishing the offender if
the State should succeed in getting him within its
power. [30]

As early as 1798 the Attorney General indicated that a person
charged with piracy on the high seas should be tried in the United
States and not extradited to England. [31] A different rationale
was relied upon in Sternaman v. Peck [32] which involved the extradition of a wife who had poisoned her husband in New York and the
ensuing death occurred in Canada. On rehearing, the argument was
raised that if a crime had been committed it was not within the
territory of Canada, but the court rejected it by citing cases
where the jurisdiction had been upheld although the crime had
been commenced in another district. [33] No attempt was made to
determine whether the crime had been perpetrated solely within
the territory of Canada. In fact, the court seems to have relied
upon the assistance of concurrent jurisdictions in the United
States and Canada. [34] Two other cases from the Ninth Circuit [35]
Ex Parte Davis and Hammond v. Sittel permitted extradition on a
non-territorial jurisdiction theory. In one case the requesting
state had jurisdiction on the subjective territorial principle
while the requested state had objective territorial jurisdiction.
The court rested its decision in both instances on the grounds
that the necessary elements to complete the offense were consummated in the requesting state. The first of these cases Ex Parte
Davis, involved the murder of one who had been fatally wounded in

Mexico but died in California. The argument was made that the offense was not complete until the death of the victim occurred, which was in California. The reasoning of the court in dismissing this contention centered on the language of the treaty requiring that the crime be committed within the jurisdiction of Mexico. Since the petitioner had done all the acts necessary for the commission of the offense within Mexico, the treaty requirement was satisfied and extradition could be granted. [36] This factual situation and the jurisdictional theory of the requesting state is the opposite of that found in Sternaman (discussed above) -- the United States having "subjective" territorial jurisdiction in Sternaman and "objective" territorial jurisdiction in Davis. Despite the difference in jurisdictional bases, the Davis court failed to distinguish between the cases and employed reasoning in support of its decision which conceivably would require an opposite result in Sternaman. In Sternaman the jurisdiction of Canada was determined by reference to United States and Canadian principles of jurisdiction, [37] while in Davis the court looked exclusively to the language of the treaty. [38]

In the second of these cases, Hammond v. Sittel, [39]= the accused forged a check drawn on a Canadian bank which was deposited in his account in California. The court determined jurisdiction by looking to where the crime was completed and concluded that Canada had exclusive jurisdiction despite the fact that the opinion relied to some extent on authorities enunciating the broad application of the "objective" principle.

The Court of Appeals in that case relied on a decision of the

Supreme Court to the effect that one who outside of a state willfully puts in motion factors to take effect in that state is an-
swerable at the place where the harm is done and that this principle is recognized in the criminal jurisprudence of all countries
and stated:

> . . . The Supreme Court in the decision from which we
>
> have quoted (Ford v. U.S., 273 U.S. 593 [1926] . . .)
>
> shows the desirability of surrendering a person for
>
> trial who puts in motion forces which operate to con-
>
> summate a crime within the territory of the demanding
>
> nation . . ., and there is no reason to suppose that
>
> the treaty was intended to exclude such a class of
>
> offenders; . . .[40]

These difficulties arise whenever a given conduct deemed criminal
produces its effects at a place other than where the original conduct took place and also whenever the offense is deemed by its
nature or affects to be continuous. The various decisions considered in this area seem to be searching for some definitive
criteria of application for the maxim *lex loci delicti*. But while
cases involving civil responsibility, conflicts of jurisdiction in
criminal cases are less susceptible to flexible rules based on
alternative policy consideration. Nonetheless it seems clear that
judicial decisions are guided by the interest displayed by prosecuting authorities and reject the claims of defendants whenever
the state having concurrent or alternative jurisdiction does not
challenge the jurisdiction of the requesting state.

In <u>Uited States ex rel. Eatessam v. Marasco</u> [41] an Israeli citizen obtained a loan in New York from a bank in Switzerland on the basis of forged securities given as collateral. The court, in holding that a crime had been committed within the territorial jurisdiction of Switzerland, interpreted the relevant treaty to allow extradition "whenever the extraditee is shown *prima facie* to have intended the harm and caused the harm to the demanding state substantially as claimed by the latter." This rule focuses entirely on the competence of the requesting nation and allows extradition whenever those jurisdictional requirements have been met. The court examined the qualifying words of the treaty with Switzerland which require that the offense be "committed in the territory of one of the contracting States [and that the offender] be found in the territory of the other State . . ." [42] The limitation that the crime took place within the territory of the requesting state is found in few United States treaties, [43] usually the words used are "jurisdiction" or as in recent conventions, [44] "territorial jurisdiction." The Italian Supreme Court (Corte Suprema di Cassazione) held in 1934, In re Amper that:

> In view of the principles of international cooperation
> for the suppression of crime, the sole duty of the
> Court of the requested State is to determine the sub-
> jective and objective existence of the crime charged
> and to see whether it is extraditable according to
> the principles which rule the relations between the
> two States in the matter of extradition. It cannot
> raise questions of territorial jurisdiction if its
> own jurisdiction is not involved. [45]

In R.v. Godfrey (1923) [46] a person was held to be a fugitive in England when Switzerland sought to have him extradited, although he had not been in Switzerland when the offense was committed. The same result applied to fugitives who had escaped to England but were sought by Germany for fraud committed by them in Holland against persons defrauded in Germany. [47]

In 1954 the French Supreme Court (Cour de Cassation) held that a certain stateless person residing in France should be extradited to Belgium for participation in a fraudulent scheme attempted to be carried out in Belgium by an accomplice in Belgium with the aid of forged documents, although he remained in France. The Court took the view that although his acts were committed in France, they were part of an ensemble of acts over which Belgian courts had jurisdiction. [48]

Decisions in the United States and in other countries do not attempt to ascertain jurisdiction under any particular theory, but rather limit their analysis to the location of the primary effect of the criminal acts. The unfortunate aspect of United States decisions, however, is not that they construe treaties to allow extradition despite concurrent jurisdiction, but their unnecessary emphasis on exclusive jurisdiction.

The theory of subjective-objective territoriality contains an inherent conflict in that it recognizes jurisdiction in more than one state without ranking priorities. The attitude of the judiciary, particularly in the United States, has been to ignore the issue of conflicting concurrent jurisdictions and to pursue a pragmatic course. Under this approach, the state which has physical

custody has *de facto* priority which is not interfered with and,
therefore, only whenever such a state does not exercise its jurisdiction is the issue of conflicts considered. Conflicts of subject matter jurisdiction are ranked so as to give priority to one
or the other prevailing theories of subject matter jurisdiction.
Among these rankings the territorial theory which is universally
recognized is considered as the ranking theory entitled to priority
over any other theory in cases of conflicts. Within.the territorial
theory, the state which has custody of the accused has priority
but this priority does not bar the state having subjective territoriality from prosecuting at a later time. The only restriction
would be that of *non bis in idem* whenever recognized (see Theories
of Defense in Chapter VI).

1.3 Floating Territoriality, the Law of the Flag

It is usually advanced that vessels, aircrafts and spacecrafts
are an extension of the territory and, therefore, the territoriality theory applies to them by extension. This approach can be
argued, if for no other reason than the fact that the object of
the extension, i.e., vessels, aircraft and spacecraft owe their
existence to technology which permitted such objects to utilize
special environments other than land. To that extent the theory
is predicated on a fiction.

Although there are obvious technological differences between
ships, aircrafts and spacecrafts before they reach outer space
and subject to the limitations set forth in 1.3 C below, there
are four factors which are common to all of them and thus permit

their joint treatment in the context of theories of jurisdiction and extradition. They are as follows:

1. Ships, aircrafts and spacecrafts operate in mediums which, with the exception of territorial airspace, the territorial sea and internal waters, are legally beyond the territorial claims of nations;

2. They enable humans to travel with great mobility and speed through these mediums;

3. They are important bases of "power" for states; and

4. They are potential arenas for criminal activities.

It is the last factor which makes ships, aircrafts and spacecrafts relevant to a study of international criminal jurisdiction, and the third factor which makes the study of the principles of international criminal jurisdiction an important concern to states, since whatever occurs on board these power bases may seriously affect the states which own or operate them. To that extent, they are relevant to a study on extradition.

The high seas, while available for use by all states, are not subject to the sovereign claims of any state. [49] The airspace above the high seas is similarly free for use by all states and is not subject to national appropriation or claim of sovereignty. A coastal state, however, in addition to claiming sovereignty over its internal waters (which all states may do), may claim a territorial sea, extending no more than twelve miles (with some exceptions) from its coastline, over which it may claim complete sovereignty, subject only to the right of innocent passage of the

ships of other states. [50] The airspace above the territorial sea
is also subject to the sovereign claims of the coastal state, [51]
but there is no corresponding right of innocent passage for aircraft. This difference in legal status is rooted in the technological fact that aircraft, being usually smaller, faster and more
maneuverable than ships, are a greater potential threat to the
security of states. [52] The airspace superjacent to a state's
land territory and internal waters, of course, is also subject to
the complete and exclusive sovereignty of the subjacent state. [53]
As with airspace over the territorial sea, there is no right of
innocent passage. Any such rights of passage must be acquired by
agreement between states. These are the basic rules of international law governing the legal status of the high seas and atmosphere of the planet earth.

The legal status of outer space is not subject to any claims of
sovereignty. This rule, developed out of United Nations resolutions, but then become part of conventional and customary international law, [54] both primary sources of international law. [55]
As of yet, there has been no agreement or decision on the separation of national airspace from outer space, although there are
some indications as to where such a dividing line should be
placed. [56]

The use of the term ("floating territory") to describe ships,
aircraft and spacecraft is, of course, an unnecessary fiction, [57]
since many difficulties arise when the territorial principle is
extended to justify jurisdiction over anything other than actual
land area. The four factors listed above are preferable for

226

analysis purposes than the term "floating territory," because they
expressly recognize, without the use of fictions, the uniqueness
of these power bases and consequently their importance to the
states. Another term employed to describe their theory is the
"law of the flag" which considers ships, aircraft and spacecraft
as territory proper because their capability of acquiring nationality, which is manifested by appropriate identifying colors, in-
signia or flag.

As a result of the carrier, nationality States have a certain
competence to prescribe and enforce rules of conduct governing all
persons aboard ships and aircrafts of their nationalities, even
when the jurisdiction of authority are within areas subject to
the territorial states. [58] This competence, however, is exclusive
when a ship is on the high seas. Skiriotes v. Florida, the Supreme
Court said that "[t]he United States is not debarred by any rule
of international law from governing the conduct of its own citizens upon the high seas or even in foreign countries when the
rights of other nations or their nationals are not infringed.
With respect to such an exercise of authority there is no question
of international law, but solely of the purport of the municipal
law which establishes the duty of the citizen in relation to his
own government." [59]

An example of such exercise of jurisdiction is the case of
United States v. Flores, in which a United States citizen was
indicted for the murder of another United States citizen aboard
an American vessel which, at the time of the offense, was anchored
in the Port of Matadi, in the Belgian Congo (at that time subject

227

to the sovereignty of the Kingdom of Belgium), about 250 miles inland from the mouth of the Congo River. The United States Supreme Court overruled the lower court decision that the place where the offense was committed was not within the admiralty and maritime jurisdiction of the United States:

"It is true that the criminal jurisdiction of the United States is in general based upon the territorial principle, and criminal statutes of the United States are not by implication given an extraterritorial effect. United States v. Bowman, 2 at 98; compare, Blackmer v. United States, supra, note 23. But that principle has never been thought to be applicable to a merchant vessel which, for purposes of the jurisdiction of the courts of the sovereignty whose flag it flies to punish crimes committed upon it, is deemed to be a part of the territory of that sovereignty, and not to lose that character when in navigable waters within the territorial limits of another sovereignty . . . Subject to the right of the territorial sovereignty to assert jurisdiction over offenses disturbing the peace of the port, it has been supported by writers on international law, and has been recognized by France, Belgium and other continental countries as well as by England and the United States." [60]

Excluding international custom, [61] the most definitive statement of the international law relating to the high seas is found in the 1958 Convention on the High Seas. After stating the basic right of states, both coastal and noncoastal, to operate ships under their respective flags on the high seas, [62] the Treaty provides that "(s)hips have the nationality of the State whose flag they are entitled to fly," but "(t)here must exist a genuine link between the State and the ship; in particular, the State must effectively exercise its jurisdiction and control in administrative, technical and social matters over ships flying its flag." [63] Article 6 of the Treaty states that ships can be under the flag of only one state and may not change flags during a voyage or while in a port of call, unless there is a real transfer of ownership or change of registry. Except as expressly provided for in the High Seas Treaty or other international treaties, the flag state has exclusive jurisdiction over the ship. [64] Warships and ships used only in governmental noncommercial service have "complete immunity from the jurisdiction of any State other than the flag State." [65]

When a ship is within a foreign state's territorial sea or inland waters, however, the competence of the flag state to prescribe and enforce rules of conduct on board is less complete than when the ship is on the high seas. The flag state, instead of having exclusive jurisdiction, usually has concurrent jurisdiction with the coastal (territorial) state.

Regarding merchant ships and governmental ships operated for commercial purposes, "(t)he criminal jurisdiction of the coastal State should not be exercised on board a foreign ship passing through the territorial sea to arrest any person or conduct any investigation in connection with any crime committed on board the ship during its passage, save only in the following cases:

"(a) If the consequences of the crime extend to the coastal State; or

(b) If the crime is of a kind to disturb the peace of the country or the order of the territorial sea; or

(c) If the assistance of the local authorities has been requested by the captain of the ship or by the consul of the country whose flag the ship flies;

(d) If it is necessary for the suppression of illicit traffic in narcotic drugs." [66]

It has not been established, however, whether international law prohibits a coastal state from exercising its jurisdiction over situations not provided for in Article 19(1) (a-d) of the Territorial Sea Treaty, since the provision is only that a coastal state "should not" exercise its jurisdiction over merchant ships and governmental ships operated for commercial purposes. Generally, however, it can be said that the coastal state may exercise criminal jurisdiction in matters which affect the "peace of the port," an imprecise therm which should be adequately provided for by Article 19(1) (a-d), but which may be extended further.

An example of the type of situation which may fall under the "peace of the port" doctrine is Wildenhus' Case, [67] in which a Belgian national killed another Belgian national below the deck

of a Belgian vessel on which they were both crew members. At the
time of the offense the ship was moored to a dock in Jersey City.
Wildenhus was arrested by local police authorities and appropriately charged. The Belgian consul applied for a writ of habeus
corpus, based upon a treaty between Belgium and the United States
which provided, in particular, that in regard to disorders aboard
merchant vessels "(t)he local authorities shall not interfere,
except when the disorder that has arisen is of such a nature as
to distrub tranquility and public order on shore, or in the port,
or when a person of the country or not belonging to the crew,
shall be concerned therein." [68]

The Supreme Court, after discussing cases which had been heard
before French tribunals under a previous treaty on the subject
between the United States and France, held that the local court
properly exercised jurisdiction over the case:

> "Disorders which distrub only the peace of the ship
> or those on board are to be dealt with exclusively
> by the sovereign of the home of the ship, but those
> which disturb the public peace may be suppressed,
> and, if need be, the offenders punished by the
> proper authorities of the local jurisdiction. It
> may not be easy at all times to determine to which
> of the two jurisdictions a particular act of dis-
> order belongs. Much will undoubtedly depend on
> the attending circumstances of the particular case,
> but all must concede that felonious homocide is a
> subject for the local jurisdiction and that if the

231

proper authorities are proceeding with the case in
a regular way, the consul has no right to interfere to prevent it." [69]

For determining whether a crime committed on board a ship disturbs the "peace of the port" of the coastal state, the Wildenhus'
Case quotes from a French case which states the following:

"Considering that every state is interested in the
repression of crimes and offenses that may be committed in the ports of its territory, not only by
the men of the ship's company of a foreign merchant
vessel towards men not forming part of that company,
but even by men of the ship's company among themselves, whenever the act is of a nature to compromise the tranquility of the port or the intervention
of the local authority is invoked or the act constitutes a crime by common law (droit commun, the
law common to all civilized nations) the gravity of
which does not permit any nation to leave it unpun-
ished, without impugning its rights of jurisdictional
and territorial sovereignty, because that crime is
in itself the most manifest as well as the most
flagrant violation of the laws which it is the
duty of every nation to cause to be respected in
all parts of its territory. 120 U.S. 1, 19 (foot-
note omitted) (1887), citing 1 Ortolan Diplomatic
de la Mer (4th ed. 455, 456, 1859). [70]

The above provisions do not affect the right of a coastal state

232

"to take any steps authorized by its laws" for the purpose of
conducting an arrest or an investigation on board a foreign ship
passing through the coastal state's territorial sea after leaving
its internal waters. [71] In this way, the coastal State retains
complete jurisdiction, not subject to the suggested general rule
of Article 19(1), to prescribe and enforce rules governing events
taking place either on board the foreign ship or on land while
the ship was in the coastal state's internal waters. If the
alleged crime or offense took place on board the foreign ship
before it entered the coastal state's territorial sea, however,
the coastal state is prohibited from taking any steps on board
the ship to arrest any person or conduct any investigation if the
ship is only passing through the territorial sea without entering
internal waters. [72] This distinction between the interest of a
state with regard to its territorial sea, on the one hand, and
its internal waters, on the other, is no doubt a realization of
the fact that when a foreign ship is in the internal waters of
a coastal state, it will probably dock at some time during the
duration of the visit, in which case the crew and, perhaps, the
passengers of the ship may go ashore where they may come in contact with the nationals of the coastal state. If any of these
interactions are criminal or even tortious in nature, the coastal
state may exercise jurisdiction even though the ship has left
the port and is passing through the territorial sea on its way
to the high seas.

Courts in extradition matters rely on the convenient fiction
that a vessel is an extension of the physical territory of a

state and, therefore, within the scope of all municipal legal provisions applicable to territory. Nonetheless the relationship between territory and jurisdiction is often at issue in extradition cases.

In R. v. Governor of H. M. Prison, Brixton, ex parte Minervini, [73] wherein in 1958 Norway requested the extradition from Great Britain of Onafrio Minervini, an Italian citizen, charged with the murder of a fellow seaman on board a Norwegian flag vessel. No specific evidence as to the geographic position of the vessel at the time of the alleged murder was submitted although it appeared that the vessel was some six days steaming from port. After his commitment for surrender by the British extradition magistrate, Minervini applied for writ of habeus corpus alleging inter alia, that the case did not come within the provisions of the Extradition Treaty of 1873 between Great Britain and Norway (63 Br. & For. St. Paps. 175) since the offense was not, in the words of Article I of the Treaty, "committed in the territory" of the requesting State. The Queen's Bench Division rejected this contention andheld that the petition should be denied stating:

> . . . This treaty is not treating "territory" in
> its strict sense but in a sense which is equivalent
> to jurisdiction, and it is only in that way that
> one can make sense of the treaty. Indeed, it is
> to be observed, though it may be said to be an
> argument the other way, that in many of these
> treaties reference is made not to territory but

to jurisdiction, but in my view in this treaty
territory is equivalent to jurisdiction . . .
The second way in which the applicant puts the
case is this: Assuming that he is wrong and that
"territory" must be given more than its ordinary
meaning, yet it is impossible to say that it
covers a ship at sea when it is within the territorial waters of a third Power because he says
that that would be a gross breach of international
comith; it would not only be legislating in respect of foreign territory, but also would be
assuming something which was within that territory
to be the territory of another foreign country.
In my view, it is quite unnecessary here to consider what is the true position of a ship, whether
the country whose flag is flown merely has jurisdiction over the ship and those on board or whether
it is to be treated for certain purposes as the
territory of that Power; because if I am right
in saying that "territory" in Article 1 of the
treaty is equivalent to "jurisdiction," then
assuming that the ship was at the time of the
alleged murder within the territory of a foreign
Power, it would be only a matter of competing
jurisdiction and no one suggests that it is wrong
to legislate to provide for competing or concurrent
jurisdiction. Accordingly, it seems to me that it

235

matters not in this case whether the ship was in the
middle of the North Sea, in the territorial waters
of Norway, in the territorial waters of this country
or in the territorial waters of any other Power; the
Norwegian government had jurisdiction and that is
sufficient to enable these proceedings to be brought.
Accordingly, it was unnecessary for any evidence to
be tendered before the chief magiastrate to show
the position of the vessel and he had jurisdiction
to make the order which he did . . . [74]

The Lord Chief Justice in the _Minervini_ case dismissed the application and held that the word "territory" in the Extradition
Treaty was synonymous with "jurisdiction," as the treaty was
not connected with territory in its strict sense but in a sense
which was equivalent to jurisdiction because the list of crimes
in the treaty included "assaults on board a ship on the high seas"
and other offenses occurring on the high seas. The same question
was at issue in _Wilheim Wolthusen v. Starl_ before the Supreme
Court of Argentina in 1926. [75] The United States requested extradition from Argentina of an individual charged with having committed larceny on board an American merchant vessel while the
vessel was moored in the harbor of Rio de Janeiro. The Extradition Convention of 1896 between the United States and Argentina
(U.S. TS 6; 31 Stat. 1883) provides for the extradition of persons accused of crimes "committed, in the territory of one of
the high contracting parties." The accused contended that the
United States had no jurisdiction, the act having been committed

in the territorial waters of Brazil. The Supreme Court of Argentina, noting that in the present case the crime, although taking place in the jurisdictional waters of Brazil, injured only the rights and interests secured by the laws of the United States, held that extradition should be granted. The Court stated that according to the principles of international law, "territory" meant not only the area within the limits of a State but also all other places subject to the sovereignty and jurisdiction of that State and with reference to the Treaty of 1896 comprised merchant or war vessels under the flag of the State as well as the house of a diplomatic agent of that State. The Supreme Court of Argentina held:

> [T]hat the term territory in the clause of the
> treaty in question includes, for the purpose of
> extradition, crimes committed on the high seas
> on board merchant or war vessels carrying the
> Argentine or United States flag; crimes committed
> on war vessels of both nations and in the house
> of a diplomatic agent of either of the countries. [76]

Both the *Harvard Draft Convention* and the *Restatement* recognize the jurisdiction of a state to prescribe and enforce rules of conduct for all persons aboard aircraft having its nationality, whether the aircraft is over the high seas or within the territorial jurisdiction of another state.

Unlike ships, there is no right of "innocent passage" for aircraft through the airspace above a foreign state's fixed territory, internal waters and territorial sea. It is, therefore, reasonably expected that the competence of the subjacent state includes the power to prescribe and enforce rules governing criminal activities in foreign aircraft and would be more complete than with respect to foreign ships in its territorial sea. The actual practices of states with respect to crimes and other offenses committed on board aircrafts of their own nationalities outside of their territorial borders, however, have been at times unusual and indicate, at least insofar as states dedicated to a strict interpretation of the territorial principle are concerned, a reluctance to exercise jurisdiction in the absence of express and specific legislative authorization.

In United States v. Cordova, [77] the defendant, Cordova, a Puerto Rican passenger on an American aircraft, which at the time was over the high seas somewhere between San Juan, Puerto Rico, and New York, assaulted another passenger and members of the crew. He was arrested when the plane arrived at New York and brought to trial. The court found him guilty but refused to convict him due to the absence of federal/jurisdiction, holding that the statutes under which jurisdiction was claimed were applicable only to vessels within the admiralty and maritime jurisdiction of the United States or to certain crimes committed on the high seas and that an airplane was not considered a vessel within the meaning of the statute and the airspace over the high seas was not part of the high seas.

In response to this decision Congress passed the Crimes in Flight Over the High Seas Act, 18 USC §7(5), in 1958 to include within the "special maritime and territorial jurisdiction of the United

States" the following:

> Any aircraft belonging in whole or in part to the
> United States, or any citizen thereof, or to any
> corporation created by or under the laws of the
> United States, or any state, territory, district
> or possession thereof, while such aircraft is in
> flight over the high seas, or over any other waters
> within the admiralty and maritime jurisdiction of
> the United States and out of the jurisdiction of
> any particular state. [78]

The English position is well expressed in <u>Regina v. Martin</u> [79]
wherein the defendants were British nationals and were charged in
1956 with being in unlawful possession of raw opium while aboard
a British aircraft enroute to Singapore from Bahrein. No violation of the law of either state was alleged. Jurisdiction was
claimed under the British Civil Aviation Act, 1949 (12, 13 & 14
Geo. 6, c. 67), 62, which provided, in part, that "(a)ny offense
whatever committed on a British aircraft shall, for the purpose
of conferring jurisdiction be deemed to have been committed in
any place where the offender may for the time being be."

The court stated that it did not have jurisdiction over the
defendants because they were not in England at the time the offense
was committed and the law under which they were indicted did not
apply to acts done on British aircraft outside of England. Section
62 did not create any offenses, but only provided the place where
an act which was already an offense, if committed on a British
aircraft outside of England (which was not the case here), might

239

be tried.

It should be noted, however, that the court did draw a distinction between "universal" offenses, such as murder and theft, which "are not thought of as having territorial limits," and offenses defined as such "only in relation to a particular place," such as the English law in question prohibiting the possession of certain drugs, which was applicable only in England. In regard to latter types of offenses the court said:

> It is most unsatisfactory if there is to be complete
> lawlessness on British aircraft, but on the other
> hand, it can hardly be satisfactory if a foreigner
> traveling from one place to another, thousands of
> miles from England, is to be held liable for in-
> fringing regulations about which he cannot possibly
> have any knowledge at all. [80]

The possibility of concurrent jurisdictional claims, including but not limited to the conflicting principles discussed above [81] caused in part the search for an effective and appropriate convention to clarify the subject. In 1963, the Convention on Offenses and Certain Other Acts Committed on Board Aircraft (hereinafter referred to as the Tokyo Convention) was adopted. [82] The Convention applies to "offenses against penal law" and other "acts which, whether or not they are offenses, may or do jeopardize the safety of the aircraft or of persons or property therein or which jeopardize good order and discipline on board." [83] In general, the Convention applies to offenses or other acts done by a person on board any aircraft registered in a state party to the treaty, "while that aircraft is in flight or on the surface of the high seas or if any area outside the territory of any State." [84] For purposes of the Convention, "an aircraft is considered to be in flight from the moment when power is applied for the purpose of take-off until the moment when the landing run ends." [85] The Convention does not apply to aircraft used in military, customs or police services. [86]

The jurisdiction of states parties to the Convention is set out in Articles 3 and 4. Article 3 reaffirms the law of the flag principle but does not make it exclusive:

1. The State of registration of the aircraft is competent to exercise jurisdiction over offenses and acts committed on board.

2. Each Contracting State shall take such measures as may be necessary to establish its jurisdiction as the State of registration over offenses committed on board aircraft registered in such State.

3. This Convention does not exclude any criminal jurisdiction exercised in accordance with national law.

Article 4 provides certain limitations upon the exercise of concurrent jurisdiction based on other principles, at least insofar as aircraft in flight are concerned:

A Contracting State, which is not the State of registration, may not interfere with an aircraft in flight in order to exercise its criminal

241

jurisdiction over an offense committed on board
except in the following cases:

(a) the offense has effect on the territory
of such State;

(b) the offense has been committed by or
against a national or permanent resident
of such State;

(c) the offense is against the security of
such State;

(d) the offense consists of a breach of any
rules or regulations relating to the
flight or maneuver of aircraft in force
in such State;

(e) the exercise of jurisdiction is necessary
to ensure the observance of any obligation
of such State under a multilateral international agreement.

The Tokyo Convention, therefore, allows states a considerable
latitude of jurisdiction. Other provisions deal with powers of
the aircraft commander, unlawful seizure of aircraft and various
powers and duties of states under the Convention.[87] Conspicuous
by their absence from the Convention are any provisions dealing
with the development of a system of priorities governing the
order in which the several possible principles of criminal jurisdiction, including the law of the flag, can be exercised, the
prevention of double jeopardy and the question of aircraft under
"bare-hull" charter to a national of a state other than the state

of registry. [88]

On December 16, 1970, the Convention for the Suppression of Unlawful Seizure of Aircraft was completed at the Hague. The Convention will be discussed below under the universality principle since it is addressed mainly to the crime of air piracy, rather than to any other common crimes committed on board aircraft, which need not be acts of air piracy.

Notwithstanding the numerous instances of aircraft hijacking, there has been no case known to this writer where extradition under the terms of the Tokyo or Hague Convention was the process by which such an offender was surrendered to the United States for prosecution. [89] In all cases, the hijacker was either returned or surrendered through one of the alternative devices of rendition (see Chapter III); or returned to the United States voluntarily. In several hijacking cases not involving the United States, the offenders were tried by the territorial state and thus extradition had been denied. [90] Even though the universality theory (discussed _infra_ in Section 5) applies, no state other than the flag state or the landing state has ever sought or prosecuted a hijacker under that theory. The greater concern of the drafters of the 1970 Hague Convention was that the "political offense exception" would not be a bar to the extradition of hijackers. This concern did not, however, materialize. The United States, for example, did not request extradition of hijackers from Cuba until 1973 even though a valid treaty existed but no diplomatic relations. [91] In other cases, the offender or offenders have either been prosecuted by the state wherein they landed, left the landing state voluntarily and returned to the flag state or were immediately granted asylum formally or welcomed in such a manner that the flag state did not bother to make any extradition request. This also reveals the cleavage between asylum and extradition as discussed in Chapter II, Section 1.

1.4 Special Environments

This descriptive label covers (a) the Arctic, (b) the Antarctic and (c) outer space. Although there are many different and contrasting environments on earth, only the Arctic and the Antarctic are so unique in terms of their use by people that they require special jurisdictional treatment. As to outer space, it is the most unique and challenging of all environments known to mankind.

A - The Arctic. Legal analysis of the Arctic depends upon an understanding of the basic physical characteristics of the area. The ice covering the Arctic Ocean is not an unbroken extension of the surrounding continents nor is it attached to any continent but exists independently in permanent form. It could conceivably be regarded as falling under the territorial principle if a state could legally claim sovereignty over it under international law. Some early legal writers on the Arctic expressed the opinion that the Arctic could be claimed as such;[92] however, scientific explorations proved that most of the ice is neither permanent nor uniform and that it is actually mobile[93] and that as a result, the Arctic is primarily of a marine character. The advent of the nuclear submarine (which unlike its predecessors does not have to surface periodically to recharge its batteries)

244

has opened the Arctic to underwater navigation. In addition, icebreakers and more recently other ships have demonstrated that the Arctic Ocean is capable of being navigated to some extent.

The Arctic states (United States, Soviet Union, Canada, Norway and Denmark) have indicated that they consider the Arctic Ocean free for use by all states and not subject to the sovereign claims of any states. [94] The pursuance of navigation by these and other states, both on and below the surface of the Arctic Ocean, as well as by aircraft flying over the area and the establishment of research stations on drifting ice islands has indicated that states consider the Arctic region as part of the high seas and not as an area capable of national appropriation. Thus, international freedom of use of the Arctic Ocean has attained the status of international custom as evidenced by a general practice. [95]

Since the Arctic is considered part of the high seas, the territorial principle does not apply except as it might relate to certain parts of the ice cap which are permanent and are attached to land areas or to those areas of the Arctic Ocean claimed by Arctic states as part of their territorial sea. Other principles of international criminal jurisdiction would have to be relied upon in order to assert jurisdiction over a particular criminal act performed or having effects thereon. [96] Due to the fact that most human activities taking place in the Arctic environment are likely to occur aboard a submarine, surface ship or aircraft, the jurisdictional principle most likely to be relied upon is the law of the flag. Activities of a criminal or even tortious nature taking place outside of these power bases can be handled by other principles. [97]

B - _The Antarctic_. The Antarctic mainland was first discovered by Captain Nathaniel Palmer in 1829, but its existence as a continent was established later. Although systematic and extensive scientific exploration of the Antarctic did not begin until the 1930's, the main thrust of activities in the area began with the International Geophysical Year from July, 1957, to December, 1958. [98]

Since the Antarctic is a continent, the territorial principle could apply as a basis for international criminal jurisdiction subject to states making proper legal claims of territorial sovereignty under international law. The 1959 Antarctic Treaty, [99] however, the basic legal document governing the activities of states in Antarctica, provides that "(n)o acts or activities taking place while the present treaty is in force shall constitute a basis for asserting, supporting or denying a claim to territorial sovereignty in Antarctica or create any rights of sovereignty in Antarctica. No new claim or enlargement of an existing claim to territorial sovereignty in Antarctica shall be asserted while the present treaty is in force." [100] Article IV (1) of the treaty provides that:

(n)othing contained in the present treaty shall be interpreted as:

(a) a renunciation by any Contracting Party of previously asserted rights of or claims to territorial sovereignty in Antarctica;

(b) a renunciation or diminution by any Contracting

246

Party of any basis of claim to territorial

sovereignty in Antarctica which it may have

whether as a result of its activities or those

of its nationals in Antarctica or otherwise;

(c) prejudicing the position of any Contracting

Party as regards its recognition or non-

recognition of any other State's right of

or claim or basis of claim to territorial

sovereignty in Antarctica.

Thus, while states may retain any claims acquired prior to the

treaty, they may not make any new claims while the treaty is in

force.[101] THerefore, the territorial principle would not be

applicable to the unclaimed parts of the Antarctic continent.

Other principles of jurisdiction would have to be utilized for

the control of criminal conduct.

Since the high seas within the area south of 60° South Latitude

are not affected by the provisions of the Antarctic Treaty,[102]

criminal jurisdiction for acts committed on board ships or

aircraft on or over the high seas would be within the ambit of

the law of the flag theory.[103] Jurisdiction over criminal

acts committed on the continent or the permanent ice shelves

attached to it is still problematic because the treaty deliber-

ately omits discussion of this aspect. However, observers who

are carrying on inspections under the treaty as designated by

Article VII (1) and scientific personnel exchanged under

Article III (1) (b), as well as staff members accompanying

such persons, are "subject only to the jurisdiction of the Con-

247

tracting Party of which they are nationals in respect of all acts or omissions occurring while they are in Antarctica for the purpose of exercising their functions." [104] Thus, the active personality principle is given exclusive application in specified cases.

With regard to other foreign nationals, the Treaty only provides that "the Contracting Parties concerned in any case of dispute with regard to the exercise of jurisdiction in Antarctica shall immediately consult together with a view to reaching a mutually acceptable solution. [195] In addition, the twelve states who are the original Contracting Parties shall meet periodically to discuss and formulate measures regarding "questions relating to the exercise of jurisdiction in Antarctica." [106]

It can be assumed, therefore, in the absence of any further guidelines drawn up pursuant to the Antarctic Treaty, that states are free to utilize any of the various principles of criminal jurisdiction, with the exception of the territorial principle, unless the act is committed in a previously claimed area. [107] States whose international criminal jurisdiction, as defined by their own municipal law, is based primarily on the territorial principle may have difficulty in finding jurisdiction in some cases. [108] The most applicable principle is probably that of active personality, although it certainly is not to be considered exclusive in application, except where the Treaty so provides. [109]

C - Outer space. The examination of jurisdictional problems of outer space has been placed under the title "special environments," because outer space, like Earth's Polar regions, is alien

248

and hostile to human existence. The analogy, however, should not be carried too far, for although an examination of jurisdictional problems in the Arctic and the Antarctic may be helpful to an understanding of those prpblems in outer space, the vast differences between these environments make any extrapolation of the analogy detrimental to the development of the law of outer space.

Outer space is similar to the Polar regions, in that there can be human activity outside of the power bases (e.g., spacecrafts, ships, etc.), but more so in outer space then outside of ships on the high seas or aircrafts flying through the atmosphere. People can function in spacesuits outside of their space vehicles and, eventually, will be able to do so upon the surfaces of other celestial bodies, just as they can function outside of shelters in the Arctic and Antarctic if properly clothed.

Since outer space, like the high seas or the airspace over the high seas, is not subject to claim of sovereignty, no state should be able to claim jurisdiction under the territorial principle. [110] Also, since the very nature of outer space confines most human activities to the interior of spacecrafts, it can be expected that the dominant jurisdictional principle in outer space, at least for the near future, will be the law of the flag.

Article VIII of the 1967 Space Treaty provides that a State Party to the Treaty on whose registry an object launched into outer space is carried shall retain jurisdiction and control over such object, and over any personnel thereof, while in outer space or on a celestial

body. Ownership of objects launched into
outer space, including objects landed or constructed on a celestial body, and of their
component parts, is not affected by their
presence in outer space or on a celestial
body or by their return to the Earth . . . [111]

This provision gives states of registry (flag states) authority
to prescribe and enforce rules of conduct governing both criminal
and non-criminal matters on board spacecrafts of all types while
in outer space, whether a spacecraft is traveling through outer
space, orbiting a celestial body, or resting upon or in a celestial
body. The same competence appears to extend to activities outside
a spacecraft, whether in outer space or on or under the surafce
of a celestial body, since the article states that jurisdiction
and control applies to the object and "any personnel thereof,"
without requiring that the personnel actually be inside the spacecraft. [112] Activities inside of research stations or other dwell-
ings of a permanent or semi-permanent nature, which rest on or
beneath the surfaces of celestial bodies and are not capable of
either landing or taking off themselves, and which may be constructed with components brought to the celestial body by spacecraft, would also be included within Article VIII, since the ownership of objects "landed or constructed on a celestial body, and
of their component parts, is not affected by their presence in
outer space or on a celestial body . . . ."

Although there is no recorded case or instance of extradition
for a crime committed in any one of these special environments,

250

crimes have been committed as between nationals and prosecution of such offenses has invariably been on one of the several other theories discussed in this chapter. The United States in its dogged instance on the territoriality theory applied the flag or floating territoriality theory to the only case reported which took place near the Arctic Circle. [113]

2. The Active Personality (Nationality) Theory

The active personality or nationality theory, like the territorial principle, is based upon state sovereignty, one facet of which is that nationals of a state are entitled to the state's protection even when they are outside its territorial boundaries. [114] Along with the right to his state's protection, a national has a corresponding duty to obey those national laws which are recognized as having an extraterritorial affect. [115] Such laws usually pertain to the duty of allegiance which some states have even found to apply to citizens and aliens as well. [116] Although such extensions of the active personality principle are based upon a constructive allegiance, they are no doubt tenuous at best and do not enjoy general acceptance in international law.

The active personality theory is universally accepted, although its precise definition and application differs widely. The Harvard Research reviewed the various legislative enactments of states implementing this principle, classified them into five basic types, according to the offenses proscribed, namely:

1-Those statutes which made all offenses punishable;

2-Those statutes which made only those offenses
   punishable which were also punishable by the
   lex loci delicti;
3-Those statutes which made all offenses of a
   certain degree punishable;
4-Those statutes which made only those offenses
   committed against co-nationals punishable; and
5-Those statutes which made only certain enumerated
   offenses punishable. [117]

Some states have given the theory even more extensive application, such as to prosecute those individuals who were not nationals at the time the offense was committed, but who later became nationals. [118] In this manner these penal laws are retroactive and in the opinion of this writer in violation of the principles of legality embodied in the prohibition against *ex post facto*. [119] Such an application of the active personality theory can result in an injustice to the defendant, particularly with regard to double jeopardy (discussed *infra* in Chapter VI, Section 4.2). International law, however, does not clearly prohibit such an exercise of jurisdictional authority since there is no principle of international law forbidding a state to exercise jurisdiction over its nationals even when abroad. [120]

A state may enforce its penal laws against its nationals even when the conduct charged as criminal was committed in a foreign jurisdiction. So far there is no international law rule prohibiting such an exercise of jurisdictional authority by a sovereign over its nationals. There appears to be no "human rights" pro-

252

tection against it other than the *rule ne bis in idem* whenever
applicable.

The question of whether such a theory will be given recognition
by a state other than the state of nationality who is seeking to
enforce its penal laws extraterritorially is when an extradition
request is lodged. In that case, the requested state would have
to decide whether the requesting state has subject matter jurisdiction over a crime allegedly committed in another state. That
other state could well be the requested state, in which case it
will have to decide whether it wishes to waive jurisdiction over
such the relator. In the event it does not waive jurisdiction,
it will have precedence because it would be relying on the territoriality principle. In the event the alleged offense was
committed in a state other than the requested state, an issue
would arise whenever that state would also request the extradition of that same relator. In this case also, priority will be
given to the state claiming territorial jurisdiction. It is
obvious that the problems of enforcing penal laws extraterritorially on the sole basis of the nationality of the alleged offender
are essentially conflicts of laws. In addition, however, they
place a burden on every national when abroad in that such a person
would fall under the sway of two penal legislations. The application of such a theory falls in four categories:

1. Laws pertaining to allegiance, national duties
    and obligations arising out of the bond of
    nationality (e.g., treason) 121

2. Common crimes which even if committed abroad

have an effect upon internal public order
(e.g., fraud).[122]

3. Common crimes committed abroad which have
a bearing upon the nationality state's outlook upon the individual (e.g., revocation
of probation).[123]

4. The prosecution of common crimes committed
abroad is a substitute to extradition of
nationals. [124]

The first category has received recognition in extradition law
as a valid basis for a request, but its application is limited
by reason of the "political offense exception" discussed in
Chapter VI. The second category could fall in the subjective
territorial theory and as such presents no difficulties other
than in cases of multiple requests and the establishment of
priority in granting extradition. The third category is applied
without difficulty because the extradition request would be based
on a penal judgment concerning another factual situation, but
wherein the offender was conditionally released. The offense
committed abroad, which the nationality state is taking cognizance
of, is only relied upon by that state to revoke the conditional
release. Considerations of such revocation are not within the
examining prerogative of the requested state and, therefore, this
instance would present no conflict of laws problems/ The fourth
category is the appropriate measure to be taken by a state which
prohibits extradition of its nationals. It is the proper application of the maxim *aut dedere aut judicare*. Such a measure

avoids the problems of non-prosecution of offenders because of their nationality and thus promote the preservation of minimum world order as discussed in Chapter I of this book. In this category the state of nationality, which becomes the prosecuting state, may require that the offense be prosecutable under the laws of the state wherein it was committed as well as under its laws.[125] This requirement of "double criminality" is one of the conditions for granting extradition and it is, therefore, important that it be applied to a procedure which is intended to be a substitute for extradition.

3. *The Passive Personality Theory*

This theory complements the active personality theory. While the exercise of the active personality theory insures nationals of a given state who have committed offenses abroad will be brought to justice, the passive personality theory insures that a state's interest in the welfare of its nationals abroad will be also protected. Since the ultimate welfare of the state itself depends upon the welfare of its nationals, it can be asserted that a state has a legitimate interest in punishing those who have been found guilty of committing crimes against its nationals while abroad.

The most famous application of the passive personality theory is undoubtedly the case of the S. S. Lotus,[126] although the decision of the Permanent Court of International Justice was based on other grounds.[127] Other states, however, have enacted statutes based upon this theory.[128] The theory has been expressly repudiated by the Restatement,[129] and it has been criticized by scholars. [130] In addition, the Brussels Convention [131] and the Geneva High Seas Convention of 1958 [132] have prohibited states which are parties to their provisions to rely on this theory to assert their jurisdictional authority. The Harvard Research, while listing the passive personality theory as one of the five general principles of penal jurisdiction in use throughout the world, does not include it in the text of the Draft Convention. [133]

As with the active personality theory, the passive personality one may lead to situations where the accused is exposed to double jeopardy. Nevertheless, the theory is relied upon by a number of states and must continue to be considered applicable in any situation in which its use is not prohibited by international law (e.g., the High Seas Convention of 1958) and in which three conditions are met:

 1-The victim is a national of the forum state (the

  state which either has the defendant in custody

  or is demanding that the state which does have

  custody extradite the defendant to stand trial; and

 2-The defendant is not a national of the forum

  state; and

 3-The offense was not committed within the terr-

  itorial jurisdiction of the forum state except

  when explicitly waived.

This theory was relied upon in part in the prosecution of Adolf Eichmann by Israel under Israeli law (for the discussion of this case, see Chapter III, Section 1) even though there was also sufficient reliance on the universality theory to avoid any

256

legal challenges to Israeli subject matter jurisdiction. In that case, however, extradition was not the mode of securing custody over the accused (see e.g., Chapter III). Many states have statutes authorizing the exercise of extraterritorial jurisdiction by virtue of conferring upon their courts jurisdiction to prosecute for acts which affect the nationals of that state. Such jurisdictional basis is, however, distinguishable from instances where a given conduct committed in a foreign jurisdiction has its effect within the state seeking to apply its laws. This later basis falls within the parameters of the objective-subjective territoriality theory discussed in Section 1 of this chapter. The passive personality theory can also be viewed as part of the protected interest theory discussed in the following section. It is distinguishable, however, in that the object of its protection is the person of nationals of the state regardless of where they may be while the protected interest theory refers to the protection of the state, its economic interest and in general harmful acts committed outside the state's jurisdiction, but which have an effect within the state. To that extent, it also can be seen as in part overlapping with the subjective-objective territoriality theory.

The passive personality theory is the counterpart of the nationality theory. Both indeed rely on nationality as a criterion, but in passive personality it is that of the victim which is relevant while in the nationality theory it is that of the offender. In both theories the state seeking to exert its jurisdiction claims the power to regulate conduct outside its territory: in the nationality theory by having certain limitations or obligations attach to the person at its nationals regardless of where they may be; in the passive personality theory by imposing limitations or obligations on others which respect its nationals regardless of where they may be.

The latest manifestation of the passive personality theory is in an Israeli law of March 21, 1972, amending its penal laws with respect to jurisdiction. Under this law conduct which affects the state (protected interest theory), its economic interests (extended protected interest theory) and is designed to harm its nationals (passive personality) subject any such actor to the jurisdiction of Israeli courts. [134] There has been much confusion over the years about the significance of the Lotus (France v. Turkey) case decided by the P.C.I.J. in 1927 [135] in respect of the passive personality theory. In that case a collision between a French and Turkish vessel resulted in the death and injury of several Turkish nationals and a French officer was prosecuted in Turkey for causing the accident. The P.C.I.J. held that Turkey could prosecute the French officer under its penal laws because the injury had occurred on the Turkish vessel (floating territoriality) and the victims were Turkish nationals (passive personality). The court indicated that the combination of these two jurisdictional theories were an adequate basis under prevailing international law. Thus, the passive personality theory cannot be solely relied upon as the exclusive basis for jursidiction to prescribe or enforce the penal laws of one state over a person whose conduct was performed outside the territory

258

of that state. However, when there is an additional jurisdictional basis the passive personality theory serves to reinforce
the jurisdictional claim of the given state. Furthermore, in
cases of conflict between two states, the one claiming passive
personality as an additional basis is to receive priority in extradition.

4. *The Protected Interest (Protective) Theory*

This is a much broader theory than the passiver personality
theory because it expands the sphere of protection afforded
national interests. It is in effect a long arm theory which
allows a state to overreach beyond its physical boundaries to
protect its interests from harmful effects engaged into abroad.
The protected interest theory allows a state to assert jurisdiction over an alien, whether an individual or jurisdicial entity, acting outside the state's territorial boundaries but in
a manner which threatens significant interests of the state. It
is a recognized theory by both the Harvard Draft Convention [136]
and the Restatement. [137] Both emphasize the potential application of this theory to cases involving counterfeiting of state
documents, by expressly stating in separate provisions that it
applies to such cases, [138] and to cases involving national
security, although each includes a limiting provision, namely:

> 1-The Harvard Draft Convention required that the
>
> alien's act "was not committed in exercise of
>
> a liberty guaranteed the alien by the law of the
>
> place where it was committed, [139] and

2-The Restatement requires that the "conduct is
generally recognized as a crime under the law
of states that have reasonably developed legal
systems." [140]

The Harvard Draft Convention and the Restatement are reflections
of the customs of the United States even though the actual practice differs at times. The protected interest principle is
likely applied by states to any acts committed by aliens which
pose either an actual or potential harm to any vital interest
of that state. The United States for one has not been reluctant
to rely on the protected interest theory, although it usually
does so under the guise of an exception to the territorial principle, rather than considering it a separate theory. [141] The
exceptions to the territorial theory as discussed above may produce the same outcomes as the protected interest theory, the
latter, however, has a much broader potential application as it
allows a state broader latitude in the exercise of extraterritorial
criminal jurisdiction. United States courts have relied on the
protected interest theory in anti-trust cases [142] and to certain
provisions of the Securities Exchange Act to transactions taking
place outside the United States which affect United States interests, provided the transactions involved stock registered and
listed on a United States securities exchange, [143] but such extensions have met with criticism about the propriety of a broad use
of this theory, particularly when it is represented as an extrapolation of the territoriality principle. [144] There is, however,
no general rule of international law which prohibits the application

of this theory on either a restricted or an unlimited basis. [145]
The potential for using this theory in extradition is very vast.
Indeed, if only the authoritative decision making process of a
given participant is without restrictions as to what constitutes
conduct performed outside its boundaries, but having an effect
on its "interests" which it deems itself competent to "protect,"
then almost every form affecting the political and economic
interest of that state could subject any such person to the
jurisdiction of that state. This is the case of the Israeli
law of March 21, 1972, which purports to grant jurisdiction to
its courts to enforce Israeli laws to acts wherever committed
which affect or are destined to affect the security of the state
or its economic interests. The requested state would be confronted with a value judgment made by the requesting state and
no basis to question its merits without challenging that very
judgment. A long arm jurisdictional theory must, therefore,
take into account its potential threat to world public order
and certain well-defined limitations to avoid creating conflict-
collision situations. This explains in fact why the United
States would rather rely on an extrapolation of the territorial
principle, even though at times strained, than explicitly recognize the protected interest theory with all its implications.

5. *The Universality Principle*

All theories previously discussed can be applied to a given
situation only if there exists some link between the state de-
siring to assert jurisdiction over the offense and the offense

itself, the offender or the victim. This link can be:

1-The *situs* of the offense, whether that location
is the territory of the state or an extension
thereof (special status territories and law of
the flag);

2-The nationality of either the perpetrator or
the victim of the offense (active and passive
personality); or

3-The effects of a given conduct outside the
state but affecting some interest that state
desires to protect (protected interest and
certain extensions of the territorial tehory).

In each of those theories the state is involved or declares
itself involved by reason of a given conduct which the state
claims as affecting it in some way. This theory, however, rests
on a different rationale.

Some offenses, which due to their very nature affect the interests of all states, even when it is committed in or against
a given state, a given victim or victims, a given interest.
Such offenses may even be committed in an area not subject to
the exclusive jurisdiction of any state such as the high seas,
air space or outer space. The *gravamen* of such an offense is
that it constitutes a violation against mankind. Such crimes
are appropriately called *delicti jus gentium*. Any state may, if
it captures the offender, prosecute and punish such a person on
behalf of the world community. The principle which gives all
states jurisdiction over certain offenses is the universality

theory, since it allows states to protect universal values and
the interests of mankind. Although the principle has been
applied to various offenses, its oldest and most common application has been to piracy.[146]

The High Seas Convention of 1958 provides that "(a)ll States
shall cooperate to the fullest possible extent in the repression
of piracy on the high seas or in any other place outside the
jurisdiction of any State."[147] Article 15 of the Convention
defines piracy as any of the following acts:

1. Any illegal acts of violence, detention or any
   act of depredation, committed for private ends
   by the crew or the passengers of a private ship
   or a private aircraft and directed:

   (a) On the high seas, against another ship
       or aircraft or against persons or
       property on board such ship or airc-raft;

   (b) Against a ship, aircraft, persons or
       property in a place outside the juris-
       diction of any State.

2. Any act of voluntary participation in the
   operation of a ship or of an aircraft with
   knowledge of facts making it a pirate ship or
   aircraft.

3. Any act of inciting or of intentionally facil-
   itating an act described in subparagraph 1 or
   subparagraph 2 of this article.

Article 19 provides that:

> (o)n the high seas, or in any other place outside
> the jurisdiction of any State, every State may
> seize a pirate ship or aircraft, or a ship taken
> by piracy and under the control of pirates, and
> arrest the persons and seize the property on board.
> The courts of the State which carried out the
> seizure may decide upon the penalties to be imposed,
> and may also determine the action to be taken with
> regard to the ships, aircraft or property, subject
> to the rights of third parties acting in good faith.

Although the provisions of the High Seas Convention relating to piracy extend to both ships and aircrafts, they are limited in their application to those vessels and aircrafts "on the high seas or in any place outside the jurisdiction of any State." While this would seem to cover ships adequately, excluding only those ships within the territorial sea or internal waters of a state, it is not sufficient to cover aircraft, since these operate not only within the airspace over territorial seas and inland waters, but within the airspace over territorial land areas as well. The characteristics of aircrafts differ from ships as to size, speed and manueverability, but also because of the steadily increasing number of incidents of aircraft piracy, many of which occurred within the territorial airspace of state. In 1970 the International Civil Aviation Organization completed the "Convention for the Suppression of Unlawful Seizure of Aircraft" (hereinafter referred to as the Hague Convention). [148]

The Convention provides that any person commits an offense who:

on board an aircraft in flight:

(a) unlawfully, by force or threat thereof or by
any other form of intimidation, seizes or
exercises control of, that aircraft, or attempts
to perform any such act, or

(b) is an accomplice of a person who performs or
attempts to perform any such act . . . [149]

Unlike the 1963 Tokyo Convention, which defines an aircraft as
being in flight "fromthe moment when power is applied for the
purpose of take-off until the moment when the landing run
ends." [150] The Hague Convention defines an aircraft as being
in flight "at any time from the moment when all its external
doors are closed following embarkation until the moment when
any such door is opened for disembarkation." [151] Also, "(i)n
the case of a forced landing, the flight shall be deemed to
continue until the compeeent authorities take over the responsibility for the aircraft and for persons and property on board." [152]
As with the Tokyo Convention, [153] the Hague Convention does not
apply to aircraft used in military, customs or police services. [154]

The Hague Convention applies "only if the place of take-off or
the place of actual landing of the aircraft on board which the
offense is committed is situated outside the territory of the
State of registration of that aircraft; it shall be immaterial
whether the aircraft is engaged in an international or domestic
flight." [155] Article 4 provides in part, that:

(e)ach Contracting State shall take such measures

as may be necessary to establish its jurisdiction

over the offense and any other act of violence

against passengers or crew committed by the

alleged offender in connection with the offense,

in the following cases:

(a) when the offense is committed on board an

aircraft registered in that State;

(b) when the aircraft on board which the

offense is committed lands in its

territory with the alleged offender still

on board;

(c) when the offense is committed on board

an aircraft leased without crew to a

lessee who has his principal place of

business or, if the lessee has no such

place of business, his permanent res-

idence, in that State.

Other provisions of the Convention set forth rules relating to

joint air transport organizations or agencies (Articles 3(4), 5),

the duties of states in regard to prosecution or extradition of

alleged offenders (Articles 3(5), 6, 7, 8, 10), duties of states

in regard to assisting the aircraft commander, crew or passengers

(Article ()), the reporting of information to the ICAO (Article 11),

and the settlement of disputes (Article 12).

Slave trading, unlike piracy, was not originally brought within

the scope of the universality principle by customary international

law. There have been a number of treaties entered into since the

266

nineteenth century, and since then slave trading has been recognized as an international crime and thus falling within the universality theory. [156] The High Seas Treaty provides that "(e)very State shall adopt effective measures to prevent and punish the transport of slaves in ships authorized to fly its flag, and to prevent the unlawful use of its flag for that purpose. Any slave taking refuge on board any ship, whatever its flag, shall *ipso facto* be free." [157] Also, under Article 22(1)(b) of the High Seas Treaty, a warship may board a foreign merchant vessel on the high seas if there is reasonable ground for suspecting that the merchant vessel is engaged in the slave trade.

Individuals, therefore, have been made subject to certain duties under international law, such as the duty not to commit piracy, the breach of which will make the individual subject to prosecution and punishment under international law. This is true even though individuals have not yet been accorded full status as subjects of international law. Since there is neither a world legislative body to enact statutory international law nor a world body to prosecute and administer punishment to those individuals found guilty of international crimes, [158] each state must act individually to enforce the universality theory. [159] The manner in which this has been accomplished takes several forms: a state may unilaterally enact municipal laws defining such offenses, giving its courts jurisdiction [160]; a state may enter into conventions which define the rights and duties of states in regard to certain universal offenses (as was done in the 1958 High Seas Treaty with regard to piracy, aircraft hijacking, international traffic of narcotics and genocide, slave trade; or states may combine their efforts and form international tribunals to try individuals who commit such crimes. An example of the last possibility occurred after World War II when the victorious Allied States, in what has probably been so far the most dramatic example of the use of the universality principle (if only because of the nature and extent of the crimes involved) formed the International Military Tribunal at Nürmberg to try the highest-ranking German officials and the International Military Tribunal for the Far East to try Japanese war criminals. [161]

The Nürmberg International Military Tribunal was established by the Charter annexed to the Agreement of August 8, 1945, for the Prosecution and Punishment of the Major War Criminals of the European Axis, which was the result of the "London Conference," conducted from June 26 to August 8, 1945, by representatives of the United States, the United Kingdom, the Provisional Government of France and the Union of SovietSocialist Republics. The concept of individual responsibility was one of the basic principles of the Nürmberg Trials. The words of the Tribunal itself are unequivocal on this point:

> It was submitted that international law is concerned
> with the actions of sovereign States, and provides
> no punishment for individuals; and further, that
> where the act in question is an act of State, those
> who carry it out are not personally responsible,
> but are protected by the doctrine of the sovereignty
> of the State. In the opinion of the Tribunal, both

268

these submissions must be rejected . . . Crimes

against international law are committed by men,

not by abstract entities, and only by punishing

individuals who commit such crimes can the pro-

visions of international law be enforced. [162]

The Tokyo war crimes trials accomplished the same function in the

Far East. [163] Other non-international war crimes trials were

held in several states such as Austria, Belgium, Italy, Hungary,

Poland, the U.S.S.R., Yugoslavia, Germany, Czechoslovakia and in

the Philippines. [164]

The growth of international criminal law is ever expanding the

application of international crimes which includes crimes against

the peace and security of humankind, war crimes, genocide, racial

discrimination, slavery, traffic in women and children, illicit

international traffic in narcotics and dangerous drugs, interna-

tional distribution of obscene material, counterfeiting, hijack-

ing, piracy. [165] These international crimes are discussed as

exceptions to the "political offense exception" in Chapter VI,

Section 1, 1.6.

The most notable example of extradition for such international

crimes under the universality theory was the attempt to prosecute

Kaiser Wilhelm II in 1919 in accordance with the Treaty of

Versailles. Article 227-228 established the principle of inter-

national accountability for waging aggressive war but the Kaiser

sought refuge in the Netherlands and his extradition was denied

on the grounds of the "political offense exception." [166] Since

World War II, however, numerous cases of extradition of war

criminals were heard but invariably the request was made by the
state wherein the alleged crime was committed. Thus, in practice,
the universality theory has not seen much application as a basis
for extradition requests, even though it was relied upon in
Nürmberg and Tokyo, but these were international rather than
national tribunals.

6. *A Policy-Oriented Inquiry into the Problems of Jurisdiction*
   in Extradition and World Public Order

When a state requests another to surrender a fugitive to its
jurisdictional control, it asserts that: (a) it has jurisdiction
over the subject matter of the conduct allegedly performed by the
actor; (b) it is a competent forum to prosecute the offender, and
(c) when the actor is surrendered, he or she will be properly
submitted to its judicial authorities for the exercise of their
competent jurisdictional authority (see, however, Chapter III
concerning unlawful seizures and irregular rendition).

These representations by the requesting state presuppose that
the requested state: 1) is competent to exercise *in personam*
jurisdiction over the relator; 2) had its legislative authority
to regulate the type of conduct allegedly committed by the
relator and deemed in violation of that state's laws is not violative of international law, and 3) that it is the competent
forum to prosecute the offender. Concerning the second point,
namely proper legislative authority, the requesting state may
rely on any one of the theories discussed above and its municipal
jurisdiction will be recognized unless it conflicts with an inter-

national law norm, in which case the latter prevails. In the event that the laws of the requesting state conflict with the laws or public policy of the requested state, in this case the question will be whether the law or policy of either state conflicts with international law and if both do not conflict with international law but only with each other, the requested state will prevail. In any event, an offender should not benefit from a conflict of laws to evade criminal responsibility and thus conflict of laws question must be resolved on the basis of the policy of *aut dedere aut iudicare.*

As to the second requirement regarding the competent forum for prosecution, international criminal law recognizes three theories which can be relied upon, they are: *forum domicilius, forum delicti commissi, forum deprehensious.* The determination of a proper prosecution forum is a policy-oriented inquiry within the framework of conflict of laws resolution.

The first formal contact between the requesting and requested state is receipt of the extradition request by the requested state who first considers whether the requesting state has: (a) jurisdiction over the subject matter; (b) is the proper prosecution forum, and (c) would have *in personam* jurisdiction once the relator is delivered. If a similar request is made by another state claiming jurisdiction over the same subject matter arising either out of the same conduct allegedly performed by that relator or by reason of another conduct allegedly committed by the same relator against the other requesting state, then the requested state has to decide the priority among these competing requests. Furthermore, the requested state may also have an interest in prosecuting the relator either by reason of the same conduct alleged in one or both requests or by reason of other alleged criminal conduct. In this case, it must weigh its interest and those of the requesting state or states.

In the case where there is only one extradition request and the requested state has no concurrent interest or claim to the same relator, the first set of policy-oriented questions proposed are as follows:

1. Does the requesting state properly assert jurisdiction over the subject matter and the relator.

2. Does such jurisdiction exist in law and in fact?

3. Is such jurisdictional claim contemplated by the treaty or the practice of reciprocity or comity upon which the request is made?

4. Does such jurisdictional claim arise under (a) international law; (b) international law as applied by the requesting state; (c) the municipal law of the requesting state, and (d) the municipal law of the requested state.

5. Does the jurisdictional basis claimed conflict with the public policy of the requested state or is so repugnant to its system so as to deny it recognition?

272

6. Is the jurisdictional claim asserted by the
   requesting state violative on its face of
   the very basis on which it allegedly rests,
   whether it be international law, municipal
   law or the application of international law
   in the municipal law of either the requesting
   or requested state.

If there is more than one extradition request for the same
relator, the requested state must first satisfy itself concerning
the first set of policy-oriented questions stated above. Thereafter the state of refuge must rank such requests. Ranking can
be made on the following basis:

1. First received, first granted.

2. The more serious offense charged receives priority.

3. The most significant state interest affected by
   the alleged crime receives priority.

4. Depends upon subject matter jurisdiction, i.e.,
   territorial has precedence over all others,
   followed by the combination of two or more
   theories (such as universality and passive
   personality or passive and active personality)
   then by universality , protective, nationality
   and passive personality.

There are no clear guidelines in extradition law and practice as
to the applicable international law rule in concurrent jurisdictional claims. The outcome is uncertainty of prosecution[167]
and potential conflict between the interested states.

International law recognizes the "equal sovereignty" of all
nation-states in the world community and does not grant any of
them a hierarchial authority over the other. Nonetheless, the
requested state must make a policy decision as to the applicability and propriety of the requesting state's three jurisdictional
requirements. Furthermore, in the event of multiple requests,
the requested state is in a position to give priority to the
request of one authoritative decision maker over the other and
thus it exercises a hierarchial authority over co-equal participants in the world community system. The requested state is,
therefore, in a vertical relationship vis-a-vis the requesting
state and pursues that role with respect to conflict of laws
issues arising out of the application of multiple theories of
jurisdiction. [168] The significance of this decision making
function is manifest whenever the requested and requesting state
have different interpretations and policies as to the theories
of jurisdiction in question and their application.

As discussed in this chapter, international criminal law has
come to recognize in varying degrees and with different applications several theories of jurisdiction. In extradition practice
jurisdictional issues are determined by the requested state
but that may not be a serious problem because there is an
anticipation that requested states will apply their domestic
theories and policies. This narrow answer to the question ignores
the broader implications with respect to the international nature
of the process. Such implications require that national theories
of jurisdiction and their application should be subordinated to

international law rules. Thus, no participant in the world constitutive process will be in a hierarchial position with respect to another co-equal participant. [169]

An underlying theme exists in jurisdiction as applicable to extradition, namely, the equal sovereignty of all participants and a logical conclusion would, therefore, be that if harmony between the laws of multiple participants in a horizontal process existed, then there would be no conflict of laws, but only conflicts of interpretation. Since, however, there is no such harmony in national approaches to jurisdiction, then there is no alternative to the establishment of a hierarchial norm to avoid conflict between co-equal authoritative decision making processes. Such a hierarchial norm would, however, be applied by each state and would not, therefore, detract from the sovereignty of any other state. Among the several problems raised by this subject is, of course, the inability, in the presently constituted world social order, to develop the type of alternative policy solution described above. The consequences arising from these problems are manifested by clashes between vertically related decision making processes. This is due to the absence of any hierarchial international resolutory norm and its implementing processes. The potential effect of such clashes is the creation of conflict situations leading to threats and disruptions of minimum world order.

These problems of conflict of criminal jurisdiction are largely due to the narrow and jealously guarded concept of sovereignty. The battles over where to prosecute an accused criminal over-

shadow the real substance of the issue, i.e., the merits in prosecuting or punishing offenders. The alternative to the present
situation is to seek the proper applicable substantive law rather
than where the accused should be tried or whether he or she should
be tried altogether.

The multiplicity of jurisdictional theories do not only result
in problems of conflict of laws but constitute an impediment to
just and effective criminal law enforcement whether nationally
or internationally while subjecting accused offenders to the risk
of multiple prosecutions and violations of their human rights.
(Indeed, under the passive personality doctrine or the nationality
doctrine more than one state can prosecute and punish a person
for the same offense and subject that person to multiple jeopardy).

The interest in preserving world public order does not conflict
with the concern for preserving municipal public order nor will
either one be impaired by preserving basic human rights. None
of these, however, can be served without shrinking national
sovereignty concepts in matters of extradition. [170]

Chapter IV

Footnotes

1. Oppenheim, International Law 263 (8th ed. 1955). Another
   authority states:

   The most important right -- and duty -- of a state

   is jurisdiction. It is solidly established in

   jurisprudence. . . . From the viewpoint of sovereign-

   ty, jurisdiction means internal sovereignty, exclusive

   control over all persons and things within its

   territory. There are, of course, restrictions,

   even upon the internal administration of a state,

   set by international law and they are constantly

   increasing in number as the needs of the community

   rise above the claims of the state. "The extent

   of both the right and the duty of a State to do

   justice within its own domain, as well as else-

   where, is also fixed by international law." The

   jurisdiction of a state is simply the amount of

   control left to that state by the community of

   nations; or, if the statement be preferred, the

   powers reserved to the states after they have

   delegated to the community the exercise of certain

   powers. In practice, vast powers are left to the

   states, and the community interferes very little

   with their internal administration. It should

   be noted that the state not only administers its

own affairs, but acts also as the agent of the community of nations to enforce international law within its territory. Eagleton, _International Government_ 87-88 (3rd ed., 1957).

(A)ll states have certain sovereign powers which they can exercise without transgressing the rights of other states under international law. If they fail to exercise these powers, it is because either they have voluntarily placed a disability on that exercise, perhaps in the form of a domestic constitutional limitation or they have not considered it necessary, as a practical matter, to exercise their powers. George, "Extraterritorial Application of Penal Legislation," 64 _Mich. L. Rev._ 609, 612 (1965-66).

Article 2 of the Draft Declaration on Rights and Duties of States, prepared in 1949 by the International Law Commission of the United Nations, recites: "Every State has the right to exercise jurisdiction over its territory and over all persons and things therein, subject to the immunities recognized by international law." Report of the _International Law Commission_, 1st Sess., 1949 (A/925), June 24, 1949, pp. 7, 8; _Yearbook of the International Law Commission_ 1949, p. 287.

2. 6 Whiteman, _Digest_, 889-890 (1968).

3. 7 Crach 116 (U. S. 1812).

278

4. 23 Fed. Cod. 281 (No. 13, 562) (C.C.S.D.N.Y., 1873).

5. 1 Moore, A Treatise on Extradition and Interstate Rendition, 135 (1891).

6. 106 F. Supp. 455 (W.D.N.Y. 1952); see also In re Martin (1925-1926) Ann. Dig. 303-304 (No. 229), wherein: Czechoslovakia requested the extradition from Hungary of one Martin M. who was accused of having committed larceny in January and February, 1921, at a place formerly Hungarian territory but which was ceded to Czechoslovakia by the Treaty of Trianon which came into force on July 21, 1921. Extradition was requested as an act of comity, there being no extradition treaty between the two countries. The Hungarian Court held that extradition could not be granted since the crime had been committed in Hungarian territory.
And United States v. I. Bardi, 140 F. Supp. 888 (D.C., 1956).

7. Bassiouni, Criminal Law and Its Processes, pp. 573-583 (1969).

8. United States Ex Rel. Keradzole v. Artukovic, 1959.

9. 130 F. Supp. 926 (D. Conn., 1953).

10. Id., 928-929.

11. 6 Whiteman, Digest, 740-748 (1968).

12. U.S.T.S. 426; I. Malloy, Treaties, etc. (1910) 360-361.

13. 61 Stat. 4019, 4026; 43 U.N.T.S. 27, 288. In Williams v. Rogers, 443 F. 2d 513 (1972), the Eighth Circuit Court of Appeals held that Article XIII of the 1947 Agreement, amended in 1965, provides the specific jurisdictional and procedural

basis for arrest, trial and custody of U. S. military personnel accused of committing offenses in the Philippines. Relying on Valentine v. U. S. Ex Rel. Neideclser, 299 U.S. 5 (1936) the court held this treaty also provides the basis for transferring to the Philippines military personnel for prosecution by Philippines judicial authority without the need for an extradition treaty or the need to pursue extradition procedures. The court, in fact, held that the agreement could serve as a substitute for an extradition treaty and that military transfers of personnel from the U. S. to the Philippines to be prosecuted under the terms of the agreement did not require following prescribed extradition procedures in the United States as would be applicable to non-military personnel. This is a novel approach which appears to be unprecedented in the anals of United States extradition practice.

14. 354 U. S. 524 (1957).

15. Girard v. Wilson, 152 F. Supp. 21, 27 (D.D.C., 1957).

16. Wilson v. Girard, 354 U.S. 524-530 (1957).

17. U.U.S.T. 1792, 1800; 1990 N.T.S. 67, 78. See, U.C.M.J., 10 U.S.C.A. for a bibliography of United States agreements. See also, Baxter, Criminal Jurisdiction in the NATO Status of Forces Agreement, 7 Int. & Comp. L. Q., 72 (1958). It should be noted at this point that most states claim jurisdiction over members of their armed forces, both nationals and non-nationals, regardless of where they happen to be. See, Restatement (Second), Foreign Relations Law of the

United States (1965) (hereinafter cited as Restatement),
§31(b), 32(1)(b). Since conflicts of jurisdiction can
result from the presence in one state of members of the
military of another state, "status of forces" agreements
are usually concluded between the two countries. See also
Bassiouni and Nanda, A Treatise on International Criminal
Law, Vol. II, Coker,"The Status of Visiting Military Forces
in Europe: NATO and SOFA, A Comparison," p. 115 (1973).

18. See, Restatement, §18 and 20.

19. Strassheim v. Daly, 221 U. S. 280, 31 S. Ct. 558 (1911);
United States v. Aluminum Co. of America 148 F. 2d 416
(2d Cir. 1945). For an earlier opinion contrary to these
cases, see American Banana Co. v. United Fruit Co., 213
U. S. 347, 29 S. Ct. 511 (1909). See, United States v. Baker,
136 F. Supp. 546 (S.D.N.Y. 1955) wherein the court distinguished the earlier case of United States ex Rel. Mavka v.
Palmer, 67 F. 2d 146 (7th Cir. 1933), and ordered deported
for having made false statements under oath to an American
Consul abroad while applying for a passport. The Court
stated: "But deporting an alien for perjury is far different
from indicting and trying him for a crime committed abroad."
136 F. Supp. 546, 548 (S.D.N.Y. 1955). In 1968 on the same
issue the Court of Appeals held in United States v.
Pizzarusso, 388 F.2d 8 (1968) that a perjured statement
before a U. S. Consul abroad subjected such a person to
prosecution in the United States. For acts of alien
committed wholly abroad, but with effect within the United

281

States, see <u>Rocha v. United States</u>, 288 F. 2d 545 (9th Cir.,
1961) <u>cert. denied</u> 366 U. S. 948, 81 S. Ct. 1902 (1961) and
for a conspiracy in Canada having effect in the U. S. See
<u>Rivard v. United States</u>, 375 F.2d 882 (5th Cir., 1967).
In this case defendants were extradited from Canada to the
United States for conspiring in Canada to smuggle heroin in
the United States.

20. See, "Harvard Draft Convention on Jurisdiction with Respect
to Crime," Art. 3, 29 <u>A.J.I.L. Supp.</u> 439 (1935), (hereinafter cited as "Harvard Draft Convention") and <u>Restatement</u>,
§17.

21. See, e.g., <u>Chandler v. United States</u>, 171 F.2d 921 (1st Cir.
1948), <u>cert. denied</u>, 336 U.S. 918 (1949); <u>Gillars v. United
States</u>, 182 F.2d 962 (D.C. Cir. 1950); <u>Kawakita v. United
States</u>, 343 U.S. 717 (1952).

22. In <u>United States v. Sisal Sales Corporation</u>, 274 U.S. 268
(1927), a federal court enjoined the defendant American
corporations from conducting in Yucatan various activities
designed to control the exportation of Sisal to the United
States from Mexico and monopolize the market both inside
and outside the United States in violation of provisions
of the Sherman Anti-Trust Act. In <u>Steel v. Bulova Watch Co.</u>,
344 U.S. 280 (1952), a federal district court in Texas was
held to have jurisdiction over a suit by an American watch
company to enjoin a United States citizen from using the
company's trademark, registered under United States law,
in Mexico on watches made in Mexico.

23. In <u>Blackmer v. United States</u>, 284 U.S. 421 (1932), the defendant, a United States citizen, was convicted upon his return to the United States for contempt of a United States court for failure to obey a subpoena of the court directing him to return home from France to act as a witness for the United States government in a criminal trial. In <u>Sachs v. Government of the Canal Zone</u>, 176 F.2d 292 (5th Cir., 1949), a United States citizen was tried and convicted for a criminal libel which he had composed in the Republic of Panama, a sovereign state, for publication and circulation in the Canal Zone.

24. Restatement, §18: Jurisdiction to Prescribe with Respect to Effect within Territory:

A state has jurisdiction to prescribe a rule of law attaching legal consequences to conduct that occurs outside its territory and causes an effect within its territory if either

(a) the conduct and its effect are generally recognized as constituent elements of a crime or tort under the law of states that have reasonably developed legal systems, or

(b) (i) the conduct and its effect are constituent elements of activity to which the rule applies;

(ii) the effect within the territory is substantial;

(iii) it occurs as a direct and foreseeable

result of the conduct outside the territory,
and

(iv) the rule is not inconsistent with the
principles of justice generally recognized
by states that have reasonably developed
legal systems.

25. See, e.g., <u>Ford v. United States</u>, 278 U.S. 593 (1927), in
which the defendants, British subjects who had been in a
British ship on the high seas about 25 miles west of San
Francisco at the time it was seized by United States
authorities, were convicted of conspiracy to violate
United States liquor laws pursuant to a treaty between the
United States and England, authorizing the United States
to seize any British vessels and persons on such vessels
suspected of such offenses.

26. In <u>Joyce v. Director of Public Prosecution</u>, 62 T.L.R. 208
(1946), the defendant, who had acted as a propagandist
radio announcer for Nazi Germany (known also as "Lord
Haw-Haw") was convicted of treason and hanged, even though
he was a United States national and, therefore, an alien
to English courts. Joyce had obtained a British passport
fraudulently in July, 1933, and held it until it expired
on July 1, 1940, after he had begun to broadcast for
Germany. The court found that the possession of even this
illegally-obtained passport gave Joyce certain rights under
British law and imposed upon him a corresponding duty of
allegiance, which he violated. In a South African case,

R. v. Neuman (1949), 8 S.A.L.R. 1238, the defendant was a
German national domiciled in the Union of South Africa who
had applied for naturalization there, but who had also re-
tained his German nationality. While in Germany he had
committed acts against the national security of South Africa
and was subsequently captured. At the time of his trial,
he was not a national of South Africa. The court found,
however, that since he had resided in South Africa and had
enjoyed its protection he "owed allegiance to that State,
breach whereof renders him liable to the penalties of high
treason." Id. at 1256.

27. See, e.g., Rek v. Godfrey (1923), 1 K.B. 24, in which the
court ordered a man in England to be extradited to Switzerland to stand trial for having procured his confederate,
who was in Switzerland, to obtain goods by false pretenses,
even though the first man had never been in Switzerland.

28. See, Art. 2, Belgian Extradition Law of 1874, Les Codes
(Trente et Unieme Édition, 1965), Loi du 15 mars 1874 sur
les extraditions, pp. 693, 694, 696.
Nevertheless, when the crime of offense for which
extradition is requested was committed outside the
territory of the requesting country, the Government
may, subject to reciprocity, surrender the prosecuted or convicted alien if Belgian law authorizes
prosecution for the same offense committed outside
the realm.
and

Art. III, Colombia–Panama Extradition Treaty of 1927, 87
LNTS 409, 415.

If the offense was committed outside the territory
of the applicant State, extradition shall not be
granted unless in like circumstances the State of
refuge authorizes the punishment of the same
offense when committed outside its own territory.

29. 211 U.S. 280 (1910).

30. Id., p. 280.

31. 1 Op. Att'y Gen. 88 (1852). A similar position was expressed
     in In re Stupp, 23 F. Cas. 281, 292–93 (No. 13,562) (C.C.S.
     D.N.Y. 1873) (dictum). In an unreported case extradition
     was refused where the victim was shot on a United States
     vessel in Canadian waters but later died in the United
     States. Clarke, The Law of Extradition, 71–72 (4th ed.,
     1903). Cf. Terlinden v. Ames, 184 U.S. 270, 289 (1902)
     (definition of extradition).

32. 83 F. 690 (2d Cir. 1897).

33. Id., at 691.

34. The same conclusion was reached in Commonwealth v. Macloon,
     101 Mass. 1 (1869) and Tyler v. People, 8 Mich. 320 (1860).
     The Tyler analysis, however, could lead to the conclusion
     that the place where a victim died would have sole juris-
     diction over the prosecution for murder.

35. Ex parte Davis, 54 F. 2d 723 (9th Cir. 1931). Hammond v.
     Sittel, 59 F. 2d 683 (9th Cir.), cert. denied, 287 U.S.
     640 (1932).

36. 54 F. 2d 683, 727.

37. *Supra*, note 32, at 691.

38. *Supra*, note 36, at 723.

39. 59 F. 2d 683 (9th Cir.), cert. denied, 287 U.S. 640 (1932).
    See also United States ex rel. Hatfield v. Guay, 11 F. Supp.
    806 (D.N.H. 1935).

40. *Supra*, note 36 at 684-686. However, in 1940, the same
    court rejected the contention of Alexander Strakosch that
    he should not be extradited to Great Britain on charges of
    fraudulent conversion and obtaining money by false pretenses
    on the grounds that even if the evidence could be said to
    show his presence in London and his participation there in
    activities of certain other accused inidviduals there was
    no evidence to show that he was there at the time of the
    actual commission of the acts constituting the offenses or
    his direct participation in those acts. The court stated:

    > Moreover, from the facts stated in the depositions,
    > it is reasonably inferable -- and, we think,
    > obvious -- that Spiro and his associates, inclu-
    > ding appellee (Strakosch), were engaged in a
    > conspiracy, and that the crimes in question were
    > committed in furtherance thereof. It therefore
    > makes no difference whether appellee was present
    > or absent at the commission of the acts consti-
    > tuting the crimes or whether he did or did not
    > directly participate in their commission.

    Cleugh v. Strakosch, 109 F. 2d 330, 334, 335 (9th Cir. 1940).

41. 275 F. Supp. 492 (S.D.N.Y. 1967).

42. Treaty with Switzerland for the extradition of criminals, May 14, 1900, Art. I, 31 Stat. 1928 (1901), T.S. No. 354.

43. Other treaties allowing extradition for crimes committed within the demanded state's territory are with Uruguay, Mar. 11, 1905, Art. I, 35 Stat. 2028 (1909), T.S. No. 501; Argentina, Sept. 26, 1896, Art. I, 31 Stat. 1883 (1901), T.S. No. 6; Colombia, May 7, 1888, Art. I, 26 Stat. 1534 (1891), T.S. No. 58 ("territories or jurisdiction").

44. See, Treaty of Extradition with South Africa, Dec. 18, 1947 (1951) 1 U.S.T. 884, T.I.A.S. No. 2248; notes 93-95 *infra*. For a list of United States extradition treaties up to 1937 see IV Treaties, Conventions, International Acts, Protocols and Agreements Between the United States of America and Other Powers 1923-1937, at 5697-730 (1965). Since that time conventions have been completed with South Africa, Brazil, Israel and Sweden.

45. (1933-1934) Ann. Dig. 353 (No. 149).

46. I.K.B. 24.

47. R. v. Jacobi and Hiller (1881), 46 L.T.R. No. 595.

48. "Case of Malinowski," 49 A.J.I.L. 267 (1955).

49. Convention on the Territorial Sea and Contiguous Zone (hereinafter cited as the Territorial Sea Treaty), Art. 1, done at Geneva April 29, 1958; 15 U.S.T. 1606, T.I.A.S. No. 5639, 516 U.N.T.S. 205. Although the Territorial Sea Treaty does not specify how wide the territorial sea may be, it is generally believed that it may be no wider than twelve miles.

See, Brierly, The Law of Nations, 202-211 (1955). If a state

claims a territorial sea of less than twelve miles from the

baseline from which the breadth of the territorial sea is

measured, in which it may exercise jurisdiction to prevent

and punish infringement of fiscal, customs, immigration and

sanitary regulations. Territorial Sea Treaty, Art. 24.

50. See, Territorial Sea Treaty, Articles 14-23. In The Schooner

Exchange v. McFaddon, 11 U.S. (1812), the Supreme Court held

that warship of a foreign state, at peace with the U.S., is

exempt from U.S. jurisdiction while in its territorial

waters. The rationale was sovereign immunity and jurisdic-

tional exemption by consent of the host state. Such consent

is implied unless there is express statement to the contrary.

Consequently, the territorial state will not exercise juris-

diction even when the matter is criminal over such vessels

and persons and property on board it.

In the Wildenhus's Case, 120 U.S. 1 (1886), the Supreme

Court held when a private vessel -- merchant ship as opposed

to a warship -- enters a port, it is subject to domestic

law unless exempted by treaty. The territorial state will

exercise its jurisdiction for crimes committed on board the

vessel even when the victim and aggressor are both foreigners.

The positions expressed in these two cases are still valid

in the United States.

51. See, the 1958 Geneva Convention, *supra*, note 49, and the

Convention on International Civil Aviation, *infra*, note 52.

52. Convention on International Civil Aviation, Art. 1, done at

Chicago, December 7, 1944; 61 Stat. 1180, T.I.A.S. No. 5191, 15 U.N.T.S. 295.

The concept of innocent passage for aircraft in a foreign state's territorial airspace was discussed at the meeting of the Institute of International Law held in Brussels in 1902, but it was never adopted as a rule of law. The effectiveness of aircraft as weapons of war, demonstrated over the fields of Europe from 1914 to 1918, no doubt contributed greatly to the early scuttling of the concept. See 4 Hackworth, Digest, 357-358 (1942).

53. Chicago Convention, supra, note 52, Articles 3(c), 6. Although Article 5 gives to states parties to the Chicago Convention a right of passage for non-scheduled flights, into and across the territory of another state, the right is very limited and cannot be compared with the right of innocent passage for ships in the territorial sea, as the territorial state may legally require the aircraft to land.

54. See, U.N.G.A. Resolution 1721 (XVI) of December 20, 1961 (adopted unanimously), at 1-b; U.N.G.A. Resolution 1962 (XVIII) of December 13, 1963 (adopted unanimously), at 2, 3; see McDougal, Lasswell & Vlassic, Law and Public Order in Space, 217 and Ch. 3 generally (1963); Brierly, supra, note 49, at 220; Gorove, "Interpreting Article II of the Outer Space Treaty," 37 Fordham L. Rev. 349, 351 (1969); Treaty on Principles Governing the Activities of States in the Exploration and Use of Outer Space, Including the Moon and Other Celestial Bodies (hereinafter cited as the 1967 Space

Treaty) Articles I, II, done at Washington, London and Moscow, January 27, 1967. 18 U.S.T. 2410, T.I.A.S. No. 6347.

55. Statute of the International Court of Justice annexed to the Charter of the United Nations, Art. 33(1); 59 Stat. 1055, T.S. 993.

56. See, Vosburgh, "Where Does Outer Space Begin?" 56 A.B.A.J. 104 (1970).

57. See, Hall, International Law, 244-49 (6th ed. 1909).

58. See, Restatement, §30(1), 31(a), 32(1)(a).

59. 313 U.S. 69-73 (1941). See, also United States v. Bowman, 260 U.S. 94 (1922); Blackmer v. United States, 284 U.S. 421 (1932); "Harvard Research in International Law, Jurisdiction with Respect to Crime," 29 A.J.I.L. Supp. 509-511 (1935) (hereinafter cited as "Harvard Research").

60. 289 U.S. 137, 155-157 (1933).

61. See, Brierly, supra, note 49 at 304-307.

62. High Seas Treaty, Art. 4.

63. Id., Art. 5. The Treaty does not define what a "genuine link" is or what would happen if such a link did not exist between a state and a ship ostensibly sailing under its flag. Restatement, at 79, 81.

64. High Seas Treaty, Art. 6. Examples of situations in which the rule of exclusive flag state jurisdiction is modified are piracy and slave trading (discussed later under the universality principle) and hot pursuit. In the last, a ship or aircraft of the coastal state may undertake uninterrupted pursuit on the high seas of a foreign vessel which is sus-

pected of having violated the laws and regulations of the coastal state if the pursuit is undertaking when the foreign vessel or one of its boats is still within the internal waters or territorial sea of the pursuing state. Id., Art. 23. See also, Ford case, *supra*, note 25; Brierly, *supra*, note 49, at 307, 311.

65. High Seas Treaty, Articles 8(1), 9.

66. Territorial Sea Treaty, Articles 19(1), 21.

67. 126 U.S. 1 (1887).

68. Id., at 5.

69. Id., at 18.

70. Id., at 18-19.

71. Territorial Sea Treaty, Art. 19(2).

72. Id., Art. 19(5).

73. 25 I.L.R. 513 (1958); 3 All English Reports 318, (1958).

74. Id., 320-321.

75. Wilheim Wolthusen v. Albert Otto Starl, (1925-1926) Ann. Dig. 305 (No. 231).

76. Id., at 306.

77. 89 F. Supp. 298 (E.D.N.Y. 1950).

78. The term "State" has been defined to mean a state of the United States, and not a foreign country. Wynne v. United States, 217 U.S. 234 (1910). For a detailed discussion of United States practice regarding aircraft crimes, see Brown, "Jurisdiction of United States Courts Over Crimes in Aircraft," 15 Stan. L. Rev. 45 (1962).

79. 2 Q.B. 272 (1956).

80. _Id_., at 284.

81. The 1958 Draft Convention on Aviation Crimes, prepared by
the Air Law Committee of the International Law Association,
provided in Article 3 a list of preferences as to what law
should apply in the case of a crime committed aboard an
aircraft:

3.01 The criminal law to be applied to the case
shall, in the discretion of the court acquiring
jurisdiction according to Article 2, be selected
from the following laws in the order of preference
stated:

3.01(1) First preference: the law of the State of
the flag of the aircraft, if such State has an
appropriate law;

3.01(2) Second preference: the law of the State
of the place where the accused person first
touches earth after the commission of the crime;

3.01(3) Third preference: the law of the State
and of the place where the aircraft first touches
down after the commission of the crime. (This
may be an emergency landing place or a scheduled
landing place).

3.01(4) Fourth preference: the law of the State
and of the place where the aircraft was first
scheduled to touch down or where a first landing
had been planned when the flight commenced as
the normal end of the flight during which the

crime was committed. (This will not be an
emergency landing place.) . . .

3.01(5) Fifth preference: the law of the place
where the aircraft last ascended into flight
prior to commission of the crime.

International Law Association, Air Law, Crimes in Aircraft,
301, 303, New York University Conference (1958).

82. Done at Tokyo, September 14, 1963, 20 U.S.T.S. 2948, T.I.A.S.
No. 6768.

83. Tokyo Convention, Art. 1(1).

84. Id., Art. 1(2). But see Chapter III of the Convention
which makes special provision for the powers of the aircraft
commander.

85. Id., Art. 1(3).

86. Id., Art. 1(4).

87. For an analysis and appraisal of the Tokyo Convention, see
Boyle and Pulsifer, "The Tokyo Convention on Offenses and
Certain Other Acts Committed on Board Aircraft," 30 J. Air.
& Com. 305, 328-354 (1964).

88. Id., at 329-330.

89. Hirsch and Fuller, "Aircraft Piracy and Extradition," 16
N.Y.L.F. 392; see appendices at 406-415 (1970).

90. Three such cases are reported in Bassiouni, "Ideologically
Motiviated Offenses and the Political Offense Exception in
Extradition -- A Proposed Juridical Standard for an Unruly
Problem," 19 DePaul L. Rev. 217 (1970), at 219, note 5.

91. See discussion of this point in Chapter I and Evans, "Air-

294

craft Hijacking: Its Causes and Cure," 63 A.J.I.L. 695
(1969).

92. Pharand, "Freedom of the Seas in the Arctic Ocean," 19
     Toronto L.J. 210, 214 (1969).

93. Id., at 218-219. There are many floating ice islands in the
     Arctic Ocean capable of human habitation, if only to a lim-
     ited degree. An example is Fletcher's Ice Island, occupied
     as a research station by the United States Air Force since
     1952. It has been drifting ever since, except for a year
     and a half when it was grounded north of Alaska. First
     spotted in 1947, by 1967, there were some 40 scientists and
     technicians working on it. Another such research statoon,
     Arlis II, was operated continuously by the Air Force for
     four years but had to be abandoned when it drifted into the
     Greenland Sea after covering more than 4,300 nautical miles
     during its drift across the Arctic Ocean. Id., at 221.

94. Id., at 227-231. The United States government has long
     held the view that the Arctic is not subject to sovereign
     claim. In 1909, it refused to accept Admiral Perry's
     "annexation" of the region. 6 Whiteman, Digest, at 1266
     (1968).

95. United Nations Charter, Art. 38(1)(b).

96. Recently, an American technician working on Fletcher's Ice
     Island (see supra, note 93) was indicted in the United
     States (Federal District Court, E. D. Va.) for the killing
     of another technician on the island. Although the floating
     iceberg was in the Arctic Ocean over 300

295

miles from the North Pole. The Department of Justice, rather than prosecute the alleged offender under active personality or protected interest theories, considered the island as a "vessel on the high seas." See, Bassiouni, "Extraterritorial Criminal Jurisdiction," The Globe (Illinois State Bar Association Newsletter), Vol. 6.1, p. 1 (1970.

97. An example of a special jurisdictional situation is Canada's recent claim of competence to enforce pollution regulations up to 100 miles from its coastline, discussed in Bilder, "The Canadian Arctic Waters Pollution Prevention Act: New Stresses on the Law of the Sea," 69 Mich. L. Rev. 1 (1970).

98. See, Bilder, "Control of Criminal Conduct in Antarctica," 52 Va. L. Rev. 231, 233-37 (1966), and sources cited therein for material on the history and physical characteristics of Antarctica.

99. Signed at Washington, December 1, 1959, 12 U.S.T. 794, T.I.A.S. No. 4780, 402 U.N.T.S. 71. As of January 1, 1971, the following states were parties to the Treaty: Argentina Australia, Belgium, Chile, Czechoslovakia, Denmark, France, Japan, Netherlands, New Zealand, Norway, Poland, South Africa, Soviet Union, United Kingdom and the United States.

100. Antarctic Treaty, Art. IV(2).

101. The Treaty is in force for at least 30 years after its date of entry into force. See, Art. XII (2)(a).

102. Id., Art. VI.

103. Aircraft flying over the Continent of Antarctica would no doubt also be under the exclusive competence of the flag

state since no state could claim sovereignty over any Antarctic airspace as long as claims of sovereignty are prohibited over the continent itself, as long as the 1959
Treaty is in force.

104. Antarctic Treaty, Art. VIII(1).

105. Id., Art. VIII(2).

106. Id., Art. IX(1)(e).

107. Seven states claim territory in Antarctica. See, Bilder,
     supra, note 98, at 260.

108. For a discussion of the application of United States law
     in Antarctica, see Bilder, *supra*, note 98, at 244-259.

109. See, Bilder, *supra*, note 98, at 260-265, for a review of
     relevant foreign law applicable to Antarctica.

110. Probably the greatest difference between Earth's Polar
     regions and outer space is that the formerare finite in
     size while the latter to the extent of human knowledge is
     infinite (or at least it is for practical purposes vis-a-vis
     Twentieth Century technology). Therefore, the use of
     "territory" in relation to outer space is not as in appro-
     priate as might seem to be the case (at least from a legal
     point of view). Also, on Earth, both territorial seas and
     territorial airspace are as much a part of a state's
     sovereign "territory" as are its actual land areas. Also,
     the surfaces of some planets would, in the absence of the
     "no sovereignty" rule currently in force in both customary
     and conventional international law be quite able to be
     appropriated as sovereign territory, just as islands in the

297

high seas can be so appropriated. It should also be noted at this point that while the United States prescribes rules of law for islands over which it claims sovereignty, it also prescribes rules of law for certain Trust Territories over which it does not claim sovereignty but exercises jurisdiction. See, Lay and Taubenfeld, The Law Relating to Activities of Man in Space, 201-202 (1970).

111. The remainder of Art. VIII states that "(s)uch objects or component parts found beyond the limits of the State Party to the Treaty on whose registry they are carried shall be returned to that State Party, which shall, upon request, furnish identifying data prior to their return." The rights and duties of states with regard to the rescue and return of astronauts and the return of objects which are launched into outer space but come down unexpectedly in a foreign state, on the high seas, or in a place not subject to the jurisdiction of any state have been clarified and elaborated by the Agreement on the Rescue of Astronauts, the Return of Astronauts, and the Return of Objects Launched into Outer Space, done at Washington, London and Moscow, April 22, 1968, 19 U.S.T. 7570, T.I.A.S., No. 6599.

112. This is apparently a greater competence than was provided by U.N.G.A. Resolution 1962 (SVIII) of December 13, 1963, which provided in part the following statement of jurisdiction: "7. The State on whose registry an object launched into outer space is carried shall retain jurisdiction and control over such object and any personnel thereon, while

in outer space . . . ." (Emphasis added).

113. See *supra*, note 96.

114. Oppenheim, *supra*, note 1, at 290, 686-689.

115. See *supra*, note 58.

116. See Joyce v. Director of Public Prosecution *supra*, note 26.

117. "Harvard Research," at 523.

118. See, e.g., German Penal Code, §4.

119. Nonetheless, the "Harvard Draft Convention," Art. 5, p. 532,
would allow such an extension of jurisdiction.

120. But for an opinion that the active personality principle
"is without any justification," see Fitzgerald, "The Territorial Principle in Penal Law: An Attempted Justification,"
1 Ga. J. Int. & Comp. L. 29, 43 (1970).

121. See Joyce v. Director of Public Prosecution *supra*, note 26.

122. In re Roquain, 26 I.L.R. 209 (1958), Belgium, Cour de Cessation
February 10, 1958. This case involved the commission of the
crime of adultery in France. Such an offense affected the
family states in Belgium and was committed between Belgian
nationals. See, also Public Prosecutor v. Van H., 19 I.L.R.
227 (1957), Netherlands, Supreme Court, January 22, 1952.

123. Schnecberger v. Public Prosecutor of the Cauton of Lucerne,
21 I.L.R. 125 (1957), Switzerland Cour de Cessation,
November 12, 1954.

124. Re Gutierrez, 24 I.L.R. 265 (1957) Mexico, Supreme Court,
October 18, 1957.

125. X v. Public Prosecutor, 19 I.L.R. 226 (1957) decided by the
Court of Appeals of the Hague March 26, 1952.

126. P.C.I.J. (1927), Ser. A, No. 10, 2 Hudson, World Court Reports 20 (1935). The case involved a collision on the high
seas between a French ship, the Lotus and a Turkish vessel,
the Boz-Kourt, near Turkish territorial waters. When the
French ship put in at Constantinople, the French watch
officer who was in charge of the Lotus at the time of the
collision was arrested ashore. France claimed that Turkey
had no jurisdiction to try the French officer, while Turkey
claimed that it was not prohibited from doing so by international law. Both states agreed to submit the case to the
Permanent Court. Turkey claimed jurisdiction under Art. 6
of the Turkish Penal Code, which provided that any foreign
who committed an offense abroad to the prejudice of Turkey
or of a Turkish subject would be punished in accordance
with the Turkish Penal Code. Hudson, "The Sixth Year of
the Permanent Court of International Justice," 22 A.J.I.L.
1, 10 (1928).

127. Although the wording of Art. 6 of the Turkish Penal Code
would support both the passive personality and protected
interest principles, the majority of the Permanent Court
based its decision upon the fact that the Turkish vessel
was assimilated to Turkish territory and that since the
effects of the crime were felt on the Turkish vessel, they
were felt in Turkey itself. See, Hudson, *supra*, note 126,
at 11. This, in effect, is a recognition of the subjective-
objective territorial principle. Brierly, *supra*, note 49,
at 308.

128. See, e.g., <u>German Penal Code</u>, Art. 4(2); <u>Chinese Criminal Code</u>, Art. 8; <u>Mexican Penal Code</u>, Art. 4. In connection with the last statute, see the discussion of the <u>Cutting</u> case in 6 Whiteman, <u>Digest</u>, 104, 105 (1968).

129. <u>Restatement</u>, §30(2): "A state does not have jurisdiction to prescribe a rule of law attaching a legal consequence to conduct of an alien outside its territory merely on the ground that the conduct affects one of its nations."

130. See, e.g., Brierly, *supra*, note 49, at 302; and Baxter, "Extraterritorial Application of Domestic Law," 1 <u>U.B.C.L. Rev</u>. 333, 335 (1960).

131. "International Convention for the Unification of Certain Rules Relating to Penal Jurisdiction in Matters of Collisions and Other Incidents of Navigation," signed at Brussels on May 10, 1952. (1960) <u>Gr. Brit. T.S</u>. No. 47, at 14, Cmnd. 1128 (entered into force November 20, 1955).

132. Convention on the High Seas (hereinafter cited as the High Seas Treaty), done at Geneva April 29, 1958, 13 U.S.T. 2313, T.I.A.S. No. 5200, 450 U.N.T.S. 82. Article 11(1) of the Treaty states that "(i)n the event of a collision or of any other incident of navigation concerning a ship on the high seas, involving the penal or other disciplinary responsibility of the master or of any other person in the service of the ship, no penal or disciplinary proceedings may be instituted against such persons except before the judicial or administrative authorities either of the flag State or of the State of which such person is a national."

301

133. "The (passive personality principle) is admittedly auxiliary in character and is probably not essential for any State if the ends served are adequately provided for on other principles." 29 A.J.I.L. Supp. 445 (1935). The "Harvard Research" also states that the principle has been opposed by writers in both common and civil law countries and that "(o)f all principles of jurisdiction having some substantial support in contemporary national legislation, it is the most difficult to justify in theory." Id., at 579. While excluding the general or unrestricted use of the passive personality principle, however, the "Harvard Draft Convention" reserves its limited use for situations where no other principle will apply, although the principle is used in the context of the universality theory. See, "Harvard Draft Convention," Art. 10(c) and "Harvard Research," at 589.

134. The Jerusalem Post Weekly of August 14, 1973, p. 4, discusses the first application of this law to a Turkish national unlawfully seized in Lebanon by Israeli commandos who was prosecuted and convicted to seven years imprisonment by a military court relying on this statute. See, also Time magazine, August 20, 1973, p. 31.

135. P.C.I.J., Ser. A, No. 10 (1927).

136. "Harvard Draft Convention," Articles 7, 8.

137. Restatement, §33. (Compare with §18 which may apply to many of the same cases, but which is considered as an exception to the territorial competence given states by §17 and which

is not considered as a separate theory in itself).

138. "Harvard Draft Convention," Art. 8; Restatement, §33 (2).

139. "Harvard Draft Convention," Art. 7.

140. Restatement, §33(1).

141. See, e.g., United States v. Archer, 51 F. Supp. 708 (S.D. Cal. 1943), where an alien who had sworn falsely before a vice consul of the United States at an American Consulate in Mexico was prosecuted under a United States statute making such false swearing a crime, the court stating that "any person who takes false oath before a consul commits an offense, not against the country where the consul is, but against the sovereignty of the United States." (Court's emphasis). Id., at 711; United States v. Rodriguez, 182 F. Supp. 479 (S.D. Cal. 1960), where defendants who had made false statements to United States officials outside of United States territory in order to obtain status as non-quota immigrants were prosecuted, the court stating that "Congress may pick and choose whatever recognized principle of international jurisdiction is necessary to accomplish the purpose sought by the (its) legislation." Id., at 491; accord, Rocha v. United States, 288 F. 2d 545 (9th Cir. 1961), cert. denied, 366 U.S. 948 (1961), involving aliens who had conspired to enter the United States illegally as pre-ferred status immigrants, the court citing the Rodriguez case and stating that "the powers of the government and the Congress in regard to sovereignty (court's emphasis) are broader than the powers possessed in relation to internal

matters." <u>Id</u>., at 549.

142. See, <u>United States v. Aluminum Co. of America</u> (the "Alcoa"
     case), 148 F. 2d 416 (2nd Cir. 1945), in which the defendant
     Canadian corporation was charged with certain violations of
     the Sherman Anti-Trust Act relating to attempts to restrain
     and monopolize interstate and foreign commerce of the
     United States; also, <u>United States v. Imperial Chemical</u>
     <u>Industries</u>, 100 F. Supp. 504 (S.D. New York, 1951). For
     an explanation of the latter case and a discussion in
     general of the United States practices with respect to
     jurisdiction over anti-trust cases, see respectively 6
     Whiteman, <u>Digest</u>, 126-27, 118-160 (1968) and <i>supra</i>, note 22.

143. <u>Schoenbaum v. Firstbrook</u>, 405 F. 2d 200 (2nd Cir. 1968) and
     <u>Securities and Exchange Commission v. Briggs</u>, 234 F. Supp.
     618 (U.S.D.C. Northern D. Ohio, 1964).

144. See, e.g., criticism of the Alcoa case in Stein & Hay,
     <u>Law and Institutions in the Atlantic Area</u>, 684 (1968); and
     Jennings, "Extraterritorial Jurisdiction and the United
     States Antitrust Laws," 33 <u>Brit. Y.B. Int'l L.</u> 146, 175
     (1957). Anglo-American practice, it can generally be said,
     still adheres to the territorial theory, with exceptions
     being made in the specific areas discussed above. This is
     reflected in the <u>Restatement</u>, §38, "Territorial Interpreta-
     tion of United States Law."

     Rules of United States statutory law, whether
     prescribed by federal or state authority, apply
     only to conduct occurring within or having effect

within, the territory of the United States,

unless the contrary is clearly indicated by

the statute.

Since the American federal system is based upon the theor-

etical premise that the federal government and Congress in

particular can act only when the power to do so is speci-

fically delegated to it in the Constitution with the non-

delegated sovereign powers remaining with the states and

the people (U.S. Constitution Amendment X), a special prob-

lem is raised within the context of American constitutional

law which is outside the scope of this discussion. See

George, *supra*, note 1, at 614-617.

For some examples of how states not following Anglo-American

jurisdictional practice have used and extended the protected

interest principle, see Sarkar, "The Proper Law of Crime

in International Law," 11 Int. & Comp. L.Q. 446, 463-64

(1962).

145. The following words of the Permanent Court in the Lotus

case seem to support such a contention: "No argument has

come to the knowledge of the Court from which it could be

deduced that States recognize themselves to be under an

obligation towards each other only to have regard to the

place where the author of the offense happens to be at the

time of the offense." P.C.I.J., Ser. A, No. 10 (1927), at

23.

Article 11 of the High Seas Treaty, however, would prohibit

use of the protective principle in the situations specified

therein.

146. See, "Harvard Draft Convention," Art. 9; _Restatement_, §34.
Although the _Restatement_ only applies the principle to
piracy, it does provide "that other crimes may become crimes
of universal interest," such as slave trading, traffic in
women for prostitution, traffic in narcotic drugs and war
crimes. _Restatement_, at 94, 97.

The "Harvard Research" in its Comment to Article 9, states
"there seems to be little or no basis for common agreement
as to which offenses should fall within the class of _delicta
juris gentium_ which are to be prosecuted and punished on
the same basis as piracy." _Id_., at 569. Some of the
offenses which are defined as such by the various laws,
codes and projects collected by the "Harvard Research" are
the slave trade, the counterfeiting of foreign moneys or
securities, traffic in women and children for immoral purposes, the use of explosives or poisons to cause a common
danger, injury to submarine cables, traffic in narcotics
and traffic in obscene publications. _Id_., at 569-571;
see also Oppenheim, _supra_, note 1, at 330; United States
practice in applying the universality principle has been
generally limited to piracy. See, 18 U.S.C. §1651 (1958);
United States v. Smith, 18 U.S. (5 Wheat.) 153 (1820);
United States v. Klintock, 18 U.S. (5 Wheat.) 144 (1820).
The United States Constitution, Art. I, Sec. 8, Cl. 9,
gives Congress the power "to define and punish piracies and
felonies committed on the high seas and offenses against the

law of nations."

147. High Seas Treaty, Art. 14. See, on the subject of immunity to ships in general The Schooner Exchange v. MacFaddon, 7 Cranch 116 (1812) (warship granted immunity); Berizzi Bros. Co. v. S. S. Pesaro, 271 U.S. 562 (1926) (governmental commercial vessel granted immunity). But cf., Republic of Mexico v. Hoffman, 324 U.S. 30 (1945) (governmental commercial vessel denied immunity because it was operated by a private corporation). On the Doctrine of Act of State, see Banco de Espana v. Federal Reserve Bank of New York, 114 F. 2d 438 (2nd Cir. 1940); Banco Nacional de Cuba v. Sabbatino, 376 U.S. 398 (1964); and Banco Nacional de Cuba v. Farr, 243 F. Supp. 957 (S.D.N.Y. 1965), aff'd 388 F. 2d 166 (2nd Cir. 1967), cert. denied, 390 U.S. 956 (1968).

148. Drafted at the Hague, December 16, 1970, T.I.A.S. 7192. As of January 21, 1971, 51 states had become parties to the Convention. For text to the Convention, see 10 Int. Legal Materials, 133 (January, 1971).

149. Hague Convention, Art. 1.

150. Tokyo Convention, Art. 1(3).

151. Hague Convention, Art. 3(1).

152. Id.

153. Tokyo Convention, Art. 1(4).

154. Hague Convention, Art. 3(2).

155. Id., Art. 3(3).

156. Oppenheim, supra, note 1, at 733-735. See the Convention to Suppress the Slave Trade and Slavery; concluded at Geneva,

September 25, 1926; 46 Stat. 2183, T.S. No. 778, 60 I.N.T.S. 253; and Protocol Amending the Slavery Convention, done at New York, December 7, 1953, 7 U.S.T. 479, T.I.A.S. No. 3532, 182 U.N.T.S. 51. See also, the Supplementary Convention of the Abolition of Slavery, the Slave Trade and Institutions and Practices Similar to Slavery, done at Geneva, September 7, 1956, 18 U.S.T. 3201, T.I.A.S. No. 6418, 266 U.N.T.S. 3 and Bassiouni and Nanda, "Slavery and Slave Trade: Steps Toward Its Eradication," 12 Santa Clara Lawyer 412 (1972).

157. High Seas Treaty, Art. 13.

158. The idea of creating an international criminal court has been discussed after World War I, and in particular, in 1937 in conjunction with the proposed draft treaty on terrorism. For the creation of an international criminal court and the enforcement machinery needed, see I Bassiouni and Nanda, International Criminal Law (1973), part V, in particular the contributions of Dautricourt and Nepote. See also Bassiouni, International Terrorism and Political Crimes, (1974) particularly Dautricourt and L. Kos-Zubkowski on the creation of an international criminal court. See, Draft Statute for an International Criminal Court, Articles 1-54, in the 1953 /Report of Committee on International Criminal Jurisdiction, General Assembly Official Records, IX, Supp. 12 (A/2645)23-26 (1954); and Klein and Wilkes, "United Nations Draft Statute for an International Criminal Court: An American Evaluation," in, International Criminal Law, Mueller and Wise, ed. (1965), p. 513-526.

159. For a detailed discussion, see Feller in Bassiouni and
     Nanda, II International Criminal Law (1973), Part I.

160. 18 U.S.C. 1651 et seq. (1958).

161. For a survey of the Nüremberg and Tokyo war crimes trials,
     see Bassiouni and Nanda I International Criminal Law (1973),
     Part V, particularly the contributions of Bierzanck and
     Röling.

162. Oppenheim, *supra*, note 1, at 342, citing Transcript of Pro-
     ceedings, pp. 16, 878.

163. See, 11 Whiteman, Digest, 962-1019 (1968). See, especially,
     In re Yamashita, 327 U.S. 1 (1946).

164. See, 11 Whiteman, Digest, 874-1017 (1968) on activities of
     the United States and other states in regard to non-interna-
     tional war crimes trials conducted both during and after
     World War II.

165. E.g., Bassiouni and Nanda, International Criminal Law (1973).

166. See, Wright, "The Legality of the Kaiser," 13 Am. Pol. Sci.
     Rev. 121 (1919).

167. Comment - "Extradition: Concurrent Jurisdiction and the Un-
     certainty of Prosecution in the Requested Nation," 14 Wayne
     L. Rev. 1181 (1968).

168. Falk, "International Jurisdiction: Horizontal and Vertical
     Conceptions of Legal Order," 32 Temp. L.Q. 295 (1959).

169. Katzenbach, "Conflicts on an Unruly Horse: Reciprocal Claims
     and Tolerances in Interstate and International Law," 65
     Yale L.J. 1087 (1956).

170. See, Bassiouni, "World Public Order and Extradition: A

Conceptual Evaluation" in <u>Aktuelle Probleme dos Internation-</u>
<u>den Strafrechts</u>, Oehler and Pötz, ed. (1970).

Substantive Requirements: Extraditable Offenses, Double Criminality, and the Doctrine of Specialty

Introduction

The principal rules and practices of international extradition constitute a significant body of international law. [1] Now almost entirely derived from treaty sources, extradition grew nonetheless to recognized stature before treaties had overtaken custom as the most important sources of that aspect of international law and practice. There are therefore considerable similarities between treaties, and also with municipal laws. In many respects, however, extradition treaties and municipal legislation contain complex rules whose variety throughout the world evidences the need for harmonization.

The two important features distinguishing modern extradition from other modes of securing jurisdiction over offenders are:

1. the conscious purpose, openly and regularly pursued, to restore a person to an authority competent to exercise jurisdiction over him or her, and

2. the observance of a body of rules imposed by international law and municipal law, governing both the prerequisites for and the consequences of extradition.

Although the obligation to extradite in the absence of treaty was supported by Bodin, Grotius, [2] and others discussed in

Chapter I, it is still not uniformly recognized as part of customary international law. States are therefore under no international legal obligation or duty to surrender a fugitive from justice in the absence of a treaty or reciprocal practice except whenever a multilateral treaty imposes such an obligation. Irrespective of the legal basis for extradition the alleged offense for which extradition is requested must be:

a.) enumerated among the "extraditable offenses," or the formula for ascertaining it is provided for in the treaty, or b.) in the absence of a treaty the offense must be reciprocally recognized as extraditable.

Extradition treaties either list the offenses for which extradition shall be granted or designate a formula by which to determine extraditable offenses. In addition to defining or designating extraditable offenses, the criminality of the conduct allegedly committed by the relator must satisfy the requirement of double criminality, i.e., that the offense charged constitutes a crime in the two legal systems. [3] The extent to which a given type of conduct shall be considered criminal in the two respective legal system varies, depending on the legal systems involved. The interpretation and application of that requirement (what constitutes an extraditable offense) will also vary according to the legal system in question.

The substantive requirements of extradition are that a person accused of or found guilty of an offense in the requesting state be surrendered to that state provided that:

1- If there is a treaty, the offense be listed or designated;

2- If there is no treaty that the respective states will

reciprocate;

3- If there is no treaty or reciprocity but the request is based on comity, the requested state will rely on its customary practice;

4- Furthermore, in all three instances the offense charged must also constitute an offense in the requested state, i.e., double criminality, either in the objective sense, *in concreto* or in the subjective sense, *in abstracto*.

The legal basis upon which extradition is practiced is either treaty, reciprocity or comity. Extraditable offenses and double criminality, however, constitute substantive requirements for the surrender of an individual by virtue of any one of these bases. The practice of listing offenses in a treaty to which participants are virtually bound is a manifestation of reciprocal obligation. Similarly, when double criminality is required by treaty or by custom, it is applicable to the practice regardless of whether the legal basis of the practice is treaty or reciprocity. Such a requirement in effect imposes a mutuality of obligation on the parties which is often referred to as a reciprocal obligation.

A corollary to these two requirements of extraditable offense and double criminality is the doctrine of specialty. That doctrine is premised on the assumption that whenever a state uses its formal processes to surrender a person to another state for a specific charge, the requesting state shall carry out its intended purpose of prosecuting or punishing the offender for the offense charged in its request for extradition and none other.

1. *Extraditable Offenses and Double Criminality*

1.1 *The Relationship of Extraditable Offenses, Double Criminality and Reciprocity.*

The term extraditable offenses means these offenses which depending upon the basis of the extradition practice existing between states, will be determined as being subject to extradition. In treaty practice these offenses will be listed in the treaty or designated in some way. Whenever the practice is not based on a treaty but on reciprocity such offenses will be those which the respective states agree upon and are willing to reciprocate on. If the basis for the practice is comity there is no application for this requirement except with respect to the binding effect of the customary practice of the requested state.

Double criminality refers to the characterization of the relator's criminal conduct insofar as it constitutes an offense under the laws of the respective states. To that extent it constitutes a form of mutuality of obligations, but should not be confused with "reciprocity" as one of the bases for the very practice of extradition.

Reciprocity as one of the legal basis for extradition is a pre-condition to the practice as well as condition subsequent in that the requesting shall correspondingly engage in the practice. It must be distinguished from the requirement of double criminality which embodies a reciprocal characterization of those offenses deemed extraditable.

314

To the extent that treaties list or designate extraditable offenses and require double criminality in addition thereto, both of these requirements characteristically contain an implicit element of mutuality, hence reciprocity.[4]

1.2 Methods of Determining Extraditable Offenses

Designation of extraditable offenses in treaties may be achieved by one of two methods, the enumerative and eliminative.

A. The enumerative method , by which the offenses are named and defined, has a limitative effect confining the application of the treaty to these offenses only.

As an example, Section 3184 of Title 18, United States Code, authorized extradition proceedings "whenever there is a treaty or convention for extradition between the United States and any foreign government," against persons charged "with having committed within the jurisdiction of any such foreign government any of the crimes provided for by such treaty or convention." All the bilateral extradition treaties and conventions to which the United States is a party thereto contain a list of offenses for which extradition shall be granted. The only multilateral extradition agreement to which the United States is a party, the Montevideo Convention of 1933,[5] concluded with other American Republics, provides for extradition of persons charged with "a crime...(which) is punishable under the laws of the demanding and surrendering States with a minimum penalty of imprisonment for one year." (Article 1(b).) However, this agreement is not operative if there is a bilateral treaty in force between the parties concerned. (Article 21.)

B. _The eliminative method_ , which is indicative rather than limitative, specifies as extraditable those offenses which under the laws of both states are punishable by an agreed degree of severity, usually a minimum penalty. The latter method is more convenient in that it avoids unnecessary detail in the treaty and obviates likely omission of certain crimes as well as eliminates problems of characterization of offenses arising from definitional differences between the laws of the requested and requesting states. It is not, however, without its difficulties when it comes to determining what actually constitutes the prescribed penalty, namely: The actual sentence, the possible sentence, or the range of the sentence. It is also problematic with respect to indeterminate sentences. The use of this method has been found to be impractical by countries such as the United States where minimum sentences are not a uniform feature of the federal laws and the laws of the different states. Illustrating this difficulty, Whiteman stated with respect to the issue arising between Columbia and the United States:

> . . .the Colombian Foreign Office . . .(proposes)
> that instead of including in the convention a list
> of the extraditable crimes it provided that crimes
> should be regarded as extraditable when they are
> punishable by the penal laws of both countries with
> a minimum penalty of deprivation of liberty for six
> months.

> . . .all of the bilateral extradition agreements
> of the United States contain lists of extraditable

316

crimes and the Department does not desire to make any exception to this practice.

The foregoing view of the matter in question is largely based upon the fact that in general recent Federal penal enactments in the United States do not prescribe a minimum sentence which may be imposed but provide merely for imprisonment for "not more" than a certain term. It is believed that similar provisions are contained in recent enactments throughout various states of the Union. Moreover, the states have penal codes which differ in many respects the one from the other and this would constitute a further obstacle to an agreement along the lines suggested by the Colombian Government.[6]

The main defects of the enumerative method arise from the fact that the list can omit certain offenses and their subsequent inclusion by supplementary treaty may prove too cumbersome. Since this method excludes an *ad hoc* determination of extraditable offenses, it is inflexable. These defects have prompted the development in some treaties to resort to the eliminative method, which define extraditable offenses by their punishment. This method has its flaws in that it is impractical to systems which have a notable disparity in penalties. Furthermore, it is not always clear whether it applies to minimum, maximum, or possible penalties. The use of such a method may also tend to eliminate the need to comply with the requirement of double criminality

317

which has some meritorious applications, particularly insofar as it concerns minor offenses in the requested state but which are aggravated in the requesting state because of more punitive or retributive approach.

The eliminative method by its very nature reflects and appeals to a retributive theory of punishment by *inter alia* ignoring enlightened theories of rehabilitation, resocialization and particularly in cases where the deviant behavior is considered an illness rather than a crime. This would be the case, for example, with respect to narcotics violations. Among many other examples are cases involving what some states will deem mental health problems and in particular juvenile delinquency violations. In addition, problems of alcoholism and drug addiction are so widely perceived that what would be a crime in some states would be considered a disease in another. The penal philosophy of states ranges in diversity from one extreme to another and the only commonality on which the eliminative approach could rest is the basic punitive orientation whenever manifested in the respective laws of the states in question.

Even though modern concepts of criminology and penology discredit a straight penalty approach to characterize offenders, the contemporary trend in extradition treaties is to designate extraditable offenses by such a method.[7]

Another significant problem raised by this method is the element of knowledge of the law attributed by legal presumption to an offender whether that person be a national or an alien. Ignorance of the law is no defense, but the presumption of knowledge of the law at an age of fast and easy travel among states with a wide divergence of penal laws strains that presumption to its utmost. It must be noted, however, that while ignorance of the law is no defense, one of the premises on which this presumption is based is the existence of notice of the proscribed conduct affording all persons the opportunity to refrain from engaging in it.[8] Double criminality provides an implicit element of notice by analogy in that the individual is held to the same proscribed conduct known to the individual in his or her own legal system. However, by allowing extradition whenever the charge contains a penalty equal to that of the other state regardless of the corresponding nature of the offense in both laws would subject people to criminal jeopardy without adequate notice.

1.3 *Rationale for Defining Extraditable Offenses*

There are two reasons traditionally advanced for the proposition of defining extraditable offenses: 1) to avoid using a cumbersome and costly procedure like extradition for minor offenses, and 2) to avoid having rhe requested state decline surrender on public policy grounds (because the conduct is not criminalized in that state) thus causing embarrassment to the respective states. Both arguments, though valid, are nonetheless challengeable if for no other reason than because their premise is predicated essentially on the interest of one state, namely, the requested state. Consider that if the requesting state deems it has a sufficient interest in the relator to request extradition to what extent should the requested state be concerned with whether it is for a serious or minor offense and whether

319

the identical offense is deemed criminal in the requested state. This is a policy question which should not be left to the determination of single states because its conflict creating potential is sufficient to make it a question of international concern. In any event, whenever the offense charged by the requesting state will be deemed contrary to the public policy of the requested state, it is likely to be because that offense is of a political character or is charged in order to effectuate a political rather than a criminological end. In this case, however, the state of refuge can deny the request on grounds of "political offense exception" (discussed *infra* Chapter VI, Section 1).

The requirement of double criminality makes the listing of offenses in a treaty a technicality which only renders the procedure more cumbersome. As a substantive matter, double criminality provides more protection to the individual and gives the requested state more flexibility than the rigid approach of listing offenses in a treaty. That approach allows for technical flaws in the process, and requires constant revision of treaties without adding anything more substantive to the requirement that the offense constitute a crime in both legal systems.

To avoid the difficulties stated above, a proposed technique of designating extraditable offenses in treaties is as follows: To list nonextraditable offenses and to designate extraditable offenses by type, category and dispositional method.

This eliminates by implication certain offenses which should not by their nature or significance be the subject of extradition. This justification is to some extent akin to the earlier rationale

320

advanced to support the practice of listing offenses. The difference between the earlier traditional justification and the one advanced here is that the list of extraditable offenses should contain those offenses which are excepted from the practice rather than list those which would support it. Furthermore, extraditable offenses should not be labeled or referred to by name but classified in a manner indicating type, category and disposition. This method would avoid most of the shortcomings discussed above and incorporate the benefits deriving from the application of the requirement of double criminality without the need to duplicate the same substantive requirement.

Another argument in support of a modified method of designating extraditable offenses arises in those cases wherein the relator is not a national of the requesting state, but a national of the requested state, and that state permits extradition of nationals. In such cases it could be assumed that listing or defining extraditable offenses is a protection for such persons insofar as offenses listed or defined constitute the same crime in his or her own state and therefore that person shall not be subjected to the application of a foreign law (that of the requesting state of which he or she is not a national) without adequate notice and knowledge. Essentially, it is an argument which extends the doctrine *nullum crimen sine legge,*[9] even though the requirement of double criminality is theoretically sufficient to provide for it. Apart from these arguments applicable to extraditable offenses in treaties, the requirement of double criminality provides the substantive basis needed to insure that the process shall not, (to this extent), be arbitrary.

1.4 Double Criminality

This requirement means that the offense charged constitutes an offense in both legal systems. There are two methods of interpreting this requirement of double criminality, namely: *in concreto* (objective) and *in abstracto* (subjective). The first approach relies on the label of the offense and a strict interpretation of its legal elements. The second approach relies on the criminality of the activity regardless of its specific label and full concordance of its elements in the respective laws of the two states.

In this context, the resolutions adopted by the 1969 Tenth International Congress of Penal Law held in Rome took the desirable lead of recommending that: the requested state set aside the requirement of double criminality, unless special circumstances exist in the requesting state such as a question of *ordre public*; in such cases that the requested state examine *in abstracto* whether or not the conduct of the relator are offenses under its law, or if it deems punishable that type of conduct. [10] According to these recommendations, however, extradition can be denied if it is manifest that the request is in the nature of a subterfuge for achieving non-penological purposes. In this case, the requested state will not be bound to adhere to the *proposed caveat*. [11]

Extradition is probably the most reciprocation oriented process and thus it is relied upon as a method of determining extraditable offenses and double criminality. It is firmly rooted in the practice even though it has long been challenged. As early as 1880

322

the Institute for International Law meeting at Oxford declared
in its Resolutions:

> La condition de reciprocite, en cette matière,
>
> peut etre commendée par la politique; elle
>
> n'est pas exigée par la justice.[12]

Indeed, justice does not require reciprocity, but politics and the
exacerbated doctrine of sovereignty do.

Even at earlier times, authors like Billot, Grotius and Vattel
had expressed a similar view,[13] and it is not therefore surprising
to find that some states reject the reciprocity approach.[14] It
would indeed be desirable that states would practice extradition
without making reciprocity a condition of the practice and an
implicit requirement of double criminality.[15] Reciprocity,
however, is upheld because it reflects and ensures the continued
preservation of co-equal sovereignty among nation-states.

Double criminality is in effect a reciprocity requirement which
is intended to insure each of the respective states that it can
rely on corresponding treatment, and that no state shall use its
processes to surrender a person for conduct which it does not characterize as a criminal.

The requirement of double criminality does, of course, benefit the
relator insofar as he or she can evade the processes of justice of
the state in which the conduct was allegedly committed if (depending
upon the interpretative formula) the same conduct is not also deemed
criminal in the requested state.

There are three approaches to determine whether the offense charged
even though criminal in both states falls within the meaning of

323

"double criminality":

1.) Whether the acts are chargeable as an offense regardless of their prosecutability:

2.) Whether the acts are chargeable and also prosecutable; and

3.) Whether the acts are chargeable, prosecutable and could also result in a conviction.

Cases show a wide divergence in the interpretation of this requirement as will be seen from the case study made in Section 3 below, but most states will, however, adhere to the first of these theories. Furthermore, as is discussed in Chapter VI, several defenses will arise which reveal that occasionally a request shall be denied on grounds that prosecution is barred by statute of limitations or that a conviction cannot be returned because of legally exonerating conditions. This indicates also that the requirement is contingent upon other factors.

The choice of any one of the above theories by which to define double criminality and the validity of any one of the defenses which can be raised are invariably a reflection of the *ratio materiae* of extradition discussed in Chapter I.

Extradition is still regarded primarily as an instrument of inter-state cooperation designed to inure principally to the benefit of the interested states. This assertion remains true even though the criminality of the relator must still be demonstrated in accordance with certain procedures and rules. Because states are co-equal sovereigns in the world order, emphasis on this characteristic aspect of the international order has pervaded the practice of extradition and imposed its consequential exigencies, i.e., reciprocity of subtantive requirements and conditions. Such form of reciprocity has characteristically been insisted upon between co-equal participants in the international order. This form of reciprocity of substantive requirements and conditions which some authors refer to as a rule of customary international law [16] has been manifested in treaty as well as non-treaty relations. If the legal basis for extradition is reciprocity, then the requirement of reciprocity of substantive requirements and conditions characterizing the mutual obligations of the respective states is tantamount to reciprocity within reciprocity. Such a situation is without apparent purpose other than to carry to its utmost extent the implications of the doctrine of sovereignty.

The requirement of double criminality is found in treaties (stated either specifically or implicitly), it is in the municipal laws and judicial practice of most states and is therefore deemed part of customary international law. Those states, such as the United States, which do not recognize extradition as part of customary international law will apply the requirement whenever its existence can be derived from a treaty. Thus, whenever a state adheres to the position that double criminality arises only from treaty obligations, the absence of any explicit or implicit language to that effect may preclude the applicability of this requirement.

The doctrine of double criminality as discussed above is the object of several definitional approaches and depending upon the choice of definitional theory it will be more or less identified with extraditable offenses. Similarly, because of the various approaches to defining extraditable offenses, the likelihood for confusion between these two requirements exists.

1.5 Definitional Theories of Extraditable Offenses and Their Relationship to Double Criminality

The term extraditable offenses applies to treaty practice where offenses are listed or designated specifically. If the practice of the respective states is based on reciprocity, then extraditable offenses are those which constitute an offense in both systems and for which there is mutual recognition. As for extradition granted on comity it is an exceptional method resorted to in special instances and whenever the respective states do not rely on a treaty of reciprocity. In these cases the requesting state does not rely on any definition or method of designating extraditable offenses and the requested state can grant or deny the request irrespective of the offense charged or its designation. It may however request that double criminality be satisfied depending upon its national legislation. In most cases involving extradition on the basis of comity the conduct of the relator constituted an offense in the requested state. It appears therefore that customary international law requires the condition of double criminality as to all bases of extradition.

Extraditable offenses are interpreted in one of two ways:

1) as requiring the offense charged to be identical to an offense in the treaty list, or 2) the offense charged is not identical to the treaty listed offense, but the acts performed which support that charge could sustain a charge under the laws

of the requested state which charge corresponds to the treaty listed offense.

The second one of these interpretative approaches focuses on the question of whether the acts performed in the requesting state and constituting an offense under its laws could also constitute an offense under the laws of the requested state and made extraditable under the treaty regardless of the actual offense charged by the requesting state. In effect, this approach produces the same result reached whenever the subjective interpretation of the requirement of double criminality is applied. Under this approach to interpreting extraditable offenses the requested state examines the category and type of offense charged to determine its counterpart under its own laws. From a practical point of view, acts which are part of the common crimes variety are likely to constitute an offense in all legal systems, Hence, if this type of conduct is charged by the requesting state and the identical charge may not exist in the requested state, the likelihood is great that the same category or type of offense exists in the requested state. Therefore, this type of broad interpretation of extraditable offenses corresponds to a subjective interpretation of double criminality.

When extradition is practiced between states which do not require listing extraditable offenses, but designate them in another manner, the requested state will also have to determine whether the offense and its counterpart fall within the treaty designation and also satisfies the double criminality requirement. Since the common crimes variety are invariably listed or desig-

nate them in another manner, the requested state will also have
to determine whether the offense and its counterpart fall within
the treaty designation and also satisfies the double criminality
requirement. Since the common crimes variety are invariably
listed or designated in treaties, the two requirements of extraditable offense and double criminality whenever broadly interpreted, are satisfied by a single test, i.e., the conduct is criminal in the jurisprudence of both states even though not defined
identically. The same outcome is produced even if a given state
is not to apply double criminality but adheres to strict compliance with the treaty list, or if that state interprets the
treaty listed extraditable offense as referring to acts which
had they been committed in the requested state would have constituted the offense charged. Under this interpretation of extraditable offenses the requirement of double criminality is also
satisfied. This indicates the close relationship of the two conditions when they are interpreted and applied in their broadest
sense.

As an indication of the interrelationship and even possible
confusion between these two elements, Whiteman states the
following:

> A common requirement for extradition is that
> the acts which form the basis for the extradition
> request constitute a crime under the laws of both
> the requesting and the requested States. This re-
> quirement exists whether the request is made under
> a treaty or apart from a treaty and whether a list

of offenses punishable by at least a certain minimum
penalty, specific provision is usually made that the
offense must be a crime in both States. Where a list
of offenses is involved in the treaty or the law, a
specific provision on the point is less common.
However, even in the absence of a specific provision,
the requirement is generally imposed. The question
whether the requirement has been met generally arises
with regard to the law of the requested State and
where the requirement is covered by a specific provision in the law or treaty it is often cast only
in terms of the law of the requested State, since,
if a State requests extradition, it must base its
request on an alleged violation of its laws. It
might be supposed that if two States agree in a
treaty to a list of offenses for which extradition
shall take place, they would include only those
acts which are crimes in both States. However,
questions nevertheless may arise. Certain acts
may, under the law of the requesting State, constitute a listed treaty offense while under the
law of the requested State, the same acts may
constitute no crime or, more frequently, one not
listed in the treaty. [17]

2. *A Case Study Analysis of Judicial Application of Extraditable
Offenses and Double Criminality with Emphasis on the Practice
of the United States, England and Canada.*

Extradition in the United States will not be granted unless the fugitive is alleged to have committed one of the offenses enumerated in the applicable extradition treaty (see Appendix A Chapter I for United States treaties). Treaties do not define these offenses but only name them; and, therefore, some body of substantive criminal law must be applied by the extradition magistrate to determine whether the act committed constitutes a treaty offense. That body of law is the jurisprudence of the state where the offense was allegedly committed. In a federal-state system, it will be the law of the *Lex Loci Delictus*, if the offense charged rests on the theory of territorial jurisdiction (see Chapter III, Theories of Jurisdiction).

The cases which follow reveal the cleavage between extraditable offenses, the interpretation given their significance, and double criminality.

In <u>Collins v. Loisel</u>,[18] Mr. Justice Brandeis stated:

<u>First</u>. Collins contends that the affadavit of the British Consul General does not charge an extraditable offense. The argument is that the affadavit charges cheating merely; that cheating is not among the offenses enumerated in the extradition treaties; that cheating is a different offense from obtaining property under false pretenses which is expressly named in the Treaty of December 13, 1900, 32 Stat. 1864; that to convict of cheating it is sufficient to prove a promise of future performance which the promisor does not intend to perform, while to con-

vict of obtaining property by false pretense it
is essential that there be a false representation
of a state of things past or present. See State v.
Colly, 39 La. Ann. 841. <u>It is true that an offense is
extraditable only if the acts charged are criminal by
the laws of both countries.</u> (Emphasis added).

It is also true that the charge made in the court
of India rests upon Section 420 of its Penal Code,
which declares: "Whoever cheats and thereby dis-
honestly induces the person deceived to deliver
any property to any person . . . shall be punished
with imprisonment of either description for a term
which may extend to seven years, and shall also be
liable to fine," whereas Section 818 of the Revised
Statutes of Louisiana declares: "Whoever, by any
false pretense, shall obtain, or aid and assist
another in obtaining, from any person, money or
any property, with intent to defraud him of the
same, shall, on conviction, be punished by imprisonment at hard labor or otherwise, not exceeding
twelve months." But the affidavit of the British
Consul General recites that Collins stands charged
in the Chief Presidency Magistrate's Court with
having feloniously obtained the pearl button by
false pretenses; and the certificate of the Secretary to the Government of India, which accompan-
ies the papers on which Collins surrender is sought,

331

describes the offense with which he is there charged

as "the crime of obtaining valuable property by false

pretenses." The law does not require that the name by

which the crime is described in the two countries shall

be the same; nor that the scope of the liability shall be

coextensive, or, in other respects, the same in the two

countries. It is enough if the particular act charged

is criminal in both jurisdictions. (Emphasis added).

This was held with reference to different crimes

involving false statements in Wright v. Henkel, 1900

U.S. 40, 58; Kelly v. Griffin, 241 U.S. 6, 14; Benson v.

McMahon, 127 U.S. 457, 465; and Greene v. United States,

154 Fed. 401. Compare ex parte Piot, 15 Cox C. C.

208. The offense charged was, therefore, clearly

extraditable. [19]

The Brandeis' opinion conformed with that of Mr. Justice Holmes

in Wright v. Henkel, [20] wherein he stated "It is enough if the

particular variety was criminal in both jurisdictions." [21]

In Gluckman v. Henkel, [22] Mr. Justice Holmes, relying on that

position, went even further and with respect to the relationship

between the complaint and the evidence represented stated that:

Neither Wright v. Henkel, 190 U.S. 40, nor

Pettit v. Wright, 194 U.S. 205, indicates that

because the law of New York in this case may

determine whether the prisoner is charged with an

extraditable crime, it is to determine the effect

of such a variance between evidence and complaint.

<u>This is a matter to be decided on general princi-</u>

<u>ples, irrespective of the law of the state.</u>[23]

(Emphasis added.)

The Holmes and Brandeis expressed majority position remained

firm in United States jurisprudence until it was exceptionally

expanded in a controversial manner in <u>Factor v. Laubenheimer</u>:[24]

In that case Great Britain requested the extradition

from the United States of John Jacob Factor for the

crime of receiving money knowing the same to have

been fraudulently obtained. The Supreme Court of the

United States upheld the decision of the extradition

magistrate in favor of extradition despite the fact

that the criminal law of Illinois, where Factor was

found and the extradition hearing was held, did not

specifically cover this offense. The Court found

that the conduct with which Factor was charged was

a crime in Great Britain, was within the provisions

of the Treaty of 1881 between the two countries,

and was 'a crime under the law of many states, if

not Illinois, punishable either as the crime of re-

ceiving money obtained fraudulently or by false

pretenses, or as larceny.'

The Factor case reaffirmed the position of the United States to

engage in extradition relatioms only by treaty and limiting the

practice to a strict interpretation of the applicable treaty
(the treaty in question, namely, the Webster-Ashburton Treaty of
1842 and its supplementary agreements of 1889, 1900 and 1905).
Each supplementary agreement *inter alia* added to the list of extraditable offenses. The offense charged in this case was not a
crime in Illinois where the accused was sought and traditional
application of double criminality would have precluded his extradition. The court reached this conclusion by finding that the
requirement of double criminality which was stated in the treaty
as applicable to some of the offenses was not applicable in the
case of this offense for which the relator was sought because it
was under one of the supplementary agreements which failed to
mention that requirement explicitly. The court in interpreting
the treaty found that under the maxim *expressio unius exclusio est
alterius*   , double criminality stated in the original treaty
had been excluded from its supplementary part which was applicable to the case at bar. The court rejected the argument that
double criminality was a requirement of customary international
law because United States extradition practice is based solely
(sic) on treaty. For all practical purposes, had the court
recognized the applicability of the double criminality requirement in reliance on many precedents including Collins v.
Loisel,[25] which it distinguished, it could have been satisfied.
The requirement would have been interpreted subjectively meaning
that: the acts charged would if charged in the requested state
constitute an extraditable offense even though it is not the
same charge proffered by the requesting state. The court con-

334

cluded that when the particular offense charged is not among those specifically required to be criminal in both states, the acts complained of heed not constitute the same crime in the state where the accused is found. It was sufficient, the court found, that the offense was specified in the treaty and considered a crime by the jurisprudence of both states.

The Supreme Court in effect set aside the argument that there was a general treaty requirement of double criminality declaring that:

> The obligation to do what some nations have
> done voluntarily, in the interest of justice and
> friendly international relationships . . . should
> be construed more liberally than a criminal statute
> or the technical requirements of criminal procedure
> . . . . It has been the policy of our own govern-
> ment, as of others, in entering into extradition
> treaties, to name as treaty offenses only those
> generally recognized as criminal by the laws in
> force within its own territory. But that policy
> when carried into effect by treaty designation of
> offenses with respect to which extradition is to
> be granted, affords no adequate basis for declin-
> ing to construe the treaty in accordance with its
> language, or for saying that its obligation, in
> the absence of some express requirement, is con-
> ditioned on the criminality of the offenses charged
> according to the laws of the particular place of

asylum.[26]

The Factor decision is a precedent to the question of treaty interpretation and only by *dicta* goes to the substance of the application and interpretation of the double criminality requirement. Justices Butler, Brandeis, and Roberts who dissented from the majority pointed out that had the court applied a broad interpretation of the requirement of double criminality the outcome would have been the same. Thus, illustrating the observation made earlier that a broad subjective interpretation of double criminality leads to the same result as its nonapplicability when it is coupled with a broad interpretation of what the requirement of extraditable offenses.

The position of the United States remained consistent: throughout the major decisions of this century, namely: Wright v. Henkel, [27] Pettit v. Walsh, [28] Gluckman v. Henkel, [29] Kelly v. Griffin, [30] Collins v. Loisel and even to some extent Factor v. Laubenheimer (subject to the reservations stated in the discussion of this case). [32] In 1952, the Second Circuit Court of Appeals in United States v. Stokinger [33] denied the application for a writ of *habeas corpus* brought by Sol and Harold Rauch whose extradition from the United States was requested by the Government of Canada for the crimes of theft and fraud. The extradition agreement between the United States and Canada included larceny as an extraditable offense. The question arose as to whether the offense charged was the same one stated in the treaty as constituting an extraditable offense. The court stated:

> . . . After an examination of the applicable

portions of the Criminal Code of Canada dealing
with theft and fraud we are convinced that the
facts set out in the depositions provided a
reasonable ground for the Commissioner to believe
that relators committed acts criminal under the
laws of Canada. It likewise seems clear to us
that the contents of the depositions provided a
reasonable ground for him to believe that relators
committed acts which would be criminal under the
laws of New York. New York Penal Law, McKinney's
Consol. Laws, c. 40, §§ 1290, 1294 and 1295. It
is immaterial that the acts in question constitute
the crime of theft and fraud in Canada and the
crime of larceny in New York State. *It is enough
if the particular acts charged are criminal in both
jurisdictions.* Collins v. Loisel, 1922, 259 U.S.
309, 42 S.Ct. 469, 66 L. Ed. 956. [34]

Thus the court did not limit its inquiry to the label of the
charge but inquired into the criminal conduct and the type of
crime it gave rise to. The following case clarifies the inquiry
of the court into the alleged criminal conduct, its relationship
to the offense charged and its corresponding offense in the law
of the requested state. Considering the application for a writ
of *habeas corpus* filed by Vincenzo Gallina who was being held
for extradition to Italy for the crime of robbery, the District
Court for Connecticut stated in 1960:

There is ample evidence in the record that
the acts participated in by relator were within
that definition. It is true that the Italian
record employs terms which translate into English
as "continuous," "reiterated," and "aggravated"
in connection with the offense of robbery, but an
examination of the record extablishes that these
words describe circumstances surrounding a robbery
or series of robberies, which circumstances, under
Italian law, indicate the nature and type and extent of the penalty to be inflicted, rather than
the nature of the crime itself. It is also clear
that the reference in the Italian record to a
charge of "attempted" robbery against relator indicates nothing more than that it was to be considered just another circumstance of the crime of
aggravated robbery, of which relator was ultimately
convicted. The offense of aggravated robbery as
encompassed in the Italian Penal Code, translated
sections of which are in the record, is extraditable under the treaty.[36]

By comparison, another decision took a more restrictive view.
In 1957, the Government of Mexico requested the extradition of
Abe Wise from the United States for the crime of fraud arising
from the giving of a check by Wise "by reason of the settlement
relative to a profit sharing association contract which was not
honored because of insufficient funds."[37] Since fraud was not

338

one of those crimes enumerated in the Extradition Treaty of 1899 between the United States and Mexico,[38] the extradition complaint referred to section 19 of Article 2 of the Treaty which provided for extradition for the offense of "Obtaining by threats of injury, or by false devices, money, valuables or other personal property . . . ." The extradition magistrate held that a proper case for extradition had not been made out, stating:

I find no crime denominated as fraud listed in the Treaty or Supplemental Conventions. That term seems to have crept into the complaint by reason of the use of the term in some of the documents and records of the Mexican Government accompanying the complaint. The offense sought to be charged here, and which the complaint should charge, if extradition is to be had, is that of obtaining money, valuables or other personal property by false devices. Mexico seems to have such a law, and Texas has such a law-- swindling, punishable by imprisonment as for theft. But the complaint does not charge Wise with obtaining money, valuables or other personal property by false devices; it charges commission of the crime of fraud more particularly referred to in Section [subd.] 19 of the Treaty." But it does not charge what Wise obtained--whether money, or what valuable or what personal property. . . .

An examination of these exhibits discloses

they do not by any stretch of the imagination charge Wise with obtaining money, valuables or other personal property by threats of injury of by false devices, the offense for which extradition is authorized by subd. 19 of Article II of the treaty. On the contrary, taking as admitted all of the fact allegations and conclusions set out in the Mexican proceedings, the record shows that Wise committed, and is charged with committing, in Mexico, the crime of 'drawing a check without funds,' in settlement of a profit sharing contract between himself and an association of collective farmers.

This is an offense for which the treaty does not authorize extradition. While the laws of Mexico, and now the laws of Texas, provide punishment for giving of a hot check, in the amount involved here ($23,241.38), with intent to defraud, even in payment of a pre-existing debt, that crime is not a treaty offense. It is not charged that Wise obtained money, valuables, or other personal property by the false device of giving a hot check. It is charged that he made a settlement of matters with the association by giving the worthless check . . .

. . . If Wise had obtained vegetables or cantaloupes by the false device of a worthless check, the offense would be extraditable; but "settlement" of a debit or controversy by worthless check does not come within the treaty . . . . [39]

This last paragraph of the Court's opinion reveals how narrowly
it construed the treaty provision and how restrictively it applied
it.

In a case having political ramifications, the Court of Appeals
for the Fifth Circuit in 1962 in <u>Jimenez v. Aristeguita</u> adhered
to the same position. [40] The relator, Marcos Perez Jimenez, was
the President of the Republic of Venezuela who had been deposed
in a coup d'etat and sought asylum in the United States. Among
the acts charged against him were those of causing improvements to
be made on his private property and work to be done in connection
with his private ventures at public expense as well as receiving,
through intermediaries, "kick-backs" and commissions in connection with the negotiation and award of contracts for the purchase
with public funds, of guns, airplanes, etc., and other articles
or property supplied or to be supplied to the Government of Venezuela. Jimenez' extradition was requested on the basis, *inter*
alia, or paragraph 14 of Article II of the Extradition Treaty of
1922 between United States and Venezuela, [41] which listed as an
extraditable offense:

> Embezzlement of criminal malversation com-
> mitted within the jurisdiction of one of the parties
> by public offenders or depositaries, where the amount
> embezzled exceeds 200 dollars in the United States of
> America or B. 1000 in the United States of Venezuela.

As to this aspect of the case, the extradition magistrate
found that there was sufficient evidence that Perez Jimenez com-

As to this aspect of the case, the extradition magistrate found that there was sufficient evidence that Perez Jimenez committed the acts charged and that these acts were within the meaning of paragraph 14 of Article II of the Treaty. On appeal from denial of a *habeas corpus* petition challenging the finding of the extradition magistrate, the United States Court of Appeals for the Fifth Circuit concluded with respect to criminal malversation:

> Criminal malversation includes a broad category of corrupt official practices. Webster's New International Dictionary defines the word "malversation" thus: 'Evil conduct; fraudulent practices; misbehavior, corruption, or extortion in office.' P. 1490 (2d ed. 1957). The Oxford English Dictionary lists two current meanings: 'corrupt behavior in an office, commission, employment, or position of trust;' and 'corrupt administration of something'-- and gives a number of instances of the use of the word in such broad senses, beginning in 1549 and continuing through the nineteenth century.

> Black's Law Dictionary sets out the accepted definition:

> > 'In French law, this word is applied to all grave and punishable faults committed in the exercise of a charge or commission, (office) such as corruption, exaction, concussion, larceny.' P. 1112 (4th ed. 1951).

342

There is evidence showing that appellant, as

chief executive of Venezuela, used his position of

power and authority to divert funds and services

belonging to Venezuela to his own use and benefit.

The offenses as to which probable cause has been

certified constituted 'embezzlement or criminal

malversation.' [42]

In a parallel construction, the Canadian Courts adopted the

same position *vis-à-vis* the United States. In 1963, the United

States, on behalf of the State of New York, sought the extra-

dition from Canada of James Pendergast, who had been indicted in

New York for the crime of larceny. It was charged that Pender-

gast had issued several checks, in large amounts, against insuf-

ficient funds. After Pendergast had been found extraditable by

the extradition magistrate he applied for discharge by way of

habeas corpus. In dismissing the application, the High Court of

Justice of Ontario considered the offense, in terms of Canadian

law, as follows:

Pendergast was indicted in the State of New

York in respect to two charges on what is called

grand larceny in the first degree. It is apparent

that this charge is the equivalent of what is known

in Canada as obtaining money by false pretences. [43]

While the other courts showed more reticence to expand the

notion of "kindred offenses," the Canadian Court found it easier

to pursue a course of interpretation of double criminality *in*

abstracto. The reciprocal experience of Canada and the United

States as neighboring states has done much to insure the satisfactory reliance of this interpretative approach to double criminality. The United States-Mexico relations have demonstrated the same consistency which is characteristic of neighboring states concerned with the mutual preservation of their internal order and cooperating in the suppression of criminality.

Some cases reveal, however, that overreliance on the spirit of cooperation between neighboring states may cause a requesting state not to fully comply with all treaty and statutory requirements. The requesting state must show that the offense charged also constitutes a crime in its own jurisdiction, otherwise extradition cannot be granted. This situation was before the Supreme Court of Quebec in United States v. Link and Green (1954)[44] in which the United States had asked for the extradition of Link and Green from Canada on the basis of indictments returned by the State of Michigan. The indictments charged the relators with obtaining money by false pretences and forgery, inducing persons residing in Michigan to buy shares in certain companies. The accused conducted their scheme from Montreal by means of postal and telephone services and at no time were they in Michigan or elsewhere in the United States. After scrutinizing carefully the facts and the evidence presented, the Court stated:

> (T)hat for an extradition application to be granted
> to surrender a fugitive for trial in a foreign jur-
> isdiction, the conduct charged as an offense must
> be punishable criminally both by the laws of the
> foreign jurisdiction and of Canada, and must also

come within the provisions of the relevant Extradition Treaty or Convention. . . .

(However,)

. . . (I)t now becomes necessary to state that
the applicant did not attempt to make any proof
that forgery, false pretences, defrauding the
public or appropriating money or property for
the benefit of the accused were offences under
the law of the State of Michigan, although they
are criminal offenses under the Canadian Criminal
Code.[45]

The unusual feature of this case is that the issue was not whether
the offense charged constituted an extraditable offense or that it
constituted an offense in the requested state but whether it was
an offense under the laws of the requesting state.

A similar decision had been reached in In Re Lamar (1940) by
the Supreme Court of Alberta, when the Court, rejecting the application for extradition stated:

The evidence does not disclose that the use of
the mails constituted any part of the unlawful obtaining as the money so unlawfully obtained, was
taken before the confirmation of purchase letter
was written or mailed. Therefore no *prima facie*
case has been made out to make the above proven
law applicable. The imputed crime has not shown
to be a crime within the law of the United States
of America.[46]

These cases, however, do not bear directly on the type of interpretation the Canadian Courts have given double criminality in
extradition practice with the United States. That interpretation
remained a subjective, *in abstracto*, interpretation.[47]

This practice goes back to 1860 in the notorious case of In re
Anderson .[48] The relator, John Anderson, was a black slave who
was sought for extradition from upper Canada to Missouri to answer a charge of murder under the laws of that state. The alleged crime had been committed when the victim, Diggs, a planter,
attempted to prevent the fugitive from escaping. Under the laws
of the requesting state, the victim was not only authorized but
under legal duty to attempt to prevent the excape of slaves. In
Canada, the institution of slavery was not recognized and, of
course, there were no laws requiring citizens to apprehend escaping slaves. Had the incident occurred in Canada, the relator
would have no culpability for killing the victim in order to retain his liberty. It was nevertheless decided in favor of surrender by the Court of the Queen's Bench of Upper Canada, on the
grounds that the victim had been acting with legal authority; and
under the law of Canada if a person kills another, who is attempting to apprehend him or her under legal authority, such a
person commits murder.[49]

A contrasting position was taken in the case of one Eisler
sought to be extradited from Great Britain on charges of perjury.
The English Court held:

> It seems to me the facts are abundantly clear.
> Eisler filled in a form as required by the law and

he made therein certain statements. He was arraigned and indicted on various matters, including making a false statement. He was tried before the District Court of Columbia in due course and he was sentenced, and he is therefore a convicted person. The point is, is he a fugitive criminal?--a person whose return to his country may be required by the United States. What is an indictable (extraditable) crime? Those matters are regulated by a Treaty between this country and the United States of America, and are set out in the Order in Council of 6th July, 1945, amongst other places. Those persons who have been accused or convicted of certain crimes or offences shall be returned, if found within the territory of either party, and in Article 3 (14) the crime of perjury is set out. It is therefore necessary to see whether by the law both of the United States and this country this man was found guilty of a crime which means perjury. Perjury is a somewhat technical matter. It is thought by certain people that if you merely tell a lie on oath, you have committed perjury. You have committed an offence which is something akin to perjury, but not necessarily perjury. The definition of perjury is contained in Section 1 of the Perjury Act. "If any person lawfully sworn as

a witness or as an interpreter in a judicial proceeding willfully makes a statement material in the
proceeding, which he knows to be false or does not
believe to be true, he shall be guilty of perjury...."
Then by Section 2 "The expression 'judicial proceeding' includes a proceeding before any court,
tribunal, or person having by law power to hear,
receive and examine evidence on oath." And Section
3--relied on by Sir Valentine Holmes--'Where a
statement made for the purposes of a judicial proceeding is not made before the tribunal itself,
but is made on oath before a person authorized by
law to administer an oath to the person who makes
the statement, and to record or authenticate the
statement, it shall, for purposes of this section, be
treated as having been made in a judicial proceeding." That was the occasion on which Eisler
made his false statement. It seems to me that
there were then contemplated no judicial proceedings
whatever. It was purely an administrative action
performed by the officer in question. He was taking and recording statements of Mr. Eisler. Mr.
Eisler, for making the statements in the form which
were false, was convicted by the District Court of
Columbia on the third indictment, and that sets out
that in the said application the defendant made
statements as set out in A, B, and C of count (1)

which were false in respect of that count. The
point is, is what he was convicted of in America,
both in America and here, an extraditable crime.
In my opinion, it is abundantly clear that in no
circumstances whatever could that offense of which
Mr. Eisler was convicted in America be brought
under the technical head of perjury in this country.

In those circumstances, the United States re-
quisitioning power(s) have failed to show that
Mr. Eisler has been guilty of an extraditable crime,
and this application fails. [50]

Commenting on this decision, the Department of State noted that
the offense of which Eisler had been convicted in the United
States was apparently also an offense in England since it appeared in the British Perjury Act of 1911 under a section entitled "kindred offences," one of which was false swearing under
oath made otherwise than in a judicial proceeding. The Department stated:

The Department of State and the Department of
Justice were aware at that time that the request
for the extradition of Eisler was made that it would
be necessary to establish the fact that the crime
for which the fugitive had been convicted was a
crime covered by the treaty according to British
law. The applicable provision in Article 9 of the
treaty is typical of the provision contained in each
of our treaties. It was thought, however, that the

British court would follow the practice of the
courts of the United States in interpreting extradition treaties liberally and that it would hold that
the crime came within the term 'perjury' as used in
the treaty in as much as the British Perjury Act of
1911 defines in Section 2 the crime as a "kindred
offense."

It is believed that the term "perjury" was
used in the treaty generically rather than technically, as the definition of the crime both by United
States and British statute was fixed many years before the treaty was negotiated and it is hardly to
be assumed that the two Governments intended to apply different meanings to it. It does not appear
from the transcript of the hearings that this view
was argued before the court or that it passed upon
it but rather that the court limited its decision
to the one point, namely that the offense was not
perjury within the meaning of Section 1 of the
British Perjury Act. [51]

The English position has remained consistent since 1865. In
Ex parte Windsor, [52] the court discharged the relator who was
wanted for forgery by the United States because the acts alleged
by the requesting state did not constitute the crime of forgery
under English law. The same rationale was followed in King v.
Dix [53] in 1902, when extradition was denied because the charge of
larceny alleged by the United States was not in conformity with

350

the required elements of that crime under English law. A second charge of embezzlement was found to be extraditable because it corresponded to the crime of larceny by fraud under English law and covered by the treaty under the term.

France in its extradition relations with the United States, adhered to a more rigid position than does Great Britain. In the Blackmer case [54] France refused extradition to the United States because the offense charged did not constitute a prosecutable offense *in concreto*, under French law. The Paris court found that the statute of limitation for similar offenses having lapsed under French law extinguished the prosecutability of the offender, and, therefore, the acts charged could not constitute an offense under French law. The French position therefore focuses on the prosecutability of the offense or *l'incrimination*, as does the United States but the difference lies in considering statute of limitations as a substantive defence to be raised at the trial. Another case involving the United States as a requesting state was In re Insull. [55] In that case, a Greek Court of Appeals in 1933 found that an extraditable offense was to be found *in concreto* and that double criminality required that all the elements of prosecution in the requested state must be satisfied. The court asserted its right to examine the substance of the charge and to determine the existence of the mental element of the offense charged. In effect, the court examined whether or not the relator could have been found guilty under

351

Greek law which was tantamount to a finding of potential conviction rather than mere prosecutability. The United States was
critical of that approach, indicating its rejection thereof. The
question of the type and quantum of evidence required in an extradition request is often confused with the issue of extraditability which requires substantively that the offense be extraditable and that the offense charged satisfy double criminality,
meaning prosecutability rather than punishability. The distinction between these approaches will be discussed in Chapter VI
with respect to substantive defenses to extradition, and the requirement of proof discussed in Chapter VII. It is worthy of
note that under common law the examining magistrate weighs the
existence of probable cause to believe the offense charged has
been committed. In civil law systems the examining magistrate
does not inquire into the sufficiency of the evidence.

All of the cases discussed in this section, as well as those
cited, [56] indicate that the meaning of extraditable offenses is
that which is listed or designated in the treaty, subject to different applications, and in the absence of a treaty, those offenses which will be the basis of reciprocal recognition. All
cases indicate that the requirement of double criminality applies
whether by treaty or not and is subject to one of the two methods
of interpretation discussed earlier, i.e., *in concreto* or *in
abstracto*. The weight of authority, however, reveals that the
subjective method, *in abstracto*, prevails.

3. *The Doctrine of Specialty*

This doctrine, often referred to as a principle, [57] stands for

the proposition that the requesting state, who secures the surrender of a person, can prosecute that person only for the offense
for which he or she was surrendered by the requested state or
else allow that person an opportunity to leave the prosecuting
state to which he or she had been surrendered.

The rationale for the doctrine rests on the following factors:

(1) The requested state could have refused extradition
    if it knew that the relator would be prosecuted or
    punished for an offense other than the one for which
    it granted extradition.

(2) The requesting state did not have *in personam* juris-
    diction over the relator, if not for the requested
    state's surrender of that person.

(3) The requesting state could not have prosecuted the
    offender, other than *in absentia,* nor could it punish
    him or her without securing that person's surrender
    from the requested state.

(4) The requesting state would be abusing a formal process
    to secure the surrender of the person it seeks by re-
    lying on the requested state who will use its pro-
    cesses to effectuate the surrender.

(5) The requested state would be using its processes in re-
    liance upon the representations made by the requesting
    state.

By reason of these factors, the requesting state is bound to
prosecute or punish (or both) the surrendered person in accordance with the reasons for which the processes of the requested

state were set in motion. Otherwise, the requested state's processes would have been set in motion under false pretences.

The Doctrine of Specialty is designed to insure against such
contingency. It developed because extradition is subject to certain requirements, such as the type of offense for which it shall
be granted as between the respective states. Without a doctrine
of specialty, the surrendering state will not in effect determine
whether the substantive requirements of extraditable offenses and
double criminality have been fulfilled. The doctrine is, therefore, a concommitant of a requested state's right to determine
the extraditability of the person sought for the offense specified. Implicitly, it protects the relator from unexpected prosecution, even though it is principally advanced as a means of protecting the requested state from abuse of its processes.[58] It is
for this reason that the doctrine does not apply to cases where
the person who may be otherwise sought for formal extradition was
delivered or brought to the requesting state through another method than extradition (see Chapter III concerning alternative extradition devices).[59] Since the requested state is designed to
benefit from this doctrine and has the right to claim its enforcement, the question arises as to the right of the relator to
insist on that requirement as a participant in the process. In
practice, when the issue arises the relator will have already
been surrendered and become subject to the authoritative processes of the prosecuting state. His or here only recourse at that
point will be limited to the remedies afforded by that very state.
Thus, unless the surrendering state objects to the variance, the

354

individual in question will not really benefit from this doctrine. The United States has adhered to that doctrine except when it is not stated in the treaty in question. In 1972 the Second Circuit Court of Appeals affirmed the doctrine in theory but held that it was designed to inure to the benefit of the requested state and not to the relator. However, it also held that the doctrine was inapplicable whenever extradition is granted on the basis of comity. The case was Ficconi and Kella v. Attorney General of the United States. [61]

Appellants were originally indicted in the District Court of Massachusetts for conspiring to import heroin in violation of 21 U.S.C. 171. Warrants at that time could not be executed; appellants later being found in Italy. Appellants, both French nationals, were extradited from Italy to the United States on charges of importing heroin into the United States. Acknowledging that there was no provision for narcotic offenses in the 1868 Extradition Convention with Italy, 15 Stat. 629 and subsequent amendments, extradition was granted by the Italian government as an act of comity, independent of the treaty.

After appellants were returned to the United States and their release on $250,000 bail each, in the District of Massachusetts, they were subpoenaed to appear before a grand jury in the Southern District of New York. When they appeared, they were arrested under an indictment issued that day charging them with receiving, concealing, selling and facilitating the transportation, concealment and sale of 37 kilograms of heroin in New York. Bail was set at $100,000 which neither could post. Appellants

355

filed petition for a writ of habeas corpus on the ground that th
their detention was on charges other than those for which they
were extradited. The Southern District of New York meanwhile
returned a superceding indictment charging appellants with conspiracy to violate the narcotics laws and two other substantive
offenses. The petition for their release was denied and appellants were tried on these charges and found guilty. One of the
questions raised was the applicability of the rule of specialty
in extradition.

Chief Judge Friendly took a restrictive view of the rule of
specialty when the re-examined the Supreme Court's decision in
U.S. v. Rauscher, 119 U.S. 407, 1866. He stated:

> Rauscher's conviction of an offense for which he was
> not and could not have been extradited did not violate
> the treaty, which was silent to the rights of a person
> extradited thereunder. It violated a rule of United States
> foreign relations law devised by the courts to im-
> plement the treaty. [62]

Judge Friendly saw no reason in principle to apply the rule of
specialty when extradition has been granted by an act of comity
by the surrendering nation.

The court found that the remedy enunciated in Rauscher must be
applied in the context for which it was designed in that the
doctrine of specialty imposes limitations upon requesting states
not to prosecute the extraditee for any offense other than for
which the accused was surrendered. The object of this rule is to
prevent the demanding state from violating its international

356

obligations vis-a-vis the surrendering state. Therefore it was essential to the present case to determine whether the surrendering state would regard the prosecution at issue as a breach of its relations with the United States. In the absence of any affirmative protest from Italy, the court did not believe that the government would regard the prosecution of appellants for subsequent offenses of the same character as the crime for which they were extradited as a breach of faith by the United States.

Although the United States has not made a preliminary showing in Italy with respect to the New York indictment, as it did concerning the Massachusetts one, the court noted:

> . . . We presume the United States is willing to submit
> such proof if Italy desires it, and with appellants
> now having been found guilty, there can scarcely be
> doubt that sufficient proof to warrant extradition
> exists. [64]

This restrictive view of the rule of specialty fails to take into account the relator as a participant in the extradition process and his right to uphold such a doctrine when a demanding state acts at variance with such obligations regardless of whether or not the surrendering state protests such actions. [65]

3.1 The Doctrine of Specialty and Variance in Prosecution

The requesting state can prosecute the surrendered individual for all included offenses in the offense charged and for which he or she was surrendered. In addition thereto, the relator can be tried for any offense established by the facts supporting the original request, provided it is a kindred offense which is based on the same facts but which would be an extraditable offense and satisfy the requirement of double criminality in accordance with the extradition relations of the respective states. Any variance from the above will be deemed a violation of the Doctrine of Specialty. In case of such a variance, the prosecuting state should allow the individual a reasonable opportunity to depart from that state or return him or her to the surrendering state before exercising its jurisdictional authority over him or her for the offense at variance with the one for which it had requested the extradition. Certainly, if the individual committed another offense pending prosecution on the charges for which extradition was granted, then the doctrine will not apply.[66] In effect, the doctrine is a form of qualified immunity from prosecution of offenses allegedly committed prior to the grant of extradition by the requested state.

The individual in question may, however, waive the application of the doctrine by consent to be prosecuted for the offense at variance with the offense charged in the extradition request.[67] In this case, it appears that the surrendering state could not claim the doctrine. This, in effect, demonstrates the ancillary dimension of the doctrine which to that extent inures to the benefit of the individual. So far, however, it is not recognized as a right of the relator which can be raised in the courts of the requesting state now exercising its jurisdiction over the relator unless the municipal laws of that state permit such a defense against charges at variance with the one stated in the extradition request. In any event so long as the maxim *mala captus bene detentus* will continue to be rocognized (see Chapter IV for a critique of this maxim) it is not likely that an individual will be likely to object to prosecution on the grounds that his or her presence was secured under reasons other than the one for which is also being prosecuted.

3.2 Extension of the Doctrine: Limitations On Re-Extradition and Death Penalty

One extension of the doctrine applies to re-extradition to a third state. In this case, whenever the state which originally sought the surrender of the individual after securing that person then considers extraditing him or her to a third state which asked that state for the same person. In this case the re-extradicting state must first secure the consent of the original surrendering state before granting the second extradition request to the third state.[68] This extension of the doctrine manifests the continued interest of the original surrendering state in the compliance with the purposes and grounds for which its processes had been set in motion and for which it granted extradition.[69] Furthermore, a surrendering state that would not exercise its jurisdictional authority over a relator and surrender him or her because the individual is likely to receive the death penalty because it is against its public policy may do so on condition that said penalty would not be imposed. The surrendering state who wishes to impose such a condition must explicitly indicate it when granting the request of the requesting state.[70] If it fails to do so the requesting state may consider it a mere recommendation for leniency.[71] It is not yet well established if such a condition is binding on the requesting state as it may be considered an infringement of its sovereignty. However, if the agent of the requesting state accepts the condition it would become part of the Doctrine of Specialty. Similarly, if a state receives a person on the basis of its request, it cannot re-extradite that person to a third state that could impose upon the relator the death penalty without either securing the first requested state's permission or in the event that first requested state would impose a condition of non-applicability of the death penalty to make its re-extradition conditioned upon non-applicability of that penalty.

The surrendering state through the Doctrine of Specialty exercises a long-arm residual jurisidction over the relator who had been subject to its exclusive jurisdiction which it had exercised for a special purpose and is entitled to see that it is not abused or misused.

Chapter V

Footnotes

1. See *supra*, Chapter I.

2. Bodin, <u>Les six livres de la republique</u>, 1576, Grotius, <u>De Jure</u> <u>Belli ac Pacis</u>, 1625, ". . . *ut non stricte populus aut rex ad dedendum teneatur, sed ut diximus, ad dedendum aut puniendum . . est enim disjunctiva obligatio.*"

3. Shearer, <u>Extradition in International Law</u>, p. 132-149 (1971) and Bedi, <u>Extradition in International Law and Practice</u> pp. 69-84 (1968).

4. The proposition that extradition when practiced on the basis of reciprocity also requires double criminality was upheld by several decisions in those countries which engage in non-treaty reciprocally based practice. See <u>in re Nikoleff</u>, Upper Court of Dresden, Germany, 1933, (1933-34) <u>Ann. Dig</u>. 351 (No. 147), wherein it was stated: "Extradition would be granted upon the principle of reciprocity and upon that of identity of extradition and prosecution, which by the way is a universally recognized principle of international law," (p. 352), and <u>Re Bachofner</u>, Columbia Supreme Court 1959, 28 <u>I.L.R</u>. 376 (1963) and <u>in re Zahabian</u>, Federal Tribunal of Bern, Switzerland, 1963, 32 <u>I.L.R</u>. 290 (1960).

5. U.S.T.S. 882; 49 Stat. 3111, 3114 (1938) 165 LNTS 45, 51.

6. 6 Whiteman, <u>Digest</u>, p. 772-3 (1968) quoting Secretary of State (Hull) to the American Ambassador at Bogata (Braden) instruction no. 37, June 9, 1939, M.S. Department of State, file 221.11/7.

7. Shearer, *supra*, note 3, p. 134-35, he states that out of 163 treaties published in the League of Nations Treaty Series, 80 have no lists but follow the eliminative method and among the 50 treaties published between Volumes 1-550 of the United Nations Treaty Series 33 have adopted the same method. The European Extradition Convention of 1957, European Treaty Series No. 24, also adopted this formula in Article 2.

8. Bassiouni, Criminal Law and Its Processes: The Law of Public Order, p. 89-90 (1969).

9. Ibid. at pp. 42, 37-43.

10. 41 Revue Internationale de droit penal, p. 12 (1970); see also, Schultz, "Rapport General," etc., 39 Revue Internationale de droit penal, p. 792 (1968).

11. Ibid.

12. I, Annuaire de l'Institut de Droit International (1875-1883) at 733 (1928).

13. *Supra*, note 2 and the authors cited in IV Travers, Le Droit Penal International, p. 389 (1921).

14. The texts of these laws reproduced in H. Grutzner, Internationaler Rechtshilfeverkehr in Strafsachen. "Die fur die Rechtsbeziehungen der Bundesrepublik Deutschland mit dem Ausland in Strafsachen massgeblichen Bestigmmungen" (1955).

15. See *supra*, note 4.

16. See *supra*, note 3.

17. 6 Whiteman, Digest, p. 773-774 (1968).

18. 259 U.S. 309, 42 S. Ct. 469 (1922).

19. Id. at 311-312.

20. 190 U.S. 40, 23 S. Ct. 781 (1902).

21. Id. at 60-61.

22. 221 U.S. 508, 31 S. Ct. 704 (1910).

23. Id., pp. 513-514.

24. Factor v. Laubenheimer, 290 U.S. 276, 54 S. Ct. 191 (1933). For a critical view of this decision see Hudson, "The Factor Case and Double Crimihnality in Extradition," 28 A.J.I.L. 274 (1934); for a supporting view see Borchard, "The Factor Extradition Case," 28 A.J.I.L. 742 (1934).

25. Supra, note 18.

26. Id. 298.

27. 190 U.S. 40, 23 S. Ct. 781 (1903).

28. 194 U.S. 205, 24 S. Ct. 657 (1904).

29. Supra, note 20.

30. 241 U.S. 6, 36 S. Ct. 487 (1916).

31. Supra, note 16.

32. Supra, note 22; for other liberal interpretations of what constitutes an extraditable offense which cite Factor v. Laubenheimer, see Collier v. Vaccaro, 51 F. 2d 17 (4th Cir. 1931); Villareal v. Hammond 74 F.2d 503 (2nd Cir. 1934). The opposite view is represented in Hatfield v. Grav 87 F.2d 358 (1st Cir. 1937) which seemed to apply an objective criteria of interpretation to double criminality (even though it restricted itself to the interpretation of extraditable offenses and did so narrowly). As to acts which preceded a treaty, it was held that the treaty list was applicable, see United States v. Hecht 16 F. 2d 955 (2nd Cir. 1927).

33. 269 F.2d 681 (2d Cir. 1959), affirmed 361 U.S. 913 (1959).

34. Id. at 685-687.

35. 177 F. Supp. 856 (D. Conn. 1959); affirmed 278 F.2d 77 (2d Cir. 1960); cert. denied, 364 U.S. 851 (1960).

36. Id. at 866-867.

37. In re Wise, 168 F. Supp. 366 (S.D. Tex., 1957); the Canadian position was the same in In re Frederico Dormberger (1935-1937) Ann. Dig. 381 (No. 178).

38. U.S.T.S. 242; 31 Stat. 1818 (1910).

39. *Supra*, note 40 at 368-369, 370-371, 372.

40. 311 F.2d 547 (5th Cir., 1962).

41. U.S.T.S. 675; 43 Stat. 1698 (1935), 49 L.N.T.S. 435-438.

42. *Supra*, note 36 at 562-563.

43. Ex parte Penderast, 6 Crim. L.Q. 394 (Canada, 1968).

44. 21 I.L.R. 234-236 (1954).

45. Id. at 235-236.

46. (1938-1940) Ann. Dig. 405 (No. 153).

47. La Forest, Extradition to and from Canada (1961).

48. 11 Upper Canada C.P. 9 (1861), discussed in Clarke, A Treatise upon the Law of Extradition (4th ed., 1903), pp. 99-103.

49. An opposing view had been taken by Great Britain in an opinion of the law officer of Her Majesty's government in an application made to the President Administering the Government of the Virgin Islands by the Lieutenant Governor of the Danish Island of Saint Thomas for the arrest and restitution of two slaves charged with burglary and felony who had fled to Tortola. The law officers said:

364

. . . [T]hat we are of opinion that according to
the Law of Nations and the laws of this country,
the Danish Government is not entitled to demand
these refugees; and it makes no difference in
our view of the case that they are slaves by the
law of Denmark or that in the event of their being
acquitted of the felony they would continue to be
held in slavery in that country. (McNair, "Extradition and Extraterritorial Asylum," 28 B.Y.I.L.
180 (1951).

50. See 6 Whiteman, Digest, pp. 797-798 (1968); Eisler v. United
States, 170 F.2d 273 (D.C. Inc., 1948); United States v.
Eisler, 75 F. Supp. 640 (D.D.C. 1948).

51. 6 Whiteman, Digest, 798-799 (1968), quoting the American
Embassy, London, to the Department of State, despatch No.
980, June 9, 1949, encl. 1, MS. Department of State, file
241.11 Eisler, Gerhart/6-949; Assistant to the Legal Adviser
(Vallance) to Gilbert F. Kennedy, Counsellor at Law, London,
letter, July 22, 1949, Ibid./7-1349.
For a discussion of the case, see Jacob, "International
Extradition: Implications of the Eisler Case," 59 Yale L. J.

52. 622 (1950).

52. 12 L.T. 307 (1865).

53. 18 T.L.R. 231 (K.B. 1902).

54. Case of Blackmer, Court of Paris, Chambre des Mises en
Accusation (1928); 284 U.S. 421 (1932).

55. (1933-1934) Ann. Dig. 344 (No. 146).

56. See *supra*, notes 4, 5 and 21 through 54; also <u>In re Gerber</u>, Federal Supreme Court of Germany, 1957, in a case involving extradition to Switzerland, 24 <u>I.L.R.</u> 493 (1957); and <u>United States of America v. Novick</u>, Quebec Superior Court, 1960, 32 <u>I.L.R.</u> 290 (1960).

57. Shearer, *supra*, note 3, p. 146.

58. In <u>Kuhn v. Staatsanwaltschaft des Kantons Zurich</u>, Switzerland, Federal Tribunal, May 12, 1961, 34 <u>I.L.R.</u> 132 (1961), it was held that:

The principle is designed to safeguard the rights of the extraditing state. This requires the restriction of the rights of the requesting state to the extent to which they would be restricted if extradition had not taken place.

59. <u>In re Karolyr</u>, Royal Hungarian Criminal Court of Budapest and Hungarian Ministry of Justice, 26 January 1928 (1927-1928) <u>Ann. Dig</u>. 345 (No. 236). Also Chapter II above, Sections 2 and 3.

60. <u>Cosgrove v. Winnery</u>, 174 U.S. 64 (1809); <u>Johnson v. Brown</u>, 205 U.S. 309 (1907); <u>Greene v. United States</u>, 154 Fed. 401 (5th Cir. 1907); <u>Collins v. O'Neill</u>, 214 U.S. 113 (1909); and <u>People ex rel. Stilwell v. Hamley</u>, 240 N.Y. 455, 148 N.E. 634 (1925); <u>United States v. Paroutian</u>, 299 F.2d 486 (1963); 319 F.2d 661 (2nd Cir. 1963).

61. 464 F.2d 475 (2d Cir. 1972).

62. <u>Id</u>. at 479.

63. Cf. cases cited *supra*, note 60.

64. *Supra,* note 61 at 481.

65. This position, which has been advanced by publicists and is found in the practice of many states, is also embodied in such multilateral treaties as the European Convention on Extradition. See Bassiouni,"International Extradition in the American Practice and World Public Order," 36 Tenn. L. Rev., 1 at 15 (1968). This decision seems to run opposite U.S. ex rel. Donnelly v. Mulligan, 70 F.2d 220 (2nd Cir. 1934), and takes a restrictive view of the rights of relators in extradition proceedings.

66. United States v. Paroutian *supra,* note 60.

67. *Supra,* note 56.

68. In Anietto et al., Italy, Court of Cassation, 1933, (1933-1934) Ann. Dig. 334 (No. 140).

69. United States ex rel. Donnelly v. Mulligan, 8 F. Supp. 262, 74 F.2d 220 (2d Cir. 1934); see also note in 35 Col. L. Rev. 295 (1935).

70. In re Cortes, Argentina, Supreme Court, 1933 (1933-1934) Ann. Dig. 356 (No. 152), where conditional release was granted to Chile and observed.

71. In re Oberblicher, Italy , Court of Cassation, 1934 (1933-1934) Ann. Dig. 354 (No. 150), wherein Italy considered the conditional extradition from Austria as a mere recommendation for leniency.

Denial of Extradition: Defenses, Exceptions, Exemptions and Exclusions

Introduction

Extradition shall be denied if any of the substantive or formal conditions of the practice are not met. In addition, extradition shall also be denied by reason of the existence of certain specific exceptions, exemptions, exclusions and defenses which arise out of a treaty or customary practice. This chapter will deal with these specific conditions, which when they exist, constitute grounds for denial of an extradition request which has otherwise met all substantive and formal requirements.

The theoretical foundation of these exceptions, exemptions, exclusions and defenses vary and they can be distinguished substantively as well as formally; but what they have in common is their outcome; namely, they constitute grounds for denial of the request.

There are four categories of such grounds which when they are found to exist result in denial of extradition request. They are:

1. Grounds relating to the offense charged:

   (a) political;

   (b) military;

   (c) fiscal.

2. Grounds relating to the relator:

   (a) nationals;

   (b) persons performing official acts and persons protected by special immunity.

3. Grounds relating to the prosectuion of the offense charged:

   (a) legality of the offense charged;

   (b) trial *in absentia*;

   (c) statute of limitation and immunity.

4. Grounds relating to the penalty and punishability of the relator:

   (a) amnesty and pardon;

   (b) double jeopardy - *ne bis in idem*;

   (c) death penalty;

   (d) cruel and unusual punishment.

A fifth category could also be advocated and would relate to the expected or anticipated violation of the relator's human rights by the requested state. These potential violations would be found in the human rights program as expressed in the United Nations Charter, The Universal Declaration, the two covenants, multilateral treaties and throughout other sources of international law which constitute a scheme for the protection of minimum standards of human rights. Since these rights, however, also find their application in the four categories described above, it is preferable to deal with them pervasively rather than particularly. This methodological choice is dictated by the contemporary stage of extradition law and practice which does not recognize

the applicability of those minimum standards of human rights to
its existing processes. Thus, mindful of not confusing what is
and what ought to be, this writer will indicate where a defense
is *lex lata* or *de legge ferenda* or even *lex desiderata*. Violations, which would fall within this category, are, however,
likely to result in the granting of asylum to the relator and the
denial of extradition on the basis of the political offense exception. For these reasons treatment of these questions is found
in the following parts of this chapter and in Chapter II, Asylum.

1. Grounds Relating to the Offense Charged

1.1 The Political Offense Exception

1.1 (1) Historical Development and Meaning

Historically, extradition was the means resorted to for the surrender of political offenders. These were persons guilty of crimes
of *lèse majesté* which included *inter alia* treason, attempts
against the monarchy or the life of a monarch and even contempt-
uous behavior toward the monarch. The first known European treaty
which dealt with the surrender of political offenders was entered
in 1174 between England and Scotland. It was followed by a
treaty in 1303 between France and Savoy. In the XVIIth century
Hugo Grotius gave the practice a theoretical framework, which
is still the cornerstone of classic extradition law. Until the
nineteenth century extradition constituted a manifestation of
cooperation between the family of nations as attested by various
alliances in existence between the reigning families of Europe.
The French Revolution of 1789 and its aftermath

started the transformationof what was the extraditable offense *par excellence* to what has since become the nonextraditable offense *par excellence*. In 1833 Belgium became the first country to enact a law on nonextradition of political offenders, and by the beginning of the XIXth century almost every European treaty contained an exception for political offenses. By 1875, the practice was sufficiently established that the determination of what constituted a political offense was reached in accordance with the laws of the requested state. This development gave rise to the increased role of the judiciary in the practice which except for England and Belgium (since 1833) had played no part in the process.

The political offense exception is now a standard clause in almost all extradition treaties of the world and is also specified in the municipal laws of many states. [1] Even though widely recognized, the very term "political offense" is seldom, if ever, defined in treaties or municipal legislation and judicial interpretations have been the principal source for its significance and application. [2] This may be due to the fact that whether or not a particular type of conduct falls within thatcategory depends essentially on the facts and circumstances of the occurrence. Thus, by its very nature it eludes a precise definition which could restrict the flexibility needed to assess the facts and circumstances of each case.

As a consequence of this preeminent role played by the judiciary in defining and applying this exception, the courts of the requested state unavoidably apply national conceptions, standards and policies to an inquiry which relates, however, to a process transcending the interests of that one participant. [4] As to the term, according to Oppenheim, it was unknown to international law until the French Revolution [5] and even when the European practice was to secure the surrender of political offenders the term was not employed. [6]

The history of the political offense exception is inexorably linked to the rise of eighteenth century political theories on freedom and democracy. Since then the development of this exception has been intricately linked to asylum (discussed in Chapter II) even though prior to the eighteenth century this relationship was very tenuous. Indeed, asylum, as practiced in the Mediterranean Basin (Egypt, Mesopotamia, Greece and Rome), had little resemblance to the later European practice bearing the same nomenclature.

The introduction of the political offense exception in the practice of extradition after Belgium's legislative initiative in 1833 was aptly discussed in the case of In re Fabijan wherein the Supreme Court of Germany in 1933 stated:

"What the Belgian legislature understoody by the term "political offense" is to be ascertained from the Belgian public and criminal law of the time when the law of 1833 was made . . . Using the term not in the legal sense but as it is understood in politics, the legislature meant essentially high treason, capital treason, acts against the external security of the state, rebellion and incitement to civil war . . .

Since these acts, because they were political,
were not listed among the offenses and crimes
enumerated in Article I of the law and were
thus not extraditable, it was not necessary to
provide specifically in Article 6 that no extradition was admissible in respect of political
offenses. This followed also from the so-called
principle of identity of extradition and prosecution, laid down elsewhere in the law. [Double
criminality discussed, Chapter V]. But special
mention of the matter had to be made because the
legislature did not merely wish to exclude from
extradition offenses against the state, but also
certain connected offenses. It was considered
that an offense against the state, especially
when it took the form of an armed rising against
the existing state authority, ought (in order to
make the principle of nonextradition effective)
to embrace other acts attending it and contributory
crimes in themselves, in particular offences
against life and property, as well as offenses
respecting the person and liberty of the individual. For persons committing such offenses in
connection with and in furtherance of an offense
against the state appeared to be not less deserving of asylum than the principal actors themselves. Looked at alone, such offenses are

"ordinary offenses." By them the Belgian legislature meant such offenses as were "ordinary"
crimes and were closely connected with a "political" offense . . . The term "connected
offense" is clearly borrowed from Article 227
of the Code d'Instruction Criminelle, where
it is used with reference to the joinder of
several courts in one indictment. In the Law
of Extradition, just as in the Code of Criminal
Procedure, the term refers to a plurality of
criminal acts which are connected by some common
feature. It follows from this that an offense
against the state in the above sense must actually exist and have taken shape. "Connection"
exists if another offense, in itself an "ordinary"
offense, stands in a particular relation to this
"principal fact." A purely external connection --
identity of time, place, occasion or person -- is
not alone enough; rather, what is required is a
conscious and deliberate relation of cause and
effect. The "ordinary" criminal act must, in
fact, have been a means, method or cloak for the
carrying out of the "political" offense. To
this extent -- and to this extent only -- the
political object of the criminal is relevant for
the determination of the question whether his
crime is a "connected" act. The antithesis of a

374

"connected" offense is an "isolated" offense,

e.g., the murder of a statesman unconnected --

or at least without the connection being dis-

cerned -- with any political revolt. Such

"isolated" offenses are extraditable notwith-

standing that the motive is political; political

asylum does not extend to them.[7]

After Belgium in 1833, France and Switzerland enacted similar

laws in 1834 and England followed in 1870.[8] The United States

did not enact special legislation to that effect save for the

provision on political asylum in Immigration Statutes,[9] but it

made the exception part of its practice as of 1843.[10]

1.1 (2) *Ideologically Motivated Offenders and Political Offenses*[11]

To secure their institutions, societies have devised laws to

punish those who seek to affect the existence or functioning of

these institutions. These laws may be designed to preclude change

altogether or to prevent change by certain means and are enacted

to protect a given social interest which presuppose a value

judgment as to the social significance of what is sought to be

preserved by this type of legislation. Paradoxically, the vio-

lators of these laws are usually committed to affecting that very

interest sought to be preserved and do not perceive their conduct

as morally blameworthy. Indeed, the converse is almost always

true. Such an offender is referred to as the ideologically mot-

ivated offender. That type of offender denies the legality of

the system, the legitimacy of a given law or the social order it

375

seeks to protect claiming adherence to a higher legitimating principle. This perception may be based on commonly understood ideals of political freedom or specific notions which may or may not reflect the common values of the ordinary reasonable person in that society or internationally recognized minimum standards of human rights. That type of violation of the law is, therefore, incidental to the ideological or political purposes of the offender and the social order that he is confronting with such conduct. In a democratic society where laws are said to embody social values and change accordingly, the element of social or moral blameworthiness will depend largely on the degree to which the violated law truly embodies prevailing social values. This is particularly true with respect to the enforcement of criminal laws, but even among such laws distinctions must be made.

Throughout the history of mankind, organized societies have characterized certain forms of behavior as offensive to their common morality. These forms of behavior have invariably included that which harmfully affects an interest commonly perceived by almost every member of society irrespective of ideology. Among these have been certain acts affecting the life and physical integrity of individuals which by virtue of their consistent recognition in the legal controls of almost all social systems are referred to as "common crimes."

Every legal system also has enactments which do not enjoy the same level of recognition granted "common crimes." These offenses may lack the foundation of commonly perceived and shared values or they may simply be regulatory norms. Furthermore, certain

offenses may embody ideological values which do not correspond
to the commonly perceived values of almost all members of a given
society, as in the case of dictatorial regimes.

Some legal doctrines would see no basis for distinguishing between these different types of legal controls on the assumption
that any violation of any law is equally reprehensible as a violation of law. Other doctrines seek to distinguish between types
of violations because such distinctions would, if nothing else,
correspond to a greater degree of individualization of the
offense which is sound criminological policy. As applied to the
ideologically motivated offender, this later approach would recognize that such an offender cannot be deterred by the penalty
attached to the transgressed legal mandate. But, the inquiry,
however, must not be limited to an examination of the professed
motivations of the actor, it must also take into account the legal
norm which was transgressed in order to have some objective basis.

Thus, there is a distinction between offenses which embody an
ideological purpose and ideologically motivated offenders. The
first applies to those legal norms designed to prohibit conduct
actuated by values which conflict with those values embodied in
or are represented by the law which is being violated. In this
case, the violation proper becomes incidental to the competing
ideological values represented on the one hand by a legal norm
designed to protect an interest albeit also socially relevant,
but other than that encompassed in the definition of common
crimes and the opposing values of the offender. However, not
every ideologically motivated offender necessarily commits an

377

ideological offense. The two concepts must be distinguished because the nature of the offense does not depend on the motives of the actor just as nature of the offense may not confer upon the actor certain motives which were not present at the commission of the violation. The character of the offense emanates from the social interest it seeks to preserve while the characterization of the actor's conduct stems from a differing individual perception of the social interest. The ideologically motivated offender, therefore, acts in a way so as to harm the legally protected social interest in order to protect or promote another interest he perceives to be more socially redeeming.

Whenever the law, which was violated, embodies the protection of socio-political structures and the actor was moved by a commitment to differing ideological values or beliefs and harms such interests without committing a "common crime," that offense is said to be "purely political." However, if such an offense also involves the commission of a "common crime," usually a private wrong, it ceases to be a purely political offense and could then be labelled either a "relative political offense" or a "common crime." [12]

The problem lies in distinguishing between types of offenses and typology of offenders. Western European doctrine makes a classification whereby it separates relative political offenses in *delits connexes* and *delits complexes*. In both cases a common crime is committed with or without the commission of a purely political offense, but is actuated by ideological motives. This approach, however, fails to appreciate the distinction between

the nature of the offense and the motives of the actor. These
approaches will be discussed below, but two general observations
must be borne in mind throughout the discussion of this exception:

1. The significance of value-oriented legal mandates

    by their very nature fluctuate in time and are

    relative to a given societal framework and, there-

    fore, cannot give rise to their international re-

    cognition except when the proscribed conduct is

    sanctioned by the common morality of mankind, as

    in the case of international crimes discussed

    below. [13]

2. It must, however, be recognized that every

    offense committed by an ideologically motivated

    offender is an attack upon the law, but not

    every attack upon the law is to benefit from

    the characterization of political offense as

    an exception to extradition.

1.1 (3) *The Purely Political Offense*

Such an offense is usually conduct directed against the sovereign
or a political subdivision thereof, and constitutes a subjective
threat to a political, religious or racial ideology or its supporting structures or both without, however, having any of the
elements of a common crime. The conduct is labelled a crime
because the interest sought to be protected is the sovereign to be
distinguished from any private wrong. The word sovereign includes all the tangible and intangible factors pertaining to the
existence and functioning of the state as an organization. It

refers to the violation of laws designed to protect the public interest by making an attack upon it a public wrong and are not to be confused with a private wrong as in the case of common crimes. Such laws exist solely because that very political entity, the state, criminalized such conduct for its self-preservation. It is nonetheless deemed a crime because it violates positive law, but it does not cause a private wrong.

Treason, sedition and espionage are offenses directed against the state itself and are, therefore, by definition, a threat to the existence, welfare and security of that entity, and as such, they are purely political offenses. A purely political offense, when linked to a common crime, loses that characteristic. This is illustrated in the following case.

In 1928, Germany sought the extradition from Guatemala of Richard Eckermann for the crime of murder. It was charged that in 1923 Eckermann was a prominent member of a secret organization of former German officers in Germany known as the Black Army whose purported purpose was to protect Germany in case of attack by its neighbors and to suppress communism and bolshevism in Germany. When one Fritz Beyer tried to join the Black Army, the other members thought him to be a spy and eventually it was alleged Eckermann gave directions to a subordinate as a result of which Beyer was shot, killed and buried. The crime was not discovered until more than a year later. The subordinate and four others who took part were tried and imprisoned, but Eckermann escaped to Mexico and then to Guatemala. The case eventually came to the Supreme Court of Justice of Guatemala,

Eckermann claiming that the crime was political, particularly in
the context of the abnormal conditions which prevailed in Germany
after World War I as a result of social, political and economic
upheavals. The Guatemalan constitution provided that "extradition is prohibited for political crimes or connected common ones."
In 1929, the court held that extradition should be granted. It
stated:

> . . . That the fact that Eckermann formed part of a
> patriotic society secretly organized to cooperate
> in the defense of his country cannot in any way
> give the character of political crimes to those
> committed by its members . . . Universal law qual-
> ifies as political crimes sedition, rebellion and
> other offenses which tend to change the form of
> government or the persons who compose it; but it
> cannot be admitted that ordering a man killed with
> treachery, unexpectedly and in an uninhabited
> place, without form of trial or authority to do it,
> constitutes a political crime. [14]

Prescinding from the question of what elements and what facts
are needed to constitute the offense of treason, the concept of
treasonous conduct gives rise to a variety of by-products which
differ from country to country. As one author noted:

> Although the Soviet formulation reflects the
> traditional law in regarding treason as breach
> of allegiance to the state, it nevertheless goes
> amazingly far in lumping together treason,

desertion and espionage, and, even more striking,

in setting up escape or flight abroad as a tre-

asonable act. [15]

Sedition in United States laws, for example, requires only a communication intended to incite a violation of public peace with intent to subvert the established form of government. The offense is complete upon the utterance and there is no necessity for any actual riot or rebellion occurring. Sedition is an insurrectionary movement tending toward treason, but wanting an overt act. It disturbs and affects the stability and tranquility of the state by means not actionable as treasonous. The distinction between treason, sedition and inciting to riot is, therefore, relative. [16]

Espionage on the other hand has a more widely recognized common denominator which is the obtaining or attempting to obtain information deemed secret or vital to the national security or defense of a given state for the benefit of another state. Unlike treason, there is no element of allegiance required on the part of the offender, hence no duty which must be breached. As with treason and sedition, it is predicated on the notion that what offends the public interest constitutes a public wrong.

Treason, sedition, espionage, peaceful dissent, freedom of expression and religion, if they do not incite to violence, are considered purely political offenses because they lack the essential elements of a common crime in that the perpetrator of the alleged offense acts merely as an instrument or agent of a political or religious thought or movement and is motivated by ideology or belief but does not cause a private harm. There is no way of defining what a purely political crime can be in a manner that would exhaust

the imagination of lawmakers but a proposed definition is as follows

A purely political offense is one whereby the conduct

of the actor manifests an exercise in freedom of thought,

expression and belief (by words, symbolic acts or

writings not inciting to violence), freedom of as-

sociation and religious practice which are in vio-

lation of law designed to prohibit such conduct. [17]

1.1 (4) The Relative Political Offense

The relative political offense can be an extension of the purely

political offense, when in conjunction with the latter, a common

crime is also committed or when without committing a purely polit-

ical offense, the offender commits a common crime prompted by

ideological motives. While the purely political offense exclu-

sively affects the public interest and causes only a public

wrong, the relative political offense affects a private interest

and constitutes at least in part a private wrong but done in

furtherance of a political purpose. The term relative political

offense is at best a descriptive label of doubtful legal accuracy

because it purports to alter the nature of the crime committed

depending upon the actor's motives (there are various theories

on the subject which are discussed below). There is nothing that

makes a given common crime political because the nature of the

criminal violation and the resulting harm constitute a private

wrong which, by definition, is a common crime. That the actor

seeks to use the offense or its impact for ulterior political pur-

poses does not alter the nature of the act or its resulting harm,

383

nor does its ulterior or ultimate purpose change its character.
The circumstances attending the commission of the crime and the
factors and forces which may have led the actor to such conduct
render the motivation of the actor complex but not the offense.
To call such crimes *delits complexes* or *delits connexes* only because the motives of the actor are taken into account even when
they deserve special consideration is to confuse the nature of
the crime with the motives of the actor. [18] Considerations fo-
cusing upon the offender's motives are not always accepted in
all criminal justice systems. For example, United States criminal laws do not include motives as part of the elements of
criminal offenses. [19] The element of intent required for all
serious crimes bears upon the state of mind of the actor at the
time the *actus reus* was committed. As such, *mens rea* does not
contemplate the reason why the ulterior purpose or the motivating factors which brought about this state of mind. [20] Certainly motive is relevant in proving intent, but it is not an element
of the crime and, therefore, has no bearing on whether or not
the actor's overall conduct, the accompanying mental state and
its resulting harm will be characterized a crime. It will,
however, be relevant in the determination of the sentence.

The criminality of an actor is determined by what he or she
did and whether he or she acted knowingly and voluntarily rather
than what the ulterior purpose for the conduct aimed at. Motive
is, therefore, a secondary factor in determining whether criminal intent exists except whenever a legal defense resting
thereon requires its proof. [21] The significance of motive in

different penal systems varies significantly, furthermore it must also be recalled that extradition is an intersystem process and, therefore, that which is significant to a given penal system may not be so with respect to another system. This therefore makes the issue of motive very complex particularly because whenever a state does not share the interest in maintaining the political ideology, system or policies of another state, it is less likely to exhibit concern or interest in the maintenance of the internal structures and public safety of that other state. In such a case the requested state is more likely to examine the motives of the offender and find some redeeming value in such conduct and eventually deem it political in order to deny extradition. There is also another problem which generally affects all theories on the relative political offense and it deals with the technical or factual multiplicity of offenses arising out of the same criminal transaction perpetrated by the ideologically motivated offender.

Most penal systems in the world have adopted a policy of grading or dividing crimes designed to protect a given social interest into various levels of accountability. The purposes of such policy vary, but, in general, they signify that the criminality of an actor, being dependent upon what he does and how he does it, must be graded in such a manner as to have punishment fit the presupposed criminality of the actor. It is further believed that because a punishment is a deterrent, the multiplicity of offenses which relate to the same social interest by virtue of such grading will induce the potential offender to perform lesser harm whenever he engages in his intended criminal conduct. Whatever the reasons for a grading policy, one thing remains certain: too many technically different offenses cover or relate to the same social interest presumably sought to be protected.

In addition to these considerations, a given social harm by reason of its significance will invariably contain lesser or included offenses which, taken independently, are the subject of separate offenses but in the context of what was actually done, may be part of the same criminal design or transaction.

The ideologically motivated offender is not likely to commit a single or isolated criminal act. Most likely, the conduct will encompass several lesser included offenses or bear upon other nonincluded but related offenses. These multiple offenses may either arise out of a single criminal act (a bomb placed in a plane which kills ten persons and destroys the plane will produce at least eleven different crimes) or from the same criminal transaction (an elaborate scheme involving several different crimes related by the single design or scheme of the actor). These related offenses technically may be considered included offenses whenever the elements of the higher degree offense are predicated on some or all of the elements of the lesser degree offense, in which case the existence of the lesser included offense would only be technical and not real. Other offenses deemed related but not included may be committed only by reason of the actor's design or by the necessity of the scheme, such as when one crime is only a stepping stone or a means to reach the

ultimate act sought to be committed. Lesser included offenses
are vertically related in that the elements of the lesser are
included in the higher offense. Other related offenses are at
best horizontally linked but only whenever the actor's design
relates them by reason of this scheme and not because of the
interrelationship between the elements of the various offenses
charged. This problem more than any other causes wide disparity
in the application of the relative political offense in municipal
laws and judicial decisions and, therefore, preclude uniform
international practice. [22] Invariably, however, three factors
are taken into account: (1) the degree of the political involvement of the actor in the ideology or movement on behalf of
which he has acted, his personal commitment to and belief in the
cause (on behalf of which he has acted), and his personal conviction that the means (the crime) are justified or necessitated
by the objectives and purposes of the idealogical or political
cause; (2) the existence of a link between the political motive
(as expressed above in (1)) and the crime committed; and (3) the
proportionality or commensurateness of the means used (the crime
and the manner in which it was performed) in relationship to the
political purpose, goal or objective to be served. The first
of these factors is wholly subjective, the second can be evaluated somewhat objectively, and the last is *sui generis*.

A dominant factor which emerges in the practice of all states
recognizing the relative political offenses as falling within
the purview of the political offense exception, namely that the
political element must predominate over the intention to commit

the common crime and constitute the purpose for the commission
of that common crime.[23]

The various theories concerning the relative political offense
have emerged from the jurisprudence of the various courts determining whether or not the request is for a relative political
offense. Three major theories have emerged: (A) the political-
incidence theory, (B) the injured rights theory, and (C) the
political-motivation theory. The European literature on the
subject usually refers only to two theories, *delits complexes*
and *delits connexes* but they encompass the distinctions made herein.

An analysis of certain landmark cases will illustrate the
application of these three divisions.

A - *The Political-Incidence Theory - The Common Law Approach*

The political-incidence theory was developed by an early English case, <u>In re Castioni</u>,[24] in which the refusal of extradition
of one whose surrender has been requested by the Swiss Government for the murder of a member of the State Council of a Swiss
canton held that "fugitive criminals are not to be surrendered
for extradition crimes, if those crimes were incidental to and
formed a part of political disturbances."[25] "Crimes otherwise
extraditable, become political offenses if they were incidental
to and formed part of a political disturbance."[26]

This case set up a two-fold standard which must be met for a
common crime to be regarded as a relative political offense:
1 - there must be a political revolt or disturbance, and 2 - the
act for which extradition is sought must be incidental thereto

388

or form a part thereof. [27] The English Court stated in this case:
"The question really is, whether, upon the facts, it is clear
that the man was acting as one of a number of persons engaged in
acts of violence of a political character with a political object, and as part of the political movement and rising in which
he was taking part." [28]

The Castioni ruling reflects the English liberal philosophy
of the late nineteenth century and is a consequence of its political theories and theories of government. English and United
States cases recognize the precedent of In re Castioni as authority. [29]

This view was confirmed in England three years after Castioni,
in the case of In re Meunier [30] where a confessed anarchist was
held extraditable for "in order to constitute an offense of a
political character, there must be two or more parties in the
state each seeking to improve the government of their own choice
on the other . . . In the present case there are not . . . for
the party with whom the accused is identified (ANARCHY) . . .
by his own voluntary statement . . . is the enemy of all governments. Their efforts are directed primarily against the general
body of citizens." [31]

Notwithstanding the validity of this position, it must be emphasized that the "political offense" concept remains essentially
a flexible one. Judge Denman, in In re Castioni, stated: "I do
not think it is necessary or desirable that we should attempt to
put into language in the shape of an exhaustive definition exactly . . . every state of things which might bring a particular

389

case within the description of an offense of a political character." [32]   This opinion presaged a recent holding of the English
courts in Ex parte Kolczysnski, [33]   that mutiny by the crew of
a small Polish fishing trawler was a political offense, notwithstanding the fact that it was not incident to a political uprising. This case indicates that (1) there is no absolute requirement that there be a political uprising in order for the political
offense exception to be applicable, but that the only indispensable ingredient is that the acts be politically motivated and
directed towards political ends; and (2) the political offense
exception legitimately can be applied with greater liberality
where the demanding State is a totalitarian regime seeking the
extradition of one who has opposed that regime in the cause of
freedom. Indeed, these two factors are closely related, particularly because in an effectively repressive totalitarian regime,
traditional political disturbances or uprisings may be unknown
despite deep and widespread hostility towards the regime. (The
United States holds a similar position). In 1973 the House of
Lords in Cheng v. Governor of Pentonville held that for the
exception to apply in addition to the predominance of a
purpose in the act it must also be directed against the opposed
government. [34]   In In re Gonzalez, [35]   the United States District
Court held "the issue is whether the acts of the relator should
be deemed politically motivated because directed towards political
ends; . . . nothing in the record suggests that the second factor is applicable as this does not appear to be a case in which
the acts in question were blows struck in the cause of freedom

390

against a repressive totalitarian regime."[36]

This approach has been followed by some Latin-American courts, even though their interpretation is often more liberal because of Western European influence and indigenous traditions towards political struggles. This position is illustrated by cases among which a case decided by the Supreme Court of Chile. Argentine had requested the extradition from Chile of Guillermo Patricio Kelly and others for murder, robbery and other offenses allegedly committed by Kelly when, during a raid on local Communist headquarters in Buenos Aires in which typewriters and other equipment were taken from the office, he shot and killed the gatekeeper. The Supreme Court of Chile, concluded that the exemption from extradition of political offenses applied only when the offense is a purely political offense or is an ordinary crime connected with a political offense. The Court held that Kelly should be extradited on the murder and robbery charges, stating:

> These crimes did not occur during an attack
> (by Kelly) on the security of the state, such as
> to be considered connected to a separate political
> offense. They took place at a time of public
> tranquility during which the murder and theft were
> isolated acts. The ultimate objective may have
> been the political one of annihilating communists,
> but the principles of public international law
> which this decision accepts do not admit that an
> ordinary crime is converted into a political one

solely because of its ultimate objective. [38]
It further stated that:

> "Political offense" does not appear to be
> defined in our positive legislation, nor in the
> international conventions and treaties previously
> enumerated, but generally accepted principles are
> in agreement that a political offense is that
> which is directed against the political organi-
> zation of the state or against the civil rights
> of its citizens and that the legally protected
> right which the offense damages is the consti-
> tutional normality of the country affected.
> Also included in the concept are acts which have
> as their end the alteration of the established
> political or social orders established in the
> state.

> A majority of the authorities consider,
> moreover, that in order to distinguish between
> ordinary and political crimes, it is necessary
> to take into account the goals and motives of
> the persons charged; that is to say, to consider
> the objective aspect of the offense as well as
> its subjective one. Political and social of-
> fenses obey motives of political and collective
> interest and are characterized by the sense of
> altruism or patriotism which animates them,
> while ordinary criminal offenses are motivated

by egoistic sentiments, more or less excusable
(emotion, love, honor), or to be reproached
(vengeance, hate, financial gain).

In this area of non-extraditable offenses
there are to be identified, purely political
offenses, which are directed against the form
and political organization of the state; improper political offenses, which embitter social
or economic tranquility; mixed or complex political
offenses, which damages at the same time public
order and ordinary criminal law, such as the
assassination of the head of state for political
reasons; and connected political offenses, which
are common crimes committed in the course of
attempts against the security of the state or
related to political offenses, it being necessary
to examine intent to determine whether the ordinary
crime is one connected, or not, to a political
one." [39]   [Emphasis added.]

The extension of the political-incidence test may often come
from the executive rather than the judiciary. [40] This was revealed in the Rudewitz case in 1908 when a Russian revolutionary,
a member of the Social Democratice Labor Party, was sought by the
Czarist Government for the common crimes of murder, arson, burglary, robbery and larceny from the United States. The Secretary
of State, subsequent to the decision of the extradition magistrate
to grant the request, concluded that the offenses charged were

political in nature and exercised his discretionary power in refusing to issue the surrender warrant. [41]

Another case of judicial-executive correlation in United States
extradition practice is the case of <u>Chandler v. United States</u>. [42]
There an American citizen was charged with treason for broad-
casting hostile propaganda to the United States from Germany during
World War II, thereby giving aid and comfort to the enemies of the
United States. Chandler claimed that his arrest having occurred
after the War while he was in Germany was a violation of his rights
of asylum conferred by International Law. The United States
Supreme Court held that in the absence of a treaty, a state does
not violate any principle of International Law by declining to
surrender a fugitive offender, but that the right is that of the
state (Germany) to offer asylum, not that of the fugitive to
claim. It also held that since treason is a violation of allegiance, such conduct may be made (consistently with intervention
of law) an offense against the United States, though the acts
were committed outside its territorial jurisdiction. The court
also found that the acts were political crimes for which extradition is not usually granted, and that had Germany claimed a
grant of asylum to the offender it is quite possible that, in
keeping with United States custom and practice Chandler would
have been returned to Germany. Chandler however was in United
States custody, the Court held that International Law principles
were not violated by his arrest in Germany and his return to the
United States and Germany did not object and therefore, there was no
his return to the United States. There was, therefore, no

opportunity to see how executive discretion would have been
exercised in this instance. (Executive Discretion is discussed
infra, Chapter VII.)

These cases, however serve to demonstrate that it is generally
within the scope of the political offense exception and in particular with respect to the relative political offense that executive
discretion finds the greatest opportunity for the exercise of its
determinative power to ultimately allow or deny extradition. The
role of the judiciary in United States practice is definitive in
finding that the exception applies, but is only conclusive in its
findings that the exception is inapplicable since executive discretion can override such findings. Consistent with this policy
and with the precedents discussed above, the United States decided the _Artukovic_ cases. [43]

In the first of these opinions, _Karadzole v. Artukovic_, [44]
the Circuit Court of Appeals affirmed a district court ruling
that the crimes charged against the petitioner, whose extradition
had been sought by the Government of Yugoslavia for the crimes
of murder and participation in murder occurring while he served
as Minister of the Interior of that country were of a political
character within the meaning of the Treaty and that, therefore,
Artukovic could not be extradited. The Yugoslav Government
charged that more than 30,000 unidentified persons and over
1,200 identified persons were killed on orders of the accused
in 1941 and 1942. The United States Court of Appeals, however,
reversing the District Court's finding held that a valid extradition treaty existed between the United States and Yugoslavia

as the successor state of Serbia with whom the extradition treaty of 1901 was in force. The District Court properly took judicial notice of the fact that various factions representing different theories of government were struggling for power during this period.

In the second opinion, Karadzole v. Artukovic,[45] the United States Supreme Court held, Justices Black and Douglas dissenting, that the judgment of the Court of Appeals should be vacated and remanded for hearings on the matter of the political offense. However, prior to this ruling, the Department of State representing the executive branch of government expressed its views to the court on the extradition issue that murder, even though committed solely or predominantly with the intent to destroy, in whole or in part, a national, ethnical, racial or religious group, is nonetheless murder within the meaning of the extradition treaty here involved, and is not thereby rendered an offense of a "political character within . . . the treaty . . . It does not appear on the face of the pleadings that all of the offenses . . . were necessarily connected with such struggle for power."[46]

The final judgment on that issue was in United States v. Artukovic,[47] where the United States Commissioner found insufficient evidence upon which to believe the accused guilty of the alleged offenses and refused extradition, holding that "the evidence presented, as well as historical facts of which I take judicial notice, proves . . . as a fact that the crimes charged in all counts of the amended complaint are political in character."[48]

396

The disposition of the case reflected the acceptance by the
United States Commissioner of the _Castioni_ standards [49] in finding
that a political offense existed in fact and, therefore, that the
relator was not extraditable. Since United States practice, however does not favor the exercise of executive discretion to grant
the request after its denial by the judiciary, a conflict was
averted which could have arisen between these two branches had
the executive department overriden the court's findings as indicated by the Department of State's views. [50] It must be noted
that this case also contained a charge that the relator committed
international crimes which should have precluded the court's findings of the political offense exception, but did not (see _infra_,
1-1-6).

In another case, the United States Supreme Court left undis-
turbed the findings of the extradition magistrate but affirmed
the position that relative political offenses are nonextraditable
and that the best test is one of "political incidence." [51] In
that case, Italy, in 1958, requested the extradition from the
United States of Vincenzo Gallina who had been convicted in Italy,
in absentia, in the court of Assizes of Caltanisetta on May 30,
1949, of the crime of robbery. After being found extraditable
at the extradition hearing, Gallina applied for a writ of _habeas
corpus_ contending, _inter alia_, that the offense was not extraditable under the Extradition Convention of 1868 between the United
States and Italy, [52] Article III, of which states that "the provisions of this treaty shall not apply to any crime or offense of
a political character . . . ." The District Court rejected the

contention. [53]

The United States Court of Appeals affirming held:

Relator contends that the hearing before the
Commissioner established beyond doubt that the offense
for which extradition is sought were of a political
character and, under Article III of the Convention
of 1868, non-extraditable. Counsel for relator has
briefed the point extensively. According to relator,
the acts to which he admitted might be ordinary crimes
in an atmosphere free of any political ramifications,
but because of the motivation for their commission,
they must necessarily be deemed of a "political
character." While the court is in general agreement
with a relator's exposition of the principles of law
governing the nonextraditability of political offenders
who have found asylum in this country, nevertheless
it is the opinion of thecourt that the Commissioner's
decision that the specific acts ascribed to relator
in the complaint of the Republic of Italy were not
of a political character, whatever his other acts
during the period in question might have been, is
supported by the evidence in the record . . . .

The claim that what appeared to be common, ordinary crimes were so admixed with political motives
and aims as to be of a political character within the
meaning of the Convention of 1868 was based solely
on testimony of relator himself. This testimony, to

the effect that relator worked for Torrese and that

Torrese and that Torrese took orders from Guiliano,

all to advance the political aims of a Sicilian sep-

aratist movement, was contradicted by statements taken

from relator's admitted accomplices after their arrest

in Italy, which tended to indicate that private gain was

the sole motivating factor in these robberies.   There

was also testimony from a Mr. Russo, a witness offered

as an expert by the Republic of Italy, who had spent

considerable time in Sicily during the years when a

Sicilian separatist organization was active, as a mem-

ber of the Office of Strategic Services, a branch of

our waritme forces. Russo testified at length and

unqualifiedly, both on direct and on cross-examina-

tion, that Guiliano was a bandit who had no legitimate

connection with the actual separatist movement, and

that Guiliano described his activities as "political"

to cloak their true purpose, i.e., private gain for

himself and his followers. With the evidence before

the Commissioner in such posture, this court cannot

say that the Commissioner's decision was not sup-

ported by competent, legal evidence. The evidence

was conflicting, it is true, but it did not pre-

ponderate so heavily in relator's favor as to require

a decision that his offenses were political as a

matter of law. [54]

In what appears to be a contrary view in a situation equally

complex and laden with political implications were the _Jimenez_
cases. [55] There a former President of the Republic of Venezuela
was sought from the United States for financial crimes and murder.
The District Court found the murder charge to be nonextraditable
on grounds of political offense exception but found that the financial crimes were not within the exception and granted extradition. Thus establishing the precedent that where multiple
charges exist and some do not fall within the political offense
exception extradition shall be granted unless all charges are related or connected to the political motive and were incidental
thereto. Where there is no such connection and the charges are
severable, extradition can be granted on the assumption that the
doctrine of specialty (_supra_, Chapter V,) shall preclude the prosecution of the relator for those charges. In view of the fact
that the ideologically motivated offender is a more wanted person
than any other person alleged to have committed a common crime,
because he struck at the very foundation of the requesting state's
existence or order, it is naive to believe that the doctrine of
specialty shall operate as a protective shield to the relator.

The position of the United States has been to consider the question of whether an offense is of a political character a mixed
question of law and facts, but chiefly one of facts. [56] This
gives, therefore, the extradition magistrate the preponderant role,
leaving reviewing courts with an examination of the interpretation
of the law and its proper application to the facts stated in the
record.

B - The Injured Rights Theory

This theory has its basis in the French Extradition Law
of March 10, 1927, and suggests that extradition cannot be granted
when the circumstances show that it is sought exclusively for a
political end. [57] It is not, however, the only theory followed
by the French courts and is considered a supplemental theory rather than an exclusive approach. The principal theory followed
in Europe is the Political Motivation Theory discussed below.
The Injured Rights Theory often appears as part of the Political
Motivation Theory. It has been evident in the reasoning of
cases in France, Belgium, San Marino, Italy, Switzerland and The
Federal Republic of Germany. The leading case following this
theory is In re Giovanni Gatti [58] wherein the extradition request
by the Republic of San Marino was for an attempted homicide by a
member of a Communist cell. The Court granted extradition and
held that: "Political offenses . . . are directed against the
constitution of the Government and against Sovereignty . . . and
disturb the distribution of powers . . . such an offense affects
the political organization of the state . . . . The offense does
not derive its political character from the motive of the offender,
but from the nature of the rights it injures." [59]

A second case, In re Colman, [60] allowed extradition upon the
request of Belgium of one sought for, and already convicted in
absentia of the Crimes of Collaboration with the enemy, carrying
arms against the state and assassination: "in a country occupied
by the enemy (in time of war), collaboration with the latter excludes the idea of a criminal action against the political organ-

ization of the state which characterizes the political offense." [61]

In the context of the discussion of executive discretion, it is interesting to note that the offenses charged against <u>Colman</u> were not covered by the extradition treaty between France and Belgium. [62] An exchange of notes between the two governments which took place after the commission of the offenses set forth the terms for the exchange of such offenders considering them as falling within the scope of the treaty. [63] The court said that "the offender . . . has no right not to be surrendered though facts which were not provided for, at the time of the consummation of the offense, by the Franco-Belgian Convention to which he is not a party, as long as both French and Belgian law render criminal and punish the offenses at the time when they were committed. [64] This insistence stretches the principle of nonretroactivity of criminal laws and somewhat subverts the legislative effect of an extradition theory by its *ex post facto* amendment.

C - The Political Motivation Theory: The European Approach

This theory was developed by the Swiss courts which attempted to modify the political-incidence theory [65] developed by the English courts. It does not look strictly to the nature of the rights injured, but it tries to correlate the ideological beliefs of the offender and the proportionate effect of his acts or offenses and the political purpose in trying to reach an equitable result which locks in the other theories.

In 1908, the Swiss Federal Tribunal stated in the case of <u>V. P. Wassilief</u> [66] that three general principles had to be met in order for an offense to be political: (1) that the offense was committed for the purpose of helping or insuring the success of a purely political purpose; (2) that there is a direct connection between the crime committed and the purpose pursued by a party to modify the political or the social organization of the state; and (3) that the political element predominates over the ordinary criminal element.

The problem of interpretation appears in the case of In re Pavan, [67] where the French Government requested extradition of an anti-Fascist journalist accused of the murder of an Italian Fascist. The Swiss court, rejecting the defense's plea of political offense, held that the crime "is invested with a predominantly political character only where the criminal action is immediately connected with its political object. Such connection can only be predicated where the act is in itself an effective means of attaining this object or where it is an incident in a general political struggle . . . ." [62]

The same reasoning was applied in the Ockert case. In 1933 the Prussian Minister of Justice requested the extradition from Switzerland of one Ockert on a charge of homicide. It appeared that Ockert, a member of the Reichsbanner, a quasimilitary organization of the Germano Social-Democratic Party, became involved in an altercation on a street in Frankfurt with certain members of the National-Socialist Party, particularly one Bleser whom he hit with his fist. Ockert then ran and when pursued by the group fired several shots at them with his pistol, two of which hit Bleser and caused his death. Ockert contended that the charge came within article 4 of the Swiss-German Extradition Treaty of 1874 which prohibited extradition for offenses of a political character. The Federal Tribunal of Switzerland agreed. The Tribunal referred to previous cases involving similar facts, particularly a case in which a Swiss Federal Court had refused extradition of a person convicted of complicity in a brawl between members of the Fascist Party in a small Italian village and their local antagonists on the basis that the clashes between such groups were not mere casual disputes arising from local or personal enmity but part of a struggle which was on such a wide scale that it came near to being a civil war. In the instant case, the Tribunal noted that reports of the incident in German newspapers spoke of "Marxist Murder Tactics" and "Sacrifice in the Service of the New Reich" and concluded that the case was essentially one of political con-flict and not extraditable. [69] Relating what is called passive resistance to political regimes and the relative political offense, the Swiss approach in the case of In re Kavic, [70] linked the non-doing of an act of opposition to the doing of an act likely to be deemed criminal.

In this case, Yugoslavia sought the extradition of the members of an airplane crew who had diverted a local flight and landed in Switzerland. They were charged with the crimes of endangering the safety of public transport and wrongful appropriation of pro-perty. The Swiss Court, in denying the extradition request, held that although the political character of the offense must outweigh its common characteristics (the danger and harm to the passengers was minimal) such need not be related to a realization of political

404

objectives or occurring within a fight for political power. [71]

"That restrictive interpretation . . . does not meet the intention of the law, nor take account of . . . the growth of totalitarian states . . . those who do not wish to submit to the regime have no alternative but to escape it by flight abroad . . . this more passive attitude . . . is nontheless worthy of asylum than active participation in the fight for political power used to be in what were . . . normal circumstances." [72]

This position is no longer valid in light of the 1963 Tokyo Convention and 1970 Hague Conventions since unlawful seizure of aircrafts became an international crime as discussed in the "exception to the exception," (*infra*, 1-1-6).

A later case illustrating this theory is the Ktir case. [73] The appellant, a French national, was a member of the Algerian Liberation Movement (F.L.N.). On November 14, 1960, he was responsible, with three other persons, for the murder in France of another member of the F.L.N. who was suspected by his chiefs of treason. He then fled to Switzerland. France requested his extradition. He contested that request on the ground that France was at war with F.L.N. and that the act he had committed was that of killing an enemy. He further contended that, if extradition were granted; it had to be made subject to the condition that he would not be executed, since the offenses would not be punished by capital punishment in Switzerland. The Court held that extradition must be granted for the following reasons:

(1) Political offences included common crimes which had a predominantly political character, from their

405

motive and factual background. However, the
damage had to be proportionate to the aim sought;
in the case of murder, this had to be shown to be
the sole means of attaining the political aim.
The offence in this case did not satisfy this requirement of proportionality.

(2) A condition that the accused would not be
sentenced to death could be attached to the extradition only if the relevant treaty expressly prohibited capital punishment.

(3) The extradition should be subject to the
condition that the appellant would not be prosecuted or sentenced for other activities. This
was required in order to give effect to the principle of specialty contained in Article 8 of the
Extradition Treaty (of July 9, 1869).

. . . .

2. According to Article 1 and 2 of the
Treaty, extradition is authorized if the acts
committed are punishable under both Swiss and
French law; if they constitute one of the offences
listed in the Convention; and if they do not constitute political offences. Political offences
include offences which, although constituting
acts falling under the ordinary criminal law, have
a *predominantly* political character as a result of
the circumstances in which they are committed, in

particular as a result of the circumstances in
which they are committed, in particular as a result of the motives inspiring them and the purpose
sought to be achieved. Such offences, akin to
relative political offences, presuppose that the
act was inspired by political passion, that it
was committed either in the framework of a struggle
for power or for the purpose of escaping a dictatorial
authority, and that it was directly and closely related to the political purpose. A further requirement is that the damage caused be proportionate to
the result sought, in other words, that the interests
at stake should be sufficiently important to excuse,
if not to justify, the infringement of private legal
rights. Where murder is concerned, such a relationship exists only if homicide is the sole means of
safeguarding more important interests and attaining
the political aim. [74]

Even though the case also involved an issue of exclusion for
military offenses and death penalty, the court found that extradition when granted for one or more offenses charged and not for
others, the Doctrine of Specialty (*supra*, Chapter V,) would preclude the prosecution of the relator for such offenses but does
not constitute a bar to his extradition for other offenses
deemed extraditable. The position of the United States is to
that extent compatible with that of Switzerland and the general
practice under customary international law. [75]

The contemporary position of western European states is still ambiguous as to what constitutes a relative political offense even though the 1957 European convention on extradition contains the exception in its Article 3. All fifteen member states of the Council of Europe recognized that it is a judicial question which depends essentially on the facts and circumstances of every case. Recent extradition legislation in several of the European states has yet to be applied and its jurisprudential significance remains to be established. This is the case with respect to Cyprus whose new law of 1970 has yet to be applied in the courts of that state, and also with respect to Denmark's 1967 Law and Norway's 1968 Law. The 1966 Extradition law of the Netherlands preserves the doctrine that the courts must determine the nature of the interests affected by the act and the motives of the actor. The variance in other laws is essentially as to the issue of whether the entirety of the criminal transaction is to be motivated by political purposes or only a portion thereof, and also their preponderance over all other motives.

Italy in Article 8 of its 1931 penal code requires the magistrate to determine whether the common crime was motivated in whole or in part by political motives. This was expressed in the 1934 decision of the Court of Appeals of Turin of In re Pavelic and Kwaternik and this position remains unchanged. This case remains a landmark because of its facts and its impact. It was based on the French government's request for the extradition of Pavelic and Kwaternik on the charge of complicity in the murder of King Alexander of Yugoslavia and the French Minister Barthou in Mar-

seilles in October, 1934. The Italian Court of Appeals held that
the offense fell within the meaning of the political offense exception embodied in Articles 2 and 3 of the Treaty of May 12, 1870
between the two states and in accordance to the Italian Criminal
Code which forbids extradition for political offenses. Even
though extradition had been denied the authors of the *attendant*
were judged in France and found guilty of common crimes. (It was
after this decision that the multilateral Convention on the Prevention and Punishment of Terrorism was drafted in 1937 and proposed *inter alia* the creation of an international criminal court
to judge such cases. Even though the convention was signed by 13
states it was never ratified by a sufficient number of states to
enter into effect and is since 1973 very discussed because of contemporary efforts to draft a convention on the same subject.)

The Law of Denmark of 1947 makes the issue dependant upon the
nature of interests affected. Switzerland also adheres to that
position but requires in addition thereto that the political motive be predominant over the intent to commit a common crime.
France adheres to its 1927 law which is vague as to its specific
requirements but its jurisprudence has closely parallelled decisions
in Belgium and Switzerland. Furthermore France requires the magistrate to inquire as to whether the extradition itself is sought
for a political purpose. Germany also has followed closely the
jurisprudence of Switzerland, France and Belgium. Sweden whose
1957 law is the broadest legislative provision in Western Europe
has been liberal in its jurisprudence. Belgium which has also
been liberal in its application of the exception which it was the

409

first state to embody in its law of 1833, had amended it in 1856
with the *clause d'attentat*. This amendment was added to the 1833
law after the Belgium courts refused to extradite to France the
author of the *attentat* against the life of Napoleon III. The
Federal Republic of Germany has a similar clause in its law on
extradition which is also embodied in Article 3.3 of the 1957
European Convention on Extradition. (The same type of provision
is found in the Caracas Convention of July 18, 1911 between the
Central American state; in Article 357 of the Bustamante Code of
February 20, 1973; in Article 3 of the Montevideo Convention of
December 26, 1933; in Article 3 of the extradition convention
of the Central American states signed in Guatemala April 12, 1934,
and in Article 23 of the Montevideo Convention of March 19, 1940.)

The *clause d'attentat* is also present in several European bilateral treaties as between Germany, France, Belgium and Monaco.
The same type of provision appears in the recent treaties of France
with for example Ivory-Coast, Dahomey, Niger, Upper Volta and
Mauritania. These recent treaties expand the original Belgium
clause of 1856 to include all forms of assassinations, excluding
such acts from the political offense exception.

The Anarchist movement of the 30's in Europe filled the annals
of European extradition and in several *causes célèbres* even the
authors of riots were extradited without benefit of the political
offense exception. This was the case with Great Britain's surrender to Italy of Rivolta and to France of Lucchesi. Italy
however did not receiprocate as witness the case of Pavelic and
Kwaternik (these cases have been referred to earlier in this

410

chapter). The latest European case was <u>Cheng v. Governor of</u>
<u>Pentonville</u> discussed above in which the House of Lords reaffirmed
its earlier position but the opinion of the court and its members
expressed a tightening of the hitherto liberal English position.
References to the rash of terrorism taking place in Europe are a
clear indication of a narrowing trend for future interpretation
of the exception. In 1974 the Council of Europe will consider
amending Article 3 of the European Convention on extradition to
take account of the contemporary problems posed by "terrorism"
and its various manifestations. This presages for all of Europe
a trend for less liberal application of the exception and for
specifying such exclusions as "terrorism" from the scope of the
exception. The problem of defining "terrorism" will of course
be the main obstacle but it is likely to be resolved by a listing
of specific acts such as aircraft hijacking, letter bombs, etc.

1.1(5) - A *proposed juridical standard of inquiry for municipal
tribunals*. [76] The determination of the relationship of all offenses committed as part of a political scheme, and particularly
under the relative political offense is, at first, as shown in
the theories discussed above, one of motive, but further inquiry
must be made into the nature of the criminal transaction. This
inquiry leads to the following questions: (1) Were all the offenses committed part of the same (political) criminal transactions? (2) What was the number or extent of these violations?
(3) How were they related in scope, time, place and social significance? (4) To what extent did the political scheme necessitate
the commission of such multiple offenses? (5) Could they readily

411

be identified as lesser included offenses, or did they appear to be realted only by the actor's design?

One interesting question which could arise at this point is: What if this inquiry concluded only partially in favor of the relator? Shall the extradition judge or executive authority weigh the degree of compliance of the relator's conduct to these tests versus his noncompliance and determine its outcome by a "preponderance of compliance" test? Or shall he disqualify the relator from the benefit of the "political offense" exception because there was a single instance of noncompliance? In this case we also see the limited chances of a juridical solution in a world system wherein the ultimate relationship between political units is predicated upon a concept of co-equal sovereigns exercising all-too-often conflicting, co-equal authority. Were the alternative a vertical jurisdictional authoritative process, the issue would then be removed from the contentious or opposing co-equal horizontal authoritative process and some opportunities for direct conflict would therefore be eliminated.

The search for an objective standard gives rise to an analogy with self-defense as commonly accepted in all penal systems, wherein a person is justified in causing harm to another to insure his own safety. The primary consideration in the law of self-defense is a value-judgment based on the inherent justification of self-preservation and its overriding exonerating effect on the consequences arising out of the potential harm to be inflicted upon the aggressor. The means authorized, the use of force, is dependent upon the nature of the potentail harm sought to be in-

412

flicted upon the aggressor. The means authorized, the use of force, is dependent upon the nature of the potentail harm sought to be inflicted by the aggressor on the victim and the latter's need to prevent such harm from occurring. Hence, if fundamental human rights are seriously violated by an institutional entity or a person or persons wielding the authority of the state and acting on its behalf without lawful means of redress or remedy being made available, then the responsibility of the individual, whose conduct was necessitated by the original transgression by reason of his need to redress a continuing wrong, is justified or mitigated and, therefore, warrants a denial of extradition.

This right to idealogical self-preservation or political self-defense is predicated on three categories of factors: First, *factors bearing upon the nature of the "rights" involved, which were originally violated and gave rise to the right to defend them.* These include: (a) the nature of those "rights" and their sources; (b) the extent to which those "rights" are indispensable or necessary to the survival or basic values of the people; (c) the historical and traditional existence of those "rights" and the degree of their availability and enjoyment by the people; (d) the extent of the people's reliance upon them in relation to their implantation in the social psychology as necessary, indispensable or fundamental to the way of life; (e) the duration of their abridgement and, if sporadic, their recurrence; (f) the potential or foreseeable voluntary termination of the transgression by the violating body or person; and (g) the existence or reasonable availability of a local or international remedy or legal method of redress of such wrongs. These factors, for the most part, can be ascertained objectively and tangibly by impartial and objective inquiry into their existence and their validity by the extradition magistrate or the executive authority in the exercise of his discretionary power to grant or deny extradition.

Second, *factors bearing upon the conduct of the nation-state which were seriously violative of these "fundamental rights."* These include: (a) the nature of the transgression, abridgement, violation, termination, subversion or abolition of the "right" or "rights" claimed; (b) the quantitative and qualitative evaluation of the violations; (c) the manner in which they were violated, the extent of the violation, the means used to accomplish it, the duration of the violation, and the frequency of their recurrence; (d) the avowed or implicit intentions of continuing these violations or their termination within a declared or foreseeable future; (e) whether these violations were conditioned, caused, prompted or forced by conditions of necessity, such as natural catastrophes, disasters, war, insurrection, or other factors affecting the physical and tangible existence or viability of the nation-state which would justify or mitigate such conduct; (f) any methods or means of redress, remedies or channels open or made available to the aggrieved party or group to which the relator belongs; (g) any repressive actions taken against those who claimed grievance and pursued legal channels of remedy in the prescribed manner or who challenged the offensive public conduct in a manner deemed lawful by the common standards of the ordinary times of that nation. The factors in this category also lend themselves to objective inquiry.

Third, assuming the existence and validity of the conditions
of the factors in the first and second categories, *factors bearing
upon the conduct of the individual who violated the positive law
of the state in defense of these "Fundamental Human Rights."*
These include: (a) exhaustion of all available remedies, local
and international, saving risks of repression; (b) the explicit
or implicit common understanding in the ordinary reasonable man
(of the nation-state in question) that no redress was available
in the reasonably foreseeable future and that such conduct was,
if not warranted, at least excusable (exonerating or mitigating)
because no other alternative existed; (c) whether the individual's
conduct was proportionate or commensurate with the nature of the
right or rights violated in terms of their objective significance
in the common understanding of the ordinary reasonable man of the
nation-state wherein the conduct took place; (d) whether the
individual's conduct was related only to the original wrong in
a negative or vengeful aspect or whether it was also intended
to terminate it or to affect its redress and, thus, have a positive aspect to it; (e) whether the means used were limited to
achieve these purposes and there was no violation committed which
was not necessitated by the attainment of such goals through the
least harmful manner; (f) whether the assumption of any risks
created would fall on the individual perpetrator, and whether
the means and tactics used would not endanger innocent persons.

This theory of ideological self-preservation is not advanced
as a means to warrant or justify lawlessness, or anarchy, but is

intended to relate an otherwise nebulous concept, which has been the subject of nefarious political manipulations, to the sphere of a legally or judicially manageable theory of law. While it is beyond the scope of this paper to expose and discuss the ramifications of such a proposition, this proposed theory is intended to lay a juridical framework to what could be considered a politically motivated offense, which would shield its perpetrator from the repressive powers of the state against which the violation was directed.

To discern between objective and subjective standards of evaluating the nature of the relator's conduct is not only a procedural question, but a substantive one, because it is outcome determinative of the issue of extraditability of the relator. Such a choice by national public policy is one which is largely determined by the overall political outlook of the nation-state in terms of its place in the relationship between the nation-states of the world community and the ideological political alignment of the nation-state in question. To promulgate an objective standard, however, requires the acceptance of a decision made in furtherance thereof and would eliminate opportunities for conflicts.

1.1(6) - *International crimes: The exception to the political offense exception.* Offenses against the Law of Nations or *Delicti Jus Gentium* by their very nature affect the world community as a whole. [77] As such, they cannot fall within the political offense exception because, even though they may be politically connected, they are in derogation to the "laws of mankind" in general and international criminal law in particular.

The concept of crimes against "the laws of mankind" is a vague generic term intending to cover all international crimes. Such vagueness however contributes to the difficulty of having that very concept accepted as an "exception to the exception", in other words, that international crimes would be extraditable offenses which are not to benefit from the political offense exception. [78] International crimes should indeed be considered extraditable offenses without the benefit of the political offense exception but in order for this position to be accepted as a rule of international law, it must be based either on conventional international criminal law or customary international law. As of yet, there is only scant indication that it is recognized as a custom evidenced by the practice of states even though there are many scholarly writings by distinguished publicists favoring it and repeated affirmation of this position in scholarly gatherings. There is therefore a growing trend towards acceptance of this position as an essential doctrine in furtherance of the pre-servation of minimum world order. [79] It must however, be emphasized that a clear definition of those international crimes falling within the doctrine of the "exception to the exception" must be set forth in conventional international criminal law. Without such clear understanding of those crimes specifically encompassed within the meaning of international criminal law the rule cannot be effectively or uniformly applied and consequently such a situation would be detri-mental to the goals of judicial assistance and cooperation in extra-dition. [80] Summarizing this problem one author noted:

In the application of extradition treaties to the cases of persons charged with, or convicted of crimes under municipal law

417

it may be essential, in the exercise of the
generally beneficent principle that political
criminals shall not be subject to extradition,
to decide whether or not a crime was political.
But where an offence is made by treaty a crime
under international law, the principle of non-
extradition of political criminals would be
contrary to public policy. [81]

The concept of international crimes while encompassing two
sources of offensive conduct: (1) that which offends the common
morality of mankind and is recognized as offensive to mankind at
large, and (2) that which by treaty has been recognized as an
international crime only the latter can be recognized as falling
within the "exception to the exception."

The process of positing international criminal law and attempting
to codify it must be credited to the United Nations, even though
certain international crimes like piracy and war crimes long
predated the United Nations.

On November 21, 1947, the General Assembly established the International Law Commission as a permanent body, having for its basic
objective "the promotion of the progressive development of international law and its codification." [82] In another resolution a-
dopted on the same day, the Commission was specifically directed
to:

"(a) Formulate the principles of international
law recognized in the Charter of the Nuremberg
Tribunal and in the judgment of the tribunal,

and

"(b) Prepare a draft code of offenses against

the peace and security of mankind indicating

clearly the place to be accorded to the prin-

ciples mentioned in sub-paragraph (a)

above." [83]

In its report of 1950, the International Law Commission, set

forth the various principles of international law recognized in

the Charter of Nuremberg and Tokyo war crimes trials and in the

judgment of these tribunals, [84] and in 1954 formulated the Draft

Code of Offenses against the Peace and Security of Mankind. [85]

Among the considerations underlying the principles of interna-

tional criminal responsibility is the belief that duties may be

imposed on individuals by international law without any inter-

position of internal law because "crimes against international

law are committed by men, not by abstract entities," [86] and that

only by punishing individuals guilty of an international crime

independently of the law of any particular country can the peace

and security of mankind be preserved. This implies that individuals

have international duties which transcend national obligations of

obedience imposed by individual states and places a duty upon each

state to prosecute or surrender for prosecution such offenders.

Put to the test this principle was not always successful. The

case in point is that of Kaiser Wilhelm II and other German

officials who under Article 227 and 228 of the Treaty of Versailles

(1919) [87] were to be prosecuted for an "offense against interna-

tional law, morality and the sanctity of treaties." The Kaiser who sought refuge in the Netherlands was not surrendered to the Allies. The Dutch Government refused his surrender on the grounds that it had a tradition of granting asylum to the "vanquished in international conflict."[88] The refusal was on the grounds of political offense exception, and no exception there to was found applicable because the crimes charged were of an international character. It is significant to note, however, that whenever the international crime does not contain elements which could be characterized as political, such as in the case of aggression,[89] and even in the case of war crimes[90] and crimes against humanity,[91] the world community found itself cooperating in such matters as: suppression of slavery and slave trade;[92] illicit traffic of narcotics;[93] counterfeiting;[94] piracy;[95] and aircraft hijacking.[96] The following is offered as a catalog of recognized international crimes, which should, therefore, constitute an exclusion from the political offense exception. They are:

1. Aggression,[97] as defined by the United Nations Charter.

2. Crimes against Humanity,[98] as defined in the formulation of the Nuremberg principles by the United Nations General Assembly[99] and the Genocide Convention.[100]

3. War Crimes,[101] as defined by the 1912 Hague Conventions,[102] and the 1949 Geneva Conventions,[103] and other rules of conduct in war and restrictions in warfare.[104]

4. Piracy.[105]

420

5. Hijacking. [106]

6. Slavery, White Slavery, and other forms of
   traffic in Women and Children. [107]

7. Counterfeiting. [108]

8. Kidnapping of internationally protected persons. [109]

9. International Traffic in Narcotics. [110]

10. Racial Discrimination. [111]

Of all these international crimes only some have a specific requirement that extradition be granted; they are: Genocide, the
1949 Geneva Conventions, the Narcotics Conventions, the Tokyo
and Hague Conventions on aircraft hijacking, the Counterfeiting
Convention and the Slavery Convention. [112] In all these cases,
however, the obligation to extradite arises by multilateral
treaty, binding only upon its signatories (subject to proper ratification) and does not constitute a self-executing obligation
but must be embodied in bilateral extradition treaties. In the
case of all other international crimes, the obligation to extradite arises under customary international law and general principles of international law. But these two sources are somewhat
challenged by those states which like the United States and England will not recognize an obligation to extradite outside their
treaties [113] as well as by other states for different reasons. [114]
There is a question as to whether or not violations of minimum
standards human rights have ripened into being a crime under international law, but so far there has been no such recognition either
by treaty or customary international law. [115] Consequently, such
violations cannot be construed, as of yet, as international crimes.

Similarly, proposals covering terrorism and conscription of minors
which have often been discussed at international conferences have
not been adopted and, therefore, are not included in this catalog
of international crimes. The issue of international crimes was
raised in the _Artukovic_ case, and the United States Court of
Appeals stated:

> We now consider the question whether
> because the offenses are also called "war crimes"
> they have lost their character as "political
> offenses" within the meaning of the treaty.
> Appellant argues that "war crimes" are crimes for
> which extradition is to be granted within the
> meaning of international acts to which the United
> States is a party. It is argued by recent legal
> writers that the "barbarity and atrocity of the
> crimes as in crimes against the law of war and crimes
> against humanity" when committed weigh so heavily upon
> the common crime element that the political act
> has practically ceased to exist and, therefore,
> that the extradition of the offender is the only
> justifiable course of action.

> Appellant in essence argues that by virtue
> of resolutions taken in 1946 and 1947 by the
> United Nations General Assembly as to the surrender
> of alleged war criminals, it is incumbent on this
> Court to hold that Artukovic is charged with an
> offense which is extraditable.

We have examined the various United Nations

Resolutions and their background and have concluded

that they have not sufficient force of law to modify

long standing judicial interpretations of similar

treaty provisions. Perhaps changes should be made

as to such treaties . . . . [116]

On appeal the Supreme Court vacated judgment and remanded the

case to the District Court, [117] but in a clear and uncompromising

decision, the District Court declined "to go into the question of

extradition for so-called war crimes," [118] and emphatically held

that Artukovic's offenses were of a political charcter and, thus,

his extradition was denied. [119] The District Court apparently

saw a close connection between the common crime with which Artukovic

was charged and his political activity. As noted by one author:

A case comparable to the Artukovic case is

that of Jan Durcansky, recently decided by the Buenos

Aires Court of First Instance, and involving a request

from the Czechoslovakian Government for the surrender

of a person accused of having participated in mass

murders of civilians in Czechoslovakia during the

period from November, 1944 to the end of the war. In

refusing his extradition, the Court said that Durcansky

was protected by extinctive prescription according

to Article 16 of the Argentine Penal Code. Though

apparently the General Assembly's resolutions urging

the members of the United Nations to surrender war

criminals were before the Argentine court in the same

manner as they were before the Court of Appeals
in the _Artukovic_ case, the result was still the
same since, admittedly, such resolutions are too
tenuous to have any legally binding force.

Apart from the countries above mentioned, it
has already been seen that Great Britain and
Australia have also refused to extradite war criminals upon essentially similar grounds, while
Italy has based its refusal to surrender on the
well established principle that a State is not
required to extradite its own nationals.[120]

On other grounds, the United States refused extradition to the
USSR of a Lithuanian national, to whom it had granted asylum.
The relator had been convicted _in absentia_ by a Russian tribunal
for the mass murder of some 50,000 civilians while in command of
a German punitive battalion in 1941. In rejecting the Soviet request, the Department of State vigorously asserted that "a person
accused of war time mass murders might not get a trial in the
Soviet Union that would be considered fair according to United
States standards."[121] This position is inconsistent with the
"rule of noninquiry" (discussed in Chapter VII). There is no case
known to this writer whose extradition was requested or granted
for an international crime, other than for war crimes and crimes
against humanity arising out of World War II. Similarly, there
is no case where after asylum was granted a state upheld the doctrine of an "exception to the exception." Even in recent hijacking cases from Poland and Czechoslovakia to Germany the re-

quested states, France and Germany, relied on the 1963 Tokyo

Convention and prosecuted the hijackers rather than surrender

them. [122]   Even in cases involving illicit international traffic

of narcotic drugs, the request and surrender of such offenders

was always on the basis of its being an extraditable offense in

current treaty practice rather than it being an international

crime. [123]

There is still difficulty, however, in determning what constitutes

international offenses, their elements, and the factual establish-

ment of their occurrence. There is, however, some international

agreemetn on the notion that such offenses constitute an "excep-

tion to the exception," [124] even though there is still no codifi-

cation of international criminal law. [125]

1.1(7) - *The political offense exception and world public

order: A proposed international solution.* The reasons for the

political offense exception rest in part upon the asylum state's

sense of humane treatment and belief in human rights and personal

and political freedom. [126]   Furthermore it is generally acknowledged

that political crimes affect the demanding state's most sensitive

interests, and, therefore, inspire a passionately hostile atmosphere

which makes an orderly and fair trial very difficult. The asylum

state also sees the political offense, unlike ordinary crimes,

as a reflection of the individual's resistance to the regime of

the requesting state and therefore the presence of the offender

in the requested state is not usually a threat to its domestic

tranquility. [127]   Consequently the requested state will not be

moved by ordinary criminological considerations but will be

suaded one or another by political reasons.

The commendable humanitarian objectives of the political offense exception have unfortunately seldom been realized. The reason for this lies in the fact that in every case the definition of political offenses and the determination of whether the crimes charged by the requesting state constitute a political offense are made by the requested state in accordance with its public policy or political interests.

In addition courts all over the world have invariably experienced difficulty in arriving at a workable definition of what constitutes a political offense.[128] The political offense exception is a double-edged sword. While it is intended to protect individual rights and personal freedom, it imposes national standards and values on other states. More significantly however, it can, for self-serving interests, deny extradition because the presence of the fugitive in the requested state serves its political purposes. The fugitive may well have committed an extraditable offense but his sudden political opposition to a foreign regime may render him so desirable to the requested state that his extradition will be denied on political offense exception grounds when under similar circumstances another fugitive may be surrendered to a friendly state.

The benefits of luring foreign defectors and offering them asylum may sometimes be commendable in terms of human rights or explainable in terms of *realpolitik* but highly explosive in terms of global strategy for minimum world order when the defector happens to have committed common crimes or international crimes to which the (political) human rights aspect is but only tenuously related. This is particularly true with respect to certain acts of terrorism

Also at times the political refugee will be a highly placed foreign official who may have committed common crimes or international crimes, but their enormity will sometimes seem to cast his acts in a political character. [129] It would seem that humane considerations and inducements to foreign exiles, defectors, or fugitives should not overshadow concern with punishability of those who have also committed common crimes and international crimes.

The realization that such problems, few and far between as they may be, are to say the least problematic and compels the search for a new outlook to avoid the potentially detrimental effects of such problems on the preservation of minimum world order. One solution is to remove the question in its entirety from the decision-making process of the nation-states involved. This presupposes an international organ such as the International Court of Justice or a specialized branch thereto or an international criminal court which would have either exclusive or review jurisdiction over such matters. This could be accomplished by a universal treaty-statute on extradition, [130] or by granting an international judicial decision-making body the exclusive jurisdiction over such cases, so as to avoid inflammatory situations which may precede a decision on the merits.

The problem of the political offense, however, goes beyond that. The definitional issue could be resolved by an international treaty-statute, but the interpretative issue remains until it can

be based on certain objective criteria designed to eliminate the
high degree of subjective evaluation presently undertaken by most
countries particularly with respect to executive discretion in
conceding or denying extradition. Admitting the difficulties in
implementing such a proposal, alternatives must nonetheless be
found for the serious question of insuring a fair trial to the
relator faced with extradition to the jurisdiction wherein the
ideologically motivated offense took place. The alternative
would be to have the state of asylum or the state of which he is
a national if it is not the requesting state, exercise jurisdiction
over the relator and prosecute him on behalf of the jurisdiction
wherein the offense took place, using the substantive laws of that
jurisdiction against which the accused relator committed the
alleged offense. [131] If found guilty, the offender could, depending
upon the situation, be confined, if the sentence is imprisonment,
either in the state where the offense was committed, or in the state
where the offense was prosecuted, or in the state of which he is
a national. Thus, *aut dedere aut punire* would be insured without
potentially violating the human rights and right to procedural
fairness of the relator and simultaneously avoiding disruptions
of world public order, since there would be an alternative to
pitting two or more nation-states against each other. [132]
Ideally, of course, the offender should be tried by an international
criminal court and imprisoned in an international institution as
in the instance of the international military tribunal at Nuremberg
and the Spandau prison which stand as primary examples of the
feasability of this proposal.

428

The attainment of world peace is dependent upon the maintenance of rules designed to safeguard world public order and to establish legal channels as alternatives to the violent means which prevail in their absence. The rule of law is not an ideological equalizer or a method of compromising opposing political doctrines, but a process of ordering and channeling conflicts through legal institutions designed for the peaceful resolution of conflicts in a judicial context. It is the gradual building of needed international legal structures, not by ideologically superimposing such structures on the nation-states, but by creating them so as to service special purposes designed to eliminate direct confrontations between states which have potential for disruption of world public order.

1.2 - Offenses of a military character.

A considerable number of bilaterial treaties and national statutes expressly prohibit granting extradition for acts punishable under the military laws of the requesting state.[133] There are, however, two conditions which limit this exemption, namely: (1) that the acts charged do not constitute a crime under the ordinary laws of the requesting state, and (2) that the acts do not constitute a violation of the laws of war which would be international crimes.

The problems arising from that category of exemption are those of draft evasion, particularly as regards the issue of evasion for political purposes.[134] The examples of such cases arose in significant number during the military involvement of the United States in Southeast Asia between 1965 and 1972 when draft evaders and deserters from the United States took refuge and were granted asylum in Canada and Sweden. These problems are usually solved between states maintaining cooperative relations by some alternative means to extradition which are discussed in Chapter III, but this was not the case with Sweden or Canada as in the example cited above.

The problem of military offenses, duty of allegiance, and extradition as between friendly or allied states is illustrated in the English case of Ex parte Duke of Chateau Thierry, [135] where a French citizen had defected to England to avoid serving in the military forces of France of which he was a national during the First World War. The English lower court held for the defendant in agreeing that the Home Secretary had no power to order an alien deported to a particular country which had been ordered as an alternative to extradition. On appeal, the decision was reversed on the grounds that although the Home Secretary had no power to order deportation to a particular country, he could select the particular ship upon which the offender must sail even if such ship should be heading for the requesting state it would be of no concern. The court concluded that the Duke was not a political refugee, [136] and, since French authorities had assured the British Government that the offender would solely be tried as a military absentee for desertion, the court, in effect, condoned disguised extradition between allies for the return of those accused of such offenses as the military crime of desertion.

The commission of a violation of military laws and regulations which does not also constitute a crime under the ordinary criminal

430

laws by a person subject to such military laws and provided that
such violation does not constitute a violation of the laws of war,
is recognized as an exclusion from extradition under customary
international law. [137]

The relationship between military offenses, common crimes and
the political offense exception with respect ot wars of national
liberation is illustrated by the _Ktir_ case, [138] wherein the Swiss
court stated:

> The question at issue, accordingly, is whether
> it is a political offense and what importance is to
> be attached to the fact that the act committed by
> Ktir was, as alleged by him, committed in a war be-
> tween France and the F.L.N.
>
> As regards the second point, the appellant pro-
> bably means to rely on Article II of the LE which
> provides that "extradition shall not be granted
> . . . for purely military offences." That provision
> is not, however, applicable, since the Treaty does not
> contain any any analogous reservation. Furthermore,
> murder has never been regarded as a "purely military"
> offense, because it affects human life and does not
> relate to military organization or military duties.
>
> As regards the political nature of the offence,
> it should be pointed out, first of all, that the
> F.L.N. is fighting for power in Algeria. It is
> active not only in that country, but also in France.
> The character of the organization is clearly political.

The appellant states that he is a member of the
F.L.N. and that he committed the act with which
he is charged by virtue of that membership and
on the orders of his superiors. His declaractions
are plausible. It may be deduced therefrom that
he acted for political, not personal, reasons.
It does not, however, follow that the act had a
predominantly political character. For this to
be the case it is necessary that the murder of
Mezai should have been the sole means of safeguarding the more important interests of the
F.L.N. and of attaining the political aim of
that organization. That is not so. It has not
been shown that the interests of the F.L.N. were
so gravely compromised by the alleged treason of
Mezai that his "suppression" was the sole means
of effectively safeguarding them. Nor is it
possible to conclude that the murder in which
Ktir took part in any way advanced the liberation
of Algeria. That murder was primarily an act
of vengeance and terror. The relationship to
the political aims of the F.L.N. is too loose to
justify it and to give it a predominantly political
character. It is, accordingly, not a political
offence in the meaning of Article 2, paragraph 1,
of the Treaty. Since the other conditions set
forth in the Treaty are satisfied, extradition must

in principle be granted. [139]

The rationale for this exlusion rests on the appraisal of the
very offense, i.e., it is peculiar rather than general and affects
a disciplinary aspect of an internal organization within a given
state without causing any private wrong as in the case of common
crimes or without causing any harm to the world community as in
the case of international crimes. It is also noteworthy to re-
assert that extradition is a means of cooperation between states
to combat common criminality and therefore such offenses are excludable from that objective. States which are bound by mutual
security pacts and other military agreements are, however, likely
to include such offenses in their treaties or in any event to
engage in the practice of disguised extradition to accomplish
their purposes of exchanging such fugitive offenders.

1.3 - *Offenses of a fiscal character.*

Theoretically the rationale for exclusion of these offenses is
said to be the same as in cases of offenses of a military character. [140] It should be stated at the outset that even though there
is little practice in extradition for fiscal offenses, there is
nothing in customary international law which prohibits it. Furthermore the term fiscal has often encompassed offenses of an
economic nature even though they involve the public interest as
opposed to a private interest. It must be recalled that extrad-
dition before the twentieth century was closely interwoven with
European history and between the sixteenth and eighteenth century
Europe's fiscal and economic structure was chaotic and oppressive,
and this explains the origin of the exclusion. Thereafter, between

the eighteenth and early twentieth century economic and fiscal
reorganization in European states was interrupted by two world
wars and the emergence of socialism and communism in Eastern and
Central Europe. These factors contributed to the continued lack
of acceptance of such violations to warrant extradition except
between compatible economic systems. The change has occurred after
the political and economic transformation of the world has been
shaped and with the recognition that states in order to carry
their public charges must enforce their economic and fiscal laws. [141]
The economic social contract theory of the twentieth century is,
however, likely to bring about a radical change in the category
of economic offenses as is the case in the socialist countries
of Central and Eastern Europe and those of Asia where such offenses
rank with the more serious common crimes as witnessed by laws on
smuggling, traffic in currency, etc. Criticizing the position
of the United States on that score as early as 1891, Moore stated:

> In the refusal to include in its treaties of extra-
> dition crimes of fraud, the government of the United
> States failed to recognize the change which, in the
> development of civilization, has taken place in the
> relative importance of criminal offenses. [142]

Such offenses are, however, gradually appearing in extradition
treaties, but the difficulty remains in satisfying the requirement of double criminality discussed in Chapter V because of the
problem of defining such offenses and determining their significance in the economic system of each particular country.

434

2 - Grounds Relating to the Person of the Relator

2.1 - Exclusion of nationals.

Unlike the political offense exception and the exception or exclusion of military and fiscal offenses, the exemption of nationals has to do with the person rather than with the offense.

The exemption of nationals takes two forms: absolute and qualified and it may be found in the Constitution of a given country, in extradition treaties, or in its municipal laws. As a general rule, European states exempt nationals while common law states do not.

United States extradition treaties contain generally three types of such provisions. The first does not refer to nationals specifically, but agrees to the extradition of " all persons," [143] and Judicial construction [144] as well as executive interpretation [145] of such a clause have consistently held that the word persons includes nationals and therefore refusal to surrender a fugitive because he or she is a national cannot be justified under such treaty provision. The second and most common type of treaty provision provides that "neither of the contracting parties shall be bound to deliver up its own citizens or subjects under the stipulations of this convention." [146] Treaties of this sort are the most numerous due to insistence by other nations. The official policy of the United States in treaty negotiations has been until lately, when possible, to prevent the surrender of nationals. [147] As construed, such a policy prohibits the Secretary of State from surrendering a citizen of the United States unless there is an explicit treaty provision providing for reciprocity. [148] The third type provides is that "neither of the contracting parties shall be bound to deliver up its own citizens under the stipulations of this convention, but the executive authority of each shall have the power to deliver them up if, in its discretion, it be deemed proper to do so." [149] Exercise of such discretion would be consistent with the treaty obligation, and the Secretary of State has both granted and denied surrender of United States nationals under a treaty of this type. An examination of some landmark cases will better illustrate the application of these provisions.

In Charlton v. Kelly the Supreme Court of the United States stated:

> That the word "persons" etymologically includes citizens as well as those who are not, can hardly be debatable. The United States-Italian treaty contains no reservation of citizens of the country of asylum. The contention is that an express exclusion of citizens or subjects is not necessary, as by implication, from accepted principles of public law, persons who are citizens of the asylum country are excluded from extradition conventions unless expressly included.
>
> . . . .
>
> The conclusion we reach is, that there is no principle of international law by which citizens are excepted out of an agreement to surrender "persons" where no such exception is made in the treaty itself. Upon the contrary, the word "persons" includes <u>all</u>

persons when not qualified as it is in some of the treaties between this and other nations. That this country had made such an exception is some of its conventions and not in others, demonstrates that the contracting parties were fully aware of the consequences unless there was a clause qualifying the word "persons." This interpretation has been consistently upheld by the United States, and enforced under the several treaties which do not exempt citizens . . . [150]

As to the obligation to surrender a national, the Supreme Court of the United States, in <u>Valentine v. United States</u>, <u>ex rel.</u> <u>Neidecker</u>, stated:

It is a familiar rule that the obligations of treaties should be liberally construed so as to give effect to the apparent intention of the parties . . . But, in this instance, there is no question for construction so far as the obligations of the treaty are concerned. The treaty is explicit in the denial of any obligation to surrender citizens of the asylum state -- "Neither of the contracting Parties shall be bound to deliver up its own citizens."

Does the treaty, while denying an obligation in such case, contain a grant of power to surrender a citizen of the United States in the discretion of the Executive? . . .

Obviously the treaty contains no express grant of the power so invoked. Petitioners point to Article

I which states that the two governments "mutually agree to deliver up persons" who are charged with any of the specified offenses. Petitioners urge that the word "persons" includes citizens of the asylum state as well as all others. But Article I is the agreement to deliver. It imposes the obligation of that agreement. Article I does not purport to grant any power to surrender save as the power is related to and derived from the obligation. The word "persons" in Article I describes those who fall within the agreement and with respect to whom the obligation is assumed. As Article I provides that there shall be no obligation on the part of either party to deliver up its own citizens, the latter are necessarily excepted from the agreement in Article I and whom the "persons" there described. The fact that the exception is contained in a separate article does not alter its effect. That effect is precisely the same as though Article I had read that the two governments "mutually agree to deliver up persons except its own citizens or subjects."

. . . .

Applying, as we must, our own law in determining the authority of the President, we are constrained to hold that his power, in the absence of statute conferring an independent power, must be found in the terms of the treaty and that, as the treaty with France fails to grant the necessary authority, the President

is without power to surrender the respondents.

However regrettable such a lack of authority

may be, the remedy lies with the Congress, or with

the treaty-making power wherever the parties are

willing tp provide for the surrender of citizens, and

not with the courts. [151]

Among the problems of nationality are those raised by its loss

and acquisition, dual nationality and the time of loss or acquisi-

tion of nationality. In the absence of a specific provision on this

point in the law of the requested state or in the extradition

treaty under which the request is made it appears that the acquired

nationality brings the accused within the nationality exemption

regardless of when it was lost or acquired. [152]

A Swiss court held that, as regards the nationality of the person

sought, the material moment was that of the extradition proceed-

ings. In this instance Italy sought the extradition from Switzer-

land of a woman who had lost her Swiss nationality after the

commission of the offense for which extradition was sought. The

Swiss-Italian Extradition Treaty provided that neither country

was bound to extradite one of its own subjects, and the Swiss

Extradition Law prohibited the extradition of Swiss citizens.

Noting that there was considerable difference of opinion as to the

extradition of a national who acquired the nationality of the

country of refuge after the commission of the offense for which

extradition was sought, the Court said that there could be no

doubt under the Swiss-Italian Treaty and the Swiss Extradition

Law that the determinative moment was that of the extradition proceedings. The Court stated that the delivering up of a former subject who was a Swiss citizen when the crime was committed or when he was convicted but who later lost Swiss nationality could not be called the extradition of a Swiss citizen and that the principal reasons for refusing to surrender citizens (i.e., special ties that bind the subject to his country and his unconditional right to remain in his own country) did not obtain with regard to a person who had lost his nationality. Accordingly, extradition was granted. [153] Extradition of nationals when prohibited by the Constitution or municipal law of a given state has been the object of a recent interpretation by the Federal Supreme Court of Germany whose Constitution prohibits extradition of nationals.

In 1954 the Federal Supreme Court of the German Federal Republic held that an undertaking by German authorities to return to Italy a German national whom Italy was willing to "temporarily extradite" to Germany (on assurances that he would in due course be returned to Italy) would not be contrary to the provision of the Constitution of the Federal Republic prohibiting the extradition of German nationals. The Court distinguished between temporary and definitive extradition and return of the person to the country which has temporarily extradited him, holding essentially that the latter restores the situation to its *status quo ante*. [154]

The rationale for this exemption rests on the notion that the requested national is likely to receive ill treatment or an unfair trial in the requesting state. To that extent it is a discriminatory practice which differentiates between nationals and non-nationals. The presupposing is that the relator will receive worse treatment in the requesting state than in the requested state of which he is a national if he were to be tried or punished therein, but without granting the same consideration to a non-national. Professor Shearer sees its contemporary rationale as follows: [156]

1- A person ought not be withdrawn from his indigenous judges; and

2- A state owes its citizens the protection of its laws. This rationalization derives to a large extent from a jealously guarded conception of national sovereignty and presupposes the existence of sharp contrasts in the administration of criminal justice between states resulting in potentially unfair treatment. The alternative to such an exemption is to try the relator in the requested state, using the substantive laws of the requesting state based on the doctrine of *renvoi*, such a proposal resembles Federal practice in the United States. [155] This approach was taken by the Supreme Court of Colombia, which stated:

The reason for prohibiting the extradition of

nationals on the request of another State is obvious.

It is due to the risk of possible grave dangers in the

trial abroad. In Colombia the prohibition rests also

on the basis that such possible risks are unnecessary,

since this Republic, with the intention of inter-

nationalizing penal law and with the laudable purpose

of beginning to make effective the solidarity of nations

in the repression of delinquency, has adopted . . .

rules enabling it to apply the Colombian penal law to

441

nationals and foreigners who have perpetrated an
offense abroad . . . Art. 7, of the Penal Code
guarantees that the homicide with which the prisoner
is charged will, if it was criminal, not remain
without consign judgment in Colombia. In that manner
the Colombian State will exercise social defense against
delinquency, as Venezuela would, leaving intact, at
the same time, the sovereignty by which the Republic
of Colombia may prohibit the extradition of Colombians
and of politico-social delinquents at the request
of another State. [157]

2.2 – *Persons performing official acts and persons
protected by special immunity under international
law.* [158]

These two categories of persons are of course very different,
but what they have in common is the immunity of the actor. The
first of these categories applies to persons why by reason of
their official capacity or functions are immune from the judicial
and administrative processes of their own state, the state wherein
they are performing such recognized official acts, or in any state
where their official acts have effects. Insofar as diplomats are
concerned, their immunity from prosecution arises under customary
international law and treaty law (e.g. The Vienna Convention on
diplomatic immunity), while that of other public officials of a
given state arises under the act of State Doctrine also recognized
in customary international law. Both forms of immunity derive from
the doctrine of sovereignty. Other persons protected by special

442

immunity are heads of state. This type of immunity applies to
prosecution as is invariably spoken of in terms of prosecution
but implicit in it is an exemption from extradition. There are
no references in extradition treaties or municipal extradition
laws to such persons covered by immunity and whenever the case
arises, the matter is determined by the international law of
immunity and the Act of State Doctrine rather than that of extradition.

3 - *Grounds Relating to the Prosecution of the Offense
Charged.*

3.1 - *Introduction to the defenses of: legality of the
offense charged, trial in absentia, statute of
limitation and immunity.*

A trial *in absentia* is valid in the state where that conviction
was rendered and a defense to extradition in such a case would depend solely on the public policy of the requested state. If that
type of a trial would be abhorrent to the public policy of the
requested state extradition would not be granted. Otherwise it
will and the conviction will be regarded as sufficient grounds
for extradition.

As to the lapse of time or statute of limitation defense, it
would depend if it were that of the requesting or requested state.
It is a valid defense if it arises under the laws of the requesting
state because it would constitute a bar to prosecution in that
state and therefore extradition would be futile and unnecessary
if the relator is to be discharged by the courts of the requesting
state after surrender. If the statute relied upon is that of the

443

requested state it is recognized in some countries as a defense, but in that case the requested state is imposing a bar on a foreign prosecution based on its own legal system which may be different. The contrary argument however is that the statute of limitation of the requested states extinguishes prosecutability in that country and that precludes satisfaction of the requirement of double criminality, (discussed in Chapter V).

With respect to the question of legality of the offense charged, this defense goes to the validity of the offense and its juridical existence. [159] It is, of course, a defense which goes to the formulation and enactment of the law in question and its substantive content. It is an argument based on certain principles of legality, which could or could not be shared by the requesting and requested state. If the law upon which the extradition request relies fails to conform in its formulation, enactment, and substance to certain principles of legality it may not be recognized as having legally valid effect and is hence unenforceable. Whenever the requested state, relies on its own principles of legality to determine the validity of the laws relied upon by the requesting state, it is imposing its standards on the requesting state. Examples of principles of legality is the prohibition against *ex post facto* laws, *nullum crimen sine legge, nulla poena sine legge,* and the requirement of promulgation of penal laws and the specificity of their language. These when adhered to in the requested state, will constitute a defense on the grounds that no state can be expected to use its processes to perform an activity which would ultimately produce a result violative of it public policy. [160]

The only relationship between a trial *in absentia* as a defense
to extradition and the issue of lack of legality of the offense
proper rests essentially on certain minimum standards of justice
perceived by a given state. Other reasons advanced are the
absence of certain procedural safeguards which may be denied the
relator condemned *in absentia*. The link between these two defenses, legality of the offense charged and trial *in absentia*
is found with respect to the issue of notice.

In the case of notice of prohibited conduct by appropriate
promulgation of the penal law in question, the relator may not
have had legal notice of his accountability for conduct deemed
criminal and consequently had not opportunity to conform his
conduct to the requirements of the law. As to a trial *in
absentia* it may be that he had no notice of the charges or the
trial, and consequently had no opportunity to defend himself
against these charges. The issue, in extradition proceeding is
whether the relator can raise these defenses upon return or have
the opportunity of presenting a defense by reopening the judgment
rendered *in absentia*. Both considerations pertain to the laws
and public policy of the requesting state and only if the effects
of such a policy are so abhorrent to the public policy of the
requested state can the latter deny the requesting state the use
of its processes to achieve such a result. [161]

3.2 - *Trial in absentia*.

This defense is not recognized in those states whose legal system
is based on civil law as opposed to common law. The issue has

however been unsuccessfully raised in the United States but it continues to resurface periodically. There is no recognized exemption by customary international law for trials *in absentia*.

One of the landmark cases in the United States is <u>Gallina v. Fraser</u>.[162] The Court's decision indicates *obiter dictum* that if the trial *in absentia* would be so fundamentally unfair by generally recognized standards of justice and not only by United States or Common Law standards the outcome would be different.[163] The Court in this and other cases[164] granted extradition where a conviction *in absentia* had been rendered against the relator but it evaded the crux of the issue by asserting that after all in order that extradition be granted, it is not necessary to advance that the relator has been convicted but only that a *prima facie* case of guilt has been proven. Furthermore, the executive may in its discretion grant extradition subject to the condition that a new trial be granted the relator.[165] This solution rests on the extension of the Doctrine of Specialty (discussed in Chapter V), as a means of insuring compliance with conditional extradition.

The position of the United States is not clear as to whether the courts,[166] in examining the request or in its re-examination in a *habeas corpus* hearing will consider the question of fundamental fairness of a relator's trial or punishment.[166] This issue will be discussed in the Rule of Non-inquiry and the scope of *habeas corpus* in Chapter VII. At present, however, it seems that a trial *in absentia* is not considered by the United States Supreme Court as sufficiently extreme a denial of fundamental fairness under universal principles to warrant denial of extradition.[167]

3.3 - *Statute of limitation and immunity in municipal law.*

Whiteman described the defense of lapse of time or statute of limitation as follows:

> One of the most common exemptions from extradition
> relates to offenses for which prosecution or punishment
> is barred by lapse of time, usually referred to as barring
> by "lapse of time," prescription, or statute of limitation.
> A provision prohibiting extradition in such cases appears
> in most treaties and laws dealing with the subject of
> extradition. In treaties, the provision sometimes appears
> in the form of a prohibition of extradition where punish-
> ment or enforcement of penalty is barred by the law of
> the requesting State or is or would be barred by the
> law of the requesting or the requested State. [168]

The manner in which the treaty or domestic-law provision is
applied may vary from country to country. [169] The requested State
may consider the case as if the offense had been committed in the
requested State and apply its own statute of limitation to determine whether prosecution would be barred. If so, extradition will
be refused. [170]

The position of the United States is that in the absence of a
specific treaty provision the defense of lapse of time is governed
by 18 U.S.C. §3282 which requires commencement of prosecution within
five years from the commission of the crime. The problem is when
that period starts and what tolls it under §3290. [171]

avoid unnecessary hardship and cost to the relator and the respective

447

Some states however accept the defense as it arises in the requesting state and require the requesting state to allege that the offense is not prescribed. [172] The European Convention on Extradition states in Article 10: "Extradition shall not be granted when the person claimed has according to the law of either the requesting or requested party become immune by reason of lapse of true law prosecution or punishment." [173] In case of doubt over the applicability of the statute of limitation, extradition should be granted, as the matter is better resolved by the courts of requesting state. [174]

There are two approaches to the legal effects of a statute of limitation. The first is that it is merely a bar to prosecution and the second that it extinguishes the offense for purposes of its legal effects; but the first is the more widely recognized. Often the legal effects of a statute of limitation and amnesty are treated alike on the assumption that both are a bar to prosecution. [175] It must be noted, however, that a statute of limitation bars prosecution but does not extinguish the criminality of the actor whereas amnesty usually does.

The question of whether the offense exists and is prosecutable goes to the requirement of whether an extraditable offense exists and if so, whether double criminality is satisfied but this will largely depend on the legal bases of the practice. If it is a treaty practice, then the treaty is controlling and in the absence of any reference to statute of limitation therein the defense may not be accepted, which is the case of the United States. [176]

If the treaty specifies that the statute of limitation is a bar
to extradition without mentioning which law is applicable, the
requested state will look at the laws of both states as it would
with respect to the question of double criminality. If the extradition practice is not based on treaty but on reciprocity, then
in the absence of prior practice, the statute of limitation of
both states will be examined. If the practice is on the basis
of comity then the requested state is free to take the statute of
limitation defense into account or reject it.

It must be mentioned, however, that when extradition is sought
for an international crime there should be no statute of limitat-
tion bar to extradition. While this principle is not yet universally accepted with respect to all international crimes, as discussed above, it has been the object of a U.N. resolution pro-
posing a convention concerning the nonapplicability to war crimes
and crimes against humanity of statutes of limitation in municipal
laws. [177]

With respect to the question of "immunity from prosecution", this
is a novel technique used primarily in the pursuit of criminal inves-
tigations, [178] and is presently almost exclusively used in the
United States particularly since 1964. [179] It is a device whereby a person is granted immunity from prosecution in exchange for
cooperation in a criminal investigation or trial. In such a case,
immunity is the *quid pro quo* for waiver of the right to remain
silent and granted in exchange of testimonial cooperation. Whenever
granted, immunity is a bar to prosecution but like a statute of
limitation, it does not extinguish the criminality of the actor

nor does it absolve him from the criminal conduct; it merely bars the state from prosecuting for such offenses as may have been disclosed under the grant of immunity.

The same rules which apply to statute of limitation presumably apply to "immunity" cases whenever they will be at issue in extradition law (since there has never been a case on this question so far due to its limited use).

4 - Grounds Relating to the Penalty and Punishability of the Relator.

These grounds for denial of extradition relate to the legal extinction or termination of the penalty, the applicability of the penalty, and the type of penalty; they are: amnesty and pardon; double jeopardy; death penalty; and cruel and unusual punishment.

4.1 - Amnesty and pardon.

Both of these are acts of executive or legislative clemency. The first is a bar to prosecution but it also extinguishes the criminality or criminal accountability of the actor. It therefore occs before guilt is determined. The second occurs after guilt is determined and either before or after the penalty is executed. Its effect is to remove the consequences of the guilty finding whether it be with respect to the execution of the sentence or other ancillary sanctions. It restores the legal status of the convicted person to that of a person not convicted. Both are a bar to prosecution and punishment. Amnesty could be said to belong in the category of a statute of limitation defense because it is a bar to prosecution, but instead it is included with pardon because it is an an act of clemency rather than a condition for responsibility set

450

forth by legislative enactment, and in addition because it extinguishes the criminality of the actor other than merely barring prosecution. It can therefore be said that it has substantive effects while a statute of limitation defense has a procedural effect. [180] In United States Conflict of Laws doctrine and in federal practice, a statute which extinguishes a cause of action is deemed substantive while one that merely precludes an action is considered procedural. Thus federal courts who apply the substantive laws of state wherein the case is brought (or the case arose) will be guided by this important distinction. Statutes of limitations are usually found in the criminal procedure laws of most states. Amnesty does not exist so far in United States laws whether it be in the federal or state laws. Pardon and clemency are executive privileges available to the President and Governors but are often treated as a part of criminal law and procedure. Because of the extensive use of probation and parole, pardon has been used essentially to erase criminal records and the civil disabilities which are imposed on persons convicted of certain crimes. It has also been used as a substitute for clemency in cases where the death penalty had been imposed or in states where certain penalties could not benefit from parole. Unlike parole, which is an institutionalized and regulated procedure, pardon, with few minor exceptions, (e.g. Federal Board recommends Pardon to the President) is almost wholly discretionary with the chief executive. Amnesty bars prosecution and extinguishes the offense as related to the category of offender benefitting from it, and pardon bars the punishment of a given person found guilty of a crime; they can

451

therefore only be considered a defense to extradition when declared by the competent authority of the requesting state. Amnesty and pardon in the requested state cannot affect extradition.

There are several analogies between amnesty and pardon and the defense of statute of limitation [181] as discussed above, but the major difference is that the latter derives from a legislative source which can be said to run into the substantive requirement of double criminality and therefore it is possible for the requested state to rely on its laws on the subject to deny extradition; while the former two are discretionary executive perogatives and can only be asserted when they originate in the very requesting state.

4.2 - *Double jeopardy - ne bis in idem.*

A Roman law maxim holds *Nemo bis in idem debet vexari* and embodies the principle that no one shall be twice placed in jeopardy for the same offense. A corollary of that principle is that society (or the victim) is entitled to but one satisfaction and that no more than a single penalty should be exacted for but a single offense. Criminal punishment has traditionally been retributive but even the *lex talio* never required more than an "eye for eye."

A universal principle developed throughout history which requires that no person shall be punished twice for the same offense. The application of this principle has been, however, different in the framework of the various legal systems. Furthermore, there has always been a question as to its applicability between legal systems. The reason has been that conduct which affected more than one state can be considered as an independent violation because each state is a separate sovereign. As a result each state seeks its satisfaction independently of the other affected state and irrespective of whether the offender is therefore placed in double jeopardy. This approach derives from the doctrine of sovereignty whereby each separate sovereign considering only the violation of its order enforces its laws regardlesss of whether the same conduct also affected another state which may have already pro-secuted or punished the offender for the same conduct.[182]

Among the problems arising out of the application of this defense are the following:

1- Will punishment in one state for a given conduct satisfy another state if the same conduct is also punishable under its laws?

2- Will acquittal by one state for a given offense satisfy another state if the same conduct is also punishable under its laws?

3- Will prosecution or any of its preceding stages preclude one state from prosecuting a person for conduct claimed criminal under both laws?

4- Will the state seeking to prosecute or punish a person already prosecuted or punished by another state for the same conduct consider itself bound by the prior prosecution or punishment, or in reliance upon a technical difference as to the offense charged will it deem itself free to pursue that same offender?

5- Will the inquiry be made as to the entirety of a given criminal transaction or will it be made as to each chargeable

offense arising out the respective laws of each state?

These threshold questions make the principle, *Ne bis in idem*
difficult to apply in extradition with any degree of uniformity
in the absence of internationally accepted doctrines of criminal
justice. So far the commonly accepted statement of this principle is that a person shall not be punished twice for the same
crime, but even that allows a wide range of interpretations and
applications.

Contemporary extradition law concerns itself with the question
but to a large extent the practice has seldom been confronted with
it because few criminal acts have a multi-state effect which are
simultaneously or concurrently pursued by more than one state.
Several extradition treaties and municipal laws refer to double
jeopardy and recognize it in varying ways as a defense to extradition. [183] Their application and judicial interpretation can be
categorized as follows:

1- The requested state shall not surrender the relator if
he was prosecuted and acquitted or prosecuted and convicted and served his sentence if he is sought for the
same offense, with the following variances:
a- regardless of the state wherein this occurred; or
b- provided it occurred in the requesting state; or
c- provided it occurred in the requested state.

2- The requested state shall not surrender the relator if
he was convicted of an offense and executed his sentence

and was sought for the same offense; with these variances:

a- by the same state which convicted him; or

b- by its own judicial authorities, or

c- by any other state.

The defense is more frequently recognized in these instances:

1- Whenever the relator has been prosecuted and punished by the requested state and is sought by the requesting state for the same, meaning identical, criminal conduct. The rationale in this instance is essentially fundamental fairness but also because it would be repugnant to the requested state to use its processes to place an individual twice in jeopardy for the same conduct particularly after that state had prosecuted and punished the offender for the said conduct.

2- Whenever the relator had been prosecuted and acquitted by the requesting state and was not a fugitive therefrom when he came to the requested state. The rationale is also fundamental fairness but also becuase the requested state is not likely to lend its processes to give the requesting state another opportunity to prosecute the same person for the same offense of which he was found innocent. A difficult problem lies in the interpretaion of the words "same conduct" and "same offense," and these two terms can be interpreted as follows:

1- Same Conduct:

a- identical acts, or;

b- a series of acts related to each other by the scheme

or intent of the actor, or;

   c- multiple acts committed at more than one place and at
different times but related by the actor's criminal design.

2- Same Offense:

   a- identical charge, or;

   b- lesser included offense, or;

   c- related offenses but not included.

This reveals the extent of the interpretative leeway which would permit any decision-making process seeking to uphold the principle in its letter to do so and concurrently surrender the relator. Various multilateral extradition conventions embody this defense in their provisions but their choice of terminology reflect the different approaches outlined above and thus do not provide a standard. The relevant provisions of these conventions follow. The Arab States Convention states in Article V:

> Extradition shall not be granted in case the person sought for has already been committed to trial for the offense for which his extradition is being requested and has not been found guilty, or has been already convicted, or if he is under investigation, or if trial had been started for the same offence in the State from which extradition is being requested.

> In case the person in question is under trial for another offence, committed in the State, which is being asked to surrender him, his extradition shall be postponed until the trial is terminated and the penalty in-

flicted has been executed. However, provisions may
be made for the temporary surrender to stand trial
in the requesting State, on condition that at the
end of such trial and before the execution of the
penalty inflicted, he will be returned to the State
applying for his extradition. [184]

The European Convention states in Article 9:

Extradition shall not be granted if final judgment has been passed by the competent authorities of
the requested Party upon the person claimed in respect of the offence or offences for which extradition
is requested. Extradition may be refused if the competent authorities of the requested Party have decided
either not to institute or to terminate proceedings
in respect of the same offence or offences. [185]

The Inter-American Convention states in Article 13:

When the person sought is under prosecution or
is serving a sentence in the requested State, his
surrender shall be deferred until his trial is ended
if found not guilty, or until the sentence has been
served, as the case may be. [186]

The Afro-Asian Convention states in Article 11:

Extradition shall be refused if the offence in
respect of which extradition is sought is under investigation in the requested State or the person sought
to be extradited has already been tried and discharged
or punished or is still under trial in the requested

457

State for the offence for which extradition is sought. [187]

The Benelux Convention states in Article 8:

Extradition shall not be granted if final judgment has been passed on the person claimed by the competent authorities of the requested Party in respect of the punishable facts for which extradition is requested. Extradition may be refused if the competent authorities of the requested Party have decided either not to institute proceedings in respect of the same facts, or to terminate proceedings already instituted. [188]

These multilateral conventions as well as bilateral treaties, municipal laws and customary practice warrant the conclusion that the principle is part of conventional and customary international law. While the principle of double jeopardy reflects the penological policy of the state applying it, its general acceptance by the world community gave it recognition as a "general principle of international law". As such it is embodied in Human Rights Conventions. The International Covenant on Civil and Political Rights states in Article 14-17:

No one shall be liable to be tried or punished again for an offence for which he has already been finally convicted or acquitted in accordance with the law and penal procedure of each country. [189]

The American Convention on Human Rights states in Article 8-4:

The American Convention on Human Rights states in Article 8-4:

458

> An accused person acquitted by a nonapplicable
>
> judgement shall not be subjected to a new trial
>
> for the same cause. [190]

The historical recognition given the principle *ne bis in idem* in
various legal systems, its enunciation in human rights conventions and its embodiment in bilateral and multilateral extradition treaties make it part of all sources of international
law and as such, it operates as a bar to extradition. The problem however lies in its application since each state will,
of course, apply its subject to its judicial interpretation
and public policy. There is no more exactitude to the principle
under international law. The various alternative applications
outlined above, subject to the different interpretations
given the words "same conduct" and "same offense" or their
equivalent in the domestic laws of the requested state which
has to grant or deny the defense.

4.3 - *Death Penalty*

Certain extradition treaties specifically state that where the
death penalty is likely to be imposed for a given offense, extradition for that offense shall be denied. An exception thereto
could be made if the surrender is conditional and the requesting
state agrees not to impose the death penalty. One example is
the United States - Brazil treaty of 1961 which provides in
Article VI:

> When the commission of the crime or offense
> for which the extradition of the person is sought is

punishable by death under the laws of the requesting State and the laws of the requested State
do not permit this punishment, the requested State
shall not be obligated to grant the extradition
unless the requesting State provides assurances
satisfactory to the requested State that the death
penalty will not be imposed on such person. [191]

Conditional extradition has been discussed as part of the doctrine of specialty in Chapter V and presents certain problems of
enforceability.

This exception for the death penalty in extradition treaties
invariably derives from the municipal laws of the requested
State particularly whenever the Constitution, national laws, or
public policy of that state prohibits the imposition of the death
penalty. This exemption from the obligation to extradition can
be total or partial as reflected in the 1962 treaty between the
United States and Israel which states in Article VII:

When the offense for which the extradition is
requested is punishable by death under the laws of the
requesting Party and the laws of the requested Party do not
permit such punishment for that offense, extradition may be
refused unless the requesting Party provides such assurances
as the requested Party considers sufficient that the death penalty
shall not be imposed or, if imposed, shall not be executed. [192]

Whenever there is no such provision in a treaty or whenever the
practice is based on reciprocity or comity the municipal laws of
the requested state shall be controlling and if these laws pro-

hibit the death penalty, it is very likely that extradition shall
be denied.

An illustration of this proposition is found in a case where
Chile requested the surrender of a fugitive from Argentina for an
offense punishable by death. Argentina had abolished the death
penalty and there was no extradition treaty in force between the
two states and the practice between these states was, therefore,
based on reciprocity. The Supreme Court of Chile informed Argentina that, if extradited, Flores would be judged according to
Chilean law and although it could not give assurance that the
lesser penalty would be imposed it would try to comply with the
Argentine conditional extradition. The lower Argentine court
held that this was not satisfactory compliance with the condition
of Argentine law. On appeal, this view was concurred in, but it
was found that under the Chilean Constitution the President had
the power to pardon and that this would thus make possible the
fulfillment of a promise to inflict the lesser penalty. On furthe
appeal, the Federal Supreme Court held that extradition should be
allowed only on a promise of pardon or commutation of sentence by
the Chilean executive in case a death sentence was imposed. The
Court stated:

> The simple manifestation of good offices of the
> Supreme Court of Justice of the requesting country does
> not amount to the promise which the Argentine law imposes
> as necessary, together with reciprocity, to concede
> extradition without treaties. [193]

The rationale for refusing extradition on the grounds that the relator is likely to incur the death penalty is twofold:

1. The abolition of the death penalty by a given
   state is predicated on humanitarian consideration
   and public policy and therefore;

2. It would be abhorrent to that state to grant extradition because it would be using its processes to
   reach an outcome which is in violation of its laws
   and public policy.

No human rights convention has so far recognized an absolute
right to life and none of the sources of international laws as of
yet elevate the right to life to an absolute. Progress in that
direction can be detected in the advances made by humanitarian
concern at the level of the municipal and international legal
orders.

In the Western European states where an increasing number of
states have abolished the death penalty the two multilateral conventions on extradition deal with the question in these terms.
The European Convention states in Article II:

> If the offense for which extradition is requested
> is punishable by death under the law of the
> requesting party, and if in respect of such offence
> the death penalty is not provided for by the law of
> the requested party or is not normally carried out,
> extradition may be refused unless the requesting party
> gives such assurance as the requested party considers
> sufficient that the death penalty will not be carried
> out. [194]

462

The Benelux Convention states in Article 10:

> If the offense for which extradition is requested
> is punishable by death under the law of the requesting
> party and that death penalty is not provided for the
> offense by the law of the requested party, or is generally
> not applied to it in actual practice, the requested state
> may grant extradition upon an undertaking being given
> by the requesting party to recommend to the head of
> state that the death penalty be committed to another
> penalty. [195]

The Western European approach is the product of a long history of
conditional extradition and has been founded on many cases over the
last half century. [196] The same approach is also embodied in the
Draft Inter-American Convention on extradition. [197] The Harvard
Research Draft on Extradition had taken the position over two
decades before the first multilateral convention was drafted. The
position of the United States is unsettled on this point even
after Furman v. Georgia [198] because of the narrow grounds on which
the death penalty was declared unconstitutional. [199]

4.4 - Cruel and unusual punishment

The treatment which the relator is likely to receive in the requesting state upon his return thereto has not been the object of
specific provisions in extradition treaties be they bilateral or
multilateral. The reason is that as between co-equal authoritative decision-making processes there can be no inquiry by one
into the internal affairs of the other. The exception which is
gradually developing is the general limitation imposed by human

rights treaties. The various human rights conventions indeed
consider cruel and unusual punishment violative of those minimum
standards of human rights which require internal protection.
Among the relevant provisions are the following excerpts.

The Universal Declaration of Human Rights states in Article 5:

No one shall be subjected to torture or to cruel,
inhuman or degrading treatment or punishment. [200]

The International Covenant on Civil and Political Rights states
in Article 7:

No one shall be subjected to torture or to cruel,
inhuman or degrading treatment or punishment.
In particular, no one shall be subjected without
his free consent to medical or scientific exper-
imentation. [201]

The European Convention for the Protection of Human Rights and
Fundamental Freedoms states in Article 3:

No one shall be subjected to torture or to inhuman
or degrading treatment or punishment. [202]

The American Declaration of the Rights and Duties of Man states
in Article XXV:

He also has the right to humane treatment during
the time he is in custody. [203]

The American Convention on Human Rights states in Article :

1. Every person has the right to have his physical,
   mental, and moral integrity respected.

2. No one shall be subjected to torture or to cruel,
   inhuman, or degrading punishment or treatment.

464

> All persons deprived of their liberty shall
>
> be treated with respect for the inherent
>
> dignity of the human person. [204]

So far, however, no multilateral extradition convention has taken up that theme nor has any bilateral treaty embodied any of these provisions. There are, of course, other provisions intended to accomplish, at least in part, the same result as is the case for provisions relating to nonextradition of nationals; double jeopardy; and the death penalty. None of these, however, cover the issue of treatment of accused offenders, whether it be in the nature of the type of corporal punishment, length of incarceration, or type of incarceration and its conditions which the relator person may be subjected to in the requesting state after surrender.

The wide divergence in penological theories and standards of treatment of offenders between countries is such that no uniform standard exists. The United Nations, however, in an effort to provide such a basis proposed the Standard Minimum Rules for the Treatment of Prisoners [205] which were adopted in the nature of a resolution and are not binding international obligations. The prohibition against cruel and unusual punishment can be said to constitute a general principle of international law because it is so regarded by the legal system of civilized nations, but that alone does not give it a sufficiently defined content bearing on identifiable applications capable of more than general recognition. The application of such a principle to sentences, type and conditions of incarceration and other correctional questions is therefore still very much in doubt in respect to extradition law and practice

465

where the rule of noninquiry precludes the extradition magistrate from inquiring into the treatment which the relator may receive in the requesting state upon his return. The rule works well in those states which do not extradite their nationals because the interest of such states in the fate of other nationals they extradite may well be limited if it exists at all. The emergence of the individual as a recognized participant in the processes of extradition and the applicability of internationally protected human rights are likely to curtail if not eliminate the rule of noninquiry.

The problems presently existing stem from the fact that there is no alternative for the requested state concerned about the fate of a surrendered person but to deny extradition. The alternative is for the requested to prosecute the relator on behalf of the requesting state and punish that person in a manner which is not cruel or unusual or to permit temporary extradition for the relator's trial in the requesting state and his or her return to the requested for sentencing or carrying out of a sentence in a manner which would not be cruel or unusual. Such an alternative would avoid the pitting of two states against each other and the accused's evasion of the process for reasons which do not arise from his or her conduct.

Footnotes

1. Whiteman states:

    . . . Most extradition laws and treaties provide that
    extradition need not or shall not be granted when the
    acts with which the accused is charged constitute a
    political offense or an act connected with a political
    offense. Generally, a distinction is drawn between
    "purely" political offenses (e.g., treason, sedition)
    and "relative" political offenses or offenses "of a
    political character" (e.g., murder committed in the course
    of a rebellion), although generally both types are
    excepted from extradition . . .

    In the case of laws and treaties which contain
    a list of specific offenses for which extradition
    shall be granted, exception of "purely" political
    offenses is usually considered unnecessary since
    such offenses may be excepted by merely not being
    included in the list. However, provision is often
    made regarding "relative" political offenses.
    6 Whiteman, Digest of International Law (1968), pp. 799-800.
    See also Shearer, Extradition in International Law (1971),
    pp. 166-198; Bedi, Extradition in International Law and Prac-
    tice, 179-191 (1968), Harvard Research in International Law,
    Draft Convention on Extradition," 29 A.J.I.L. Supp. p. 21,
    107 (1935).

2. Deere, "Political Offenses in the Law and Practice of Extradition," 27 <u>A.J.I.L.</u> 247, 240 (1933); Garcia-Mora, "The Present Status of Political Offenses in the Law of Extradition and Asylum," 14 <u>U. Pitt. L. Rev.</u> 371-372 (1953); Evans, "Reflections upon the Political Offense in International Practice," 57 <u>A.J.I.L.</u> 1, 15 (1963); Garcia-Mora, "The Nature of Political Offenses: A Knotty Problem of Extradition Law," 48 <u>Va. L. Rev.</u> 1226, 1230 (1962).

3. <i>Id.</i>, Garcia-Mora, "The Nature of Political Offenses: A Knotty Problem of Extradition Law," at 1229.

4. Evans, <i>supra</i>, note 2 at 17.

5. I. Oppenheim, <u>International Law</u> (Lauterpacht, 8th ed., 1955), p. 704.

6. See <i>supra</i>, Chapter I, notes 5-6. As late as 1834 a treaty between Austria, Prussia, and Russia called for the surrender of persons accused of high treason, armed rebellion, acts against the security of the throne or the government and acts of <i>lèse majesté</i>, see 15 Martens, <u>Nouveau Recevil des Traites</u> 44.

7. [1933-1934] <u>Ann Dig.</u> 360-361-363 (No. 156); and Billot, <u>Traite de L'extradition</u> 109 (1874); Shearer, <i>supra</i>, note 1 at 166-167.

8. 33-34 Vict. S. 52 S. 53 (1878).

9. Section 213.

10. Malloy, <u>Treaties</u> 26; also 4 Moore <u>Digest</u> 332 (1906),

11. This section is based in part on Bassiouni, "Idealogically Motivated Offenses and the Political Offense Exception in

Extradition - A Proposed Juridical Standard For an Unruly Problem," 19 DePaul L. Rev. 217, 218-226 (1969).

12. This distinction between *delits complexes* and *delits connexes* was first made by by Billot in his Traite de L'Extradition 104 (1874).

13. See Donnedieu de Vabres, Introduction a L'Etude du Droit Penal International (1928); and Donnedieu de Vabres, Les Principes Modernes du Droit Penal International (1938).

14. In re Richard Eckermann, [1929-1930] Ann. Dig. 293, 295 (No. 189); and Garcia-Mora, Treason, Sedition and Espionage as Political Offenses under the Law of Extradition, 26 U. Pitt. L. Rev. 65 (1964); In re DeBernonville, (1955) I.L.R. 527, holds that "treason to country is among political crimes, the authors of which are not subject to extradition." Accord, Ex parte Kolcynski, 1 Q.B. 540 (1955): "Treason is an offense of a political character." In Chandler v. United States, it was held *inter alia* that political offenders include persons charged with treason. 171 F. 2d 921 (1st Cir. 1948). In In re Ockert, [1933-1934] Ann. Dig. 268 (No. 157), it was said, "high treason, capital treason and the like are political offenses because the offense is against the state and its principal organs."

15. *Id.*, Garcia - Mora, at 74. Compare the Soviet Criminal Goddarts, 68-98 (and 10 U.S.C. § 791-97 (1965); and 18 U.S.C. 951-69 (1965); see also, Bassiouni, "The Criminal Justice System of the U.S.S.R. and the Peoples Republic of China," 11 Revista de Derechho Puertorriqueno 168 (1971); and

Berman, <u>Soviet Criminal Law and Procedure</u> 178-86 (1966).

16. For sedition in American law, see Bassiouni, <u>Criminal Law and Its Processes</u>, 289-91 (1969).

17. Civil disorders in the United States, such as the riots of the sixties in major American cities, could be considered common crimes, relative political offenses, or purely political offenses depending upon one's ideological position. The United States government considers such acts common crimes as witnessed by the Chicago Conspiracy trial of the seven defendants accused of such crimes during the 1968 Democratic Convention in Chicago under 18 U.S.C.A. § 231, 232 (1968). All states have legislation which prohibits conduct such as disturbing the peace and arson which is used against rioters engaging in ideologically motivated demonstrations, e.g. See Bassiouni, <u>The Law of Dissent and Riots</u> (1971).

18. But see <u>Youssef Said Abu Dourrah v. Attorney General</u>, 8 <u>Palestine Law Reports</u> 43 (1941): "We know of nothing in the criminal law of this country or of England that creates a specific offense called political murder;" also in [1941-1942] Ann. Dig. 331 (No. 101) at 336.

19. See Bassiouni, *supra*, note 16, at 62.

20. *Id.*, at 51-88.

21. *Id.*, at 134-137.

22. G. Whiteman, <u>Digest</u> at 779-857 (1968); and I. Oppenheim, *supra*, note 5 at 707.

23. See Belgian Extradition Law of Oct. 1, 1833, <u>Les Codes</u> 698 (31st ed. 1965); and <u>In re Fabijan</u>, <u>supra</u>, note 7.

24. 1 Q.B. 149 (1891).

25. *Ibid.*, p. 152.

26. *Ibid.*

27. Bassiouni, "International Extradition in the American Practice and World Public Order," 36 Tenn. L. Rev. 1, 17 (1968).

28. *Supra.*, note 24, p. 159.

29. In re Ezeta, 62 F. 2d 198 (9th Cir., 1957) rev'd on other grounds, 355 U.S. 398, 78 S.Ct. 381 2 L. Ed. 2d 356 (1958), which stated that "the general rule is that there must be an 'uprising,' and that the acts in question must be incidental to it." See also, 1 Hyde, International Law, p. 573 (1922); Garcia Mora, "The Nature of Political Offenses: A Knotty Problem of Extradition Law," *supra*, note 2 at p. 1240; and Deere, *supra*, note 2, at p. 266.

30. In re Meunier, 2 Q.B. 415 (1894); see also Re Aston, 1 Q.B. 108 (1896).

31. *Ibid.*, p. 419.

32. *Supra*, note 24 at p. 155.

33. 16 B. 540 (1955), 21 I.L.R. 240 (1954); see also, Schtrak v. The Government of Israel, 3 All English Reports 529 (1962); see also Oppenheim, *supra*, note 6 at 784-785.

34. 2 All Eng. Rep. 204 (1973).

35. 217 F. Supp. 717 (1963).

36. *Ibid.*, the same position was held in Ornelas v. Ruiz, 161 U.S. 502, 165 at 689 (1996).

37. Garcia-Mora, *supra*, note 6, p. 378.

38. "In the Matter of Extradition of Hector Jose Campora and

and Others," 58 <u>A.J.I.L.</u> 690, 694-695 (1957).

39. *Ibid.*, at 698-694.

40. Compare, <u>In re Fabijan</u>, *supra*, note 7, stating at 367:

. . . Neither the actual attack on the policeman

engaged in the lawful discharge of his duties,

nor the "demonstration" of the accused and his three

companions against the Carabinieri barracks,

constitute a "political crime" in the strict sense

of the term. Both parts of the whole act were

directed, not against the central political

authority, but only against individual organs

of the State . . . There is no proof of a prin-

cipal political crime with which the acts of the

prisoner could possibly be connected. Moreover,

he himself has not sought to allege the existence

of any such crime, but has merely contended that

he had a "political motive". However, as has been

explained already, proof of political motive does not

make an act a "connected" act when there is no

"concrete" political act.

And the case of Rudewitz, *infra,* note 35 and corresponding

text.

41. Letter from Secretary of State Elihu Root to Russian Ambassa-

dor Rosen, 1908, on file in Department of State, File No.

16649-9, 4 Hackworth, <u>Digest</u>, 316, pp. 49-50 (1942).

42. *Supra*, note 14.

43. <u>Ivancevic v. Artukovic</u>, 211 F. 2d 565 (9th Cir. 1954);

Artukovic v. Boyle, 140 F. Supp. 245 (S.D. California, 1956);

Karadzole v. Artukovic, 247 F. 2d 198 (9th Cir., 1957);

Karadzole v. Artukovic, 355 U.S. 898 (1958), United States

v. Artukovic, 170 F. Supp. 383 (1959).

44. Karadzole v. Artukovic, 247 F. 2d 198 (1957).

45. 355 U.S. 383 (1958).

46. "Letter from the Legal Advisor of the Department of State
to the Acting Assistant Attorney General McLean," M.S. Dept.
of State, Dec. 16, 1957, file 611.6926/11- 57; also "memorandum for the United States," submitted in Karadzole v. Artukovic, and appended to the opinion *supra*, note 44.

47. 170 F. Supp. 383 (1959).

48. *Ibid.*, pp. 392-393.

49. *Supra*, note 24.

50. See Positions of the Department of State, *supra*, note 4; and
6 Whiteman, Digest, p. 826 (1968).

51. Gallina v. Fraser, 177 F. Supp. 356 (D. Conn. 1959); *aff'd*
278 F. 2d Cir. 1960; *cert. denied* 364 U.S. 851 (1960).

52. U.S.T.S. 174; 15 Stat. 629; I. Malloy, Treaties, 966-967
(1910).

53. *Supra*, note 48.

54. *Supra*, note 48 at 73.

55. Jimenez v. Aristeguieta, 311 F. 2d 547 (5th Cir., 1962).

56. Ornelas v. Ruiz, *supra*, note 36; see also, Ramos v. Diaz and
Ramoz Covreta, 178 F. Supp. 459 (S.D. Fla. 1950).

57. See Levasseur, 2 Juris Classeur de Droit International, 405-
410 (1965); this position is also the common law position

but the latter is not limited thereto.

58. <u>In re Giovanni Gatti</u> [1945-1947] <u>Ann. Dig.</u> 145 (No. 70).

59. *Ibid.*, the Court of Appeal of Grenoble, France, further
stated at 145:

> Political offenses are those which injure the
> political organism, which are directed against the
> constitution of the Government and against sovereignty,
> which trouble the order established by the Fundamental
> laws of the state and disturb the distribution of
> powers. Acts which aim at overthrowing or modifying
> the organization of the main organs of the state,
> or at destroying, weakening or bringing into dis-
> repute one of these authorities, or at exercising
> illegitimate pressure on the play of their mechanism
> or on their general direction of the state, or which
> aim at changing the social conditions created for
> individuals by the constitution in one or all of
> its elements, are also political offenses. In brief,
> what distinguishes the political crime from the common
> crime is the fact that the former only affects the
> political organization of the state, the proper rights
> of the state, while the latter exclusively affects
> rights other than those of the state.

60. <u>In re Colman</u> [1945-1947] <u>Ann. Dig.</u> 139 (No. 67).

61. *Ibid.*, page 141.

62. <u>Franco-Belgian Extradition Treaty</u> of August 15, 1874 cited
in <u>In re Colman</u>, *supra*, note 59.

63. A case decided by the same court nine months prior to the
    Colman, *supra*, note 59, decision, refusing the extradition
    request of Belgium for the crime of economic collaberation
    with the enemy, held that the exchange of notes between the
    countries could not be considered since it was not mentioned
    by the requesting government as a grounds for granting
    surrender. Also, that "such a convention (the notes) . . .
    cannot, without ratification and publication, have force of
    law in the meaning of Article 26 of the Constitution of the
    French Republic of 1946." In re Talbot [1945-47] Ann. Dig.
    142 (No. 68).

64. *Supra,* note 60, at 140. For opposite holding, see Denmark
    (collaboration with the enemy), [1945-1947] Ann. Dig. 146 (No.

65. The Federal Tribunal of Switzerland has stated concerning
    relative political offenses:

    A relative political offense is one which, while
    having the characteristics of a common offense, acquires
    a political character by virture of the motive inspiring
    it, or the purpose for which or the circumstances in
    which it has been committed; in other words, it is in
    itself a common offence but has a predominantly political
    character.

    In re Ficorilli, 18 I.L.R. 345 (No. 110) (1951), and In re
    Barratini, [1938-1940] Ann. Dig. 412 (No. 159).

    Frequently, the term "political offense" is used to cover
    both "purely" political offenses and "relative" political
    offenses. Thus, the Belgian Court of Appeal stated in 1936:

475

A political offence is one which, in essence,
is directed against the political regime or which,
though normally constituting an ordinary crime
("crime de droit commun"), assumes the character of
a political crime because the aim of the author of
the crime was to injure the political regime. However, an ordinary crime committed under the influence
of party passion against an adversary cannot be
regarded as political unless it occurred as an episode
in a civil war between combatants engaged in a violent
struggle in which the constitution of the State was
in issue.

66. U.S. Foreign Relations, 1909, pages 520-521 (Dept. State).
Also, Deere, *supra*, note 2 at 253.

67. In Re Pavan 1923 Ann. Dig. 347 (No. 239) and In Re Peruze
1952 I.L.D. 369 (No. 79).

68. *Ibid.*, pages 347-349.

69. In re Ockert, [1933-1934] Ann. Dig. 369 (No. 157). In the
case referred to above, Italy unsuccessfully sought the extradition, for attempted homicide, of one Ragni who took part
in an encounter between fascists on the one hand and Socialists,
communists, and 'Popolari' on the other, in which a number of
persons were injured by shots and otherwise. In re Ragni,
[1923-1924] Ann. Dig. 286 (No. 166).

Similarly, A Swiss Federal Court refused an Italian request
for the extradition of one Camporini, former mayor of Corresio
and secretary of the Social-Democratic party, accused of

476

shooting and fatally wounding one Tizzoni, a Fascist, during

disturbances accompanying the Italian parliamentary elections

in 1924. In re Camporini, [1923-1924] Ann. Dig. 283 (No. 164).

The Swiss Federal Tribunal recognizing this deficiency has

said in the Kavic, Bjelanove and Arsenijevil case, 39 I.L.R.

371 (No. 30) (1952):

> That restrictive interpretation . . . does not meet
> the intention of the law, nor take account of recent
> historical developments, such as the growth of total-
> itarian States . . . Those who do not wish to submit
> to the regime have no alternative but to escape it by
> flight abroad . . . This more passive attitude for the
> purpose of escaping political constraint is no less
> worthy of asylum than active participation in the
> fight for political power used to be in what were
> earlier considered to be normal circumstances . . .
> Recent pracitce has been too restrictive in making the
> relative political character of an offense dependent
> on its commission in the framework of a fight for
> power.

70. 39 I.L.R. 371 (1952).

71. 6 Whiteman, Digest, 371 (1968).

72. *Supra*, note 70 at 372.

73. 34 I.L.R. 143 (1961).

74. *Ibid.*, 143-144.

75. See *supra*, note 54-55 and corresponding text.

76. From Bassiouni, *supra*, note 11, pp. 254-257.

77. I Bassiouni and Nanda, <u>A Treatise on International Criminal Law</u> (1973), Part I, "The Meaning of International Criminal Law."

78. See Garcia-Mora, "Crimes Against Humanity and the Principle of Nonextradition of Political Offenders," 62 <u>Mich. L. Rev.</u> 927 (1964); Garcia-Mora, "War Crimes and the Principle of Nonextradition of Political·Offenders," 9 <u>Wayne L. Rev.</u> 269 (1963); Green, "Political Offenses, War Crimes and Extradition," 11 <u>Int. & Comp. L.Q.</u> 329 (1962); Neuman, "Neutral States and the Extradition of War Criminals," 45 <u>A.J.I.L.</u> 495 (1951).

79. E.g., McDougal and Feliciano, Law and Minimum World Public Order (1961).

80. <i>Supra</i>, note 77 and Volume II, <u>Jurisdiction and Cooperation</u>.

81. Johnson, "The Draft Code of Offenses Against the Peace and Security of Mankind," 4 <u>Int. & Comp. L.Q.</u> 445, 456 (1955).

82. G.A. Res. 174 (II) (1947).

83. G.A. Res. 177 (II) (1947).

84. G.A.O.R., V, Supp. 12 (A/1316), 11-14 (1950).

85. G.A.O.R., IX, Supp. 9 (A/2693), 11-12 (1954) and Johnson, <i>supra</i>, note 81.

86. <u>Trial of the Major War Criminals Before the International Military Tribunal</u>, Vol. I, p. 223 (1947).

87. For text see 13 <u>A.J.I.L.</u>, Supp. 151 (1919).

88. For comments, see Garner, "Punishment of Offenders Against the Laws and Customs of War," 16 <u>A.J.I.L.</u> 70 (1931); Wright, "The Legal Liability of the Kaiser," 18 <u>Am. Pol. Sci. Rev.</u>

121 (1919).

89. For a summary of its development, see I Bassiouni and Nanda, *supra,* note 77, Part II, Chapter I, and Stone, <u>Aggression and World Order</u> (1958).

90. Garcia-Mora, *supra,* note 78; see also, 12 <u>Dept. State Bull.</u> 160 (1945).

91. *Ibid.*

92. Nanda and Bassiouni, "Slavery and Slave Trade: Steps Toward Its Eradication," 12 <u>Santa Clara L.Rev.</u> 423 (1972).

93. Bassiouni, "The International Narcotics Control Scheme - A Proposal," 46 <u>St. John's L. Rev.</u> 218 (1972).

94. Convention for the Suppression of Counterfeiting Currency, 20 April 1920; for text see 4 Hudson, <u>International Legislation</u> 2692-705 (1931).

95. See the 1958 Geneva Convention on the High Seas, 13 U.S.T. 2312, T.I.A.S. No. 0200 (1962) 450 U.N.T.S. 82 and 4 Whiteman, <u>Digest</u> 657 (1963).

96. See, *ibid.*, 1958 Geneva Convention, Article 15; the 1963 Tokyo Convention, 20 U.S.T. 2941, T.I.A.S. No. 6768 (1969), and the 1970 Hague Convention, T.I.A.S. 7192 and 4 Whiteman, <u>Digest</u>, 657-659 (1963); see also:

    Hirsch and Fuller, "Aircraft Piracy and Extradition," 16 <u>N.Y.L.F.</u> 392 (1970); Evans, "Hijacking: Its Causes and Cure," 69 <u>A.J.I.L.</u> 695 (1969).

97. See Bassiouni, "Aggression, The Crime Against Peace," in I Bassiouni and Nanda, *supra,* note 89.

98. See Garcia-Mora, "Crimes Against Humanity and the Principle

of Nonextradition of Political Offenders," *supra*, note 78;
and Johnson, *supra*, note 81.

99. *Supra*, note 83.

100. The Convention on the Prevention and Punishment of the Crime
of Genocide states: "Genocide and the other acts enumerated
in Article III shall not be considered as political crimes
for the purpose of extradition," it goes on to say that "The
Contracting Parties pledge themselves in such cases to grant
extradition in accordance with their laws and treaties in
force." G.A.O.R. Res. 260 at 174 (A./181) (1948). Two implications would seem to follow from this provision. The
first is that under no circumstances can the parties to the
Convention regard genocide as a political offense. The overriding purpose of the Convention is to punish genocide as an
ordinary crime and the states cannot invoke their laws and
practices to reach a different result. To this extent, one
category of crimes against humanity has become an ordinary
crime by the consensus of mankind. The second implication
indicates that the contracting parties have assumed the explicit obligation to extradite persons accused of genocide
to any government requesting their surrender. This is clearly
a mandatory provision and no exception can be engrafted into
its terms.

See, "Genocide as a Crime under International Law," Lemkin,
41 A.J.I.L. 145 (1947); Drost, The Crime of State: Genocide
185-190 (1951); on Reservations to the Convention on the
Prevention and Punishment of the Crime of Genocide, (1951)

I.C.J. Rep. 15, and Bassiouni, "Genocide, Slavery and Racial

Discrimination," in I Bassiouni and Nanda, *supra*, note 77,

Part V, Chapter I.

101. See Garcia-Mora and Greene, note 78.

102. For summary of the customary rules of warfare, see United

States Army Field Manual, 27-10 (1956).

103. See, Pictet, The Geneva Conventions of August 12, 1949 (1958),

and the Commentaries on the Third Geneva Convention Relative

to the Protection of Civilian Persons in Time of War, wherein

Article 146 states:

Each High Contracting Party shall be under the obligation

to search for persons alleged to have committed, or to

have ordered to be committed, such grave breaches and

shall bring such persons, regardless of their nationality,

before its own courts. It may also, if it prefers, and

in accordance with the provisions of its own legislation,

hand such persons for trial to another High Contracting

Party concerned, provided such High Contracting Party

has made out a prima facie case.

The same provision is found in the other three Geneva Conven-

tions as follows: Convention for the Amelioration of the

Condition of the Wounded and Sick of Armed Forces in the

Field, Art. 49 (1955), 3 U.S.T. & O.I.A. 3114, 3146, T.I.A.S.

No. 3362; Convention for the Amelioration of the Condition

of Wounded, Sick and Shipwrecked Members of the Armed Forces

at Sea, Art. 50 (1955), 3 U.S.T. & O.I.A. 3217, 3250, T.I.A.S.

No. 3364. These "grave breaches" are enumerated in Article

147 of the Geneva Convention Relative to the Protection of Civilian Persons in Time of War:

Grave breaches to which the preceding Article relates shall be those involving any of the following acts, if committed against persons or property protected by the present Convention: willful killing, torture or inhuman treatment, including biological experiments, willfully causing great suffering or serious injury to body or health, unlawful deportation or transfer or unlawful confinement of a protected person, compelling a protected person to serve in the forces of a hostile power, or wilfully depriving a protected person of the right of fair and regular trial prescribed in the present Convention, taking of hostages and extensive destruction and appropriation of property, not justified by military necessity and carried out unlawfully and wantonly.

The other conventions also contain provisions enumerating the grave breaches which are punishable, e.g., for the wounded and Sick in the Field, see Article 50; for the Wounded, Sick and Shipwrecked at Sea, see Article 51; and for Prisoners of War, see Article 180.

104. See I Bassiouni and Nanda, *supra,* note 77, Part III, "The Regulation of Armed Conflicts."

105. *Supra,* note 95.

106. *Supra,* note 96.

107. *Supra*, note 92.

108. Convention to Prevent and Punish the Acts of Terrorism Taking
the Form of Crimes Against Persons and Related Extortions
That Are of International Signficance - OAS/Off. Rec./Ser. P./
Doe. 68, Jan. 13, 1971; and Convention on the Prevention and
Punishment of Crimes Against Internationally Protected Persons
Including Diplomatic Agents. G.A. Res. A/3166 (XXVIII) 5 Feb.
1974.

109. October 12, 1923.

110. See Bassiouni, *supra*, note 93.

111. International Convention on the Elimination of All Forms of
Racial Discrimination, Dec. 21, 1965, U.N. Doc. A/Conf. 3214
at 23.

112. See, *supra*, notes 92 to 111.

113. See Chapter I.

114. In the case of neutral states, for example, see, Neumann,
supra, note 78.

115. See Bassiouni, "The Human Rights Program: The Veneer Of
Civilization Thickens," 21 DePaul L. Rev. 271 (1971). Future
developments will depend largely on what the late Professor
W. Friedmann wrote in his article entitled, "The Use of
'General Principles' In The Development of International Law",
47 A.J.I.L. 279 (1968); See also Bin-Cheng, General Principles
of Law as Applied by International Court and Tribunals, (1958).

116. Karadzole v. Artukovic, 247 F. 2d 193, 204-205 (9th Circ. 1957).

117. 355 U.S. 393 (1958).

118. United States v. Artukovic, 150 F. Supp. 383, 392 (S.D. Cal.

1959).

119. *Ibid.*, at 393.

120. Garcia-Mora, *supra*, note 78, at 290-291. The author further
states:

The reluctance to extradite war criminals is
almost universal among the States as excellently
illustrated by the Brazilian case In re Kahrs et
al., involving the request for the extradition of
certain Norwegian nationals accused of having been
members of an organization guilty of war crimes.
In denying their extradition, the Brazilian Supreme
Court firmly hold that "The accused . . . are
charged with genuinely political crimes. They are
being prosecuted for their political ideas, such
as supporting a nationalist organization or sympa-
thizing with the ideas propogated by the same
. . . There arises a question of crimes distinctly
political in nature when Norwegian law punishes
expressions of thought, opinion, or related
matters. This decision is quite consistent with
the previous Denmark (Collaboration with the Enemy)
Case, involving the extradition of certain Danish
nationals convicted in Denmark of collaborating
with the German occupation forces. In refusing their
extradition, the Brazilian Supreme Court succinctly
said that the crime of assisting the enemy in time
of war is a political one *lato sensu* because it is

484

a crime against the State in its supreme function,
namely, its external defense and its sovereignty."
The difference between these two cases and the
Artukovic Case is radically important, for while
the latter involved the commission of atrocities
allegedly in the pursuit of a political end, the
Brazilian cases, on the other hand, dealt with the
expression of unpopular political opinion and the
crime of treason, both of which have been generally
regarded as purely political offenses. Thus, the
reason for giving asylum to the offenders in the
Brazilian cases appears fairly plain. (Page 291-292).

121. N.Y. Times, Sept. 17, 1962, p. 12, Col. 6; 2 Hyde,
International Law (2d ed. 1945). The note of Secretary of State Lansing to the Governor of Texas
explaining the refusal to extradite General Huertas
to Mexico. The Department of State rejected a demand
for his extradition because of the probable doubt as to the
political character of the crimes charged, the lack of orderly machinery of justice by which a fair trial could be expected, and the possibility that accomplices in Mexico may
take this means of obtaining the release and return of their
leader. July 7, 1915, U.S. Foreign Relations, 1915 at 834
(Dep't State, 1924).

122. Cited in Bassiouni, *supra,* note 11, at 219, note 5.

123. The latest was the extradition of one August Ricord from
Paraguay, charged with smuggling some two tons of heroin in

485

the United States. The Paraguayan Supreme Court granted his extradition September 2, 1972.

124. The late Judge Hersch Lauterpacht said in this connection that Acts which per se constitute common crimes and which are contrary to the rules of war cannot legitimately be assimilated to political offenses. See Lauterpacht, "The Prosecution and Punishment of War Crimes, 21 Brit. Y.B. Int'l L. 88 at 91 (1944).

125. See, however, Johnson, *supra*, note 81; and Mueller, "The United Nations Draft Code of Offenses Against the Peace and Security of Mankind: An American Evaluation" in International Criminal Law, Mueller and Wise eds. (1965), pp. 602 ff.

126. Garcia-Mora, International Law and Asylum as a Human Right (1956); see also, *supra*, Chapter II, Section 1 on "Asylum."

127. See Garcia-Mora, "The Present Status of Political Offences in the Law of Extradition and Asylum," 14 U. Pitt. L. Rev. 371-373-74 (1953).

128. For the intricacies and complexities in determining the nature of a political offense, see Garcia-Mora, "The Nature of Political Offenses: A Knotty Problem of Extradition Law," 48 Va. L. Rev. 1226 (1962).

129. See the Artukovic cases discussed above and note 116-118, where the estimates of the number of persons the relator was accused of being responsible for their death is 200,000; see also the case of Tedeekoslovak General Jan Sejna, who sought asylum in the United States in 1968 after Dubcek took over. General Sejna was accused of the death of some 10,000 persons,

but he was granted asylum. See Time magazine, March 15, 1968, p. 27.

130. This was proposed by this writer at the 1968 Freiburg International Colloquium on extradition and was submitted to the Xth International Congress on Penal Law, held in Rome in 1969; see Bassiouni, "Rapport, Etats-Unis d'Amerique" 39 Revue Internationale de Droit Penal, 496 at 516-517 (1968); and the resolution at 855; see also resolutions of the Xth International Penal Law Congress of Rome 1969 in 40 Revue Internationale de Droit Penal (1969); and the International Pre-conference held in Siracuse Italy, Pre-congresso Internazionale di Diritto Penale (1969), Bassiouni, "Rapporto di sintezi," p. 473.

131. For an analogy, see Jessup, "The Doctrine of Erie Railroad v. Tomkins Applied to International Law," 33 A.J.I.L. 740 (1939).

132. See Chapter I, Section 3.

133. Bedi, Extradition in International Law and Practice, p. 196 (1968).

134. Tate, "Draft Evasion and the Problem of Extradition," 32 Albany L. Rev. 337 (1968).

135. Ex parte Duke of Chateua Thierry, 1 K.B. 552 (1917).

136. Ibid.

137. In re Girardin, [1933-1934] Ann. Dig. 357 (No. 153).

138. Supra, note 73.

139. Supra, note 73, p. 145.

140. Bedi, supra, note 133, at 138.

141. Sack, "Non-Enforcement of Foreign Revenue Laws in International Law and Practice," 81 U. Pa. L. Rev. 559 (1933).

142. I. Moore, A Treatise on Extradition and Interstate Rendition, p. 111 (1891); such offenses are extraditable under the Rustamante Code (1928), 86 U.N.T.S. 120, 4 Hudson, International Legislation 2283 (1931); see also, In re Munes, Supreme Court of Peru 1934 [1933-1934] Ann. Dig. 335 (No. 142).

143. Jay's Treaty with Great Britain.

144. Charlton v. Kelly, 229 U.S. 447-457 (1912) (Italy).

145. Id., at 475-76 and Memo from Secretary of State Knox.

146. Treaties with France, Iraq and Venezuela (see Appendix A, Chapter I).

147. See 4 Hackworth, Digest 318 at p. 55.

148. Valentine v. United States ex rel Neidecker, 299 U.S. 5 (1936); see also, Garner, "Non-extradition of American Citizens --The Neidecker Case," 30 A.J.I.L. 430 (1936).

149. Treaties with Mexico, Argentina and Japan, see Appendix A, Chapter I.

150. Supra, note 144 at 467-468: Canadian courts have taken the same view, re Burley, 1 Can. L.J. 34 (1865).

151. 29 U.S. 5, 7-8, 10-11, 13 (1936). It appears that in the case of the treaty with Canada and Great Britain, the court considered surrender of nationals discretionary with the Executive of those Governments. See LaForest, Extradition To and From Canada, 23-24, 37 (1961). It should be noted that in Canada and Great Britain the authority to surrender individuals to foreign governments is found in municipal legislation.

152. See, In re D.G.D. [1933-1934] Ann. Dig. 335 (No. 141). In 1932

Bulgaria requested the extradition from Greece of one D.G.D.,

who had been convicted and sentenced in Bulgaria in 1930 but

had escapted to Greece and acquired Greek nationality. The

Court of Thrace held that extradition must be refused, stating:

"By Article 2 of the Extradition Treaty . . . the Contracting

Parties do not extradite their own nationals. No distinction

is made between nationality acquired before and nationality

acquired after the act for which extradition is requested."

In another case the Court of Appeal of Aix-En-Provence held,

in 1951, that France could surrender to Italy an individual

charged with having committed certain offenses in Italy in

1945 who had acquired French nationality by neutralization in

1950, although the French-Italian Extradition Treaty of 1870

provided for the non-extradition of nationals of the contracting

parties. In re A., 18 I.L.R. 324 (No. 101) (1951).

153. In re Del Porto, [1931-1932] Ann. Dig. 307 (No. 167). In 1929

a Greek court refused the request of Albania for the extradi-

tion of a person of Albanian nationality but of Hellenic race

on the ground that Article 3 of the Extradition Treaty between

Greece and Albania which prohibited the surrender of Greek

"nationals" must be understood to include persons of Hellenic

race though of a different nationality. Albanian National,

Extradition Case, [1929-1930] Ann. Dig. 281 (No. 173).

In opposing their extradition to Italy from Palestine, one

Goralschwili and another contended that they should be treated

as British subjects and thus, under the British-Italian Extra-

dition Treaty of 1873, applicable to Palestine, not extraditable. It appeared that the accused were ex-Ottoman subjects
who had applied for and obtained provisional certificates of
special citizenship issued by the Government of Palestine
pending the enactment of the Palestine Citizenship Order.
The High Court of Palestine rejected their contention, holding
that the Crown had not acquired sovereignty by accepting the
Mandate for Palestine and that the subjects of the mandated
territory did not become British subjects. They could,
therefore, be extradited to Italy, if it were found that an
extraditable offense had been committed by them. Attorney-
General v. Goralschwili and Another, [1925-1926] Ann. Dig.
47 (Nc. 33).

154. Extradition of German National Case, 21 I.L.R. 232, 234 (1954).

155. Erie R.R. Co., v. Tompkins, 304 U.S. 64 (1938), and Rule 16
Federal Rules of Civil Procedures; see also, Jessup, supra,
note 131.

156. Shearer, Extradition in International Law, p. 118 (1971).

157. In re Arevalo, [1941-1942] Ann. Dig. 329-330 (No. 99). In
in re Rojas, the Supreme Court of Costa Rica advised the
executive to refuse the request of Nicaragua for Rojas'
extradition for the crime of swindling made under the Central
American Extradition Convention of 1923 on the grounds that
Rojas was a Costa Rican and that under Article 4 of the
Convention the contracting parties are not obliged to
surrender their nationals but must prosecute them for the
offense. [1941-1942] Ann. Dig. 330-331 (No. 108).

In _in re Artaza_, the Court of Second Instances of Argentina
reversed the decision of the lower court in favor of granting
the extradition of Artaza, an Argentine national, to Brazil
where he was charged with homicide. The Court noted that ther
was no extradition treaty in force between the two countries
and stated: ". . . In the absence of an extradition treaty
with the demanding State, the provisions of Title V, Chapter
II, of Book IV, Section II, of the Code of Criminal Procedure
governing the proceedings. According to Article 669 of this
Code an Argentine citizen has the right to request a trial
before an Argentine court. As the appellant has exercised
this right, the extradition request is denied." 18 _I.L.R._
333 (No. 106) (1951).

In 1932 Tom Coumas, a naturalized American of Greek origin,
fled to Greece after allegedly committing a murder and an
assault with a deadly weapon in the State of California.
In 1934 the United States, on behalf of California, requested
his extradition from Greece under the United States–Greece
Extradition Treaty of 1931 (U.S.T.S. 355; 47 Stat. 2185).
Coumas successfully resisted extradition on the ground that
he was a Greek citizen since he had never divested himself
of his Greek citizenship; and that under the 1931 Treaty his
extradition was not obligatory and was, under Greek law, prohibited. He was, however tried in Greece for the crimes for
which his extradition had been sought, convicted, and sentenced
to 4 years' and 4 months' imprisonment. After serving his
sentence in Greece, he returned to the United States where

he was arrested in 1947 for trial on the same charges. The Supreme Court of California held that his prosecution in California was barred by California law which provided that conviction or acquittal in another State or country also having jurisdiction over an offense within the jurisdiction of California is a bar to prosecution therefore in California. Coumas v. Superior Court, 192 p. 2d 449 (1943), cited in 6 Whiteman, Digest 377-378 (1968). See also, The Bustamante Code of Private and International Law, supra, note 142, which makes extradition of nationals optional.

158. 6 Whiteman, Digest 1-66; 342-351; 428-636 (1968).

159. Bassiouni, Criminal Law and Its Processes, pp. 37-45 (1969).

160. The United States Supreme Court held in Wilson v. Girard, 354 U.S. 524, 77 S.Ct. 1409 (1953) that surrender of a person for trial to another which does not have the same procedural safeguards is not violative of due process.

161. Id., and supra, note 164.

162. 177 F. Supp. 356, 867-68 (D. Conn. 1959). Relator claimed that he committed the robberies to collect funds for the Sicilian separatist movement, and therefore that he could not be extradited since his offenses were of a political character. The Commissioner, however, apparently found that relator and his associates used the separatist movement to further their real objectives of personal gain. Following the arrest of his associates in 1946, relator went into hiding. He was tried in absentia in 1949 and 1951. His whereabouts were apparently unknown until 1955 when he entered the United

States, probably as a stowaway, *id.* at 861-62.

Although relator was an American citizen by birth, his
extended residence in Italy and connection with the separatist
movement might raise some questions about his citizenship.
66 Stat. 267 (1952), as amended 8 U.S.C. 1481 (1959 . The
District Court, however, proceded on the assumption that he
was a citizen, 177 F.Supp. at 861.

163. 278 F. ed. 77 (ed. 1950), *cert. denied* 364 U.S. 851, 81
sup. et. 97 (1960). In Argento v. Horn, 241 F. 2d 253 (6th
Cir. 1957), no constitutional issue was raised. In United
States ex rel. Argento v. Jacobs, 176 F. Supp. 877 (N.D.
Ohio 1959), the court rejected *in dictum* a constitutional
argument similar to that advanced by Gallina, saying that while
a trial *in absentia* "does not comport with our ideas of justice or fairness, it must be remembered that petitioner is an
Italian National and alleged to be a fugitive from that
country. The offense was committed in Italy and is governed
by Italian law which permits the trial of a criminal case
in absentia." *Id.* at 879. The requested person was discharged, however, for lack of sufficient evidence of guilt.
The constitutional issue was apparently raised in in re
Extradition of D'Amico, 177 F. Supp. 648 (S.D.N.Y. 1959), but
became moot when the Italian Counsel represented to the court
that D'Amico would be tried anew if extradited. The court
of appeals in reviewing these decisions also considered
Wilson v. Girard, 354 U.S. 524 (1957); Grin v. Shine, 187
U.S. 181 (1902); Holmes v. Jennison, 39 U.S. (14 Pet.) 540

493

(1840), and a number of interstate extradition cases. The court correctly noted that nothing in those cases supported relator's claim, with the exception of the *dictum* in United States ex. rel. Argento v. Jacobs neither is there anything in them directly contrary to relator's claim. The interstate extradition cases, in particular, are irrelevant because a fugitive claiming his conviction violated due process would be told that he can test his claim in the courts of the state where he was convicted. Cf. Sweeney v. Woodall, 344 U.S. 86 (1952). In Ex parte Fudera, C.C.S.D.N.Y. 1903, 162 F. 591, a *habeau corpus* proceeding, the very treaty now in question was asserted as the basis of a request for extradition of the petitioner. From a reading of the case it seems clear that the person who had committed the crime had been convicted *in contumacium* in his absence by the Italian Government. Yet the court expressed not the slightest doubt that extradition would have been granted under these circumstances had sufficient evidence of the criminality of the petitioner been presented to it. The fact that petitioner was discharged from custody was due to the lack of competent evidence that the crime charged had been committed.

164. In Ex parte La Mantia D.C.S.D.N.Y. 1913, 206 F. 330 again involving extradition under this same treaty, the court had said that it made no difference whether there was a conviction *in contumacium*: insofar as the hearing on the criminality of the accused was concerned, he was to be regarded as only charged with the crime. Although in that case the

494

accused was discharged for lack of competent evidence of identity, there can be no doubt that had such evidence been produced, the court would have ordered the accused held for extradition despite the fact that he had already been tried for the offense and would in all probability, be incarcerated immediately upon his return to Italy. See also, in re Mylonas (Greece) 187 F. Supp. 710 (1960) for the same position.

165. Italy's willingness to make such agreements is illustrated by in re Extradition of D'Amico, 177 F. Supp. 648 (S.D.N.Y. 1959). In that case the Italian Counsel, apparently without waiting for a request from the State Department, assured the court that the requested person would receive a new trial. Id. at 651 n. 3.

166. Despite the desirability of giving the executive maximum discretion in extradition matters, and despite the difficulty of finding an appropriate remedy, judicial intervention should be available to protect the rights of the requested person when the alternatives have been exhausted. Cf. Johnson v. Zerbst, 304 U.S. 458, 467, (1938). Johnson v. Dye, 175 F. 3d 250 (3d Cir.), rev'd per curiam on procedural grounds, 338 U.S. 364 (1949) (remedies in state courts had not been exhausted).

167. In Gallina v. Fraser, supra, notes 162-163, the district court stated that "regardless of what constitutional protections are given to persons held for trial in the courts of the United States or of the constituent states thereof, those protections cannot be claimed by an accused whose trial and

conviction have been held or are to be held under the laws
of another nation, acting according to its traditional processes and within the scope of its authority and jurisdiction
. . . For the present we hold that extradition of a person
convicted (*in absentia*) . . . is not contrary to due process
of law even where it appears that the extradition will not
be followed by a new trial, but rather by immediate incarceration for the offense charged upon a sentence previously imposed
. . . " [177] F. Supp. at 866. This statement could also be
interpreted as holding that the test of due process in this
context is whether the foreign procedure is lawful and in
accord with the traditional processes of that country. If
this latter interpretation of the holding is correct, then
the district court decision is based upon a rejection of
relator's second argument.

168. 6 Whiteman, <u>Digest</u> p. 859 (1968).

169. See Bedi, *supra*, note 133 at 168-171.

170. <u>In re Weill</u>, Supreme Court of Argentina 1939, [1941-1942] <u>Ann.</u>
<u>Dig.</u> 334 (No. 104), <u>in re Addis</u>, Court of Appeals of Belgium, 1931,
[1931-1932] <u>Ann. Dig.</u> 306 (no. 166); <u>in re Romaguera de Mouja</u>
Supreme Court of Venezuela, 1952, 19 I.L.A. 373 (No. 84 (1952);
<u>in re Plevani</u>, France, 1955, 22 <u>I.L.R.</u> 514 (1955).

171. Jhirad v. Ferrandina, 486 F. 2d 442 (2nd circ. 1973), <u>cf.</u>
<u>U.S. v. Kelly</u> 96 F. 2d 787 (1938).

172. In re Gicca [1933-1934] <u>Ann. Dig.</u> 354 (No. 151) (Argentina).

173. European treaty series no. 24 (1957) 359 U.N.T.S. 273 (1959);
see also the position of Arab Convention on extradition of

496

1953, Article 6, quoted in Bedi, *supra*, note 133 at 168.

174. See <u>Lazzeri v. Schweizerische Bundesanwaltschaft</u>, Federal
     Tribunal June 29, 1961; 34 <u>I.L.R.</u> 134 (1961) where the appellant
     was sentenced *in absentia*, on May 13, 1956, to six months'
     imprisonment for fraudulent bankruptcy and fraud. His extra-
     dition was requested by the Italian authorities. He was
     arrested on August 6, 1960, on arrival in Switzerland from
     Germany. He contested his extradition on a number of grounds.
     First, it was contended on his behalf that the proceedings
     which had led to his conviction were vitiated by procedural
     faults and could accordingly not be recognized. Secondly,
     it was argued that further proceedings must be assumed to be
     timebarred, since the date of the original offense was not
     known. Thirdly, it was claimed that on extradition, the
     appellant would run the risk of being prosecuted for a new
     offense, namely, bigamy. The court held that extradition
     should be granted and examined the Statutes of Limitations
     applicalbe to the offenses charged in the two countries
     concerned and found that they did not prevent extradition;
     for one offense there was a doubt under Italian law, but
     extradition had to be granted so that the doubt, relating to
     the application of Italian law, could be resolved by the
     Italian courts.

175. In the <u>Lazzeri</u> case, *id.*, the relator contested his extradi-
     tion on the grounds that an amnesty of July 11, 1959, com-
     bined with one of December 23, 1949, would have wiped out
     his sentence. The Federal Tribunal has previously recognized

that amnesty is not a bar to extradition to Italy, since this
is not provided for in the Treaty. On the other hand, (Professor)
Schultz Schweizerisches Auslieferungsrecht, at p. 340
considers that an amnesty must be taken into account even in
the absence of express provision, since its effect is a bar
to prosecution, and the basis for extradition thus disappears.
Whether this is a justifiable criticism of past case-law does
not need to be decided here. If the Court were to follow
Schultz, it must accept also his further view that a general
amnesty is not sufficient to bar extradition; an individual
order making it applicable to the prosecution of the particular
fugitive is necessary. Such an order has not been made in the
present case. 34 I.L.R. 133 at 137 (1961).

176. See, *supra,* note 170.

177. Convention on the Nonapplicability of Statutory Limitations
to War Crimes and Crimes Against Humanity, G.A. Res. 291
(XXIII) Dec. 9, 1968.

178. Bassiouni, *supra,* note 159 at pp. 452-3.

179. Bassiouni, "Recent Supreme Court Decisions Strengthen Illinois
Law Enforcement," 2 Ill. Cont. Leg. ed. 111 (1964); see also,
Albertson v. Subservice Activities Control Board, 382 U.S.
70, 86 S. Ct. 120 (1965), and Giancana v. United States,
352 F. 2d 21 (7th Cir. 1965), *cert. denied* 382 U.S. 959
(1965). These decisions as well as many in state practice
followed the incorporation of the Fifth Amendment privilege
against self-incrimination in the Fourteenth Amendment due
process clause and held applicable uniformly to State and

Federal courts in <u>Malloy v. Hogan</u>, 377 U.S. 1, (1964), and
its application to the first interstate immunity case, <u>Murphy</u>
v. <u>Waterfront Commission</u>, 378 U.S. 52, (1964). The latest
opposition of the United State Supreme Court was expressed
favoring the practice in <u>Kastigan v. United States</u>, 408 U.S.
931 (1972).

180. In certain municipal legislations like Germany, consider that
a bar to prosecution or punishment, i.e., statute of limitation, amnesty or pardon is a bar to extradition. See
Grützner, "Rapports: Allemagne," <u>39 Revue International de
Droit Penal</u>, p. 379 (1969), and <u>in re Zanini</u> [1935-1937] <u>Ann.
Dig</u>. 372 (No. 173) and <u>in re Issel</u>, 18 <u>I.L.R.</u> 331 (No. 104)
(1951).

181. See <u>Lazzeri</u> and <u>Amnesty Cases</u>, *supra*, note 174-175.

182. Bassiouni, *supra*, note 159 at p. 126 (1969) particularly
the case of <u>Bartkus v. Illinois</u>, 359 U.S. 121, 795 ct. 679
(1959) which upholds the doctrine of separate Sovereigns even
as between states and Frank, "An International Lawyer Looks at
the Bartkus Rule," 34 <u>N.Y.L. Rev.</u> 1096 (1959).

183. Bedi, *supra*, note 133 at pp. 172-179.

184. 159 B.F.S.P. 1952 p. 606, League of Arab States Treaty Series
p. 27-32, reprinted in 8 <u>Revue Egyptienne de droit Internation-
al</u>, 328-332 (1952).

185. 24 <u>European Treaty Series</u>, (1957), 359 U.N.T.S. 273 (1959).

186. <u>Second Draft Convention on Extradition</u>, adopted by the Inter-
American Juridical Committee, July 10, 1957.

187. Articles containing the principles concerning extradition of

fugitive offenders, Asian-African Legal Consultative Committee (1961).

188. "The Benelux Convention of 27 June 1962 on Extradition and Judicial Assistance in Penal Matters," Tractatanblad No. 97 (1962).

189. Gaor, XXI, Supp. 16 (A1 6316) pp. 52-53.

190. OAS Treaty Series No. 36.

191. U.S. T.I.A.S. 1691; 15 U.S.T. 2893, 2100.

192. U.S. T.I.A.A. 5476; 14 U.S.T. 1707, 1718.

193. In re Pedro Alejandrine Flores [1929-1930] Ann. Dig. 229 (No. 185).

194. Supra, note 135.

195. Supra, note 188.

196. See supra, note 193 for the Flores Case and see the cases cited in Chapter IV notes, 57-65 and corresponding text.

197. Supra, note 186, Article 10.

198. 408 U.S. 238 (1972); Bassiouni, and Lahey and Sang, "La peine de mort aux Etats-Unis-L'Etat de la question en 1972", Revue de Science Criminelle et de Droit Penal Comparé No. 1 (1973) pp. 23-43.

199. Supra, note 1.

200. Adopted Res. 217A (III) G.A. 10 December 1948, GAOR III. 1, Res. (A.310) pp. 71-7.

201. Adopted Res. 220 (XXI) G.A. 16 December 1966. GAOR, XXI, Supp. 16 (A/6316), pp. 52-58.

202. Signed at Rome, 4 November 1950, entered into force 3 September 1953, European Treaty Series, 213 U.N.T.S. 221.

203. Adopted by the Ninth International Conference of American States, Resolution, Washington, D.C. 19 U.S.

204. Signed at San Jose, Costa Rica, 22 November 1962, not yet in force.

205. United Nations Conference on the Prevention of Crime and the Treatment of Offenders in 1955, Res. 663 c (XXIV), July 31, 19 See also Fourth United Nations Conference held in Kyoto, Japan 17-26 August 1970, A/Conf. 4910 (1970).

Extradition Procedure in the United States

1. Sources and Content of Procedural Rules: Some Comparative Aspects

In almost all countries procedural rules in extradition emanate
from one or more of the following three sources: 1) treaty,
2) specific (extradition) legislation or 3) general criminal law
and procedure legislation (applicable to extradition by analogy).
Treaties are probably the most characteristic sources because
extradition is most frequently practiced by international agreements. However, treaties seldom, if ever, prescribe internal
procedural rules, consequently many states have enacted specific
legislation relating to extradition procedure. In the United
States where extradition treaties are deemed self-executing, the
United States Code directs the judicial officer (a United States
magistrate) and the Secretary of State to act "according to the
stipulations of the treaty or convention." [1] By comparison, in
England, where treaties are not self-executing but require implementing legislation in all cases where private rights may be
created or affected, the provisions of the applicable treaty are
incorporated by reference into the municipal legislation. Such
legislation is then applied to each new treaty by means of an
Order-in-Council which must recite the terms of the new treaty

and the applicability of the act is subject to the limitations and qualifications contained in the new treaty. [2] In England, if the scope of the treaty is broader than municipal law, the latter prevails, while in the United States treaty provisions supersede municipal law. The reason for this divergence in these two common law systems is that the United States Constitution provides for the supremacy of treaties while England has no constitution.

Some national extradition laws apply only in the absence of treaties where extradition is granted *ex gratia* (comity) or on a basis of reciprocity. Such is the case in the French Law of 1927 which provides that: "in the absence of a treaty, the conditions, the procedure and the effects of extradition are determined by the provisions of the present law. The present law applies as well to matters which are not regulated by treaties." [3]

In the now prevalent treaty practice of most states, municipal laws set forth the conditions under which an extradition request will be considered in the absence of a treaty and in all cases establish the basis for the mechanics of seizure of the relator and his or her surrender to the requesting state.

General municipal laws are comparatively less important than the three other sources of procedural norms governing extradition because they would only apply by analogy whenever such an analogy is permissible. In such cases, the interpretation of general statutes will be subject to the same considerations applicable to special extradition legislation.

Special extradition statutes will usually exclude the application of other laws by analogy, [4] but on occasion courts will resort to general municipal laws applicable to criminal proceedings to fill gaps and aid in judicial interpretation.[5] This approach to judicial interpretation is more akin to the jurisprudence of common law countries than to civil law countries. In this respect, however, the United States Supreme Court warned against judicially inspired innovations in federal procedure with respect to extradition proceedings because these are amply regulated by United States statutes. [6] The extradition magistrate, however, may develop by analogy situations which make it essential for the determination of the particular case. [7]

Treaties are generally silent as to the designation of organs competent to handle extradition proceedings. Apart from the almost standard recourse to diplomatic channels in the presentation of the requisition and the supporting documents, the requested state determines under its laws all other questions, arising under the treaty. The requested state may choose to deal with extradition matters entirely at the executive level or to assign them exclusively or partially to its judicial organs. This issue may conceivably become a question of international interest if in order to advance the rule of law and the protection of fundamental human rights extradition is to become a wholly judicial question. Indeed, it is arguable that judicial bodies are more appropriate to decide questions affecting individual liberties than those which are designed to carry out govern-

mental policy. This was not always the case since until the
nineteenth century exclusive control was with the executive.
France, for example, surrendered fugitive criminals under its
treaties without any reference to the courts until 1875. In
the United States exclusive executive control was maintained
from 1794 until 1842. The surrender of one Robbins to Great
Britain under the Jay Treaty of 1794 was bitterly attacked at
the time because of the denial of a judicial hearing, but the
action was legally sustained. [8] Until 1815 the same view was
held in Great Britain as the prerogative of the King to expel
aliens was held to exclude even the requirement of a treaty. [9]
The denial of the existence of this prerogative came after 1815.[10]
It was followed by the conclusion of the Webster-Ashburton Treaty
of 1842 in which both Great Britain and the United States committed
themselves to the policy of making a judicial hearing an essential
part of the extradition process. [11] Very few countries retain a
system of exclusive executive control (e.g., Ecuador, Portugal
and Spain).

Belgium was the first state to introduce a measure of judicial
control in extradition proceedings in a law promulgated in 1833
which required that all extradition cases be submitted for judicial
consideration. It did not, however, make the judicial determination conclusive either for or against extradition.

The system established by this legislation has remained in
effect and, consequently, the executive is empowered to decide
requests for extradition on its own after seeking only an advisory
opinion from the *chambre des mises en accusation* of the Court of

Appeal. Since the court's opinion is not binding, whether it favors extradition or not, there is, therefore, no right of appeal from it. [12] A similar measure of nonbinding judicial direction prevails in some other countries (e.g., Japan, Mexico, the Netherlands and Peru).

Judicial control assumed a different role in the Anglo-American system. Instead of making the judicial function purely advisory, legislation has had the effect of making judicial determination conclusive as to refusal of extradition and advisory as to its concession. Where the court rules that extradition is admissible, the executive may nonetheless refuse surrender because that becomes a matter of foreign policy which is within its prerogatives. This approach was first adopted by Great Britain in legislation implementing the treaties of 1842 and 1848 [13] and by the United States in its first extradition statute of 1848. [14] Not only does this system give adequate opportunity to the fugitive to contest extradition before the ordinary courts, but in effect it gives him or her a further opportunity of making representations to the executive in the event of an adverse judicial determination. This may be of special significance in the case of political offenses.

France, which had adopted the Belgian judicial advisory system in 1875, moved in its Law of 1927 to judicial control somewhat similar to the Anglo-American pattern. Other states employ the same system and include *inter alia*, Argentina, Austria, Brazil, Chile, Costa Rica, Finland, Greece, Haiti, Italy, Luxemborg, Norway, Sweden, Switzerland, Turkey, Uruguay and the Member States

of the Commonwealth. In the case of Brazil it is possible for
the courts to attach certain judicial conditions to the surrender
of a person with at least the tacit consent of the executive. [16]
This is an application of the Doctrine of Specialty discussed in
Chapter V. Such conditions are implicit in the doctrine and are
prevalent with respect to restrictions on the death penalty by
several states such as Italy.

Germany stands at the opposite end of the spectrum in
assigning exclusive competence in all extradition matters to its
judicial authorities. [17] Although it follows that the fugitive
is thereby deprived of a last resort approach to the executive,
which is a feature of the Anglo-American system, it is nonetheless true that German law since 1949 offers a wider scope for
judicial inquiry than the laws of any other country other than
the United States. [18]

In most countries of the world there are two processes in extradition matters and, therefore, two sets of procedures applicable
to the executive and the judiciary. These two levels of author-
itative-decision-making-process are separate processes operating
within a single system. It is an almost foregone conclusion
that procedures governing both of these levels should differ
from state to state as sharply as do the contrasting legal systems of the world. There are, however, remarkable similarities.
For example, almost all states initiate a request (or requisition)
through their executive branch and these requests are received
by the executive branch of other states. The executive of the
requested state sets in motion or allows the requesting state

to set in motion the judicial machinery to adjudicate the surrender of the person sought after. Thereafter, the executive proceeds with the actual surrender of the person. The differences between states arise in great variety within these stages. The most significant difference arise in respect to the quantum of evidence required by the requested state and other judicial formalities required to adjudicate the surrender of the relator. All other distinctions are, in comparison to these questions, of limited significance.

The practice of states, as to the required documents, proof of guilt, and all the concomittant evidentiary questions are as may be expected drastically different between common law and civil law inspired systems. This is due to the fact that extradition proceedings are essentially penal and the criminal processes of these two legal systems are contrasting in scope and means as one is inquisitorial and the other is accusatorial. Consequently, the requirement of proof of guilt, its substantive content and procedural methods differ sharply. Basically, the civil law inspired systems do not inquire into proof of guilt while the common law inspired systems do so.

The rationale for the civil law inspired systems is that extradition is a tool of judicial cooperation in penal matters, hence no inquiry is made into the issue of guilt not even a *prima facie* one. The common law inspired systems consider that the use of their judicial processes must meet their threshhold standards of criminal responsibility, hence they inquire into the existence of "probable cause." To a large extent the requirements of these two systems are a reflection of their thresh-hold standards of criminal responsibility as applied to the pro-secutability of the relator. Certainly, the more a given system inquires into the guilt or innocence of the relator, the more the extradition process is likely to shift from inquiry into extradit-ability to inquiry into punishability.

The contract between the two types of systems can be seen through the following two decisions of the United States and Switzerland. The Supreme Court of the United States held in Benson v. McMahon the test as to whether such evidence of crim-inality has been presented is the same as that

> of those preliminary examinations which take place
>
> every day in this country before an examining of
>
> committing magistrate for the purpose of deter-
>
> mining whether a case is made out which will justify
>
> the holding of the accused, either by imprisonment
>
> or under bail, to ultimately answer to an indictment
>
> or other proceeding in which he shall be finally
>
> tried upon the charge made against him. 462-463,
>
> 8 S. Ct. at page 1243. [19]

It is in essence the same as the test of whether "there is prob-able cause" to believe that an offense has been committed and that the relator is the person believed to have committed it. [20]

In a case in which the Federal Republic of Germany sought the extradition from Switzerland of a Polish national charged with the crime of forgery, the accused contended that the offense fell within the competence of American occupation authorities and that

509

Germany was not competent to seek extradition. The Swiss Federal
Tribunal stated:

> It is for the Federal Council to decide whether a
> request for extradition complies in form with the
> requirements of treaty or law. The Federal Tribunal,
> therefore, does not have to deal with the question
> whether the present request has been made by the
> competent authority or whether the warrant attached
> to it was issued by a competent organ. Similarly,
> it is not for the Federal Tribunal to examine
> whether the court before which the person extra-
> dited is to be tried has jurisdiction under the
> law of the requesting State; the only argument
> which could be taken into consideration would be
> that that court was a tribunal with special powers
> (Ausnahmegericht) . . . [extradition for trial by a
> special court being prohibited by Swiss law].
> The Federal Tribunal is also not competent to
> decide the question of guilt. Extradition is
> granted on the basis of the facts alleged in the
> indictment attached to the request for extradition . . .[21]

The civil law inspired systems do not inquire into the issue
of "probable cause," with few exceptions, and accept the formal
requisition as *prima facie* evidence sufficient to grant extradition without more than the fulfillment of those formal obligations embodied in the treaty. This is usually limited to:

1. Proof of identity of the relator;

510

2. Conformity of the requisition to treaty

   requirements.

Proof of such requirements are found in the requisition and accompanying documents such as the indictment or its counterpart charging document or a court's validated judgment and are not subject to review by the authorities of the requested state.

2. *Procedure in the United States*

2.1 *Initiation of the Process*

The power to extradite is a national one, vested exclusively in the federal government and held to require a treaty before it can be exercised. [23] The extradition procedure prescribed by federal statute may be summarized briefly as follows: [24] Extradition proceedings must be initiated by the competent authorities of a requesting state that will: (1) present a requisition to the Department of State in accordance with treaty stipulations, and (2) file a verified complaint in the Federal District Court wherein the relator is found charging him or her with an offense under the terms of the treaty and in accordance with treaty stipulations, the procedural laws of the United States and the substantive laws of the state wherein the Federal District Court is located.

The process operates at two levels, the executive and the judiciary, each independently of the other, though both are interrelated and indispensable to the system. [25] There can be no extradition until both levels, executive and judicial, agree to it. [26] However, a finding by a judge of insufficient evidence of criminality and the subsequent discharge of the relator terminates extradition proceedings. [27] The converse, however, is not true because after a judge commits a relator for extradition, the Secretary of State can refuse to surrender the relator to the requesting state. [28]

2.2 The Initial Executive Process

At the executive level the requisition is a formal diplomatic request, [29] even though there is no specific form for it, except that it must be addressed to the Secretary of State by the competent authorities of the requesting state. [30] Treaties differ as to the substantive requirements of the requisition but these questions are of limited significance because the diplomatic note embodying the requisition can always be amended or supplemented because the critical stage is the judicial hearing. Even substantive errors in the requisition are not fatal to the case of the requesting state since it is possible to submit more than one requisition even after its denial and that includes an adverse judicial finding. [31] The United States Supreme Court held that double jeopardy did not attach in such cases. [32]

There is no time limit required for the submission of the requisition to the Secretary of State and it can, therefore, be before, during or after the judicial proceedings. It must, however, be submitted before the Department of State can certify the surrender of the relator. [33] This, of course, is subject to specific treaty stipulations and most treaties require that it be filed no later than two calendar months after the relator has been arrested and confined on the extradition warrant. The Supreme

Court held that after this lapse of time the relator is to be

released and the surrender warrant quashed. [34]

In the event that requisitions are received from two countries

for the same accused, priority may be given by the treaties either

to the first request received, [35] or to the request which alleges

the most serious crime. [36]

The Secretary of State, upon request by the requesting state,

may issue a preliminary mandate to the judge who will conduct the

judicial hearing on that motion. This is not, however, the usual

practice and such a preliminary mandate is not a determination

of the issue of extraditability nor is it a prerequisite for the

initiation of the judicial proceedings. The practice is for the

requesting state to initiate such proceedings on its own motion. [37]

2.3 *The Judicial Process*

The judicial proceedings are initiated by a complaint made by an

authorized representative of the requesting government. It is

not necessary that the representative be a consular or diplomatic

officer, provided that the person making the complaint is author-

ized to do so by the requesting state. In United States ex rel

Caputo v. Kelly, [38] the second circuit held that:

Extradition proceedings must be prosecuted by the

foreign government in the public interest and may

not be used by a private part for private vengeance

or personal purposes; but if in fact the foreign

government initiates the proceedings, no reason is

513

apparent why it may not authorize any person to make
oath to the complaint on its behalf. [39]
An order for the provisional arrest of the relator may be made
but must be issued by a competent judicial officer subject to
constitutional limitations. [40] The court must have *in personam*
jurisdiction before proceeding with the hearing. [41]

(1) - <u>The complaint</u>. The complaint which must be sworn or
affirmed to, [42] is akin to an indictment or information, [43] and
as such it must inform the relator of the charges brought against
him or her to allow the preparation of a defense. [44] The complaint
should set forth the following facts (but it can be amended to
comply with these requirements or any other order by the court
for further information) they are:

1. The name of the relator;

2. The existence of a treaty in force; [45]

3. Allege the commission of an extraditable
   offense under the treaty; [46]

4. The offense constitutes a crime under the
   laws of the state wherein the Federal District
   Court is located; [47]

5. Attached thereto a certified copy of the indictment
   (or its counterpart) or conviction of the relator
   in the requesting state by its competent authorities, showing the offense charged; [48]

6. Accompanying affidavits, documents and evidence
   proving the foreign law and the facts alleged
   thereunder. [49] (The quantum of proof needed

for the determination of surrender is discussed

below).

Upon the filing of such a complaint, the magistrate will issue a

warrant for the arrest of the relator. That warrant is valid

anywhere in the United States and any authorized judicial officer

can hear the case even if he did not issue the warrant. [50] The

relator is not entitled to bail, but can be released on bond at

the discretion of the magistrate. [51]

(2) - The hearing. The scope of the hearing is not to deter-

mine guilt or innocence but to determine that:

1. The relator is the person sought after;

2. The offense charged is extraditable;

3. The offense charged is a crime under the

    laws of that state wherein the hearing is held;

4. There is "probable cause" to believe the relator

    committed the offense charged.

What a requesting state has to come forth with is stated by

Whiteman in these terms:

. . .The requirements regarding what documents must

be submitted by a requesting State in support of its

extradition request vary depending on whether the

person sought has already been tried and convicted

in the courts of the requesting State and then

escaped or whether he is merely charged with an

offense but has not yet been brought to trial.

Further, in the case of one merely charged with

an offense, the documentation required varies

depending on whether the requesting State must, under the laws of the requested State or the applicable treaty, establish a *prima facie* case of the guilt of the accused in order to obtain his extradition. Under the laws and treaties of many countries, it is sufficient merely to show that the person sought is charged in the requesting State, and a warrant of arrest or similar document issued by the authorities of that State is sufficient evidence, insofar as possible guilt is concerned, to warrant extradition. In the case of other countries, notably the United States, Canada and Great Britain, it is necessary to submit some further evidence of the person's guilt. [52]

Under United States law in 18 U.S.C. §3184 it is stated that the extradition magistrate hears and considers "the evidence of criminality" and commits the accused for surrender if "he deems the evidence sufficient to sustain the charge under the provisions of the proper treaty or convention." The extradition treaties and conventions to which the United States is a party provide that extradition shall take place only if the evidence against the fugitive is sufficient to justify commitment for trial had the offense been committed in the requested State. The Supreme Court of the United States in Benson v. McMahon stated:

> . . . we are of opinion that the proceeding before
> the commissioner is not to be regarded as in the

nature of a final trial by which the prisoner could
be convicted or acquitted of the crime charged
against him but rather of the character of those
preliminary examinations which take place every day
in this country before an examining or committing
magistrate for the purpose of determining whether
a case is made out which will justify the holding
of the accused, either by imprisonment or under
bail, to ultimately answer to an indictment, or
other proceeding, in which he shall be finally
tried upon the charge made against him. [53]

Furthermore, Mr. Justice Holmes in Glucksman v. Henkel, said:

It is common in extradition cases to attempt to
bring to bear all the factitious niceties of a
criminal trial at common law. But it is a waste
of time. For while of course a man is not to be
sent from the country merely upon demand or sur-
mise, yet if there is presented, even in somewhat untechnical form according to our ideas,
such reasonable ground to suppose him guilty as
to make it proper that he should be tried, good
faith to the demanding government requires his
surrender. Grin v. Shine, 187 U.S. 181, 184.
See Pierce v. Creecy, 210 U.S. 337, 465. We are
bound by the existence of an extradition treaty
to assume that the trial will be fair. The
evidence in this case seems to us sufficient to

require us to affirm the judgment of the Circuit
Court.[54]

The position of the United States is on this point unchanged.

(3) - _The evidence_. The question of sufficiency of the
evidence has invariably been a difficult one since it relates
not only to the nature of "probable cause" in United States law
but also because it depends on the offense charged and its elements under the law of the state whose substantive law is being
applied. In a landmark case, Collins v. Loisel, the Supreme
Court held:

> The function of the committing magistrate is to
> determine whether there is competent evidence to
> justify holding the accused to await trial, and
> not to determine whether the evidence is sufficient
> to justify a conviction. Grin v. Shine, 187 U.S. 181,
> 197; Benson v. McMahon, 127 U.S. 461, Ex parte Glaser,
> 176 Fed. 702, 784. In In re Wadge, 13 Fed. 864, 866,
> cited with approval in Charlton v. Kelly, _supra_, 461,
> the right to introduce evidence in defense was
> claimed; but Judge Brown said: "If this were recog-
> nized as the legal right of the accused in extradi-
> tion proceedings, it would give him the option of
> insisting upon a full hearing and trial of his case
> here; and that might compel the demanding govern-
> ment to produce all its evidence here, both direct
> and rebutting, in order to meet the defense thus
> gathered from every quarter. The result would be

that the foreign government, though entitled by the
terms of the treaty to the extradition of the accused
for the purpose of a trial where the crime was committed, would be compelled to go into a full trial
on the merits in a foreign country, under all the
disadvantages of such a situation, and could not
obtain extradition until after it had procured a
conviction of the accused upon a full and substantial trial here. This would be in plain contravention of the intent and meaning of the extradition treaties." The distinction between evidence
properly admitted in behalf of the defendant and
that improperly admitted is drawn in Charlton v.
Kelly, *supra*, between evidence rebutting probable
cause and evidence in defense. The court there
said, "to have witnesses produced to contradict
the testimony for the prosecution is obviously a
very different thing from hearing witnesses for
the purpose of explaining matters referred to by
the witnesses for the government." And in that
case evidence of insanity was declared inadmissible as going to defense and not to probable
cause. Whether evidence offered on an issue
before the committing magistrate is relevant is
a matter which the law leaves to his determination,
unless his action is so clearly unjustified as to
amount to a denial of the hearing prescribed by law.

The phrase "such evidence of criminality" as used in the treaty refers to the scope of the evidence or its sufficiency to block out those elements essential to a conviction. It does not refer to the character of specific instruments of evidence or to the rules governing admissibility. Thus, unsworn statements of absent witnesses may be acted upon by the committing magistrate, although they could not have been received by him under the law of the State on a preliminary examination. Elias v. Ramirez, 215 U.S. 398; Rice v. Ames, 180 U.S. 371. And whether there is a variance between the evidence and the complaint is to be decided by the general law and not by that of the State. Glucksman v. Henkel, 221 U.S. 508, 513. Here the evidence introduced was clearly sufficient to block out those elements essential to a conviction under the laws of Louisiana of the crime of obtaining property by false pretenses. The law of Louisiana could not and does not attempt to, require more. It is true that the procedure to be followed in hearings on commitment is determined by the law of the State in which they are held. In re Farez, 7 Blatchf, 345, Fed. Cas. No. 4645; In re Wadge, supra; In re Kelley, 25 Fed. 268; In re Ezeta, 62 Fed. 972, 981. But no procedural rule of State could give to the prisoner a right to introduce evidence made irrelevant by a treaty. [55]

In another frequently cited case, the relator raised the question of sufficiency of the evidence and the District Court, after reviewing the evidence presented by the requesting government at the hearing, remanded the case to the extradition magistrate for further proceedings including the talking of further evidence, stating:

. . . It is plain that the evidence presented
against D'Amico was unsatisfactory to say the
least. There is at the least grave doubt on the
present record as to whether there was any evidence
warranting a finding that there were reasonable
grounds to believe D'Amico guilty of the crime
charged.

In this state of the record it becomes of significance that there is real doubt as to whether the
Commissioner actually made a finding that there
was probable cause to believe that D'Amico committed these crimes. A careful reading of his
findings indicates that he passed directly only
upon the two questions raised by the relator at
the hearing--whether the crime charged was extraditable under the treaty and whether relator was
in fact the Vito D'Amico "mentioned in the judgment filed in Italy." The Commissioner found
against the relator on both of these points but
his findings go on to say "accordingly" there is

probable cause to believe that the offense charged
was committed by the respondent.

This does not seem to me, in the light of the circumstances here, to be an independent finding that
there was probable cause to believe that the offense
was committed by the relator. The explanation of
the omission of any independent finding on this
point may well be that the sole question of fact,
raised by relator's previous counsel on the hearing was the question of identity. Nevertheless,
the Commissioner was required under the statute
and the treaty to make a specific finding as to
the sufficiency of the evidence to establish
probable cause that relator had committed the
offenses. See Benson v. McMahon, 127 U.S. at
page 463, 8 S.Ct. at page 1243, 32 L.Ed. 234; . . .

In the light of this record and the circumstances
of this case, such an ambiguity in the findings
cannot be viewed as merely a harmless technicality. The relator is entitled to evaluation of
the evidence on the issue of whether it establishes that there is probable cause to believe
that relator committed the offenses charged and
to an independent finding on that issue. [56]

The concomittant of "evidence of guilt" is "evidence in defense"
and clearly if the former is grounded in a "probable cause"
standard, then the later is its corollary and cannot be excluded

from the context of the required standard and bear on the same.
As stated in <u>Jimenez v. Aristeguita</u>:

> The accused is not entitled to introduce evidence
> which merely goes to his defense but he may offer
> limited evidence to explain elements in the case
> against him, since the extradition proceeding is
> not a trial of the guilt or innocence but of the
> character of a preliminary examination held before
> a committing magistrate to determine whether the
> accused shall be held for trial in another trib-
> unal. [57]

Summarizing the position of the United States, Whiteman states
that:

> Inasmuch as the actual trial of the accused (assuming
> he is merely charged with an offense) is to take
> place in the requesting State if and when he is
> extradited, the extradition hearing which the
> requested State may accord the accused normally
> limits the scope of its inquiry to whether a
> proper case for extradition has been made out
> under the applicable law and/or treaty on the
> basis of the evidence furnished by the requesting
> State in support of its extradition request. While
> the accused may introduce evidence to show that the
> case comes within a prohibition against extradition
> contained in the applicable treaty and/or law (e.g.,
> political offense, national of asylum State,

prosecution barred by lapse of time) or to show

that he is not, in actuality, the person sought

by the requesting State, he may not, generally,

introduce evidence in defense to the merits of

the charge or merely to contradict the evidence

of guilt submitted by the requesting State. [58]

It is established that extradition proceedings are not a trial
of the guilt or innocence of the relator but an inquiry into
whether he or she should stand trial. What is at issue, therefore, is not punishability but prosecutability. In this respect,
a unique case in the annals of extradition is the Insull case
where a Greek court examined the guilt of the relator. [59] The
United States opposed this ruling as inconsistent with its treaty
with Greece. Subsequently, however, it had to add a protocol to
that treaty which in Article I prohibits inquiry into ultimate
guilt or innocence. [60]

(4) - Review and Habeas Corpus. No appeal lies from the decision to commit the relator for surrender, however, the relator
may challenge the lawfulness of the order and the legality of his
detention by means of applying for a writ of habeas corpus. [61]
The Supreme Court as early as 1896 declared:

By repeated decisions of this court it is settled

that a writ of *habeus corpus* cannot perform the

office of a writ of error, and that, in extradition

proceedings, if the committing magistrate has juris-

diction of the subject matter and of the accused,

and the offense charged is within the terms of the

treaty of extradition, and the magistrate, in
arriving at a decision to hold the accused, has
before him competent legal evidence on which to
exercise his judgment as to whether the facts
are sufficient to establish the criminality of
the accused for the purposes of extradition, such
decision cannot be reviewed on *habeas corpus*.
* * * Whether an extraditable crime has been
committed is a question of mixed law and fact, but
chiefly of fact, and the judgment of the magistrate,
rendered in good faith on legal evidence that the
accused is guilty of the act charged, and that it
constitutes an extraditable crime, cannot be reviewed on the weight of the evidence, and is final
for the purposes of the preliminary examination,
unless palpably erroneous in law. [Emphasis added].

Further defining the limits of *habeas corpus*, Mr. Justice Holmes
in Fernandez v. Phillips stated:

* * * That writ as has been said very often cannot
take the place of a writ of error. It is not a
means for rehearing what the magistrate already
has decided. The alleged fugitive from justice
has had his hearing and *habeas corpus* is available
only to inquire whether the magistrate had jurisdiction, whether the offense charged is within
the treaty and, by a somewhat liberal extension,
whether there was any evidence warranting the

finding that there was reasonable ground to believe
the accused guilty. [63]

In <u>Gallina v. Fraser</u>, the Court, seeing the need for guidelines
for *habeas corpus* limits the inquiry into what is required to
surrender the relator, and sees that function as such:

1. that the Commissioner was duly authorized to
   issue the warrant for relator's arrest and
   conduct a hearing pursuant to Section 3184,

2. that the Commissioner had jurisdiction over
   the person of the relator,

3. that the extradition to the demanding nation
   was requested pursuant to a treaty of extradition then in force between the demanding
   nation and the United States,

4. that the offenses of which the relator was
   charged were within the terms of such a
   treaty and not excluded from its operation by
   any exceptions expressed therein,

5. that there was competent, legal evidence of
   the criminality of the relator presented to
   the Commissioner on which to base his decision
   to commit relator, and

6. that the Commissioner committed no error of
   law prejudicial to the rights of the relator,
   then the petition for a writ of *habeas corpus*
   must be dismissed. [64]

A writ of *habeas corpus* can also properly challenge the detention of the relator beyond the two months period and appropriately issue for his or her release as soon as this period elapsed. [65]

(5) - <u>Habeas corpus and the rule of non-inquiry.</u> *Habeas corpus* is not a valid means of inquiry into the treatment the relator is anticipated to receive in the requesting state and this is known as the "rule of non-inquiry."

In <u>Neely v. Henkel</u>, [66] the relator contended that amendments to the extradition statutes were unconstitutional in that the accused was not assured the rights, privileges and immunities guaranteed by the United States Constitution upon surrender to the requesting State. The protections specifically alluded to by Neely were the United States constitutional prohibitions against bills of attainder and *ex post facto* laws and the "due process" clause of the Fourteenth Amendment. The Supreme Court held that:

> These provisions have no relation to the crimes
> committed without the jurisdiction of the United
> States against the laws of a foreign country.
> In connection with the above proposition we are
> reminded of the fact that the appellant is a
> citizen of the United States. But such citizen-
> ship does not . . . entitle him to demand, of right,
> a trial in any other mode than that allowed to its
> own people by the country whose laws he has vio-
> lated and from whose justice he has fled. [67]

The "rule of non-inquiry" is brought into sharp focus in the line of cases dealing with convictions *in absentia*. In such

527

cases, the United States follows the general practice in international law and that convictions *in absentia* are not conclusive of the individual's guilt, but regarded as indictments or formal charges against the individual sought to be extradited. [68] A careful reading of the decisions applying the rule of non-inquiry in such cases reveals that while the courts prefer not to inquire into the treatment to be received by the relator upon surrender or the quality of justice he or she is expected to receive, there is nonetheless in some instances a finding of nonextraditability on "other grounds." Three such cases are particularly revealing.

In the first case, Ex parte Fudera, [69] involving a conviction *in absentia* of a fugitive found guilty and sentenced for the crime of murder by the Italian courts, the District Court, on a writ of *habeas corpus*, chose to pass over the question of the propriety of the *in absentia* criminal prosecution and sentencing. The court instead rejected the Italian government's evidence of guilt on the grounds that it was based on "pure hearsay" and released the relator on the grounds of insufficient evidence.

The second case, Ex parte LaMantia, [70] similarly involved a murder conviction by an Italian tribunal. This time the fugitive alleged that the Sixth Amendment to the United States Constitution had been violated since he had been denied the right of confrontation and cross examination. The federal district court held that "this did not apply to persons extradited for trial under treaties with foreign countries whose laws may be entirely different." [71] However, the fugitive again was ordered released and extradition refused for insufficiency of evidence presented by the Italian government.

In the third case, the District Court in the case of In re Mylonas, [72] consistent with prior authority, ruled that Mylonas' conviction *in absentia* did not preclude extradition, even though the fugitive, convicted of embezzlement, was not represented by counsel, and had no one appear for him. Again, however, the court found grounds upon which it ordered the accused discharged from custody - namely, that under Article V of the 1931 treaty of extradition with Greece, the Greek government's long-delayed effort to take the accused into custody exempted Mylonas from extradition "due to lapse of time or other cause."

Thus, in the three above cases, the courts, though recognizing the limited scope of *habeas corpus* and the rule of non-inquiry, freed the relators and denied extradition upon other grounds. Notwithstanding these cases, United States law and recognized practice allows extradition based on *in absentia* convictions. Two opinions, however, voiced disenchantment with the established rule.

In Argento v. Horn, [73] the United States Court of Appeals for the Sixth Circuit felt constrained to submit to precedent on this question but expressed its doubts about it. Argento, the fugitive, had been convicted *in absentia* for the crime of murder by Italian courts. The murder had occurred in 1921 and the conviction obtained in 1931, but not until the 1950's did the Italian government initiate proceedings for Argento's extradition. The court stated:

The appellant has apparently been a law abiding

529

person during the thirty years that he has been
in this country. To enter a judgment that will
result in sending him back to life imprisonment
in Italy, upon the basis of the record before the
Commissioner, does not sit easily with the members
of a United States court, sensible of the great
Constitutional immunities . . . however, we con-
ceive it our obligation to do so. [74]

The test of the "rule of non-inquiry" will be in cases where
the relator is likely to encounter such treatment in the requesting State that it is likely to be deemed significantly offensive
to the minimum standards of justice, treatment of individuals
and preservation of basic human rights, as perceived by the requested State. [75]

In Gallina v. Fraser, [76] the United States Court of Appeals
for the Second Circuit bowed to precedent and followed the rule
of non-inquiry, but indicated that given a proper case, that
rule might not be rejected. In this case, Gallina had been
tried and convicted *in absentia* by the Italian courts for the
crime of robbery. Gallina petitioned the federal district
court for a writ of *habeas corpus*, contending that if extradited
to Italy, he would be imprisoned without retrial and without an
opportunity to face his accusers or conduct any defense. Judge
Waterman stated:

We have discovered no case authorizing a federal
court in a *habeas corpus* proceeding challenging
extradition from the United States to a foreign

nation, to inquire into the procedures which await

the relator upon extradition . . . <u>Nevertheless, we</u>

<u>confess to some disquiet at this result. We can</u>

<u>imagine situations when the relator, upon extradi-</u>

<u>tion, would be subject to procedures or punishment</u>

<u>too antipathetic to a federal court's sense of</u>

<u>decency as to require re-examination of the prin-</u>

<u>ciple set out above.</u> [77] [Emphasis added].

This was not such a case, however, because Gallina had been

represented by counsel at his trial, and was tried along with

his alleged associates who were present before the Italian court

and were also convicted.

The United States courts have so far refused to undertake a

factual inquiry into the individual's prospective treatment by

the requesting State but in the event Judge Waterman's views

prevail in some future case, the court might refuse to surrender

the fugitive to an oppressive or arbitrary system. In this case

the alternative must be to prosecute the relator in the United

States. In some ways a contrasting position is taken by the Courts

in refusing to examine or review a foreign extradition decision

whereby surrender to the U.S. is secured [<u>McGann v. U.S. Board of</u>

<u>Parole</u>, 488 F. 2d 39 (3d circ. 1973) following <u>Johnson v. Browne</u>

205 U.S. 309 (1907)].

(6) - <u>Executive discretion</u>. The executive level operates at

both ends of the system. Initially, it is the requisition stage

and the diplomatic level and ultimately it reserves itself a

veto right. Prior to 1871, the function of the Secretary of

State upon receiving the magistrate's certification was considered purely ministerial. Once the Secretary had satisfied himself as to the regularity of the proceedings before the magistrate, his duty was to issue the warrant. Thus, in effect, the sole power to commit for extradition or to discharge was vested in the extradition magistrate. [78]

Executive discretion was first exercised in 1871, when the Secretary surrendered only four out of seven persons awaiting extradition to Great Britain on charges of piracy and assault with intent to commit murder. No reason for the refusal to surrender the other three prisoners was given. [79]

The first judicial recognition of this discretion came in In re Stupp, [80] where it was found that federal law endowed the Secretary with the power to refuse the surrender of the relator. Stupp's extradition to Prussia had been certified to the Secretary by the magistrate, although Prussia's jurisdiction over the offense was not territorial but was based on Stupp's Prussian nationality. The Secretary refused to issue the warrant on advice of the Attorney General that the extradition treaty applied only when the alleged offense had occurred within the territory of the requesting country.

The extent of the Secretary's discretion is not clear, for both the statute and the courts are silent as to its limits. Usually, the treaty obligation to extradite is absolute, but the extradition statute might be interpreted to grant the Secretary discretion to refuse surrender by his interpretation of the treaty obligation.

532

Although extradition treaties are considered self-executing, the extradition statute supersedes prior inconsistent treaty provisions under the rule that treaties and statutes are legislation having coordinate authority. [81] Executive discretion should be interpreted as granting the Secretary only limited discretion to differ from the courts in the interpretation of the political aspects of the treaty. The Secretary, whenever he exercised discretion has, however, always based his refusal to surrender upon a determination that the treaty did not require extradition in that given instance. Thus, a formulation of the limits of the Secretary's discretion can be derived only indirectly from executive and judicial construction of treaty obligations. [82]

The Secretary of State, in fact, acts as an authority for *de novo* reconsideration of the precise issues, previously resolved by the extradition magistrate. Thus, this discretionary authority is coextensive with the judiciary as to the same issues and invades the judiciary's province.

The United States extradition treaties generally provide that the requesting State must present to the magistrate sufficient evidence of the accused's guilt as would justify the apprehension and commitment of the accused for trial according to the laws of the requested State and it is to this question that the Secretary's discretionary refusal to surrender is most frequent. Although the extradition magistrate would determine that the evidence is sufficient, the Secretary could reach a contrary conclusion and refuse extradition. The Secretary may also exercise his discretion in the refusal to extradite United States citizens to demanding states that have historically refused to extradite their nationals at the United States' request. The refusal to extradite for crimes deemed by the Secretary to have constituted "political offenses," or the deferment of extradition while the fugitive is undergoing prosecution or is imprisoned within the United States are the most frequently exercised grounds of executive discretion. [83]

Despite its power of review, the Executive (the Secretary of State) has refused surrender of nationals infrequently and only then when discretion to refuse surrender of nationals was expressly granted by the treaty. [84] Three reasons may be suggested for this infrequent exercise of executive discretion. First, as the law of extradition has become more highly developed, extradition magistrates have been more effective in eliminating those cases that do not give rise to an obligation to surrender. Second, the courts, examining such extradition proceedings on writs of *habeas corpus* are asserting a greater supervisory role, despite their earlier protestations to the contrary. Third, the State Department wishes to defer to the requests of the other nations in an effort to maintain good foreign relations and conform to an orderly process of preservation of minimum world order.

(7) - <u>Procedure for requests by the United States</u>. The Department of State in May, 1969, issued a "Memorandum relative to applications for the extradition from foreign countries of fugitives from justice" [85] (hereinafter referred to as "Memorandum"). This document is the first revision of such State Department guidelines since a similar memorandum was issued in July, 1949.

534

The Memorandum outlines the requirements set forth by the Department of State (the proper agency empowered to act on behalf of the United States government in extradition matters) whenever the Justice Department of the United States, the governors of the states and territories of the Union seeking the extradition of a person in a foreign country.

Every requisition application must contain specific statements and allegations which must meet a test analogous to the sufficiency of a complaint and must be accompanied by certain specified documents. There is, however, no statement in the Memorandum indicating whether an applicant's failure to comply with the requirements set forth in the document would result in the denial of the application. For that matter, there is no indication as to whether these requirements are mandatory or recommendatory. However, since the Department of State has discretionary power in accepting or rejecting a requisition application, the conclusion is that the requirements are mandatory unless waived by the Department of State.

The machinery of extradition is set in motion when the Secretary of State presents a formal request to another government for the surrender of a person sought by the United States. This means in fact that the applicant must satisfy the Department's requirements before any action will be taken. To that extent, no applicant will see his application for requisition granted and acted upon until it has in fact satisfied the moving authority. An applicant does not possess the right to compel the Department of State to grant its application. The only remedy in case the Secretary of State fails to request extradition would be for an applicant to secure a writ of <u>mandamus</u>. The federal judiciary would be empowered to issue such a writ, but in all probability would decline to do so on the grounds that it is a question of "foreign affair." Federal courts will abstain from substituting their judgment to a decision which, in addition to having political ramifications, is one which under the constitution is within the powers of the Executive (President and his delegated authority within the Executive). The judiciary, especially in matters of foreign affairs involving execution of treaties, is very careful not to transcend the constitutional limits of separation of power.

The Memorandum has no binding effect on the Department of State which has the power to revoke, amend or substitute it at its discretion. The question arises, however, as to its binding effect when, in reliance upon it and in good faith, an applicant goes through the trouble and expenses of complying with it and finds its application blocked or rejected because the Department seeks new, different or additional documents or forms. It is doubtful whether an administrative recourse is available since the question may still be deemed one of foreign policy. However, since the document regulates the internal practice of the United States in relation to its internal political subdivisions, it is not within the purview of international law but solely a municipal law question.

On March 19, 1970, the President issued an Executive Order (11517) "providing for the issuance and signature by the Secretary of State of Warrants appointing agents to return fugitives from justice extradited to the United States." [86] The President, by

virtue of his own constitutional authority and by the authority

of Section 301, Title 3, United States Code, designated the

Secretary of State to issue and sign all warrants appointing

receiving agents, thereby relieving his office from that function.

This is the only amendment so far to the procedures set forth by

the Memorandum.

Chapter VII

Footnotes

1. See discussion of United States procedure, *infra* Section 3.

2. 33 & 34 Vict. c. 52, ss. 2, 5 (1870); <u>Regina v. Wilson</u> (1877) 3 Q.B.D. 42.

3. Law of March 10, 1927, Art. 1.

4. In the United States, the Federal Rules of Criminal Procedure on admissibility of evidence are inapplicable to extradition proceedings; nor do depositions need to conform to the ordinary rules of admissibility; <u>United States ex rel. Karadzole v. Artukovic</u>, 170 F. Supp. 383 (S.D. Calif. 1959). See also <u>re Johnstone and Shane</u>, 18 C.L.R. (2d) 102 (1959) where a Canadian court declared that all the technical rules of our criminal procedure are not to be imported into extradition matters. The European Convention on Extradition, 24 <u>European Treaty Series</u> in Article 22, permits one application of the requested state relating to procedural matters and provisional arrest except insofar as the treaty may provide otherwise.

5. <u>In re Diaz</u>, 22 <u>I.L.R.</u> 517 (1954) (Venezuela); <u>in re Lobo</u>, 18 <u>I.L.R.</u> 277 (1949) (Brazil); <u>re Alvarez</u>, 20 <u>I.L.R.</u> 390 (1960) (Chile).

6. <u>Miner v. Atlass</u>, 363 U.S. 641, 650 (1960).

7. 1 Moore, <u>Extradition</u>, p. 556-561 (1891).

8. 1 Moore, <u>Extradition</u>, p. 90 (1891).

9. I Blackstone, <u>Commentaries</u>, 366; Chitty, <u>Pleas of the Crown</u>, 49 (1820); <u>East India Company v. Campbell</u>, I Ves Snr. 246

(1749); Mure v. Kaye, 4 Taunt. 34 (1811).

10. Opinion of the Law Officers of the Crown, October 4, 1815,
    II McNair, International Law Opinions, 44 (1956).

11. 1 Malloy Treaties 650. See also In the Matter of Metzger,
    5 How. 176 (1857).

12. In re Rozzoni, 24 I.L.R. 506 (1957) (Belgium).

13. 6 & 7 Vict. cc. 75, 76. See now 33 & 34 Vict. c. 52.

14. Act of August 12, 1848. See also 1 Moore, Extradition,
    p. 551-556 (1891) and in re Strupp, 12 Blatchford 501 (1875).

15. Lemontey, Du role de L'autorite Judiciaire dans la procedure
    d'extradition passive (1966).

16. Case of Stagl, The Times (London) June 21, 1967, p.4.

17. Law of December 23, 1929, Harvard Draft on Extradition, 29
    A.J.I.L. Supp. (1935).

18. Constitution of the Federal Republic of Germany, 1949, Art. 16
    (2); Extradition (Yugoslav Refugee in Germany) Case 28 I.L.R.
    347 (1959).

19. 187 U.S. 455, 462-463.

20. See discussion infra, section 3.2(3).

21. In re Wyrobnik, 379 I.L.R. 330 (No. 86) (1952).

22. Shearer, Extradition in International Law, p. 157-58 (1971).

23. In 18 U.S.C. §3184 (1968) (Fugitives from foreign country to
    the United States) it is stated that:
    Whenever there is a treaty or convention for extra-
    dition between the United States and any foreign
    government, any justice or judge of the United States
    or any magistrate authorized so to do by a court of

539

the United States, or any judge of a court of
record of general jurisdiction of any state, may,
upon complaint made under oath, charging any person
found within his jurisdiction with having committed
within the jurisdiction of any such foreign government any of the crimes provided for by such treaty
or convention issue his warrant for the apprehension of the person so charged that he may be
brought before such justice, judge or magistrate
to the end that the evidence of criminality may
be heard and considered. If, on such hearing,
he deems the evidence sufficient to sustain the
charge under the provisions of the proper treaty
or convention, he shall certify the same together
with a copy of all the testimony taken before
him to the Secretary of State that a warrant may
issue upon the requisition of the proper authorities
or such foreign government for the surrender of
such person, according to the stipulations of the
treaty or convention; and he shall issue his
warrant for the commitment of the person so
charged to the proper jail there to remain until
such surrender shall be made.

See also, Valentine v. United States ex rel. Neidecker, 229
U.S. 5 (1936); United States v. Rauscher, 119 U.S. 407 (1886);
4 Hackworth, Digest 305 (1944).

24. 18 U.S.C. (1968) §3181 et seq., agent to receive fugitive,

§3182; authority over offenders, §3193; extraterritorial jurisdiction of United States, §3188; protection of accused, §3190; Secretary of State, surrender of fugitive to foreign government, §3186; transportation, §3194; application of rules, Rule (54(b)); arrest, §3190; extraterritorial jurisdiction, §3042, 3183; Provisional arrest and detention, §3187; foreign countries, §3184; provisional arrest and detention, extraterritorial jurisdiction, §3187; certificates and certification; diplomatic officer, §3190; evidence, §3190; extraterritorial jurisdiction of United States, §3183; fees and costs, §3195; foreign countries, §3184; indictment, etc., §3182; state or territory to state, district or territory, §§3182, 3183; witness fees and costs, §3195; commissioner, fees and costs, §3195; continuance of law in force, §3181; costs, payment, §3195; country under control of the United States, §3185; discharge of prisoner committed, §3188; escape, retaking accused, §3186; evidence, §3190; countries under control of United States, §3185; expenses, §3195; extraterritorial jurisdiction of United States, provisional arrest and detention, §3187; foreign countries, §3184; continuance of law, §3181; country under control of United States, §3185; payment of fees and costs, §3195; Secretary of State, surrender of fugitives, §§3185, 3186; hearing, §3189 et seq.; witnesses for indigent fugitives, §3191; indictment, state or territory to state, district or territories, §3132; indigent fugitives, witnesses, §3191; juvenile offenders, §5001; orders of court, discharge or person committee, §3188; payment of fees and costs, §3195; place of hearing, §3189; protection of accused, §3192; provisional arrest and detention within extraterritorial jurisdiction, §3187; resistance to extradition agent, §1502; retaking accused, escape, §3186; Secretary of State; fees and costs certified to, §3195; foreign country under control of United States, order of secretary, §3185; surrender of fugitives, agent of foreign country, §3186; time of commitment pending extradition, §3188, transportation of accused, §3192; extraterritorial jurisdiction of United States, §3183; receiving agent, §§3193, 3194; venue, hearing, §3189; witnesses, fees and costs, §3195; and indigent fugitives, §3191.

25. 18 U.S.C. §3184 (1968).

26. Grin v. Shine, 187 U.S. 181 (1920).

27. Discussed, *infra*, notes 3.3(3) and corresponding text.

28. See executive discretion, *infra*, 3.3(6).

29. 6 Whiteman, Digest 906 (1968).

30. 18 U.S.C. §3184 (1968).

31. Ex parte Schorer, 197 F. 67 (S.D. Wis. 1912).

32. Collins v. Loisel, 262 U.S. 926, (1923); cf. in re Lobo (1949) Ann. Dig. 277 (No. 91) Brazilian Supreme Court.

33. Ex parte Schorer, *supra*, note 9 and 6 Whiteman, Digest 905 (1968).

34. See in re Normano, 7 F. Supp. 329 (D. Mass. 1934); in re Dawson, 101 Fed. 253 (D.C.N.Y. 1900); on when commitment starts see United States v. Chan Kain-Shu 477 F. 2d 333 (5th cir. 1973).

Charlton v. Kelly, 229 U.S. 447 (1913).

35. See, e.g., Treaty with Great Britain on Extradition, Dec.
    22, 1931, and Art. X, 47 Stat. 2122, 2125 (1932), T. S.
    No. 849 (effective Aug. 9, 1932), which provides:
    If the individual claimed by one of the High Con-
    tracting Parties in pursuance of the present Treaty
    should be also claimed by one or several other
    powers on account of other crimes or offenses
    committed within their respective jurisdictions,
    his extradition shall be granted to the power
    whose claim is earliest in date, unless such
    claim is waived.

36. See, e.g., Pan American Convention, Art. 7, 49 Stat. at
    3115, T.S. No. 882, 165 L.N.T.S. at 53 which reads:
    When the extradition of a person is sought by
    several states for the same offense, preference
    will be given to the state in whose territory
    said offense was committed. If he is sought for
    several offenses, preference will be given to the
    state within whose bounds shall have been committed
    the offense which has the greatest penalty according
    to the law of the surrendering state.
    If the case is one of different acts which the
    state from which extradition is sought esteems
    of equal gravity, the preference will be deter-
    mined by the priority of the request.

37. 4 Hackworth, _Digest_ 93 (1944), and 6 Whiteman, _Digest_ 916

(1968). See also Ex parte Van Goven, 28 F. Case 1020 (No.

16, 858) (c.c.d. Minn. 1876); Grin v. Shine, *supra*, note 26;

in re Schlippenbach, 169 F. 783 (S.D.N.Y. 1908); in re Lo

Dolce 106 F. Supp. 455 (S.D.N.Y. 1952).

38. 92 F. 2d 605 (1938), cert. denied, 303 U.S. 635 (1938).

39. Id. at 605.

40. In Valentine v. United States ex rel. Neidecker, 299 U.S. 5
(1936) at 8-9, the Supreme Court held:
It cannot be doubted that the power to provide for

extradition is a national power; it pertains to the

national government and not to the states . . .

But, albeit a national power, it is not confided to

the executive in the absence of treaty or legislative

provision. At the very beginning, Mr. Jefferson, as

Secretary of State, advised the President: The laws

of the United States, like those of England, receive

every fugitive, and no authority has been given to

their Executives to deliver them up. As stated by

John Bassett Moore in his treatise on extradition -

summarizing the precedents - the general opinion

has been, and practice has been in accordance

with it, that in the absence of a conventional

or legislative provision, there is no authority

vested in any department of the government to

seize a fugitive criminal and surrender him to a

foreign power. Counsel for the petitioners do

not challenge the soundness of this general opinion

544

and practice. It rests upon the fundamental con-

sideration that the Constitution creates no executive

prerogative to dispose of the liberty of the indiv-

idual. Proceedings against him must be authorized

by law . . .

See also Ex parte Charlton, 185 F. 880 (C.C.N.J. 1911),

aff'd 229 U.S. 447 (1911).

41. A judge of a United States District Court has jurisdiction

to hear extradition proceedings under 18 U.S.C. §3184 (1964).

Bernstein v. Gross, 58 F. 2d 154 (5th Cir. 1932). A judge

of a state court has jurisdiction under 18 U.S.C. §3184

(1964) even though the accused is a federal official, in re

Keene's Extradition, 6 F. Supp. 308 (S.D. Tex. 1934). A

United States Commissioner has jurisdiction when authorized

by a United States District Court and the accused is within

the commissioner's district. Vaccaro v. Collier, 38 F. 2d

862 (D. Md. 1930).

42. 18 U.S.C. §3184 (1968).

43. Bassiouni, Criminal Law and Its Processes, 448-450 (1969).

44. In the case of in re Wise, 168 F. Supp. 366, 369 (S.D. Tex.

1967), a district court held that the complaint must be

sufficient to inform the accused of the charges against

him. The court stated:

Despite intimations to the contrary in some of the

cases, a complaint seeking the issuance of a warrant

for extradition to a foreign country must allege

facts sufficient to apprise the defendant of the

nature of the charge against him and to show that
an extraditable offense has been committed. While
it is not necessary to charge the offense with the
particularity of an indictment, it should be sufficiently explicit to inform the accused of the
nature of the charge. This principle is best set
out in Ex parte Sternaman . . . It is implicit in
all of the cases announcing the rule that the
complaint need not meet the requirements of an
indictment. P. 369.

The complainant should set forth clearly and
briefly the offense charged. It need not be
drawn with the formal precision of an indictment.
If it be sufficiently explicit to inform the
accused person of the precise nature of the
charge against him it is sufficient. The extreme
technicality with which these proceedings were
formerly conducted has given place to a more
liberal practice, the object being to reach a
correct decision upon the main question -- is
there reasonable cause to believe that a crime
has been committed? The complaint may, in some
instances, be upon information and belief. The
exigencies may be such that the criminal may
escape punishment unless he is promptly appre-
hended by the representatives of the country
whose law he has violated. From the very nature

of the case it may often happen that such representative can have no personal knowledge of the
crime. If the offense be one of the treaty crimes
and if it be stated clearly and explicitly so that
the accused knows exactly what the charge is, the
complaint is sufficient to authorize the commissioner
to act . . . P. 596.

45. United States v. Rausher, *supra*, note 23; Terlinden v. Ames,
184 U.S. 270 (1902); Argento v. Horn, 241 F. 2d 158 (6th
Cir. 1957); cert. denied 355 U.S. 318; rehearing denied
355 U.S. 385 (1957) and Chapter I.

46. Collins v. Loisell, *supra*, note 32; see also Chapter IV.

47. United States v. Stockinger, 269 F. 2d 681 (2nd Cir. 1959)
and Chapter IV for the rule on double criminality; see,
however, Factor v. Laubenheimer, 290 U.S. 276 (1933).

48. Any foreign documents presented either to the executive or
judicial branch in an extradition proceeding must be authenticated by the principal diplomatic or consular officer
of the United States in the requesting state. This
officer must certify that the documents are entitled to be
received for similar purposes, i.e., as evidence of criminality, see in re Cortes, 136 U.S. 330, 336 (1890), in the
requesting state. See 18 U.S.C. §3190 (1964).

49. In Desmond v. Eggers, 18 F. 2d 503 (9th Cir. 1927), the
Court of Appeals said:
The complaint filed before the judge or committing
magistrate in this country was upon information and

belief, but it set forth the source of information,
by referring to cert n affidavits and documents
which were later received in evidence upon the
hearing. Assuming for the present that such affidavits were properly authenticated, the sufficiency
of the complaint is amply supported by authority . . .
P. 504.

See also Rice v. Ames, 180 U.S. 371, 375-76 (1901);
Glucksman v. Henkel, 221 U.S. 508, 514 (1901). But cf. in
United States ex rel. McNamara v. Henkel, 46 F. 2d 84
(S.D.N.Y. 1912), it was held that a complaint based on
information and belief made pursuant to telegraphic request
without supporting documents was sufficient, provided the
request was made by a person whom the United States authorities were justified in believing.

One of the most frequent objections to an extradition complaint based on information and belief is that the information, the certifications, the depositions, etc., are all
hearsay. However, such testimony is admissible in the
extradition hearing. In Argento v. Horn, *supra*, 241 F. 2d
258 (6th Cir. 1957) at 263, the court held that:

The sworn statements were taken ex parte in Italy
without the knowledge of the appellant or his
counsel. They were obviously hearsay, and clearly
would have been inadmissible in a criminal trial in
the United States. [However], that is not the test.
The only question to be answered under the statute

is whether the statements were "properly and legally authenticated so as to entitle them to be received for similar purposes by the tribunals" of Italy . . . It was the unambiguous testimony of an expert in Italian law that they were.

50. _In re Farez_, 8 F. Cas. 1001, 1005 (No. 4,644) (C.C.S.D.N.Y. 1869), held that if the warrant was issued by a commissioner, his authority to do so had to appear on the warrant; _in re Henrich_, 11 F. Cas. 1143, 1146 (No. 6,369)(C.C.S.D.N.Y. 1867). _Pettit v. Walshe_, 194 U.S. 205 (1904): The appellee, Walshe, was arrested in Indiana by a United States marshal acting under the authority of a warrant issued by a commissioner in New York City. The warrant directed the marshal to return the accused to the New York commissioner to hear evidence of criminality. Petitioner challenged the validity of the requirement that the marshal return him to a New York commissioner. In affirming the grant of _habeas corpus_, the Supreme Court ruled that the petitioner had to be brought before the nearest authorized judicial officer in the place where he was found, i.e., Indiana. The Court stated that:

. . . T he alleged criminal shall be arrested and delivered up only upon such evidence of criminality as, according to the laws of the place where the fugitive person so charged is found, would justify his apprehension and commitment for trial, if the crime or offense had been there committed. As applied to the present case, that stipulation means

that the accused, Walshe, could not be extradited
under the treaties in question, except upon such
evidence of criminality as, under the laws of the
state of Indiana -- the place in which he was
found -- would justify his apprehension and commitment for trial, if the crime alleged had been there
committed . . . P. 217

[I]t is made the duty of a marshal arresting a
person charged with any crime or offense to take
him before the nearest Circuit Commissioner or
the nearest judicial officer, having jurisdiction
for a hearing, commitment or taking bail for trial
in cases of extradition. P. 219

Jimenez v. Aristeguieta, 311 F. 2d 547, 553 (5th Cir. 1952),
the court held that the warrant was returnable before any
justice, judge or magistrate authorized to hear evidence of
criminality in extradition cases under 18 U.S.C. §3184 (1964).

51. In re Gannon, 27 F. 2d 362, 363 (E.D. Pa. 1928); the court
held that the right to bail in extradition proceedings is
purely statutory and since the statutes fail to expressly
give this right, it does not exist as a right of the prisoner.
The district court in in re Mitchell, 171 F. 289 (S.D.N.Y.
1909), in admitting the petitioner to bail said:

In several cases in this district commissioners
and judges have issued bail under similar circumstances, and while I quite agree with the learned
counsel for his Majesty's government that the

550

right is a dangerous one, and ought to be exercised with great circumspection, it seems to me that the hardship here upon the imprisoned person is so great as to make peremptory some kind of enlargement at the present time, for the purpose only of free consultation in the conduct of the civil suit upon which his whole fortune depends. These special circumstances alone move me to allow him to bail, and his enlargement is to be limited strictly to the period of that suit . . . I am also moved to this disposition from the fact that he has long known of these proposed proceedings and has made no effort to avoid them or to escape. P. 290.

52. 6 Whiteman, Digest, p. 954 (1968).

53. 127 U.S. 457, 462, 463 (1887).

54. 2 21 U.S. 508 (1910); see also Cleugh v. Strakosch, 109 F. 2d 333-335 (9th Cir. 1940); and United States ex rel. Argento v. Jacobs, 176 F. Supp. 877 (M.D. Ohio E.D. 1959), wherein the court held:
Recognizing fully the right of the Republic of Italy, under the treaty, to extradite its subjects to make them answer to a criminal charge, it is something else where the extradition, in effect, seeks to execute on an in absentia conviction. In such a case the Court must scrutinize the evidence carefully to determine at least a reasonable probability

that the petitioner was guilty of the crime. P. 883.
In my judgment, there was not sufficient evidence
to warrant a reasonable belief that petitioner was
guilty of the crime of murder, and the Commissioner's
finding to the contrary is not supported by the
evidence. P. 879.

55. 259 U.S. 309, 316-317 (1921).

56. Application for the extradition of D'Amico, 185 F. Supp. 925,
930-931 (S.D.N.Y. 1960), appeal dismissed, U.S. ex rel.
D'Amico v. Bishopp, 286 F. 320 (2d Cir. 1961).

57. 311 F. 2d 547, 556 (1962); see also, Collins v. Loisel,
supra, note 32 and Charlton v. Kelly, 229 U.S. 447 (1913).

58. 6 Whiteman, Digest, 998-999 (1968); see also Chapter V; on
this question the United States does not differ from the
practice of almost all other countries, see e.g., in re
Janssens, (1950) Ann. Dig. 266 (No. 84). In seeking to prevent his extradition from Venezuela to Belgium where he stood
convicted of "abuse of confidence" for having converted certain sums entrusted to him, Frederick J. J. A. Janssens contends that his conviction had been improper since the alleged
abuse of confidence was a civil matter which had been settled
by gradual payment. The Supreme Court of Venezuela held
that extradition should be granted stating:"It is settled
law in this Court that the issues raised by the interested
party on the merits are bey ond its powers to decide since
final judgment on these matters should properly be rendered
by the courts of the demanding country."

552

The United States holds that in an extradition proceeding evidence in defense of the charge for which the fugitive's surrender is sought is not admissible, even if the evidence can be characterized as an affirmative defense, such as justification in re Ezeta, 62 Fed. 972, 986 (N.D. Cal., 1896), insanity, Charlton v. Kelly, 229 U.S. 447 (1913); the defense of insanity was also rejected by the Supreme Federal Tribunal of Brazil, in re Santucci Lazaro (1929-1930) Ann. Dig. 288 (No. 184); or alibi, Desmond v. Eggers, 18 F. 2d 503, 506 (C. A. 9, 1927), motion for stay of execution denied, 274 U.S. 722 (1927); in re Wadge, 15 Fed. 864 (S.D.N.Y., 1883), aff'd, 16 Fed. 332 (C.C.S.D.N.Y., 1883) or amounts only to a denial of the demanding government's charges through evidence contradicting or impugning its witnesses. See Desmond v. Eggers, supra; in re Ezeta, supra. Under Collins v. Loisel, 259 U.S. 309 (1922), the leading Supreme Court case on the subject, the defendant is permitted to explain, through his testimony and that of others, any ambiguities there may be in the evidence offered by the demanding government. See Application of D'Amico, 135 F. Supp. 925, 930 (S.D. N.Y., 1960), appeal dismissed sub nom. United States ex rel. D'Amico v. Bishopp, 286 F. 2d 320 (C.A. 2, 1961). The defense of superior orders was rejected in in re Gonzalez, 217 F. Supp. 717 (S.D.N.Y., 1963);

The "Act of State" defense was rejected in <u>Jimenez v.</u>
<u>Artisteguita</u>, 311 F. 2d 547 (5th Cir. 1952).

59. Hyde, "The Extradition Case of Samuel Insull," 28 <u>A.J.I.L.</u>
307 (1934).

60. 31 Stat. 357 (1967).

61. Bassiouni, *supra*, note 43, p. 512-518.

62. <u>Ornelas v. Ruiz</u>, 161 U.S. 502, 589 (1896); see also <u>Wright v.</u>
<u>Henkel</u>, 190 U.S. 40 (1903).

The writ of *habeas corpus* cannot perform the office
of a writ of error, but the court issuing the writ
may inquire into the jurisdiction of the committing
magistrate in extradition proceedings, <u>Ornelas v. Ruiz</u>,
181 U.S. 502; <u>Terlinden v. Ames</u>, 184 U.S. 270; and it
was on the ground of want of jurisdiction that the
writ was applied for in this instance before the
commissioner had entered upon the examination; as
also on the ground that petitioner should have been
admitted to bail.

The contention is that the complaint and warrant
did not charge an extraditable offense within the
meaning of the extradition treaties between the
United States and the United Kingdom of Great
Britain and Ireland, because the offense was not
criminal at common law, or by acts of Congress, or
by the preponderance of the statutes of the states.
Treaties must receive a fair interpretation according
to the intention of the contracting parties and so

554

as to carry out their manifest purpose. The
ordinary technicalities of criminal proceedings
are applicable to proceedings in extradition only
to a limited extent. Grin v. Shine, 187 U.S. 181;
Tucker v. Alexandroff, 183 U.S. 424. P. 57.

63. 268 U.S. 311, 312 (1925).

64. Gallina v. Fraser, 177 F. Supp. 856, 860 (D. Conn. 1959).
Affirmed, 278 F. 2d 77 (2d Cir. 1960), cert. denied, 364
U.S. 851 (1960); Application for the extradition of
Vito D'Amico, 185 F. Supp. 925, (S.D.N.Y., 1960); appeal
dismissed, U.S. ex rel. D'Amico v. Bishopp, 286 F. 2d 320
(2d Cir. 1961); the District Court stated:
Habeas corpus in extradition proceedings is limited
in scope. It does not afford a rehearing of what
the Commissioner has already decided. The alleged
fugitive has had his hearing before the Commissioner
and habeas corpus is available only to inquire
whether the magistrate had jurisdiction whether
the offense charged is within the treaty, and by
a somewhat liberal extension, whether there was
any evidence warranting the finding that there
was reasonable ground to believe the accused
guilty. Fernandez v. Phillips, 268 U.S. 311,
312, 45 S. Ct. 541, 542, 69 L. Ed. 970. See
also, Benson v. McMahon, 127 U.S. 457, 8 S. Ct.
1240, 32 L. Ed. 234; re Luis Oteiza v. Cortes,
136 U.S. 330, 10 S. Ct. 1031, 34 L. Ed. 464,

Bryant v. United States, 167 U.S. 104, 105, 17

S. Ct. 744, 42 L. Ed. 94; Elias v. Ramirez, 215

U.S. 398, 406, 30 S. Ct. 131, 54 L. Ed. 253. P. 927.

The Court of Appeals affirmed the action of the

District Court saying "habeas corpus is not a rigid

and inflexible proceeding in which the court must

either order release of the prisoner outright or

direct his return to custody." The Court concluded:

. . . the district court, after a careful

study of the record, has determined that an

essential finding has not been made and that

the case should be remanded to the Commissioner

to supply the defect. Such action is entirely

within the power given the court by 28 U.S.C.

§2243, and we think Collins v. Miller, . . .

252 U.S. 364, 40 S. Ct. 347, 64 L. Ed. 616,

requires us to hold such orders nonappealable.

(994-997).

65. In re Factor's extradition, 75 F. 2d 10 (1934).

66. 180 U.S. 109 (1901).

67. Id. at 122-123.

68. See Chapter VI.

69. 162 Fed. 591 (C.C.S.D.N.Y., 1908).

70. 206 Fed. 330 (D.C.S.D.N.Y., 1918).

71. Id. at 332.

72. 187 F. Supp. 716 (N.D. Ala. 1960).

73. 241 F. 2d 258 (6th Cir. 1957).

74. Id. at 263-64.

75. See Chapter VI on Defenses.

76. 278 F. 2d 77 (2d Cir. 1960).

77. Id. at 78, 79.

78. 1 Moore, Extradition, §361 (1891).

79. Id. 363.

80. 23 Fed. 281 (C.C.S.D.N.Y., 1873).

81. Executive Discretion in Extradition, *supra*, note 76 at 1313, 1316 (1962).

82. Id. at 1319-1321.

83. Id. and 1 Moore, Extradition, §366 (1891).

84. *Supra*, note 59 at 1328.

85. For text, see 63 A.J.I.L. 799 (1969).

86. For text, see 64 A.J.I.L. 650 (1970).

Chapter VIII

A Policy-Oriented Framework for Inquiry into the Processes
and Values of Extradition

1. The Individual in International Law and in the Scheme of
   Extradition

Since World War II, the peoples of the world have become, more
than ever, in the history of Humankind, conscious of the need to
insure their collective safety and survival.

The extraordinary technological advancements in mass communi-
cations produced popular attitudinal changes and developed world
public opinion into an instrument of coercion and a sanctioning
process in the world social process.

It takes one seventh of a second for the mass media communication to flash around the globe some item of information which,
from a local issue, may suddenly acquire a world-wide significance. One can hardly forget the almost instantaneous pictures
sent from the moon which were received almost everywhere in the
world by Satellite communication. The significance of these
pictures was not as much for what was seen of the moon's surface,
but what was seen of the earth from outerspace. Indeed, it was
never clearer to mankind that this is a small world. The impact
of the attitudinal change in the world community's perception of
its interrelationship is difficult to assess. One reason is
that conflicts between nation-states, from their origin to their

outcome, have historically been institutionalized. They have always been affairs of state and found their rationalization in claims of sovereignty, national interest, and interests of the national security, while the interests of the individual, who always wound up as *Chair-a-Cannon*, had little or no impact on the decision-making process which translates national goals and values into specific policy. [1] The awareness amongst peoples of the world that the individual is the ultimate bearer of the consequences of state action created the need for reappraising the framework and structures of international law. But to actuate this perception into world order strategy requires first a re-evaluation of values underlying existing world order strategy. [2] To Professor McDougal, that strategy is: the obtaining in particular situations and in the aggregate flow of situations of outcome of a higher degree of conformity with the security goals of preservations, deterrence, restoration, rehabilitation and reconstruction [3] (of all societies comprising the world community). A corollary to that approach is the implicit, if not explicit, recognition that the individual is a subject of international law. [4] Its inarticulated premise, however, is that modern international law is the common law of mankind wherein the individual is a participant in its processes because he is the ultimate party at interest. [5]

While theoretically recognizing the importance of the individual, international law is yet unable to fit him in the constitutive framework of that discipline which was historically developed out of the need to regulate institutional and not

559

interpersonal relationships. The realization that all deeds which threaten the peace and security of mankind and which are violative of world public order are committed by individuals whether immediately or ultimately, challenges the assumption that only nation-states are and should exclusively be the subjects of international law.

The difficulty of fitting the individual in the framework of a discipline (international law) which rejects him *a priori* has been apparent in the search for a definition of international law. In fact, even the descriptive label is unsettled. As stated by this writer: "International law, as a body of law, has changed rapidly with the increased needs of mankind to strengthen its ties in search of objectives highlighting commonality of purpose. Significantly also, the label has changed: *Jus Gentium, Droit des gens, Volkrrecht,* Transnational Law, World Law and Common Law of Mankind; and if I may be permitted the license of my own, universal intersocial public order." [6]

The emergence of the individual in the sphere of international law has been attributed primarily to a humanitarian concern which was described by Judge Jessup as follows:

> The international society has come more slowly
> to recognize that what is involved is really a con-
> cern for the individual who has been the victim of
> barbarous treatment. In our traditional international
> system of inter-state relationships, we were impelled
> to confine ourselves largely to the legal issue that

560

the state was injured through the injury inflicted

upon its citizen. But this was a procedural, not

a substantive problem. [7]

This assertion is only partially true, because the recognition

given the individual equally sprung out of the world community's

desire to assess international responsibility. As between

humanitarian concern and the desire to impose individual respon-

sibility, the latter has probably been the most significant

factor which brought about the re-appraisal of the entire frame-

work of the discipline. Just as individuals can be the direct

beneficiaries of rights created by a nation-state or by multi-

lateral conventions, [8] they are also the subjects of direct

obligations before the international community. [9] Consequently,

the significance of the recognition of the individual's place in

the framework of international law should, however, be *intrinsic*

and not derivative. That framework will depend on perceived

goals of minimum world order and its methodology.

However, theories on world public order, world order, and

world peace through law differ, [10] even though to this writer,

only as to methodology and not as to goals. Minimum world order

methodology rests on three factors, namely:

1- A process of identification of factors bearing

   upon the internal decision-making process of a

   given nation-state;

2- Appraisal of the interaction between national

   decision-making processes;

3- The extent to which values affect those pro-

cesses can be perceived, appraised and their
impact on outcomes measured. Thus, this
process is intended to channel a conflict-
creating situation through an analytical
framework designed to prevent a disruptive
result which would have otherwise occurred.

The analytical methodology is the means for acquiring standards
of foreseeability needed to evaluate and balance those factors
and circumstances which lead to potential conflict. Ideological
differences are not at issue in this approach; instead situations which are likely to lead to conflict collision courses are
channelled to alternative tracks to avoid threats to minimum
world order. Thus, efforts should be directed toward the
development of such structures and institutions which are likely
to identify conflict creating issues and place them within a conflict resolution context offering alternatives to the pitting of
opposing decision-making processes against each other.

The acceptance of minimum world order factors gives rise to
the opportunity to develop a juridically oriented regulating
framework for world relations regardless of ideological or
political distinctions. As a consequence of this approach, it is
opportune to reappraise the purposes and structures of extradition in the present state of international law.

Extradition is still regarded, with some variations in application but not in substance, as an institutional practice.
States are the subjects of its regulation, while individuals are
the objects of its outcome. The individual who is contemplated

562

by extradition proceedings is not the primary party contemplated by extradition law and practice. Restrictions, limitations, or defenses which exist under extradition law are not, with a few exceptions, primarily designed for the benefit of the individual, instead they are designed to inure to the benefit of the states involved.[11] While it is sustainable to argue that the individual is the beneficiary of certain protections such as the political offense exception, the fact that such a claim is limited only to the right to raise the issue and not a particular outcome is indicative of the real center of interest.[12] The requested state has the right to accept or reject the relator's contention that the alleged conduct falls within the scope of the defense and does so in accordance with its own self-serving standards.[13]

To further emphasize the interstate nature of the concept of extradition, nowhere in extradition law and practice can the individual--the object of the proceedings--compel the requesting or requested state to adhere to internationally recognized principles of extradition law if either state wishes not to apply them or to circumvent them.[14] Many states, in fact, deny that extradition and asylum are subject matters which fall within customary international law and, therefore, that no international obligation exists other than specific duties created by treaty or accepted through reciprocal practice.[15] There is, however, no direct right conferred upon the individual by international extradition law which he can claim, let alone enforce, against either of the respective states involved. The

individual is always dependent upon the good faith and benevolence of the states. [16] The application and enforcement of
individual rights is considered a matter of municipal law even
though it might involve certain human rights recognized and proclaimed by the world community. [17] This problem arises from the
fact that the individual is still not considered a full-fledged
subject of international law, and hence, no practical means for
the implementation of human rights have been developed which
would allow individual redress of wrongs against a given state
which is still shielded by the doctrine of state sovereignty. [18]
Even the failure of a given state to abide by its treaty or
other legal obligations will not create a right under international law which the individual can raise against that state,
other than whenever the municipal law of that state allows him
such a right. A mutual or consentual failure by the respective
states engaged in the extradition proceedings to abide by a
treaty obligation designed to inure to the relator's benefit
does not constitute a breach of international law or of a specific treaty provision, since the individual although bearing
the consequences is not a party to the treaty. However, lack
of fairness or good faith by the parties in the application of
rights which they have stipulated in favor of third parties, or
conceded to individuals as parties beneficiary under the treaty,
may be said to violate the principle of *Ex Acquo et Bono*. [18]
Treaty rights created by the respective nation-states which
contain a stipulation for the benefit of the individual, are, to
that extent, rights running in favor of a third party, even

564

though "the individual" is neither a party to the treaty nor a fully recognized subject of international law. [19]   A claim could be asserted that a state's failure to grant the relator those rights created for his benefit by treaty, or by general principles of international law regarding extradition, create implications of illegality, in addition to which in certain cases a moral stigma would attach to that action. [20]   To avoid possible loss of political face by the given state which could be embarrassingly used by other states (whether they are parties to the proceedings or not) most rights conferred upon or granted the individual in most extradition treaties are couched in terms which are vague and indefinite so as to insure against the certainty of their claim and assertion. This is particularly true in the case of provisions relating to the political offense exception. [21]

The development of the human rights program is likely to have a significant effect on the lingering of classicists who are unwilling to adhere to such a transformation of a discipline whose main thrust has been conservative. When the recognition of human rights will be followed by their implementation, the participant states in the process of extradition will find their traditional unchallenged sovereign prerogatives withering away. But this development, however, will cause extradition to back into a new situation where the individual will become an absentee participant whose representation will be vicarious and whose role will be derivative. This development is not what policy planning would opt for, if for no other reason than as a

565

policy choice all participants to a process must be intrinsi-
cally part of that process with well-defined rights and obligations and not be relegated to positions outside the framework of
the process affecting their interests.

2. *A Policy Inquiry into Factors Bearing on the Framework and*
    Processes of Extradition

The first policy consideration is the identification of what
justifies extradition as an institution. [23] Two hypotheses
arise: (a) the supposition of a *civitas maxima*, whereby states
have mutually complementary duties in combatting common forms of
criminality on the grounds that minimum world order rests in
part on a minimum level of municipal order and the impact of
common criminality on the latter ultimately affects the former;
(b) the existence of a limited self-serving interest in all
nation-states where concern for the punishability of common
criminality arises out of the impact of criminality on the
municipal order.

Whatever the choice between these two assumptions, certain
factors must be considered which condition, qualify or limit
resort to the practice of extradition.

The question arises first with respect to conditions giving
rise to the practice, not in terms of what these conditions are,
but whether they are truly conditions precedent or merely regulating norms of the practice proper, such as with the requirement of reciprocity or the insistence on the existence of a
treaty as a condition precedent for extradition. The answer
will, of course, depend on the choice of either one of the two

assumptions stated above which support the very practice. This writer proposes adherence to the first assumption, i.e., mutuality of concern in combatting common forms of criminality as part of the larger framework of preservation of minimum world order. Thus extradition becomes one of the means of implementing world order and not a privileged practice. Consequently, all its conditions are in the nature of functional factors, even though sometimes of an organic nature, and should therefore be considered as factors which qualify or limit the practice and as factors bearing upon the very nature of the institution of extradition.

The factors which qualify or limit the practice are based on four considerations: (A) public policy; (B) political; (C) human rights and humanitarian concern; and (D) practical.

A. *Public policy considerations*: are those aspects resting on constitutional law and other municipal laws, which warrant, limit or qualify the conduct of a sovereign in the use of his processes and prerogatives to seize the body of a person and deliver him to another sovereign. While the issue of individual seizure is a question of human rights, it is still primarily one of municipal public policy with respect to the rights and obligations arising out of the course of conduct of a public body acting under color of law.

The means by which extradition is to be accomplished affect the practice but not its nature or purposes. The difference between the common law and civil law countries is vast with respect to public policy. Some policy consid-

567

erations in common law countries are so outcome determinative of the process that the *modus operandi* itself appears to thwart the basic notions of the practice proper and are said to raise to the level of a conceptual limitation. [24]

The first question of public policy arises with respect to the attitude of the requested state toward the requesting state. [25] Three views prevail: (a) extradition on the basis of a treaty only; (b) on the basis of reciprocity; (c) comity. The choice between these views stems from the original choice of either one of the two hypotheses outlined above which justify the practice. It is clear that if a state conceives of the practice as a question of mutual cooperation and assistance in penal matters, it will grant extradition with lesser formalities than if it deems it as a matter of self-serving interest, in which case it may insist on more formalities and depending upon its perceived interests.

Whenever a state accepts a requisition for extradition, the policy considerations which affect the process, are: (1) the choice of a jurisdictional theory; [26] (2) the extraditability of the offense, and the requirement of double criminality, interpreted either *in concreto* or *in abstracto*; [27] (3) limitations on certain types of offenses such as: political, fiscal, economic and military offenses (which stem more often from policy rather than humane considerations, even if an element of the latter is implicit in the formulation of the policy), [28] (4) inquiry into the sufficiency of the charge, or the evidence refuted.[29]

B. *Political considerations*: as the name suggests, are factors
    which have no relationship to the nature of the practice or
    its rationale but derive from purely political decisions or
    sometimes from concern for human rights, which is a value-
    oriented judgment grounded in an exclusively one-sided
    subjective evaluation. Whether to grant or deny extradition
    for a real or alleged political offense exception frequently
    has little to do with the actual conduct of the relator or
    his criminality, but is often predicated on the nature of
    the political relations between the respective states.[30]
    The integrity of the practice is affected in this respect as
    it is when, for the political and practical convenience of
    the interested states, forms of disguised extradition take
    place.[31] A distinction must be made as between policy and
    political decisions. For example, the discretion available
    to the executive branch to refuse extradition after a judi-
    cial determination permitting it is made, is seldom based on
    extradition policy, rather it is a political discretionary
    power.[32]

C. *Concern for human rights and humane considerations*: This
    refers to the treatment that awaits the relator in the
    requesting state.[33] Such considerations violate the rule
    of non-inquiry into the criminal processes of the state
    wherein the relator is alleged to have committed a violation
    and where he or she is expected to be prosecuted or punished.[24]
    In light of the absence of recognized international standards

of fairness, [35] this factor allows the requested state to set itself up as a judge or evaluator of another state's legal or judicial processes. Essentially, the requested state balances the rights of the relator to fairness against the interest of the requesting state in prosecuting or punishing that relator. This observation, however, will depend on the nature of the human right in question and thus may transcend such considerations when it bears on issues of fundamental justice such as in the case of *ne bis in idem*. [36]

D. *Practical questions*: These arise most significantly as to the type of offense for which extradition will be granted. It has to do mostly with the realization that the process is both costly and cumbersome and, therefore, should for all practical purposes be limited to more serious offenses and to cases where the prosecutability of the offender is seriously intended and not remote or illusory. This situation arises with respect to petty offenses and whenever, under the law of the demanding state, the prosecution is barred by prescription, statute of limitation or subject to amnesty or pardon. [37] Under those circumstances, there is justification for the requested state to deny putting its processes in motion to effectuate a surrender for a doubtful legal outcome.

3. *Appraisal of the Conceptual Framework of Extradition as an International Process*

International law in the twentieth century is entering a pronounced phase of changing structures which entails the broadening of its scope and application. The individual who had been alien to the scope of this discipline is acquiring a limited place therein. This is manifested by the recognition and proclamation of certain fundamental human rights and by the subjection of the individual to personal accountability before the world community. Relations between nation-states are ceasing to be a matter of limited interest and exclusive concern to the parties immediately involved, but are broadening to encompass some aspects of the world community's interests in the maintenance and preservation of minimum world order. The impact of these factors on classical norms of extradition laws and practices are causing a re-evaluation of this institution's purposes and functions.

The proposed conceptual framework for extradition is premised on five interlocking factors, which are: (1) the recognition of the national interest of the states who are parties to the extradition proceedings; (2) the existence of an international duty to preserve and maintain minimum world order; (3) the effective application of minimum standards of fairness and justice to the relator in the extradition process; (4) a collective duty on the part of all states to combat criminality; and (5) the balancing of these factors within the juridicial framework of the Rule of Law.

The relationship of these five factors is founded on the following rationale: (1) the existence of a duty to preserve and maintain minimum world order does not destroy national sovereignty because the interests of the world community can be considered within the scope of the national interest since this latter is founded on the notion that national interests are better served within a framework of international interdependence. (2) The enforcement of individual rights in extradition proceedings is not only a matter of humanitarian concern, but also a recognition that the individual is a party at interest vis-a-vis the respective states and the world community and that such recognition does not detract from state sovereignty because the individual is the ultimate bearer of the consequences of institutionalized conflicts and personally accountable before the world community for acts in violation of international law. (3) Mutual cooperation and assistance in penal matters between states reinforces the effectiveness of the municipal public order of all states and does not have to depend for its effectiveness on political compromises or denial of individual rights. (4) Adherence to the Rule of Law as part of international due process of law is the ultimate safeguard and guarantee for the survival of all human beings regardless of race, religion, creed or national origin and such a framework lends credence and legitimacy to the process of decision making. Legitimacy and credibility of a decision-making process make acceptance of its results more likely and thus greatly diminish opportunities for conflict over decisional outcome.

In our contemporary politically factionalized world, it would be naive to believe that in balancing the five factors of this proposed concept of extradition all said factors are equal; some are more equal than others. The first of these factors, the nationally perceived interest of states will remain the foremost consideration. The second factor, the duty to combat criminality, will be largely shaped by considerations ancillary to the first and, therefore, of lesser impact in the course of the authoritative decision-making process leading to the granting or denial of extradition. The third, concern for the individual, will remain the least considered factor in the over-all balancing of the equities and interests involved, as weighted by the value-oriented goals of institutional authoritative decision-making processes. The fourth, concern for the preservation of minimum world order if it is considered, will be regarded as part of nationally perceived interest and not as an independent international obligation. As to the Rule of Law and international due process, it is likely to be treated in a perfunctory manner by adherence to certain forms and formalities with little regard for its substance. However, in the history of law, forms and formalities as part of adjective law are likely to determine outcomes which can ultimately shape substantive rights.

Minimum world order is all too often threatened when processes and practices, such as extradition, create conditions which are likely to pit two opposing authoritative decision-making processes against each other without alternative courses of conduct.

The balancing of all factors underlying extradition is not likely to find an objective application by a given nation-state. The acceptance of one nation-state of another's decision to deny extradition may lead to the disruption of the respective states'

573

relations.

The alternative is the formulation of a universal convention on extradition in the spirit of the following resolution, introduced by this author at the 1968 Freiburg International Colloquium on Extradition, which recommended it to the Tenth International Penal Law Congress and which was embodied in a similar resolution adopted by the 1969 International Penal Law Pre-Congress of Siracuse (Italy). It states:

It appears hopeful to substitute to the strictly national concepts of criminality and to the intransigent consequences of national sovereignty an international concept of forms of criminality which (by their very nature) endanger fundamental human and social values and for the preservation of which a closer cooperation between the states is indispensable.

Consequently and in conformity to the contemporary trend to attribute to the individual the quality of subject of International Law, it is suitable to recognize that the individual who is the object of an extradition procedure may uphold before national and international jurisdictions the prerogatives recognized to him by the Universal Declaration of Human Rights and by international treaties.

To this effect and with a view to foresee a general international convention, it might be use-

ful that there be organized regional or
international jurisdictions capable of hearing individual recourses directed against
the decisions of national authorities
rendered in violation of the aforementioned
individual rights.

These jurisdictions could also be seized
with a procedure inspired by *habeus corpus*
which would permit and give a more effective
and practical remedy for the establishment of
the Rule of Law on a worldwide basis. [38]

1. McDougal, Lasswell and Reismah, "The World Constitutive Process of Authoritative Decision," <u>19 J. of Legal Ed.</u>, 253 (1967).

2. See, e.g., the series of four volumes on the <u>Strategy of World Order</u>, by Falk and Mendlovitz, I - <u>Toward a Theory of Prevention</u>, II - <u>International Law</u>, III - <u>The United Nations</u>, and IV - <u>Disarmament and Economic Development</u>, (1968); Clark and Sohn, <u>World Peace Through Law</u> (1965); McDougal and Associates, <u>Studies in World Public Order</u> (1960); McDougal and Feliciano, <u>Law and Minimum World Public Order</u> (1960).

3. McDougal and Feliciano, <u>Law and Minimum World Public Order</u>, p. 268, (1960); see also Bassiouni, "International Extradition in American Practice and World Public Order," 36 <u>Tenn. L. Rev.</u> 1 (1960), at 30, "Order is the product of a system of action through the inter-reactions of pluralistic values in the perception realization of the need for an inter-social criteria of an acceptable conduct." And Carlston, "World Order and International Law, 20 <u>J. of Legal Ed.</u> 2 (1967).

4. Kelsen, <u>Principles of International Law</u>, 2nd Rev. ed. by

R. W. Tucker (1966); Tucker, "Has the Individual Become the Subject of International Law?" 34 <u>Cin. L. Rev.</u> 341 (1965); Korowicz, "The Problem of the International Personality of Individuals," 50 <u>A.J.I.L.</u> 533 (1956); Lauterpacht, "The Subjects of the Law of Nations," 63 <u>L. Q. Rev.</u> 438 (1947) and 64 <u>L. Q. Rev.</u> 97 (1948); Jessup, "The Subjects of a Modern Law of Nations," 45 <u>Mich. L. Rev.</u> 383 (1947); Eagleton, "Some Questions as to the Place of the Individual in the International Law of the Future," 37 <u>A.J.I.L.</u> 642 (1943).

5. Jencks, <u>The Common Law of Mankind</u> (1958); Jessup, <u>Transnational Law</u> (1956).

6. Bassiouni, "Islam: Concept, Law and World *Habeas Corpus*," 1 <u>Rutgers Camden J.</u> 163 at 191 (1969).

7. Philip C. Jessup, Ambassador at Large, "The Conquering March of an Idea," address delivered before the 72nd Annual Meeting of the American Bar Association, St. Louis, Mo., September 6, 1949; 31 <u>Department of State Bulletin</u>, No. 533, September 19, 1949; pp. 432, 433-434.

8. Judge Jessup further stated that: "A very large part of international affairs and, thus, of the process of inter-national accommodation, concerns the relations between legal persons known as states. This is necessarily so. But it is no longer novel for the particular interest of the indi-vidual human being to break through the mass of interstate relationships. *Idem.* See also, De Visscher, <u>Theory and Reality in Public International Law</u>, 125 (Corbett Trans.

1957). The Universal Declaration of Human Rights, Dec. 6, 1948, U.N. General Assembly, 2d Sess. Doc. A/811. "The General Assembly proclaims this Universal Declaration of Human Rights as a common standard of achievement for all peoples and all nations, to the end that every individual and every organ of society, keeping this Declaration constantly in mind, shall strive by teaching and education to promote respect for those rights and freedoms and by progressive measures, national and international, to secure their universal and effective recognition and observance, both among the peoples of Member States themselves and among the peoples of territories under their jurisdiction."

For the U.N. debates, see U.N. Gen. Assembly Off. Rec. 3d Sess., 1st pt., Summary Record, Dec. 9, 1948, 180th meeting, p. 862. For a survey of human rights conventions, see Bassiouni, "The 'Human Rights' Program: The Veneer of Civilization Thickens," 21 DePaul L. Rev., 271 (1971).

9. For the principle of individual accountability for international crimes, see Chapter V, Section 1.

10. Compare authors cited, *supra*, note 3.

11. See Chapter VI.

12. See Chapter VI.

13. See Chapter VI.

14. See Chapter III.

15. See Chapter I for arguments on this concept and Friedmann, "The Use of 'General Principles' in the Development of International Law," 57 A.J.I.L. 279 (1963).

16. The only exception is under the European Court of Human Rights and the European Commission on Human Rights which hears individual petitions and gives individuals standing to present claims against states under the European Convention for the protection of Human Rights and Fundamental Freedoms was signed at Rome, Nov. 4, 1950, 213 U.N.T.S. 221 and became effective September 3, 1953.

17. See "Symposium on Human Rights," 21 DePaul L. Rev. (1971).

18. The basis for this principle of the common law, which subjects parties to an agreement to the duty of good faith, is found in 3 Blackstone's Commentaries 163. For its recognition and application in international law, see 1 Whiteman, Digest, 98 (1963).

19. On the subject of treaty rights and interpretation of treaties, see McDougal, Lasswell and Cheng, World Public Order and Treaty Interpretation (1968). Professor Dehaussy feels that individuals can claim their rights from their states through the principle of invoking the binding coligations and laws of the state against the state itself. 1 Juris-Classeur de Droit International, chs. 10 and 14 (1958).

20. See, e.g., Bin Cheng, General Principle of Law as Applied by International Courts and Tribunals (1948).

21. See Chapter VI.

22. See Bassiouni, supra, note 8.

23. Wise, "Some Problems of Extradition," 39 Revue Internationale de Droit Penal 518 (1968), reprinted in 15 Wayne

L. Rev. 709 (1968).

24. See Chapter VII.

25. See Chapter I.

26. See Chapter IV.

27. See Chapter IV.

28. See Chapter VI.

29. See Chapter VII.

30. See Chapter VI.

31. See Chapter III.

32. See Chapter VII.

33. See Chapter VI.

34. See Chapter VI.

35. Mueller and Wise, eds., International Criminal Law, p. 135 (1965).

36. See Chapter VI.

37. See Chapter VI.

38. 39 Revue Internationale de Droit Penal, p. 516 and p. 855 (1968). The original text was in French, and this translation may reveal the difficulty of remaining faithful to a verbatim translation.

SUBJECT INDEX

A

Abduction and kidnapping   121, 124-28

   Causes celebres   124-25

   Definitions   124, 172-28

   State responsibility for   150-51

Active personality theory, see Jurisdiction

Aircraft, see Jurisdiction, Principles, Territoriality,

  Floating territoriality

Aliens in international law, 193, state responsibility

  for   199

Alternative to non-extradition proposed   331

Alternatives to extradition

   Application of municipal immigration laws   134-42

    (See also Exclusion, Expulsion)

   Appraisal of   176-85

   Arguments against using irregular means   183-84

   Considered as practical supplements   184-85

   Factors influencing   179-81

   Questions raised by frequent use of   177-79

   Unlawful seizures and irregular rendition

    devices   121-85

     Rationale   123-24

     Typology   121-22

    (See also separate entry, Unlawful seizures)

    Used for military offenses   430

   See also Abduction and kidnapping

SUBJECT INDEX

Amnesty and pardon, defenses 450-42, 497-98

Antarctic, see Jurisdiction, Principles, Terri-

 toriality, Special environments

Antarctic Treaty, 246-47; list of nations signing 296

Apprehension of fugitive criminal by irregular

 means, classification 122

Arab League Extradition Agreement, 19; list of

 nations signing and ratifying, 20; quoted on

 double jeopardy 456-57

Arbitral tribunals 169-70

Arctic, see Jurisdiction, Principles, Terri-

 toriality, Special environments

Assassination, excluded from political offense

 exception 410

Astronauts, agreement on the rescue and return of 298

Asylum 2, 3, 86-113

 Committee on the Legal Aspects of 106

 Definitions 86, 91, 114-115

 Diplomatic asylum 96-97

 Ecclesiastic vs. political 90

 Factors affecting decision on 110-11

 History of 86-90

 Human rights approach 117-18

 Individual right to 102-103

 International common law of 97-100

SUBJECT INDEX

Asylum (continued)

    Legal basis for   97–103

    Origin of term   86

    Rationale for   90–97

    Relationship with extradition appraised   107–113

    Territorial vs. extraterritorial   91–93

    United States position on   104–106

    Vs. denial of extradition   108–109

    See also Political asylum

Aut dedere aut punire (iudicare) maxim   7, 254, 271,
                                         331, 428

Authoritative process, term defined   46

B

Bilaterial treaties   13–18, 23–24

C

Characteristics of the extradition process

    In international law and practice   6–24

        Absence of a treaty   9–13

        Bilateral treaties   13–18

        Duty to extradite   6–9

        Multilateral regional arrangements   19–24

    In United States law and practice   24–52

        See also United States procedures

Comity, a basis for extradition   1, 2, 8, 25,
                                         43, 279, 326

        and passim

SUBJECT INDEX

Competing requests for extradition, problem   272-73

Conceptual framework for extradition, proposed   570-75

Conditional extradition   460-61, 463

Constitution, United States, and extradition   29-34

Conventions and other documents affecting extradition

    See Separate list   1, 7

Counterfeiting, an extraditable offense   13-14

Cruel and unusual punishment exception   450, 463-66

    Problems and proposed solution   466

    References in human rights conventions   464-65

    United Nations resolution on Standard

        Minimum Rules for the Treatment of Prisoners 465

D

Death penalty exception   359-60, 407,

    450, 459-63,

    507

Decision-making process, term defined   46

Defenses, see Denial of extradition

Definitions

    Abduction and kidnapping   124, 127-28

    Asylum   86, 91, 114-15

    Disguised extradition   133-34

    Double criminality   312-13, 322,

    323-26

    Extraditable offenses   326-29

Definitions (continued)

    Extradition 2, 27, 47

    Informal rendition 128–29

    Piracy 263–64

    Political offense 371–72, 378, 383, 402–407, 474, 476

    Relative political offense 383ff., 392–93, 475

    Specialty doctrine 313

    Terms used in this book 45–46

    Treason and related crimes 381–82

    Treaty 28

Denial of extradition, grounds for 368–466

    Political self-defense, theory proposed 412–16

    Relating to human rights 369–70

      (See also Asylum)

    Relating to the offense 368, 370–434

      (See also Fiscal offense; Military offense; Political offense)

    Relating to penalty and punishability 369, 450–66

      (See also Amnesty and pardon; Double jeopardy; Death penalty; Cruel and unusual punishment)

    Relating to prosecution 369, 443–50

(See also Legality of offense; In absentia

  trial; Statute of limitations)

Relating to the person of the relator   369, 435–43

  (See also Nationals; Officials)

Deportation, see Expulsion

Difficulties of extradition, cause of evasion   123, 132, 177–81,

                      184, 185

Disguised extradition   133–43

  Condoned in case of Duke of Chateau Thierry   430

  Definition   133–34

  Used frequently by United States   184–85

Double criminality requirement   255–56, 320–26

  And extraditable offense requirement   317–19, 326–29

  And reciprocity   314–15, 322–23,

                      361

  And specialty doctrine   354

  Case study analysis   329–52

  Definitions and interpretations   312–13, 322,

                      323–26, 346,

                      352

Double jeopardy defense (Non bis in idem)   224, 252–53,

                      319, 450, 452–59,

                      512, 570

  List of conventions embodying   456–59

  Problems   453–54, 455–56,

                      459

Rationale — 455

Treaty interpretations categorized — 454–55

"Due process" issue — 30, 168, 182, 496

Duty to extradite — 6–9

E

Eichmann case — 124–30, 150, 175, 178, 188, 189, 198, 256

Eliminative method of determining extraditable offenses — 316–19

    enumerative method — 315, 317

European Convention on Extradition — 20–22, 367

    List of nations ratifying — 21

    Quoted on death penalty exception — 462

    on double jeopardy — 457

European Convention on Human Rights — 51, 169, 200, 579

    List of nations ratifying — 76

    Source of law on human rights — 165–66

European Court of Human Rights — 169

Evidence required by requested state — 508–510

Ex acquo et bono principle — 564

Ex injuria ius non oritur principle — 144–45, 151, 174–75

Exceptions, exemptions, and exclusions, see

 Denial of extradition

Exclusion, irregular rendition device   141-42, 188,
193, 194, 197

Executive discretion

    Amnesty and pardon   450-51

    Dependent on treaty provisions   438

    Deportation cases   141

    Granted by domestic laws   43

    In absentia trial defense   446

    Limitations on   544-45

    Political offense evaluation   428

    Reasons for infrequent use   534

    Surrender of nationals   436

    Veto of extradition order   32, 93

Executive vs. judicial power in extradition   32-35, 44, 67,
68, 109, 111,
393-97, 495,
504-508, 511-
12, 536

Exhaustion of ordinary remedies rule   143-44

Extradition defined   2, 27, 47

Extradition processes, need for streamlining   123, 132, 177-
81, 184, 185

Expressio unius exclusio est alterius maxim   334

Expulsion, irregular rendition device   134–41, 188, 197–98

    Statements on, in international conventions   162–65

    See also Refoulement

Extraditable offense requirement

    And double criminalty   314–29

    And reciprocity   314–15

    And specialty doctrine   354

    Case study analysis of judicial application   329–52

    Definitional theories and interpretation   326–29

    Interpretation, literal vs. broad   326–27

    See also Legality of offense charged

Extraditable offenses

    Counterfeiting   13–14

    Identified in treaties or reciprocally recognized   312

    Methods of determining   315–19

      proposed technique   320–21

    Narcotics traffic   14

    Rationale for defining   319–22

    Slavery   14

    See also International crimes

F

Factors qualifying extradition   566–70

Concern for human rights   569–70

Political considerations   569

Practical questions   570

Public policy considerations   567–69

Factors underlying proposed framework   47–52

Failure to act, state responsibility for   149

Fiscal offense exclusion   433–34

Flag, Law of the, see Jurisdiction, Principles,

  Territoriality, Floating Territoriality

Floating territoriality theory, see Jurisdiction,

  Principles, Territoriality

Forum for prosecuting fugitive offender, question

  of competency   270–71

G

General principles of international law   160

Geneva conventions, provisions on bringing

  criminal offender to court   481–82

Genocide, not a political offense   14, 171

H

Habeas corpus in extradition proceedings   36–37, 41,

    336, 337, 342,

    356, 524–27,

    555

History of extradition   1–6

Human rights

And asylum   100-102

And extradition   93-94

And state responsibility   151-73

And state sovereignty   46-52, 152-
                                                    53, 565, 571-
                                                    72

International sources of law on   154 ff.

Justiciability affirmed by court action   168-70

Violated by irregular alternatives to extradi-

   tion   123, 124, 145,
                                                    157, 182-83

Violations not yet recognized as international

   crime   421

  See also Individual vs. state under international law

Human rights documents - See separate list

Humanitarian international law, emergence of   2, 4-5

I

Ideological self-preservation, see Political self-defense

Ideologically motivated offender, term defined   45-46

Ideology, term defined   45

Immigration laws, used for disguised extradition   121-22, 133-
                                                    34, 142-43

Immunity from prosecution, in exchange for coopera-

   tion   449

In absentia trial, defense   40, 41, 443,
                                                    445-46, 496

SUBJECT INDEX

Individual vs. state under international law   2, 46-52, 74-
77, 267-69,
419, 558-66

  (See also Human rights)

Informal rendition   128-33

 defined   128-29

Injured rights theory   401-402

International Court of Justice   99-100, 144,
155, 157-58,
168-69, 170,
291

International courts' decisions, source of law   154, 168-70

International crimes

  Catalogue of   269, 306, 420-
21

  Clear definition needed   417

  Extraditable offenses   416-25

  Extradition for, not yet a reality   424-25

  Piracy   263-66, 267

  Slave trading   266-67

  United Nations attempts to codify   418-19

International criminal court, proposed   409, 427, 428

International tribunals   268-69

Irregular rendition devices, see Alternatives to
extradition

J

Judicial control in extradition, states employing   506-507

Judicial vs. executive power, see Executive vs.

 judicial power

Jurisdiction as related to extradition   202-276

   Aircraft, ships, and spacecraft, see infra

     Principles, Territoriality, Floating territoriality

   And sovereignty   204-205, 207,

                                    275-76

   Balancing of interests theory   202

   Military bases in foreign countries and military

     occupation   212-15

   National theories vs. international law rules   274-75

   Principles

     Active personality (nationality)   205, 248,

                                    251-55

     Flag state   291-92

     Passive personality   205, 237-38,

                                    255-59, 300

     Protected interest   205, 259-61,

                                    300, 305-306

     Territoriality   205-251, 253,

                                    304-305

       Floating territoriality (law of the flag) 224-44, 245,

                                    247, 249, 251,

		258
Special environments		244–51
	Antarctic	246–48
	Arctic	244–46, 295–96
	Outer space	248–50
Special status territories		211–17
Subjective-objective territoriality		217–24, 254, 257, 300
	Universality	205, 243, 256–57, 261–70, 302, 306
Subject-matter conflicts		224
Subject-matter jurisdiction vs. jurisdiction over person		126, 203–204
Term "territory" synonymous with "jurisdiction"		234–37
Theories listed		205
Jurisdictional problems		270–76
Jurisdictional requirements of requesting state		271–74

K

Kaiser Wilhelm II, political offense exemption   269, 419–20

Kidnapping, see Abduction and kidnapping

L

Lapse of time defense, see Statute of limitations

Legal framework of extradition   1–85, 313

(See also Procedural rules and practice, Srouces and content)

Legality of offense charged, defense 444-45

Legislation clarifying extradition proceedings 30-31

Legislative clemency, in amnesty and pardon 450

M

Mala captus bene detentus maxim 122, 126, 128,

143-45, 182,

186, 359

Military deserters, deportation of 139

Military offense exemption 400, 407, 429-

33

Military personnel 280-81

Multilateral regional arrangements for extradition 19-24

Multilateral treaties 154, 156,

160-68

Multiple jeopardy 276

(See also Double jeopardy)

Multiple requests for extradition 543

N

Narcotics traffic, an extraditable offense 14

narcotics conventions 58

Nationality theory, see Jurisdiction, Principles,

Active Personality

Nationals, exclusion of 34, 60, 435-

42, 533-34

In Socialist Bloc treaties 24

Problems | 439–40

Proposed alternatives | 441–42

Rationale for | 440–41

Non bis in indem, see Double jeopardy

Noninquiry rule | 424, 463, 466, 569

Non-refoulement principle | 102, 164–65

Nordic States scheme, reciprocal national legislation | 19–23

Novation of extradition agreements | 18

Nullum crimen sine legge doctrine | 321

Nurmberg International Military Tribunal | 268–69

O

Offenses, see Extraditable offenses

Officials and others protected by immunity | 442–43

Order, term defined | 46

Origin of term "extradition" | 3

Outer space | 297–98

see also Jurisdiction, Principles, Territoriality, Special environments

P

Pardon, see Amensty and pardon

Passive personality theory, see Jurisdiction, Principles

Peace treaties, used to revive lapsed extradition treaties | 16–17

SUBJECT INDEX

Permanent Court of International Justice   99, 255, 258,
     300, 305

Piracy, an international crime   263-66

     Defined   263-64

     Early efforts to combat   5

Political asylum

     United States immigration laws applicable to   105-106

     United States policy and practice   104-106

     Vs. humanitarian asylum   107-108

Political offense exception   93, 109, 198,
     254, 269, 320,
     370-429

     And asylum   97, 372

     And ideologically motivated offenders   375-79

     And individual human rights   50

     Applied to disguised extradition   140

     Assassination excluded from   410

     Definitions   371-72, 402-
     407, 474, 476

     History   370-75

     International crimes an exception to the
     exception   416-25

     Problems threatening world order and proposed
     solution   425-29

     Purely political offense   378, 379-83

     proposed definition   383

Relative political offense   383-411

    Ambiguous position of western European states 408-410

Definitions   383 ff., 392-
                                                    93, 475

    Juridical standard of inquiry proposed   411-12

    Political-incidence theory   388-400

    Political motivation theory   402-411

    Problem of multiplicity of offenses involved 385-88

    Questions for determining extraditability   411-12

    Theories concerning   388-411

    Treaty provisions   467

Political refugees

    Deportation of   138

    Extradition in ancient times   4-5

    Still most vulnerable to disguised extradition 143

    See also Political offense exception; Refugees

Political self-defense, factors determining the
right of   413-15

Procedural rules and practice

    In the United States   502-537, esp.
                                                    511-37

    Initiation of request and actual surrender 507-508

    Sources and content   502-511

    Time limits   527

      (See also Statute of limitations)

SUBJECT INDEX

See also Legal framework; United States procedure

Proposals

    Alternative to exemption of nationals   441-42

    Alternative to nonextradition   331

    Conceptual framework for extradition   45-52

    Criteria for state responsibility in interna-

        tional relations   150-51

    Enforcement of individual rights stated in

        treaties   52

    Framework for inquiry into processes and values   558-75

    International criminal court   427, 428

    Juridical standard of inquiry for relative

        political offense   411-12

    Policy-oriented questions on jurisdictional

        problems   272-73

    Remedies for unlawful seizures   173-85

    Rule of law, worldwide   572, 575

    Solution to political offense problems threaten-

        ing world order   425-29

    Universal convention (treaty-statute) on

        extradition   427, 574-75

Protected interest theory, see Jurisdiction, Principles

R

Rationae materiae vs. Rationae personae for asylum   94-97

Reciprocity, a basis for extradition   1, 2, 8

And double criminality   314-15, 322-
23, 361

And sovereignty   323-25

List of nations requiring reciprocity guarantee   11

List of nations with no legislative provisions

    for   57

Reciprocal national legislation   19-23

Refoulement   164-65

Refuge, see Asylum

Refugees   100-105, 163-
56

Relative political offense, see Political offense exception

Remedies for international injuria   173-85

Rendition devices other than extradition, classified 121-22

Requested state and requesting state, relation

 between   568

Rule of Law, worldwide, proposed   572, 575

S

Sanctuaries in ancient times   87-89

Ships, see Jurisdiction, Principles, Territoriality,

 Floating territoriality

Slavery, an extraditable offense   14

 documents on   307-308

Sovereignty doctrine   278, 564-65

   And Asylum   94-96

And double jeopardy   453

And exclusion of nationals   441

And immunity for officials   442

And reciprocity   324-25

Harmonized with mininum world order andindividual

   human rights   47-48, 565,

                                                   571-72

 Violated by irregular alternative to extradition 124, 145, 182

Spacecraft, see Jurisdiction, Principles, Territoriality,

 Floating territoriality

Special status territories, see Jurisdiction, Principles,

 Territoriality

Specialty doctrine   352-60, 406,

                                                   407

And multiple charges   400

And variance in prosecution   357-59

Applied in conditional extradition   507

   in disguised extradition   140

   in re-extradition   359-60

Convenience for the states, not an individual

   right   50

Defined   313

Rationale for   353

Relation to requirements of extraditable offense

   and double criminality   354

SUBJECT INDEX

State responsibility in international relations

    Categories of wrongful acts   146-48

    Criteria proposed   150-51

    For enforcing universality theory   267-68

    For its agents and individuals international

      behavior   149-51

    For unlawful seizures   145-51

    Toward aliens   193, 199

State succession and extradition treaties   17-18, 33,

        35-39

    Nations agreeing to treaty continuity   61

Stateless persons   163

Status of Forces agreements   216-17, 281

Statute of limitations (lapse of time) defense   351, 443-44,

        447-50

Subjective-objective territorial theory, see Juris-

  diction, Principles, Territoriality

Substantive requirements   311-60

  (See also specifically Double criminality; Extraditable

  offenses; Specialty doctrine)

Superior orders, defense of obedience to   151

Surrender without formal process   121

T

Temporary extradition   440

Territorial asylum, see Asylum

SUBJECT INDEX

Territoriality, see Jurisdiction, Principles

Terrorism problems   123-24, 127, 409-411, 422

Tokyo International Military Tribunal for the Far East   268-69

Treason and related crimes, defined   381-82

Treaties, as basis for extradition   2-4, 311-13

    Lapses and revival   15-18, 60

    List of nations requiring   11

    Problems involved   26

    Sole basis in United STates   24-29

    United States treaties   26-30, 60, 288, 334, 505

        list of those currently in force   78-85

    See also Procedural rules, Sources and content

U

United Nations Charter and resolutions, a source of law on human rights   154-56, 170-71

United States positions

    On asylum   25, 104-106

    On comity   43

    On evidence permitted at extradition trial   523-24

    On exclusive right of immigration laws   134

    On in absentia trials   446, 529

    On jurisdiction over Arctic   295-96

SUBJECT INDEX

On political asylum   104–105

On political offense determination   400

On protected interest theory   261

On specialty doctrine and political offenses   407

On state succession   39

On statute of limitations defense   447–48

On surrender of nationals   435–39

On treaty requirement   9, 10, 29, 32

United States procedures in extradition   502–537

Executive discretion   531–34

Habeas corpus and the rule of noninquiry   527–31

Hearsay information admissible as evidence   548

Initiation of the process   511–13

Judicial process   513–37

Noninquiry rule   527–31

Re in absentia convictions   527–31

Re multiple requests   513

Re requests by the United States   534–37

Time limits   512–13

Unlawful seizures

And human rights   143–73

Categories   146

Human rights vs. state sovereignty   152–53

Internal law vs. international law dichotomy   152

Mala captus bene detentus maxim   122, 126, 128,

SUBJECT INDEX

	143-45, 182,
	186, 359
Remedies established	151
Remedies proposed	173-85
State responsibility for	145-51
See also Alternatives to extradition	
Universal convention (treaty-statute) on extradition proposed	14, 19, 427, 574-75

V

Values and value-judgment, terms defined	45

W

War, effect on extradition treaties	15-17, 39-41, 60, 71
World public order	
Defined	46
Extradition's relationship to	566-67
Factors	561-62
Harmonized with national sovereignty and individual human rights	47-48, 276, 565, 571-72
Threatened by denying extradition or granting asylum	111-13
by irregular alternatives to extradition	124, 181-83

A., In re   489

Abel case (Col, Abel/Pilot Francis Gary

  Powers exchange)   141, 197

Addis, In re   496

Adsetts case   56, 190

Ahlers case   124, 178, 188-89

Albertson v. Subservice Activities Control

  Board   498

American Banana Company v. United Fruit

  Company   281

Amper, In re   222

Anderson, In re   346

Anietto et al., In re   367

Arevalo, In re   490

Argento v. Horn,   16, 39-40, 493, 529-30,

                              547, 548

Argoud case   124, 188

Arguellos case   56

Artaza, In re   491

Artukovic cases   132-33, 395-97, 422-24,

                              485, 486

Artukovic v. Boyle   75, 473

  (See also Ivancevic v. Artukovic,

  Karadzole v. Artukovic, United States

  v. Artukovic, United States ex rel.

  Karadzole v. Artukovic, infra.)